The War On Freedom
THE 9/11 CONSPIRACIES

Also by Jim Marrs

Crossfire: The Plot That Killed JFK
Alien Agenda
Rule by Secrecy
Psi Spies

Acknowledgment for assistance over and beyond the call of duty should be given to Gary Beebe, Ericca Feste, Dan Foster, Thomas L. Mattingly, Mark Mawrence, Richard Scheck, and that Queen of Tolerance, my wife, Carol.

THE WAR ON FREEDOM
THE 9/11 CONSPIRACIES

Jim Marrs

ARES
Publishing

First edition published in May, 2003.

Cover design by Ericca Cordier

Library of Congress Cataloging-in-Publication Data

Marrs, Jim
        The War on Freedom: The 9/11 Conspiracies/by Jim Marrs
        p.   cm.
        Includes bibliographical references and index.
        ISBN 0-9727131-1-5
        1. Current Events-United States. 2. Conspiracies - United States. 3.
        History - United States. 4. United States - Foreign relations - 1989—.
        4. Secret societies - United States. I.Title

ISBN 0-9727131-1-5

The War On Freedom

Jim Marrs

Contents

INTRODUCTION * 3
    The National Security State * 4
    Democracy or Republic? * 6

Part I - The Events of September 11, 2001 * 9
    Chronology of Events * 9
    Unresolved Issues and Questions * 11
    The Tracks of Foreknowledge * 22
    FBI Couldn't or Wouldn't Connect the Dots * 30
    Missed Opportunities at the CIA * 39
    Selling Stocks Short Indicates Foreknowledge * 48
    Israeli Foreknowledge? * 53
    Remote-Controlled Aircraft a Reality * 63
    Remote Viewers Look at 9/11 * 63

Part II - War for Oil and Drugs * 76
    The Central Asian Gas Pipeline * 78
    Afghan Action Planned Long Ago * 81
    Wag the Dog in Iraq? * 88
    Destroyed Crops Impact World Drug Trade * 107
    Who and Where is Osama bin Laden? * 112
    Bin Laden Replies * 116
    Bin Laden Family and Friends * 118

Part III - Reaction to September 11, 2001 * 131
    Creating Homeland Security * 134
    The PATRIOT Act * 164
    Son of PATRIOT Act * 178
    Big Brother's Technology * 182
    Governing by Secrecy and Decree * 190
    The Crimes of Henry Kissinger * 200
    Secret Societies * 205

Part IV - Historical Precedents* 226
      The Gulf War * 226
      The Reichstag Fire * 232
      Pearl Harbor * 237
      Would Americans Allow Attacks on Americans? * 240
      War as an Economic Boost * 244

Part V - Qui Bono? Who Benefits? * 252
      The Mass Media * 252
      A Dismal Foreign Policy Record * 258
      Manufactured Enemies * 262
      The Hegelian Dialectic * 264
      What Do We Know Now? * 266

SOURCES * 273

INDEX * 297

INTRODUCTION

"Our nation must come together to unite."
- President George W. Bush, June 4, 2001

Being free is like being pregnant.

You either are or you're not. There's really nothing in between.

Some people argue that in a populous nation some curtailment of freedom is both necessary and acceptable. It seems only proper that the person in the car next to you on the freeway must demonstrate some minimum driving ability to obtain a state-granted license.

Having said that, most people also argue that freedom is too precious to toss out in the hope of security or government efficiency. If an error is to be made, it must be on the side of freedom.

Today in America, the new War on Terrorism might more truthfully be called a War on Freedom, and it began long before the events of September 11, 2001.

In fact, it may have begun ages ago, but for our purposes consider that it began at the end of World War II in the euphoria following the Allied victory over the Axis (Germany, Italy and Japan) military forces.

American GIs returning home from far-flung battlefields looked forward to getting on with their lives, while civilians were ecstatic over the prospect of unrationed gasoline, meat and tires. In 1952, the war's supreme allied commander, General Dwight D. Eisenhower, was elected president and all seemed right with the American way of life.

During the 1950s, despite the ever-present danger of nuclear war with the Soviets and a certain "police action" for the United Nations in Korea, most Americans paid scant attention to events around the world and most of the public could not have cared less about what happened in Washington.

In the hustle and bustle following the war, Americans failed to see that the basic structure of their nation was changing. A predominantly rural nation became urban. New technology, especially television, brought a hurried aspect to everyday life. Large businesses slowly evolved into giant multinational corporations.

And, spurred by the anticommunism of the Cold War, a certain sense of paranoia entered the body politic. Senator Joseph McCarthy and FBI director J. Edgar Hoover led the stampede to brand anything contrary to their worldview as communistic.

The National Security State

Immediately following the still-controversial crashes of unusual aerial objects near Roswell, New Mexico, in the summer of 1947, a National Security Act was rushed into effect and the American national security state was born.

On September 15 of that year - less than four months after pilot Kenneth Arnold reported "saucers" soaring over Mount Rainier and only two months after the New Mexico crashes - President Harry S. Truman hurriedly signed into law the National Security Act of 1947. It was the greatest reformation of the U.S. government up to that time.

This legislation established the National Security Council (NSC), made the air force a separate branch of service, united the military branches under a Department of Defense and created America's first peacetime civilian intelligence organization, the Central Intelligence Agency (CIA).

The NSC is a prime example of the tight inner-government control that has come to dominate U.S. policy decisions to include the use of armed force. Most Americans have no idea who exactly makes up the powerful NSC. They might be surprised to learn that council principals are the president, vice president and secretaries of state and defense, all positions appointed by the sitting president. This has placed unprecedented power in the hands of the nation's executive branch.

Anything that can be construed to affect national security - from foreign conflicts impacting oil supplies to unidentified aerial phenomena - can and has been placed under the jurisdiction of "national security."

It might also be noted that the NSC has been predominantly controlled by members of the Council on Foreign Relations and/or The Trilateral Commission, secretive organizations with a globalist agenda. (See my book *Rule by Secrecy* for more details on these organizations.)

Many government "alphabet" agencies also are susceptible to tight control from this inner circle of top government officials. These include the Central Intelligence Agency (CIA), the National Security Council (NSC), Federal Bureau of Investigation (FBI), National Security Agency (NSA), Defense Intelligence Agency (DIA), National Reconnaissance Office (NRO), Drug Enforcement Agency (DEA), Bureau of Alcohol, Tobacco, Firearms and Explosives (ATF), Internal Revenue Service (IRS), Federal Emergency Management Agency (FEMA) and many others. These agencies are themselves quite secretive, citing reasons of national security, executive privilege or the need to protect informants or criminal case files.

Under such centralized control, the activities of subservient agencies and divisions are of little consequence. Government bureaucrats - honest and well intentioned for the most part - simply follow orders and policies set by their superiors.

Many government employees have lost their jobs or resigned in the face of directives that bewilder and perplex those not privy to the inner secrets and agendas.

In Korea, American military men and women for the first time fought under the leadership of non-American officers in a dirty little war that was never declared as such and ended only with a stalemate and armistice.

The multinational aspect of the Korean conflict set the precedent for what occurred later in Vietnam, Beirut, Afghanistan, Iraq, Kuwait, Kosovo, and Bosnia.

And these actions set the stage for the recent terrorist attacks on America.

Everyone agrees that the world changed on September 11, 2001.

But to whose world are they referring?

For more than a year following the tragic attacks in New York and Washington and military operations in Afghanistan, Osama bin Laden remained a fugitive from justice, just as he had during the 1990s. The al-Qaeda terrorist network continued to be sought by the governments of several nations. Afghanistan remained a war-ravaged and impoverished Third World nation. Their worlds did not change.

It was the American way of life that changed. Freedoms long taken for granted, such as habeas corpus, legislative oversight, search and seizure laws and separation of military and police authority, are today under attack. Rule by executive fiat seems to be the order of the day. Congress, by its own admission, is largely out of the loop.

Thomas Jefferson wrote, "I know of no safe depository of the ultimate powers of the society but the people themselves, and if we think them not enlightened enough to exercise their control with a wholesome discretion, the remedy is not to take it from them, but to inform their discretion."

Few people in the United States today have been informed that they have been living under a State of Emergency since September 11, 2001.

This was quietly and officially declared by President George W. Bush three days later when he issued a proclamation stating, "A national emergency exists by reason of the terrorist attacks at the World Trade Center, New York, New York, and the Pentagon, and the continuing and immediate threat of further attacks on the United States.

"Now, therefore, I, George W. Bush, President of the United States of America, by virtue of the authority vested in me as President by the Constitution and the laws of the United States, I hereby declare that the national emergency has existed since September 11, 2001, and pursuant to the National Emergencies Act (50 U.S.C. 1601 et seq.), I intend to utilize the following statutes: sections 123, 123a, 527, 2201(c), 12006, and 12302 of title 10, United States Code, and sections 331, 359, and 367 of title 14, United States Code."

It was with this proclamation that Bush made public the "shadow government," unelected officials and appointees who can determine the future of this former republic. This shadow government had been mentioned many times in the past by researchers and journalists such as Bill Moyers but had been generally perceived as mere conspiracy theory.

The United States suddenly found itself in a new war - a War on Terrorism. This is a war Americans never asked for and never envisioned. It is a war predicated on the premise that a sneak attack was made on the United States. This new war effort has now been added to a previous ongoing war, the War on Drugs. The result is an ever increasing assault on liberty and freedom. Is this assault desirable? Is it necessary? Must individual freedom be given away in the hope of protecting it? And what of the 9/11 attacks? Have we caught the culprits? Have any of the guilty been punished? For that matter, has there been any definitive proof of precisely who orchestrated and carried out the attacks?

Osama bin Laden in separate news broadcasts naturally denied any involvement. A videotape produced two months later by the CIA hinting at his involvement has been called into question by many people, including experts in Canada and Europe. By mid March 2002, concern over bin Laden had noticeably decreased. President George W. Bush indicated he had lost interest in finding the man. "We haven't heard from him in a long time," Bush told reporters at the White House. "I truly am not that concerned about him." Even an audio recording produced in late 2002 failed to stir up much enthusiasm for continuing the search for bin Laden.

Whether or not bin Laden is the ultimate guilty party is only one of the many questions being raised by thoughtful people concerning what really took place in New York City and Washington. Questions and speculation are rampant on the Internet as well as in private conversations. The corporate mass media, on the other hand, has been satisfied to parrot the official party line and not ask embarrassing questions.

Are these attacks and their aftermath merely another example of the violence inherent in human nature or the result of evil forethought and planning? There certainly cannot be any question that the 9/11 attacks were a conspiracy, a term that has been largely kept out of national debates until now.

But exactly what kind of conspiracy are we dealing with?

It has been said that truth is the first casualty of war. Could this be why a terrorist hijacking attack was quickly transformed into a new "war" with an accompanying decrease in individual liberties? Why did we not proclaim war after the 1993 World Trade Center bombing or the truck bombing of the Khobar Towers in 1996 or the U.S. embassy bombings in Tanzania and Kenya in 1998?

Truth has a way of belonging to whomever controls the flow of information.

Democracy or Republic?

Would you rather live in a democracy or a republic?

Before you answer that question, you might want to seriously consider your response.

Today, Americans find themselves at the mercy of a mass media controlled by a mere handful of giant multinational corporations, whose ownership is concentrated in a few wealthy families. With such control over television, radio, newspapers, magazines, movies, advertising and publishing, carefully chosen corporate executives can manipulate the thinking of the masses. Words can be used as psychological weapons. One clear example is the name of the government organization charged with the conduct of military operations. Since 1865, the old War Department fought a declared war on only three occasions: the Spanish-American War, World War I and World War II. Since changing the name to the Defense Department in 1947, the United States has sent troops to fight in Korea, Vietnam, Cambodia, Laos, the Dominican Republic, Haiti, Grenada, Panama, Colombia, Lebanon, Saudi Arabia, Iraqi, Kuwait, Bosnia, Kosovo, Afghanistan and other countries.

Another slight, but most significant, name change lies at the heart of efforts to siphon freedoms from the American public.

One rarely hears national leaders refer to the "republic" anymore. Instead national debate today has been centered about the idea of "democracy," rule by the majority. While the word "democracy" has a nice egalitarian ring to it, there are definite drawbacks. Perhaps the clearest example of "democracy" in action is an old-fashioned lynch mob. Everyone cries "Hang him!" and the majority has its way.

Our forefathers, terrorists themselves in the battle to overthrow their British controlled government, clearly understood the drawbacks of pure democracy. They had the forethought to create a republican system of laws, checks and balances within their new nation. Under a law-abiding republic, a person accused of a crime must be afforded some basic niceties such as an investigation, legal representation and fair trial before he can be hanged. With this understanding of the principles of a democratic republic and the more clear vision of hindsight, a close inspection must be made of the current War on Terror.

Unlike previous wars, there is no Berlin or Tokyo to capture and hence, no victory to be won, except for those who profit from war. The real victim of this war is the average American citizen, right along with the starving Afghan or Iraqi.

This new war might well be compared to the failed War on Drugs and the nearly forgotten War on Poverty. No clear victory has yet been achieved over the misuse of drugs or the ravages of poverty within our own nation. Our prisons are overflowing with drug offenders with no appreciable lessening of either demand or supply and our basic civil rights have been badly mauled.

Just like those failed campaigns, the War on Terrorism for the foreseeable future will set us all on a costly course of restrictions on individual freedom, ever more centralized authority and omnipresent fear. All this derived from a tiny wealthy elite that nevertheless dictates to both politicians and the public. According to the nonpartisan Center for Responsive Politics, less than one-tenth of one percent of the United States population gave 83 percent, or $728 million, of all itemized campaign contributions in the 2002 elections. A little more than 600,000 people - 0.28 percent of the adult population - gave contributions large enough to be counted. The Federal Election Commission requires donations of more than $200 to be itemized. Needless to say, Republicans raised more of this total than Democrats.

And where are the voices of those who would stand for the vast majority of hardworking Americans, who would argue the merits of this new war? The corporate owned airwaves and newspapers only ratchet the fear factor upward each day with little or no effort to hear the many thoughtful Americans who are asking themselves, "Do I really need to give up my freedoms in order to save them?"

With this question in mind, let us seek the answer by taking a long and thoughtful look at what has been happening in the United States.

Part I- The Events of September 11, 2001

"Had I known that the enemy was going to use airplanes to kill on that fateful morning, I would have done everything in my power to protect the American people."
- President George W. Bush at the White House, May 17, 2002

Superficially, the attacks of September 11, 2001, horrible and tragic as they were, all seemed straightforward enough.

According to official pronouncements, about nineteen suicidal Middle Eastern Muslim terrorists, their hearts full of hatred for American freedom and democracy, hijacked four airliners, crashing two into the twin towers of New York City's World Trade Center and a third into the Pentagon. The fourth reportedly crashed in western Pennsylvania after passengers attempted to overcome the hijackers.

However, a closer look at the events of 9/11 brings only many unanswered questions. As pointed out by thoughtful students of history, one must ignore the details, which often are contradictory or erroneous, and instead concentrate on the overall process by which these events transpired.

A Chronology of Events

Sometime between 7:45 A.M. and 8:10 A.M. on September 11, 2001, American Airlines Flight 11 and United Airlines Flight 175 were hijacked and by 8:15 A.M. both were obviously off course. This was known to air traffic controllers.

American Flight 11, a Boeing 767 with 92 persons on board out of a possible 351, had taken off from Boston's Logan International Airport en route to Los Angeles. United Flight 175, another Boeing 767 carrying 65 passengers out of a possible 351, also departed from Logan to Los Angeles.

During that same time frame, American Flight 77, a Boeing 757 with 64 passengers out of a possible 289, took off from Dulles International Airport in Washington destined for Los Angeles, while United Flight 93, a Boeing 757 with 45 passengers out of a possible 289, headed for San Francisco from Newark Airport.

By 8:43 A.M. the Northeast Air Defense Sector (NEADS) of the North American Aerospace Defense Command (NORAD) was alerted to the hijackings of Flights 11 and 175 by the FAA and, according to a NORAD statement, two F-

15 jet fighters were scrambled from the Otis Air National Guard Base in Falmouth, Massachusetts.

Moments after 8:45, it was known to authorities that the four airliners had been hijacked, an unprecedented occurrence.

About 8:46 A.M., just as the Otis jets were taking off, Flight 11 struck the north face of the 110-story north tower of the World Trade Center at the 96th floor. Also at this time, the two F-15s from Otis were redirected to New York City.

At 8:47 A.M.., despite having its tracking beacon turned off by the hijackers, air traffic controllers could see that American Flight 77 had reversed course and was moving back toward the East Coast.

At 9:03 A.M., with the evacuation of the WTC towers proceeding amidst fear and confusion, United Flight 175 careened into the southeast corner of the south tower at the 80th floor, sending burning fuel into the air over lower New York. The F-15s were reported as being seventy-one miles away. According to official sources, the jets arrived over NYC at 9:10 A.M., seven minutes too late.

According to the *New York Daily News* of September, 12, 2001, at 9:06 A.M., the NYPD broadcast this message to key officials, "This was a terrorist attack. Notify the Pentagon." At 9:08 A.M., it was added, "Freeze all the airports. Freeze all the airports. Nothing in or out."

Although there were reports of people inside the Pentagon watching the attack on New York and speculating about the possibility of such attacks on themselves, no one was warned and the Pentagon was not evacuated. However, at 9:30 A.M. two F-16 fighters were scrambled from Langley Air Force Base in Hampton, Virginia.

At 9:31 A.M., President Bush declared the disaster in New York an apparent terrorist attack.

At 9:35 A.M. American Flight 77, its transponder turned off, began making a complicated 270-degree circular spiral turn while descending seven thousand feet. At 9:40 A.M., it reportedly crashed into the west side of the concrete and limestone Pentagon, destroying two of its five rings of offices.

By 9:48 A.M. key officials of the White House and the Capitol were evacuated and taken to secure but undisclosed locations. One minute later, in an unprecedented action, the FAA ordered all airline flights across the nation grounded.

Shortly after 10 A.M. the south tower of the World Trade Center collapsed, covering lower Manhattan with tons of ash, dust, smoke and debris. At that same time, United Flight 93, also with transponder turned off or disabled, crashed in western Pennsylvania about eighty miles southeast of Pittsburgh near Shanksville after passengers reportedly used cell phones to report that they intended to fight the hijackers. This event was followed about twenty-three minutes later by the collapse of the WTC north tower, the upper floors of which had been burning for about an hour and a half.

By noon, there were closings at the United Nations, Securities and Exchange Commission, the stock markets, some skyscrapers in several cities and even some large tourist attractions such as Walt Disney World, Mount Rushmore, the Seattle Space Needle and St. Louis's Gateway Arch.

At 1:04 P.M., speaking from Barksdale Air Force Base in Louisiana, President Bush proclaimed, "Make no mistake, the United States will hunt down and punish those responsible for these cowardly acts."

At 5:25 P.M. the 47-story Building Seven of the WTC collapsed and, after about an hour and a half, disaster relief crews began moving into the area searching for survivors.

Unresolved Issues and Questions

The attacks have prompted a lengthy list of questions, many of which have still not been satisfactorily answered. Due to the premature cleansing of "Ground Zero," many of them probably will never be answered.

How could an obviously sophisticated terrorist plan involving perhaps more than one hundred persons, and in the works for many years, escape the notice of our intelligence services, especially the FBI and CIA?

The fact is, it didn't, as will be discussed later.

And why, instead of cashiering those responsible for this intelligence failure and totally restructuring these agencies, are we doubling their budgets? Will we now get twice as much failure as before?

To many thoughtful people, it is unsettling and even a bit suspicious that not one individual within the federal government or military has been fired or even reprimanded for the obvious intelligence and reactionary missteps of that day.

Why did there appear to be a consistent failure of response on the part of defense authorities?

Both American Flight 11 and United Flight 175 were off course by 8:15 A.M. yet NORAD was not notified for fifteen or twenty minutes. It was another fifteen minutes before jet interceptors were ordered off the ground at Otis AFB, a delay of more than thirty minutes.

Yet in October 1999, when golf pro Payne Stewart's Learjet went off course due to a failure of the plane's oxygen system, the air force announced that two F-15s from Elgin Air Force Base, Florida, intercepted the plane within twenty-four minutes after it lost contact with aircraft controllers, and followed it until it crashed. In 2001, a private plane that merely passed too close to the Bush ranch in Texas was immediately ordered to land.

Why was a FEMA disaster relief team dispatched to New York City, arriving the day before the attacks? Was this a stroke of luck, a coincidence, part of an unreported training exercise or something else?

What are the odds that four transcontinental flights on two major airlines

- American Flights 77 and 11 and United Flights 175 and 93 - would have 78, 74, 81 and 84 percent empty seats respectively on September 11, 2001?

And why did Defense Secretary Donald Rumsfeld mention a "missile" when describing the Pentagon attack to *Parade* Magazine?

How did the terrorists obtain top-secret White House and *Air Force One* codes and signals, the excuse for hustling President Bush from Florida to Louisiana to Nebraska on September 11?

At 9:00 A.M. on September 11, just about the time Flight 175 slammed into the south tower of the WTC, Secret Service agents in Washington received this chilling message: "*Air Force One* is next." Within minutes Vice President Dick Cheney was hustled from his seat in front of a television down to the president's nuclear-bomb-proof emergency operations center and the White House evacuated.

The warning was transmitted in that day's top-secret White House code, indicating that whoever was behind the transpiring attacks had access to the highest level of security codes. It meant that whoever had the codes could track and accurately pinpoint the president's plane.

After several days of investigation, the picture grew even darker. Someone had penetrated the National Security Agency's (NSA) hush-hush Echelon surveillance system. In fact, they appeared to have more electronic capability than even the NSA, including the use of "steganography," technology that allows its user to bypass Echelon and other electronic monitoring by hiding messages randomly in otherwise innocent digital files such as music, online advertisements, e-mail headers or even Internet pornography. Such buried messages leave no trace of their presence. The idea that someone had access to such high-level codes provoked speculation that there were "moles," deep-cover secret agents, within the U.S. government. It also could mean that whoever was behind the attacks had access to the latest and most sophisticated electronic equipment.

While hundreds of people around the world were rounded up by national authorities in the wake of the 9/11 attacks, why were about two dozen members of Osama bin Laden's family allowed to fly by private jet to a reunion in Washington and then Boston? And was this during the no-fly time in the week following the attacks? According to the *New Yorker* magazine, the bin Ladens grouped in Boston, where they eventually flew their private jet to Europe once the FAA reinstated overseas flights.

More questions have been raised concerning the hijackers themselves and the people behind them.

The day following 9/11, FBI director Robert Mueller announced some astonishingly swift police work. "We have, in the last twenty--four hours, taken the [passenger] manifests and used them in an evidentiary manner. And have successfully, I believe, identified many of the hijackers on each of the four flights that went down," he told newsmen. Sounding like a 1940s police detective,

Mueller added, "We will leave no stone unturned to find those responsible for the tragedies."

Yet, at the same time, Mueller acknowledged that the list of named hijackers might not contain their real names. If they all used aliases, how did the FBI identify them so quickly? Isn't everyone required to show a photo ID to claim a boarding pass? Where was the normal security? And how did the FBI learn the names of five of the hijackers and obtain their photographs the day of the attacks?

Not one of the accused hijackers' names appeared on the passenger lists made public by American or United Airlines. In fact, several of those named as the culprits in the attacks have been found alive and well in the Middle East.

Saudi pilot Waleed al-Shehri was identified by the U.S. Justice Department as one of the men who crashed American Flight 11 into the WTC. But a few days later, Waleed al-Shehri contacted authorities in Casablanca, Morocco, to proclaim that he was very much alive and played no part in the attacks. He said he did train as a pilot in the United States but left the country in September 2000, to become a pilot with Saudi Arabian Airlines.

Another man identified as one of the hijackers of Flight 11, Abdulaziz al-Omari, also turned up alive in the Middle East, telling *BBC News* that he lost his passport while visiting Denver, Colorado. Actually two turned up, as yet another Abdulaziz al-Omari surfaced in Saudi Arabia very much alive and telling newsmen, "I couldn't believe the FBI put me on their list. They gave my name and my date of birth, but I am not a suicide bomber. I am here. I am alive. I have no idea how to fly a plane. I had nothing to do with this."

Yet another man identified as one of the hijackers of United Flight 93, Saeed al-Ghamdi, was reported alive and well and working as a pilot in Saudi Arabia. "You cannot imagine what it is like to be described as a terrorist - and a dead man - when you are innocent and alive," said al-Ghamdi, who was given a holiday by his airline in Saudi Arabia to avoid arrest.

There were even reports that another identified hijacker, Khalid al-Midhar, might also be alive. "It was proved that five of the names included in the FBI list had nothing to do with what happened," announced Saudi Arabia's foreign minister Prince Saud al-Faisal, after meeting with President Bush on September 20, 2001.

Mueller acknowledged within days of the attacks that the identities of the hijackers were in doubt but this gained little notice in the rush to publicize the culprits. Despite initially saying he was "fairly confident" that the published names of the hijackers were correct, Mueller later admitted, "The identification process has been complicated by the fact that many Arab family names are similar. It is also possible that the hijackers used false identities."

In September 2002, during testimony before a joint congressional committee, Kristin Breitweiser, whose husband, Ronald, died in the WTC, asked a most pertinent question, which continues to go unanswered. She cited a *New*

York Times article the day after the strikes stating that FBI agents arrived at flight schools within hours to gather biographies on the terrorists. "How did the FBI know where to go a few hours after the attacks?...Were any of the hijackers already under surveillance?"

None of the accused hijackers' names appear on any of the passenger lists and there was a discrepancy of thirty-five names between the published passenger lists and the official death toll on all four of the ill-fated flights. Internet columnist Gary North reported, "...the published names in no instance match the total listed for the number of people on board." Why the discrepancy?

And as none of these listed passengers had Arabic-sounding names, how did the government know who the hijackers were?

Why did one of the named hijackers, Mohammed Atta, reportedly leave behind in his parked car a suitcase containing incriminating documents? Why even take a suitcase on a suicide mission? And if the suitcase was camouflage to present the appearance of a normal tourist, why did he leave it behind?

Why did Council on Foreign Relations notables such as Henry Kissinger, Wesley Clark, Strobe Talbott and Alexander Haig all appear on national television within three hours of the attacks with the same admonition that 9/11 represented a new type of warfare and that all nations should band together under the United Nations to defend against international terrorism?

How could the "black box" flight recorders on both WTC planes, designed to withstand crashes, have been damaged beyond use but a paper passport was fortuitously found on the ground blocks from the WTC?

CNN reported on September 16, "In New York, several blocks from the ruins of the World Trade Center, a passport authorities said belonged to one of the hijackers was discovered a few days ago, according to city Police Commissioner Bernard Kerik. That has prompted the FBI and police to widen the search area beyond the immediate crash site." What happened to the passport and this story? Both seemed to have disappeared. Some suspicious researchers smelled planted evidence.

Furthermore, in light of media stories concerning the discovered passport, a Koran left on a bar stool, flight school materials and even "suicide notes" left behind, why did FBI director Robert Mueller in an April 19, 2002, speech before the Commonwealth Club in San Francisco declare that the hijackers "left no paper trail"?

On the night before the attacks, the *Boston Globe* reported, four of the suspected hijackers called several escort services asking how much it would cost to acquire prostitutes for the night. Other news sources stated that other suspects spent time in bars and strip clubs in Florida, New Jersey and Las Vegas.

Heavy drinking and a search for hookers by some of the hijackers sounds more like mercenaries carousing before a mission than pious religious fundamentalists about to meet their maker.

Why did the seat numbers of the hijackers given by a cell phone call from flight attendant Madeline Amy Sweeney to Boston air traffic control not match the seats occupied by the men the FBI claimed were responsible?

Why did news outlets describe the throat cutting and mutilation of passengers on Flight 93 with box cutters when *Time* magazine on September 24 reported that one of the passengers called home on a cell phone to report, "We have been hijacked. They are being kind"?

Since Saudi Arabia's foreign minister claimed five of the proclaimed hijackers were not aboard the death planes and in fact are still alive, and a sixth man on that list was reported to be alive and well in Tunisia, why are these names still on the FBI list?

As for the overall investigation into the September attacks, by late October U.S. authorities conceded that most of their promising leads for finding accomplices and some of their long-held suspicions about several suspects had unraveled, according to the *New York Times*. More than eight hundred people had been arrested and more than 365,000 tips received from the public, yet nothing substantial has been forthcoming in this, the largest U.S. criminal investigation in history.

Why, according to several experts, did the destruction of the World Trade Center towers appear more like a controlled implosion than a tragic accident?

Such questions concerning the collapse of the towers were advanced by experts in demolition and firefighting immediately, only to die away in the subsequent media blitz. Many people, experts and laymen alike, asked why the south tower collapsed first when it was not as extensively damaged as the north tower, which burned for almost an hour and a half before its collapse.

Numerous sources have claimed that bombs rather than the planes caused the collapse of the World Trade Center towers.

Van Romero, vice president for research at the New Mexico Institute of Mining and Technology and a former director of the Energenic Materials Research and Testing Center said televised images of the collapse of the WTC towers suggested that explosives were used to create a controlled demolition.

"My opinion is, based on the videotapes, that after the airplanes hit the World Trade Center there were some explosive devices inside the buildings that caused the towers to collapse," Romero told the *Albuquerque Journal* on September 11, 2001.

Romero, who ironically was in the Washington area during the 9/11 attacks, said the collapse of the WTC was "too methodical" to be the chance result of airplanes colliding with the structures. He said it appeared more like the controlled implosions used to demolish old buildings.

"It could have been a relatively small amount of explosives placed in strategic points," he said, adding that the detonation of bombs within towers is consistent with common terrorist strategy. "One of the things terrorist events are noted for is a diversionary attack and secondary device. Attackers detonate an

-15-

initial, diversionary explosion that attracts emergency personnel to the scene, then detonate a second explosion," he explained.

Many have wondered about the witnesses who claimed to have heard multiple explosions within the buildings. One such witness was the head of WTC security, John O'Neill, who stated shortly before he himself became a victim that he had helped dig out survivors on the 27 [th] floor before the building collapsed. Since the aircraft crashed into the 80 [th] floor, what heavily damaged the 27th floor?

Another of those mentioning bombs was Louie Cacchioli, a fifty-one-year-old fireman assigned to Engine 47 in Harlem. "We were the first ones in the second tower after the plane struck," recalled Cacchioli. "I was taking firefighters up in the elevator to the twenty-fourth floor to get in position to evacuate workers. On the last trip up a bomb went off. We think there were bombs set in the building." The fireman became trapped in an elevator but managed to escape with the use of tools.

Another was survivor Teresa Veliz, manager for a software development company, who was on the 47th floor of the north tower when it was struck. "I got off [the elevator], turned the corner and opened the door to the ladies' room. I said good morning to a lady sitting at a mirror when the whole building shook. I thought it was an earthquake. Then I heard those banging noises on the other side of the wall. It sounded like someone had cut the elevator cables. It just fell and fell and fell."

Veliz reached ground level with a coworker when the south tower collapsed, knocking them down. In near total darkness, she and the coworker followed someone with a flashlight. "The flashlight led us into Border's bookstore, up an escalator and out to Church Street. There were explosions going off everywhere. I was convinced that there were bombs planted all over the place and someone was sitting at a control panel pushing detonator buttons. I was afraid to go down Church Street toward Broadway, but I had to do it. I ended up on Vesey Street. There was another explosion. And another. I didn't know which way to run."

Ross Milanytch watched the horror at the WTC from his office window on the 22nd floor of a building a couple of blocks away. "[I saw] small explosions on each floor. And after it all cleared, all that was left of the buildings, you could just see the steel girders in like a triangular sail shape. The structure was just completely gone," he said.

Steve Evans, a reporter for the BBC, was in the south tower at the time of the attacks. "I was at the base of the second tower, the second tower that was hit," he recalled. "There was an explosion - I didn't think it was an explosion - but the base of the building shook. I felt it shake…then when we were outside, the second explosion happened and then there was a series of explosions….We can only wonder at the kind of damage - the kind of human damage - which was caused by those explosions, those series of explosions."

Fox 5 News   in NYC shortly after 10:00 A.M. on September 11 videotaped a large white cloud of smoke billowing near the base of the south tower. The commentator exclaimed, "There is an explosion at the base of the building...white smoke from the bottom...something has happened at the base of the building...then, another explosion. Another building in the World Trade Center complex..."

The most compelling testimony came from Tom Elliott, who was already in his office at Aon Corp. on the 103rd floor of the WTC South tower before the planes struck.

Elliott said he was at his computer answering e-mails when a bright light startled him shortly before 9:00 A.M. A rumble shook the building and he could see flames accompanied by dark smoke that appeared to be crawling up the outside of the building. He also felt heat coming through the windows. Strangely, there were no alarms.

"I don't know what's happening, but I think I need to be out of here," Elliott recalled thinking to himself.

Elliott and two others began walking down the building's stairwell when they ran into a few others. The absence of more people and the lack of alarms made them feel they had prematurely panicked.

He recalled that as his small group reached the 70th floor, they heard the announcement that the building was secure and there was no need to evacuate. "Do you want to believe them?" one woman said to Elliott. "Let's go!" He followed the woman down the stairs.

After descending three more floors, Flight 175 crashed into the south tower. An article in the *Christian Science Monitor* described what happened next:

"Although its spectacularly televised impact was above Elliott, at first he and those around him thought an explosion had come from below. An incredible sound - he calls it an 'exploding sound' - shook the building, and a tornado of hot air and smoke and ceiling tiles and bits of drywall came flying up the stairwell."

"In front of me, the wall split from the bottom up," Elliott said. He said people in the stairwell panicked and tried to flee upward until some men pointed out that the only escape was downstairs. By about 9:40 A.M., Elliott managed to stumble out of the south tower and make his way to his roommate's office in Midtown, where he broke down sobbing upon learning of the tower's collapse.

A CNN video of the scene at the WTC showed smoke boiling up from the street level prior to the collapse of the towers, apparently from the eight-story WTC building six, more popularly known as the Customs House building.

Due to a delayed broadcast, there was some initial confusion about just when the blast occurred. However, CNN's Public Affairs Department confirmed that the video footage of an apparent explosion at ground level was made at 9:04 A.M., just one minute after Flight 175 struck the south tower and long before either tower collapsed.

Asked what might have caused the smoke seen in the video, the CNN archivist replied, "We can't figure it out."

According to news reports, the FEMA team of engineers commissioned to investigate the WTC tragedy were barred from entering the Custom House building. FEMA officials reported that because the structure was considered "very dangerous," there was "no data collection" from building six. Yet, the FEMA report blithely stated, "Building five was the only building accessible for observation [by the team of engineers]...the observations, findings and recommendations are assumed to be applicable to all three buildings."

A spokesman for the Export-Import Bank of the United States confirmed the 9:04 A.M. time of the blast but said all of the eight hundred or so employees of the Custom House building had already been evacuated after the WTC north tower was struck.

Other occupants of the building, which included the Customs Service, the Departments of Commerce, Labor, Agriculture and the Bureau of Alcohol, Tobacco and Firearms, declined to explain either the early blast or the massive crater at the center of the Customs House ruins.

No explanation for this explosion or crater has been forthcoming.

Who exactly ordered that broadcast over the loudspeakers in the south tower as workers were trying to evacuate, "Remain calm, damage is in Tower One. Return to your desks"? Many people lost their lives because of these announcements.

An audiotape of New York firefighters at the scene, unpublicized until mid-2002, indicated that fire officials managed to reach the 78th floor of the south tower - very near the crash scene - and seemed convinced that the fire was controllable.

The tape was briefly mentioned by the *New York Times* but was kept from the public by the U.S. Justice Department who claimed it might be needed in the trial of the "twentieth hijacker," Zacarias Moussaoui, even though Moussaoui was in custody at the time of the attacks.

The tape was made from radio transmissions made on the morning of September 11, 2001. The tape reportedly was found two or three weeks after 9/11 in offices of the Port Authority of New York and New Jersey in WTC building five. Apparently, Port Authority personnel were monitoring and recording the NYFD channel.

Two fire officials mentioned by name in the tape were Battalion Chief Orio J. Palmer and Fire Marshal Ronald P. Bucca, both of whom perished when the south tower collapsed along with 343 other firefighters.

According to the *Times* article both firemen "showed no panic, no sense that events were racing beyond their control...At that point, the building would be standing for just a few more minutes, as the fire was weakening the structure on the floors above him. Even so, Chief Palmer could see only two pockets of fire and called for a pair of engine companies to fight them."

As noted by *American Free Press* reporter Christopher Bollyn, "The fact that veteran firefighters had a 'coherent plan for putting out' the 'two pockets of fire,' indicates they judged the blazes to be manageable. These reports from the scene of the crash provide crucial evidence debunking the government's claim that a raging steel-melting inferno led to the tower's collapse."

More evidence of ground explosions causing the WTC collapse came from seismographs at Columbia University's Lamont-Doherty Earth Observatory in Palisades, New York, twenty-one miles north of the WTC. Just prior to the collapse of the twin towers, seismic equipment recorded two "spikes" indicating large bursts of energy that shook the ground beneath the WTC towers just before their collapse.

Additionally, according to Mark Loizeaux, president of Controlled Demolition, Inc. of Phoenix, Arizona, who consulted on removing the WTC debris, "hot spots" of molten steel were found as many as five weeks after the collapse when rubble was removed from the elevator shafts seven levels down.

Loizeaux speculated that steel-melting fires were generated by "paper, carpet and other combustibles packed down the elevator shafts by the towers as they 'pancaked" into the basement."
Since construction steel's melting point is about 2,800 degrees Fahrenheit, other experts disputed this idea, saying that due to the lack of oxygen, such debris would have been only a smoldering pile.

Speculating further, Loizeaux told the *American Free Press*, "If I were to bring the towers down, I would put explosives in the basement to get the weight of the building to help collapse the structure."

Considering the total destruction, reports from survivors and firemen and the seismic shocks just prior to the collapse, many people believed that Loizeaux's description was exactly what happened on September 11, 2001.

Columbia's seismic equipment recorded a 2.1-magnitude ground shock during the ten-second collapse of the south tower and a 2.3 quake during the eight-second collapse of the north tower. However, the strongest shocks, or "spikes," on the data recorder both occurred at the beginning of the tower's collapse, well before falling material struck the ground. The two spikes were more than twenty times the amplitude of the other seismic shock waves associated with the falling buildings. One seismologist said the 1993 truck bomb at the WTC did not even register on seismographs because the explosion did not cause shock waves through the ground.

Seismologist Arthur Lerner-Lam, director of Columbia's Center for Hazards and Risk Research, added to this by saying, "During the collapse, most of the energy of the falling debris was absorbed by the towers and the neighboring structures, converting them into rubble and dust or causing other damage - but not causing significant ground shaking." Asked about the two unusual shocks, Lerner-Lam was noncommittal. "This is an element of current research and discussion. It is still being investigated," he told the media.

So the public was left with the official explanation that high-temperature fires caused by burning jet fuel melted structural steel beams, causing the towers to fall. No one will ever know for certain since none of the engineers hired by FEMA inspected or tested the steel before it was hauled away for salvage.

"I am not a metallurgist," explained Dr. W. Gene Corley, head of the FEMA engineer team.

According to FEMA's "Building Performance Assessment," temperatures at the crash site - only two floors above Chief Palmer and Marshal Bucca - were as high as 1,700-2,000 degrees Fahrenheit, so intense as to melt the structure's steel frame girders.

"If FEMA's temperature estimates are correct, the interiors of the towers were furnaces capable of casting aluminum and glazing pottery," declared researcher and author Eric Hufschmid. Yet the firemen were able to work for an extended period of time in close proximity and believed the fires they encountered were manageable.

Citing a severe fire in Philadelphia's Meridian Plaza in 1991, Hufschmid noted, "The Meridian Plaza fire was extreme, but it did not cause the building to collapse.

"The fire in the south tower seems insignificant by comparison to both the Meridian Plaza fire and the fire in the north tower. How could the tiny fire in the south tower cause the entire structure to shatter into dust after fifty-six minutes while much more extreme fires did not cause the Meridian Plaza building to even crack into two pieces?"

Perhaps there are more reasonable explanations for two modern buildings to collapse into nothing but dust, but now no one will ever know for certain.

The public might know more of what really happened to the WTC if the New York Police Department and New York Fire Department had been allowed to do their jobs. But, as with the JFK assassination, their work was taken from them by federal officials, who immediately closed doors and shut out the public from their consultations.

The FBI took charge of the criminal investigation while the little-understood Federal Emergency Management Agency took responsibility for determining what happened to cause the collapse of the twin towers. FEMA seemed determined to haul away the evidence, even before a full and impartial investigation could be made. Such premature destruction of evidence was called into question by Bill Manning, editor of the 125-year-old firemen's publication *Fire Engineering* in its January 2002 issue

"For more than three months, structural steel from the World Trade Center has been and continues to be cut up and sold for scrap," wrote Manning. "Crucial evidence that could answer many questions about high-rise building design practices and performance under fire conditions is on a slow boat to China, perhaps never to be seen again in America until you buy your next car."

Challenging the theory that the twin towers collapsed as a result of crashed airplanes and fires, Manning added, *"Fire Engineering* has good reason to believe that the 'official investigation' blessed by FEMA and run by the American Society of Civil Engineers (ASCE) is a half-baked farce that may already have been commandeered by political forces whose primary interests, to put it mildly, lie far afield of full disclosure.

"Except for the marginal benefit obtained from a three-day, visual walk-through of evidence sites conducted by the ASCE investigation committee members - described by one close source as a 'tourist trip' - no one's checking the evidence for anything."

"The destruction and removal of evidence must stop immediately," Manning declared.

In that same issue, a number of fire officials, including a retired deputy chief from New York's fire department, called on FEMA to "immediately impanel a 'World Trade Center Disaster Review Panel' to coordinate a complete review of all aspects of the World Trade Center incident."

These fire officials noted that the WTC disaster was the largest loss of firefighters ever at one incident; the second largest loss of life on American soil; the first total collapse of a high-rise during a fire in United States history and the largest structural collapse in recorded history.

"Now, with that understanding, you would think we would have the largest fire investigation in world history," they wrote. "You would be wrong. Instead, we have a series of unconnected and uncoordinated superficial inquiries...Ironically, we will probably gain more detailed information about the destruction of the planes than we will about the destruction of the towers. We are literally treating the steel removed from the site like garbage, not like crucial fire scene evidence."

Complaints from the federal investigating team of engineers supported these accusations.

Citing delays by federal agencies and incomplete information, the twenty-six-member team of ASCE engineers that was formed to study the collapse of the WTC towers finally produced a 296-page report by early May 2002.

But even as the report was issued, team leader and structural engineer Dr. W. Gene Corley told Congress there were still many questions left unanswered by his study.

"We didn't have time and resources," Corley complained. He said his team didn't have enough data to create a computer model of the interior damage caused by the aircraft, nor could they model the spread of the fires. The team also griped that federal agencies feuded over funding and to whom the team should be reporting.

The team never had access to 911 emergency calls, which could have helped determine exactly what happened where in the minutes prior to the collapse of the buildings, and, this can not be emphasized enough, they confirmed reports that much of the structural steel was removed from the site, cut up and sold as scrap before they had a chance to examine it.

The team could not even obtain a complete set of building plans until early in 2002. Then they found that floor supports were attached to exterior columns by strong welds and not, as widely believed, relatively small bolts.

Corley did say the team learned just enough to know that more answers were desperately needed to design protective measures for similar structures that might be future terrorist targets.

His quest for more answers coupled with congressional outrage over the obstacles thrown in front of the engineering team prompted Presidentto pledge $16 million for a follow-up study by the National Institute of Standards and Technology.

In light of the results of such panels in the past, many researchers are not holding their breath in expectation of real answers.

The Tracks of Foreknowledge

Following the devastating attacks of 9/11, U.S. leaders said we should avoid "finger pointing" to place blame, yet advance warnings were too numerous and specific to do otherwise.

During 2001, the United States spent $30 billion on intelligence gathering plus an additional $12 billion aimed specifically at counterterrorism. This total of $42 billion exceeds most nation's total gross national product, yet Americans were told that none of its two dozen alphabet intelligence agencies had any inkling that we were about to be attacked.

Information available today seriously disputes this claim. It was disputed within days of the attacks by people both in and outside the government.

Questions as to why there had been no warning came quickly. The day after the attacks, Congressional Research Service antiterrorism expert Kenneth Katzman was quoted as saying, "How nothing could have been picked up is beyond me."

Something must have been picked up. How else to explain the fact that the State Department on September 7, 2001, issued a worldwide caution to Americans that they "may be the target of a terrorist threat from extremist groups with links to Osama bin Laden's al-Qaeda organization....Such individuals have not distinguished between official and civilian targets. As always, we take this information seriously. U.S. government facilities worldwide remain on heightened alert."

As months passed, more and more evidence accumulated until it became overwhelmingly clear that persons within the U.S. federal government were warned of terrorist attacks, including the use of airplanes against buildings.

One year after the attacks, an unusual joint House and Senate investigating committee received testimony that U.S. intelligence agencies had received at least twelve warnings of coming offensive action by terrorists. And as will be seen, this is a low figure.

By April 2002, leaks in the news media damaging to the official explanation and a public clamor for an investigation of the 9/11 attacks prompted congressional leaders to agree to a joint investigation by both the Senate and House Intelligence Committees. Limited in scope, the probe was only to review intelligence failures and recommend corrections. It got off to a rocky start when retired CIA inspector general Britt Snider resigned under pressure from committee members who believed his close connection to CIA director George Tenet might interfere with an impartial investigation.

Further frustrating congressional efforts to investigate the attacks was the apparent bumbling and sluggishness of the federal bureaucracy.

According to the *Los Angeles Times*, "Small teams of investigators have been at the Justice Department and the CIA, gathering documents and conducting interviews. They have come back with a litany of complaints about tactics they say are designed to slow their progress and restrict their access to documents and potential informants, sources said."

During these hearings, it was learned that from 1998 onward, both the CIA and FBI received ever-increasing warnings concerning al-Qaeda using hijacked aircraft to attack targets within the United States. Despite the serious nature of the issue of official foreknowledge, the Bush administration continued to stonewall and hamper the congressional investigation, even launching an investigation of the investigators.

After word leaked to the public in June 2002 that communications in Arabic intercepted by the National Security Agency on September 10, 2001, contained phrases such as "Tomorrow is zero hour" and "The match is about to begin," the FBI swung into action.

But instead of going after the authors of the notes indicating foreknowledge, they went after the persons on the joint committee who leaked the information.

Even as White House spokesman Ari Fleischer was calling the notes "alarmingly specific," bureau agents were asking committee members to take lie detector tests regarding the leaks. The *Washington Post* reported that nearly all of the thirty-seven members of the joint committee were questioned. Some members declined to take the lie detector tests, citing constitutional separation of powers and the unreliability of such tests.

Eleanor Hill, staff director of the joint House and Senate intelligence committee, spoke out about advance notice of the attacks passed to ranking leaders. She noted that a briefing for "senior government officials" in July 2001 specifically warned that Osama bin Laden "will launch a significant terrorist attack against U.S. and/or Israeli interests in the coming weeks. The attack will be spectacular and designed to inflict mass casualties against U.S. facilities or interests. Attack preparations have been made. Attack will occur with little or no warning."

She said it was unknown if President Bush received specific information regarding the possibility of airliners being used as flying bombs because the director of the CIA would not declassify the information. The unusual joint hearings were scheduled for June 2002 but then delayed until late September. "Are we getting the cooperation we need? Absolutely not," charged the senior Republican on the Senate Intelligence Committee, Republican Senator Richard Shelby of Alabama.

Florida Democratic Senator Bob Graham echoed Shelby's complaint, saying the Bush administration told them they can "only talk to the top of the pyramid." "Well, the problem is, the top of the pyramid has a general awareness of what's going on in the organization, but if you want to know why Malaysian plotters were not put on a watch list...you've got to talk to somebody at the level where those kinds of decisions were made." Graham referred to Hill's report, which pointed out that two of the hijacking suspects, Khalid al-Midhar and Nawaf al-Hazmi, lived openly in San Diego even after being observed in a Malaysia meeting with known terrorists. Bush and Cheney had long opposed any independent investigation of the 9/11 attacks, claiming it would impede the War on Terrorism by leading to leaks of security measures and tying up personnel needed in the war.

But with the revelations of irregularities in investigations by government agencies that came to light in the spring and summer of 2002, Congress was finally moved to action. "The attacks of September 11...highlighted a failure of national policy to respond to the developments of a global terror network implacably hostile to American interests," thundered Senator John McCain, who, along with Senator Joseph Lieberman, cosponsored a bill to create an independent commission to investigate everything from visa procedures to airline security. Legislation to create this ten-person panel, armed with subpoena power and a $3 million budget, was approved by the Senate in a 90/8 vote late in September 2002.

The Hill report, described as preliminary, was based on a review of 400,000 government documents and testimony taken during four months of closed-door hearings. Hill stated that while investigators found no specific warning of the 9/11 attacks, collectively the warnings "reiterated a consistent and critically important theme: Osama bin Laden's intent to launch terrorist attacks inside the United States."

The report showed that in addition to knowing of terrorist plots to use hijacked jets as flying bombs, "senior U.S. officials" were advised two months before the attacks that bin Laden was planning a major operation, possibly inside the United States. Illinois Republican Representative Ray Lahood said it was possible that U.S. intelligence agencies had enough information to have prevented the attacks, but there were "no guarantees."

Actually, warnings of a domestic attack had been coming in for some time.

In December, 2000, the Congressional Advisory Panel to Assess Domestic Response Capabilities for Terrorism Involving Weapons of Mass Destruction issued a report stating, "We are impelled by the stark realization that a terrorist attack on some level within our borders is inevitable."

One clear warning came eight years before the 9/11 attacks in the form of a book written by Yossef Bodansky, director of the U.S. House Task Force on Terrorism and Unconventional Warfare.

In his book, *Target America: Terrorism in the U.S. Today,* Bodansky detailed the airfields in Iran and North Korea where Muslim terrorists trained and noted, "According to a former trainee in Wakiland [Iran], one of the exercises included having an Islamic Jihad detachment seize (or hijack) a transport aircraft. Then, trained air crews from among the terrorists would crash the airliner with its passengers into a selected target."

Wiretaps on suspected al-Qaeda terrorists in Italy as far back as 2000 also gave indication of plans for a major attack on the United States involving airplanes and airports. "This will be one of those strikes that will never be forgotten..." was the comment recorded from Abdelkader Mahmoud Es Sayed, an Egyptian accused of being a ranking al-Qaeda member in Italy and a man convicted of the 1997 massacre of fifty-eight tourists at Luxor, Egypt. Es Sayed also mentioned danger in airports and flying. In another taped conversation on January 24, 2001, a Tunisian terrorist spoke about fake identification papers to Es Sayed and asked, "Will these work for the brothers who are going to the United States?" Es Sayed also stated the war against the enemies of Islam would be fought "with any means we can combat them, using...airplanes. They won't be able to stop us even with their heaviest weapons."

According to the *Los Angeles Times*, several U.S. officials said they were unfamiliar with the wiretap messages but "one Justice Department official noted that a small cadre of U.S. intelligence agents might have been privy to them." What is most enlightening about these Italian wiretaps is not that they evinced foreknowledge - they were too vague to be considered a precise warning - but that they gave indication of the many and varied alerts coming into the United States as well as the fact that many foreign intelligence services were monitoring al-Qaeda cells.

Spain got in on the act. In August 2001, the voice of an unidentified man in London was taped speaking with the head of a Madrid terrorist cell. The man said he had entered the field of aviation and was taking flying lessons.

According to a report on MSNBC, just two weeks before the 9/11 attacks, a radio station in the Cayman Islands received an unsigned letter warning of a major attack against the United States involving airliners. It was reported that U.S. government officials went to investigate but no further information was forthcoming. As will be seen, the Cayman Islands is an offshore banking haven to many factions, including the CIA and international bankers.

Even the much disparaged Taliban apparently tried to give warning. According to a story posted September 7, 2002, by Independent Digital, an aide to then Taliban foreign minister Wakil Ahmed Muttawakil tried to warn U.S. authorities weeks prior to the 9/11 attacks. Muttawakil, unhappy with the glut of foreign Arab militants in Afghanistan, told his aide he was concerned over the prospect of U.S. military action against his country. He was quoted as saying, "The guests are going to destroy the guesthouse."

The aide, unidentified for his own safety by the British publication, said Muttawakil was shocked in the summer of 2001 to learn of a coming attack from fundamentalist Islamic leader Tahir Yildash. "At first, Muttawakil wouldn't say why he was so upset," explained the aide. "Then it all came out. Yildash had revealed that Osama bin Laden was going to launch an attack on the United States. It would take place on American soil and it was imminent. Yildash said Osama hoped to kill thousands of Americans."

The aide said he first traveled across the Pakistan border to meet with American consul general David Katz late in July 2001. "They met in a safe house belonging to an old Mujahideen leader who has confirmed to the *Independent* that the meeting took place," reported the news outlet. Katz declined to discuss the matter.

Next, the aide was sent by Muttawakil to the Kabul offices of the United Nations, where he again issued his warning.

Apparently since the aide failed to make it clear that he was sent by Foreign Minister Muttawakil, both American and United Nations officials thought his warning more propaganda from the warring factions within Afghanistan and did nothing.

Similar warning signs came from the Far East. In 1995, when Manila authorities answered a fire call they discovered bomb-making materials in the apartment of Ramzi Yousef, later convicted for his role in the 1993 WTC bombing. Yousef escaped but another suspected al-Qaeda member, Abdul Hakim Murad, was taken into custody.

Murad told his interrogators that Ramzi had a plan to hijack a commercial airliner in the United States and crash it into CIA Headquarters or the Pentagon. Philippine investigators also found evidence that Ramzi's plan, code-named "Project Bojinka," also involved targeting the White House, Sears Tower in Chicago, the Transamerica Tower in San Francisco and the World Trade Center.

Apparently Muslim fanatics had already attempted to put Ramzi's plan into effect. On Christmas Eve 1994, four men thought to be connected to bin Laden's terrorist network hijacked Air France Flight 8969 bound from Algiers to Paris. The plane landed in Marseilles, where the hijackers demanded that it be loaded with explosives and extra fuel. Their plan, apparently to crash the craft into the Eiffel Tower, was derailed when commandos stormed the plane and killed all four hijackers.

Warnings continued to pour in from the Philippines, a hotbed of terrorist activity. According to the *Manila Times*, Philippine defense and police intelligence officers warned American authorities of an alliance between Abu Sayyaf (ASG) terrorists there and the al-Qaeda network. The paper said American officials ignored the warnings until September 11, 2001.

The report went on to describe a 1994 meeting between ASG cofounder Edwin Angeles and WTC bombing mastermind Ramzi Yousef that included convicted Oklahoma City bombing accomplice Terry Nichols, who was married to a Philippine national. The topics of discussion were terrorist targets. The Murrah Federal Building in Oklahoma City was mentioned as well as another attack on the World Trade Center.

It appears that everyone from the Chinese to our own FBI tried to warn Washington authorities that an attack was imminent, yet nothing was done.

Chinese military officers wrote about just such an attack as 9/11 three years before the fact. In a military manual entitled *Unrestricted Warfare*, People's Liberation Army colonels Qiao Liang and Wang Xiangsui noted, "Whether it be the intrusions of [computer] hackers, a *major explosion at the World Trade Center, or a bombing attack by bin Laden* [emphasis added], all of these greatly exceed the frequency bandwidth understood by the American military..."

A CIA translation of this Chinese manual was published on September 11, 2002, the one-year anniversary of the attacks. The manual is a recipe book of unorthodox methods for weaker nations to humble America. It discusses multilevel attacks on America's social, political and economic systems using strategies involving computer hackers, the infiltration of illegal immigrants, stock market manipulation and even the use of weapons of mass destruction.

The Chinese leadership, and particularly its military chiefs, has long viewed the United States as their principal enemy, a fact that has been marginalized by both the U.S. Congress and the corporate mass media due to the close business and trade relations between the nations.

Exactly one month following the 9/11 attacks, China was quietly approved as a member of the World Trade Organization after fifteen years of negotiation. It was a move that had previously prompted many and widespread protests due to that Asian nation's abysmal human rights record. This time, with Americans in shock over the 9/11 attacks, little notice was given to this action.

With the heightened security due to the attacks, there was no opportunity for demonstrations against this WTO action. According to CNN, WTO ministers meeting in the Persian Gulf state of Qatar were protected by a U.S. helicopter ship, other vessels and inside a cordon that included more than two thousand U.S. Marines.

WTO director-general Mike Moore declared China's entry into the trade organization "a major historic event," yet there was minimal publicity in the United States.

Even the Russians seemed to be aware that something big was coming.

Dr. Tatyana Koryagina, a senior research fellow for the Institute of Macroeconomic Researches under the Russian Ministry of Economic Development and reportedly close to President Putin's inner circle, predicted that an "unusual catastrophe" would strike the United States in late August, 2001. Her prediction appeared in a *Pravda* story published on July 12, 2001.

"The U.S. has been chosen as the object of financial attack because the financial center of the planet is located there. The effect will be maximal. The strike waves of economic crisis will spread over the planet instantly and will remind us of the blast of a huge nuclear bomb."

Asked about the discrepancy of dates in a later interview, Dr. Koryagina explained, "I did not make a serious mistake. Indeed, between 15 and 20 August, the dollar started trembling under the pressure of multiple bad news about the U.S. and economy. And within weeks, the Manhattan skyscrapers fell down.

"As a result, a significant part of the world financial network was paralyzed. This strike was aimed at destabilization and destruction of America and (in domino fashion) all the countries making countless billions of dollars." She advised Russian citizens not to invest in American dollars.

She also said the 9/11 attacks were not the work of nineteen terrorists but a group of extremely powerful private persons seeking to reshape the world. This group, she added, has assets of about $300 trillion, which it will use to legitimize its power and create a new world government.

Many persons have taken Dr. Koryagina's comments very seriously when considering both her credentials and her knowledge of Russia's close contacts with nations identified with terrorism, such as Iraq, Iran, Syria, Libya, and North Korea.

As reported by the *Washington Times* on September 28, 2001, "U.S. intelligence agencies have uncovered information that Russian criminal groups have been supplying Osama bin Laden and his al-Qaeda terrorist network with components for chemical, biological and nuclear weapons."

Arabic sources too seemed to have been able to discern that bin Laden was preparing to launch a major attack.

In mid-2002, Egyptian president Hosni Mubarak revealed that his intelligence service warned U.S. officials about a week before the 9/11 attacks that bin Laden's organization was in the last stages of preparing a major operation against an American target.

Mubarak said Egyptian intelligence chiefs tried unsuccessfully to thwart the operation using an unnamed agent who had penetrated the al-Qaeda network. They passed the information regarding this penetration to U.S. intelligence between March and May 2001, he said, adding, "We informed them about everything."

An American intelligence official told *The New York Times* that they had received no such warning but Mubarak said he was informed that security at the

U.S. embassy in Cairo was tightened just before the attacks. Mubarak's interview with the *Times* apparently was the first time that a foreign leader admitted that an intelligence service had penetrated the al-Qaeda terrorist network.

The *Times* writers noted dryly, "At a minimum, Mr. Mubarak's account adds detail and drama to a list of warnings about potential terrorist attacks that American intelligence fielded in the days, weeks and months before September 11."

Within hours of the attacks Abdel-Barri Atwan, editor of the London newspaper, *al-Quds al-Arabi*, told Reuters News Service, "Osama bin Laden warned three weeks ago that he would attack American interests in an unprecedented attack, a big one...Personally we received information that he planned very, very big attacks against American interests. We received several warnings like this."

Although Atwan said he did not notify the authorities of this warning because he did not take it seriously, it raises the question - if a London newspaper knew of impending attacks, why not the American intelligence services?

An article in the June 23, 2001, issue of *Airjet Airline World News* noted another Arabic source as claiming that "a big surprise" was expected in coming weeks.

A reporter from Arabic satellite television channel MBC who had recently met with bin Laden was quoted as saying, "A severe blow is expected against U.S. and Israeli interests worldwide...There is a mobilization among the Osama bin Laden forces. It seems that there is a race of who will strike first. Will it be the United States or Osama bin Laden?"

Another source may have been an Iranian being held in Germany at the time of the 9/11 attacks. According to the German newspaper *Neue Presse,* prior to 9/11 the man asked to contact American authorities to warn them of an imminent attack. It was reported that when the man told the Secret Service that he was facing deportation from Germany, they hung up on him. On September 14, the man was finally interrogated by U.S. agents.

Closer to home, in a 1993 letter to the *New York Times*, the Middle Easterners who bombed the World Trade Center in that year made it plain that they would try again. Their letter read:

We are, the fifth battalion in the LIBERATION ARMY, declare our responsibility for the explosion on the mentioned building. This action was done in response for the American political, economical, and military support to Israel the state of terrorism and to the rest of the dictator countries in the region.

Our demands are: 1 - Stop all military, economical, and political aid to Israel. 2 - All diplomatic relations with Israel must stop. 3 - Not to interfere with any of the Middle East countries interior affairs.

If our demands are not met, all of our functional groups in the army will continue to execute our missions against the military and civilian targets in and out the United States.

For your own information, our army has more than hundred and fifty suicidal soldiers ready to go ahead. The terrorism that Israel practices (Which is supported by America) must be faced with a similar one. The dictatorship and terrorism (also supported by America) that some countries are practicing against their own people must also be faced with terrorism.

The American people must know, that their civilians who got killed are not better than those who are getting killed by the American weapons and support.

The American people are responsible for the actions of their government and they must question all of the crimes that their government is committing against other people. Or they - Americans - will be the targets of our operations that could diminish them.

The conspirators also drafted a second letter, which was later recovered from an erased file on a computer disk seized from Ayyad's office. This second letter, which the conspirators apparently did not send, proclaimed that the World Trade Center bomb did not do as much damage as had been intended, because their "calculations were not very accurate this time." They warned, however, that they would be more precise in the future and would continue to target the World Trade Center if their demands were not met.

After his arrest, Ramzi Yousef was more specific. He said that the conspirators had intended for the bomb to topple one of the towers and hoped that it would crash into the other, bringing them both down and killing one quarter of a million people.

It is now clear that the FBI had numerous warnings of what was to come.

FBI Couldn't or Wouldn't Connect the Dots

Despite the use of an electronic eavesdropping system originally named Carnivore, the top tier of the FBI couldn't seem to piece together the available information, which would have led any reasonable person to the conclusion that Middle Eastern terrorists were working diligently on plans to attack the United States.

Just six days after the 9/11 tragedy, FBI director Robert Mueller stated, "There were no warning signs that I'm aware of that would indicate this type of operation in the country."

The Carnivore electronic monitoring system created so much consternation from persons concerned with individual rights and privacy that it is now called simply DCS-1000. In at least one instance, Carnivore actually prevented the bureau from gaining information on a suspected terrorist.

The Electronic Privacy Information Center in May 2002 acquired FBI memos under the Freedom of Information Act, which showed that a 2000 bureau wiretap aimed at an unnamed suspect was ineffective because a low-level FBI technical person destroyed the information.

According to David Sobel, general counsel for the center, "The FBI software not only picked up the e-mails under the electronic surveillance of the FBI's target...but also picked up e-mails on non-covered targets." One of the obtained memos showed that an FBI supervisor explained, "The FBI technical person was apparently so upset [over intercepting unauthorized e-mails] that he destroyed all the e-mail take."

The FBI had previously issued assurances that Carnivore could only capture a narrow field of information authorized by a court order. "This shows that the FBI has been misleading Congress and the public about the extent to which Carnivore is capable of collecting only authorized information," Sobel said.

Even a secret court order provoked fallout that may have hampered anti-terrorist efforts by the bureau.

When Chief Judge Royce Lamberth, heading the special - and mostly secret - Foreign Intelligence Surveillance Court, which reviews national security wiretaps, found out that in 2000 the FBI had been misrepresenting information in their requests for eavesdropping, an investigation was ordered forcing many FBI wiretaps to be shut down.

Despite the problems with their Carnivore system and bungled wiretaps, many agents within the bureau were actively working on the problem of terrorism.

Perhaps the most knowledgeable person within the FBI on Middle Eastern terrorism in general and Osama bin Laden in particular was John O'Neill.

In 1995 O'Neill was promoted to head the FBI's counterterrorism section and began working out of FBI Headquarters in Washington. One of his initial jobs was the capture of Ramzi Yousef, then a key suspect in several acts of terror including the 1993 bombing of the World Trade Center.

Through the late 1990s, O'Neill, according to Lawrence Wright writing in the *New Yorker*, became "the bureau's most committed tracker of Osama bin Laden and his al-Qaeda network of terrorists".

But O'Neill came to believe that his superiors did not carry the same verve against terrorism as he did. "John had the same problems with bureaucracy as I had," said Richard A. Clarke in a 2002 magazine interview. Clarke had served as White House coordinator for counter terrorism since the Bush administration in the late 1980s. "The impatience really grew in us as we dealt with the dolts who didn't understand."

Despite the 1996 defection of Jamal Ahmed al-Fadl, a long-sought al-Qaeda terrorist, and his subsequent detailing of the network to both the CIA and FBI, the State Department refused to list al Qaedaas a terrorist network. Recall that the State Department has been under the control of the Council on Foreign Relations since before World War II.

"When it comes to foreign affairs, [the Council on Foreign Relations] *is* the eastern Establishment," noted Rockefeller family biographer Alvin Moscow. David Rockefeller, along with Henry Kissinger, met with Saddam Hussein more often the U.S. government officials in the months leading up to the Gulf War of 1991.

Despite O'Neill's growing ire over perceived indulgence of terrorists by higher authorities and his contentious personality, he accepted the post of special agent in charge of the National Security Division in New York City. Here he created a special "al-Qaeda" desk and worked doggedly to pinpoint Osama bin Laden. O'Neill, one of the top-level terrorism experts within the FBI, knew well who and what he was up against.

"Almost all of the groups today, if they chose to, have the ability to strike us here in the United States," O'Neill said in a 1997 Chicago speech.

By the summer of 2001, O'Neill had been passed over for promotion and was growing weary of fighting his superiors on the issue of terrorism. Adding to his disillusionment was O'Neill's experience trying to conduct an investigation of the bombing of the U.S. destroyer *Cole*, which had been severely damaged by a small boat filled with explosives and two suicide bombers.

O'Neill, commanding about three hundred heavily armed FBI agents, claimed his investigation was being hampered by everyone from Yemen president Ali Abdullah Saleh to U.S. ambassador Barbara Bodine. The FBI force believed they were never given the authority they required to conduct a strenuous investigation.

"...O'Neill came home feeling that he was fighting the counter-terrorism battle without support from his own government," noted the *New Yorker*. When he tried to return to Yemen in early 2001, O'Neill was refused entry.

"The last two years of his life, he got very paranoid," writer Lawrence Wright was told by Valerie James, a close friend of O'Neill's. "He was convinced there were people out to get him."

In the end, it appears it was his old arch-enemy, Osama bin Laden, who got him.

By the summer of 2001, events and O'Neill's career were coming to a head. Someone had leaked information on some of O'Neill's bureau gaffs to the *New York Times* and information on terrorism was pouring into government agencies. "Something big is going to happen," he told a friend.

"It all came together in the third week of June," recalled Clarke. "The CIA's view was that a major terrorist attack was coming in the next several weeks." Clarke said orders to beef up security were passed to the FAA, the Coast Guards, Customs, the INS and the FBI.

But O'Neill had had enough. By August 23, he had retired from the FBI and accepted a job paying twice his bureau pay - chief of security for the World Trade Center. When the first tower was stuck, O'Neill ordered the building evacuated but stayed behind to help others in the north tower. He used a cell phone to speak to a few friends and relatives. He assured them he was okay. He was last seen walking toward the tunnel that led to the south tower.

John O'Neill was not the only FBI agent to see definite warning signs.

Twelve-year FBI veteran Robert G. Wright Jr. in mid-2002 charged the bureau's counter terrorism efforts were ineffective and "not protecting the American people." Going further, Wright charged that FBI superiors had derailed investigations that could have prevented the 9/11 attacks, saying the bureau had evidence that the World Trade Center was a possible target.

On May 9, 2002, Wright, who worked out of Chicago, called a news conference in Washington to publicly accuse the bureau of not properly investigating terrorists in America, despite orders from FBI director Robert Mueller for him to stay home and stay quiet. At the same time he filed a lawsuit against the bureau in Washington's U.S. District Court accusing the bureau of violating his First Amendment rights by prohibiting him from speaking out about FBI wrongdoing.

He charged senior bureau officials "intentionally and repeatedly thwarted and obstructed" efforts to root out terrorists and that they prevented the filing of cases that could have broken up their operations.

Wright's suit was filed just one day after Congress berated the FBI for failing to vigorously act on a July 2001 recommendation from its Phoenix field office that aviation schools should be checked for Middle Easterners seeking flight training.

Counterterrorism experts in Phoenix were concerned after noting that several Middle Eastern men were seeking information on airport operations, security and flight training. One wrote in a memo to Washington, "FBIHQ should discuss this matter with other elements of the U.S. intelligence community and task the community for any information that supports Phoenix's suspicions."

The memo was written by Phoenix Special Agent Kenneth J. Williams and noted, "Osama bin Laden and Al-Muhjiroun supporters [were] attending civil aviation universities/colleges in Arizona."

FBI officials merely passed the memo, which actually pointed to bin Laden by name, along to about a dozen of its offices for "analysis."

A much more serious issue concerning the FBI arose when five people including a former and a current bureau agent, were charged in May 2002 with using confidential government information to manipulate stock prices and extort money from businesses.

In indictments brought in Brooklyn, San Diego stock adviser Amr Ibrahim Elgindy was accused of bribing FBI agent Jeffrey A. Royer to give him information on publicly traded companies. Royer, who had worked for the FBI between 1996 and 2000, subsequently left the bureau and went to work for Elgindy's firm, Pacific Equity Investigations. Another FBI agent, Lynn Wingate, was also indicted, accused of passing information to Royer and helping to track investigations of Elgindy through FBI computers. Elgindy reportedly supported Muslim refugees in Kosovo.

According to Assistant U.S. Attorney Kenneth Breen, Elgindy tried to sell $300,000 in stock on September 10, 2001, and told his broker the market was about to drop. Authorities were investigating to see if Elgindy may have had some foreknowledge of the 9/11 attacks.

An FBI spokesman said the bureau was "distressed" by the charges of obstruction of justice, racketeering, extortion and insider trading.

"I love America, and likewise I love the FBI, particularly its purpose and mission," Agent Wright told newsmen, echoing the thoughts of many bureau personnel. "However, the mission has been seriously jeopardized to the point where American lives have been needlessly lost."

"Knowing what I know," Wright added, "I can confidently say that until the investigative responsibilities for terrorism are transferred from the FBI, I will not feel safe."

Former FBI agent Gary Aldrich described the bureau's top management as "incompetent lunkheads and deadheads." Aldrich too said many opportunities to stop the attack were missed.

Aldrich blamed Bill and Hillary Clinton for the breakdown of the FBI as well as other federal agencies. He said the Clintons' blatant disregard for national security procedures made the government weak and vulnerable and that they showed more concern for political opponents than foreign enemies.

According to several FBI sources, when the Clinton administration arrived, emphasis in the bureau shifted from antiterrorism to investigating militias, white supremacists, anti-abortion groups and other "right-wing" extremists.

"When I left [the FBI] in 1998, domestic terrorism was the number one priority," said retired agent Ivan C. Smith, former head of the analysis, budget and training sections of the FBI's National Security Division. "And as far as I know, it was still a higher priority than foreign terrorism on September 11."

With the advent of the Clintons, FBI probes were aimed everywhere except at foreign terrorists. Veteran agents said some forty boxes of evidence gathered in the 1993 World Trade Center bombing were never analyzed, including almost ten boxes of material from the Philippine side of the investigation.

And the Clinton-era disinterest in foreign terrorism was not limited to the FBI. Commerce Department officials told reporter Paul Sperry they were ordered to "sanitized" a Y2K counterterrorism report by removing mention of Islamic threats. Only "right-wing" groups were included in the report.

By mid-2002, even FBI director Robert Mueller was forced to acknowledge that the FBI had missed many "red flags," including the Phoenix memos as well as two from the Oklahoma City office. There agents and one FBI pilot reported "large numbers" of Middle Eastern men receiving flight training at local airports and warned this activity might be related to "planned terrorist activity."

The revelations of FBI malfeasance prompted an unusual two-hour press conference in late May 2002 in which a defensive Mueller told reporters, "There was not a specific warning about an attack on a particular day. But that doesn't mean there weren't red flags out there, there weren't dots that should have been connected to the extent possible." Mueller even admitted that he had misspoken in fall 2001 when he denied the existence of any pre-9/11 attack warnings.

Mueller outlined his plan to reorganize the FBI, which consisted primarily of shifting agents from the War on Drugs to the War on Terrorism and to create a new Office of Intelligence headed by a CIA analyst. Many observers saw this plan as an attempt to merge the FBI and CIA into a terrorist-fighting force that would only bring more centralized authority to Washington. This same plan - to combine the worst of two worlds - was later echoed in proposals for the new Homeland Security Department.

One government informant, a self-confessed Florida con man named Randy Glass, said he worked undercover for the bureau for more than two years and learned specifically that the World Trade Center twin towers were to be the target of terrorists.

Hoping to lessen a prison term for a conviction of defrauding jewelry wholesalers out of $6 million, Glass in 1998 contacted federal agents and said he could set up illegal arms deals. Aided by veteran Alcohol, Tobacco and Firearms agent Dick Stoltz, Glass began to arrange deals with a variety of persons. He claimed he had acquired heavy weapons such as Stinger and TOW missiles stolen from military facilities.

Business was good but none of the deals seemed to work out until Glass contacted a Pakistani-born New Jersey deli owner. This man helped arrange arms deals with Pakistanis who claimed contacts to Pakistani intelligence, the Taliban and even Osama bin Laden. Many hours of tapes were made of their meetings.

However, during lengthy and detailed maneuvering to arrange the financing in early 2001, the Pakistanis grew suspicious and left the country. Only the deli owner and one other man were arrested. The other man pled guilty to trying to sell weaponry and was sentenced to thirty months in jail, while the deli owner went free and his court records sealed from the public.

ATF agent Stoltz said cases against the men were hampered by the fact that government prosecutors had to remove references to Pakistan in court filings because of diplomatic concerns.

Glass told news reporters that on one occasion in 1999 he met with one of the Pakistanis in the Tribeca Grill in Manhattan. "At the meeting, [he] said Americans are the enemy and they would have no problem blowing up this entire restaurant because it is full of Americans," Glass recounted. "As we left the restaurant, [he] turns and says, 'those towers are coming down.'" The man was indicating the World Trade Center.

Perhaps the most provocative evidence of governmental foreknowledge came from the man who led the prosecution of President Bill Clinton during his impeachment.

Chicago attorney David Schippers, who by mid-2002 was representing Wright and other disgruntled FBI employees, said in a late October 2001 interview that he had been approached by FBI agents a month and a half prior to the 9/11 attacks. The agents revealed that they had knowledge that lower Manhattan was to be the object of a terrorist attack using airplanes as flying bombs and they wanted to prevent this.

They were seeking legal advice because their FBI superiors had ordered them off the case and threatened them with the National Security Act if they spoke out. Schippers said he tried in vain to warn Attorney General John Ashcroft.

"[A]gain I used people who were personal friends of John Ashcroft to try to get him. One of them called me back and said, 'All right, I have talked with to him. He will call you tomorrow morning.' This was like a month before the bombing. The next morning I got a call. It wasn't from Ashcroft. It was from somebody in the Justice Department....He said, 'We don't start our investigations at the top. Let me look into this and I will get back to you.' As I sit here today [October 10, 2001], I have never heard from him."

Schippers said interference with official government investigations regarding terrorism is nothing new. He mentioned seeing a warning issued in February 1995 from an unofficial group researching terrorism that a federal facility in America's heartland was to be attacked. Government officials ignored it until the April 19, 1995, bombing of the Murrah Federal Building in Oklahoma City.

The attorney echoed Agent Aldrich's charge that national security precautions were stripped away during the Clinton administration. Speaking of his attempts to warn authorities, Schippers said, "I tried the House, I tried the Senate, I tried the Department of Justice. I didn't go to the FBI because I know there is a roadblock there and I didn't go to the Justice Department until Ashcroft got in there because I know there are roadblocks out there. These are the very same people who put up roadblocks on the attack against the terrorists under Clinton, they are still there. They still constitute, almost like a moat, between the people with the information and the people who should hear the information...

"As a human being, as a former prosecutor, as a lawyer and a guy who represents police and agents all over the United States, it is inconceivable to me that those bureaucrats in Washington would turn their back on the obvious for their own purposes," concluded Schippers, "But, I don't know"

It is clear that other bureau agents also tried to send warnings upstairs regarding the flight training of terrorists but got nowhere. In August 2001, the FBI did arrest Zacarias Moussaoui after a Minnesota flight school warned the bureau that Moussaoui appeared to be the type of person who might fly a plane loaded with fuel into a building. One unnamed FBI agent wrote more than one memo to superiors stating that Moussaoui, a French citizen of Moroccan descent, was the type of individual to take a plane and hijack it, perhaps even fly it into the World Trade Center. There was a general disbelief in the FBI that al-Qaeda had much of a presence here," explained White House terrorism coordinator Clarke. "It just hadn't sunk through to the organization, beyond O'Neill and (the assistant director of the counterterrorism division)."

In fall 2002, President Clinton's national security adviser, Samuel R. Berger, told a joint congressional committee that the FBI had repeatedly assured the Clinton White House that the al-Qaeda organization lacked the ability to launch a strike on U.S. soil.

CBS's *60 Minutes II* reported on May 8, 2002, that a ranking French jurist and terrorist expert sent a report on Moussaoui, a French citizen, to the FBI weeks before 9/11.

U.S. authorities denied there was anything in the report to alert them. One FBI supervisor even questioned the French report, asking how many men named Zacarias Moussaoui must live in France. When informed that there was only one listed in Paris, the supervisory special agent continued to stall any action. Meanwhile, FBI attorneys turned down a request from their agents to search Moussaoui's computer and apartment.

As a result of all this inaction, Moussaoui was simply held on immigration charges until after 9/11 when FBI agents finally were able to make their search. They recovered incriminating financial records linking Moussaoui to al-Qaeda, flight simulators and information on crop dusters.

Moussaoui, whose trial was postponed until early 2003, is known as the "twentieth hijacker" based on the theory he was to replace an original "twentieth hijacker," Ramzi Ben al-Shibh, a former roommate of Mohamed Atta, who reportedly sent $14,000 to Moussaoui. Al-Shibh, who also was unable to gain entry into the United States, was arrested in Pakistan in late September 2002. Moussaoui and al-Shib were the only two men in custody believed to be directly involved in the 9/11 attacks.

Considering Moussaoui's French citizenship, controversy quickly arose in legal and political circles over how to handle a foreign citizen in an American court with little to link him directly to anyone's death. Further confusion came in September 2002 when the Arab TV station Al-Jazeera aired tapes of the only known contact between Moussaoui and al-Shibh. In another e-mail exchange with al-Shib, Atta used phrases like, "The first semester starts in three weeks. Nothing has changed. Everything is fine. This summer will surely be hot. Nineteen certificates for private study and four exams." These seem hardly the words necessary to obtain the death penalty that federal prosecutors were seeking.

The feds were further embarrassed in 2002 when government prosecutors left forty-eight classified documents, summaries of FBI interviews, with Moussaoui. They were later found in searches of Moussaoui's Alexandria, Virginia, jail cell. The top-side interference in the Moussaoui case briefly made headlines in the late spring of 2002 with the publication of a scathing thirteen-page letter from FBI special agent and Minneapolis chief division counsel Coleen M. Rowley to Director Robert Mueller. In her May 21 letter, Rowley, a twenty-one-year veteran of the bureau, described a top-heavy FBI management bureaucracy riddled with "many who were failures as street agents" and "careerists" who placed advancing their own careers over integrity and truth.

"I know I shouldn't be flippant about this, but jokes were actually made that the key FBIHQ personnel had to be spies or moles, like Robert Hanssen, who were actually working for Osama bin Laden to have so undercut Minneapolis' effort...

"I have deep concerns that a delicate and subtle shading/skewing of facts by you and others at the highest levels of FBI management has occurred and is occurring in an effort to avoid or minimize personal and/or institutional embarrassment on the part of the FBI and/or perhaps even for improper political reasons," she told Mueller. She added, "I'm hard pressed to think of any case which has been solved by FBIHQ personnel and I can name several that have been screwed up!"

Rowley, after hearing the news media continually quote Director Mueller as saying the bureau would have taken action if only they had had advance warning of the attacks, sent a message informing him of the intelligence sitting in the Minneapolis files. She said when the same denials of knowledge continued, she and other agents again attempted to inform Mueller of the facts.

"Finally, when similar comments were made weeks later we faced the sad realization that the remarks indicated someone, possibly with your approval, had decided to circle the wagons at FBIHQ in an apparent effort to protect the FBI from embarrassment and the relevant FBI officials from scrutiny," Rowley wrote the director.

She also pointed out that the only difference between when informed FBI agents were denied a search warrant on Moussaoui and when one was approved was the fact of the 9/11 attacks, events that certainly could not be swept under the rug.

Rowley was one of many persons who pointed out the fact that FBI headquarters personnel "were privy to many more sources of intelligence information than field division agents." Despite this fact, she said, "key FBIHQ personnel whose job it was to assist and coordinate with field division agents on terrorism investigations continued to, almost inexplicably, throw up roadblocks and undermine Minneapolis' by-now desperate efforts to obtain a FISA [Foreign Intelligence Surveillance Act] search warrant, long after the French Intelligence Service provided it's information and probable cause became clear."

Even after the 9/11 attacks had begun, Rowley said higher authorities still would not untie their hands. Taking a call from a bureau superior just after the attacks had begun, Rowley said she told him in light of the attacks it would be the "hugest coincidence" if Moussaoui were not involved with the terrorists. Her superior replied that coincidence was the right term; it was just that and the

Minneapolis office should not do anything without headquarter's permission because "we might 'screw up' something else going on elsewhere in the country."

Rowley's insightful and damning critique of FBI inefficiency in light of the 9/11 attacks prompted widespread, though brief, mass media coverage. One Internet columnist noted that the Bush administration took advantage of the cover of the "Rowley firestorm" to announce a reversal of some of the government's meager rules against indiscriminate domestic spying, rules prompted by the many abuses of the FBI during the 1960s.

Steve Perry with *Counterpunch*, a biweekly newsletter, wrote that the Bush team defused Rowley's revelations by choosing that time to announce plans to reorganize the entire intelligence apparatus. Such a move would be time-consuming and require much preparation yet the administration requested no funding for its proposal this year, indicating the timing of the announcement may indeed have been meant to distract attention from Rowley's accusations.

It might also be added that any failures at the FBI cannot be laid off on lower level agents and supervisors. In August 2001, Attorney General Ashcroft, apparently more concerned with the long-lost War on Drugs and pornography, turned down a bureau request for $50 million to beef up its counterterrorism efforts.

All information flowing upward within the FBI ended at Director Mueller and his boss, Ashcroft, both of whom we were told worked closely with President Bush.

Missed Opportunities At The CIA

The CIA by many accounts also had their share of pre-attack warnings.

Like the FBI, the CIA has its own electronic eavesdropping satellite and computer system, called Echelon. This system tracks international calls, faxes and e-mail messages all around the world. It was so secret that the government would neither confirm nor deny its existence until 2001. According to a study by the European Union, Echelon accumulates electronic transmissions like a vacuum cleaner using keyword search software in conjunction with massive computer data banks.

The Echelon system, headquartered in the United States with the National Security Agency at Fort Meade, Virginia, has caused protests in several nations, excluding the United States whose population rarely gets any news concerning this global wiretapping system.

In 2000, French prosecutor Jean-Pierre Dintilhac ordered his country's counterintelligence agency to see if Echelon was being used to steal foreign business secrets, to spy on citizens, and to see if it was "harmful to the vital interests of the nation." The Italian Parliament also opened inquiries into Echelon, saying, "The scope is not military." According to a German newspaper, the *Frankfurter Allgemeine Zeitung*, the Echelon spy system provided both U.S. and Israeli intelligence services warning of the impending terrorist attacks at least three months before the fact. The newspaper reported that Echelon, with its 120 satellites, has been used extensively by Israeli intelligence to monitor Arab terrorist groups.

Largely unreported in the American media was a story that Osama bin Laden himself was overheard telling his stepmother on September 9, 2001, "In two days you're going to hear big news and you're not going to hear from me for a while." This telephone interception, attributed to a "foreign intelligence service," undoubtedly was the product of Echelon. Yet no one in America was alerted to bin Laden's "big news?"

The CIA also had another high-tech weapon in their arsenal for use against terrorists. The Predator, an unmanned surveillance aircraft, has been used under the Clinton administration to track the movements of Osama bin Laden. There had even been talk of using the craft to unleash Hellfire missiles on the al-Qaeda leader. But Donald Rumsfeld, among other things when he took office as secretary of defense, chose not to launch any further Predator drones.

There is enticing evidence that tied Osama bin Laden directly to the CIA back at the time the agency was funding and training fighters against the Soviets in Afghanistan. While it has been widely acknowledged that the CIA helped found and fund the al-Qaeda network during the Soviet invasion of Afghanistan, the agency steadfastly denied any direct dealings with bin Laden.

Internet sources claimed that bin Laden, under the name Tim Osman, actually was brought to the United States in the late spring of 1986 for a meeting with government agents at the Hilton Hotel in Sherman Oaks, California. Former FBI senior special agent Ted L. Gunderson confirmed this meeting and said he was one of the attendees. Gunderson said he was contacted by a "top figure" in the Reagan administration and asked to meet with Afghan insurgents to "see what we might do to help them." The four men at the hotel meeting, according to Gunderson, were himself, a quiet Tim Osman (bin Laden), Michael Riconosciuto, a CIA scientific "asset" with connections in the arms business, and a man identified as Ralph Olberg, who was purchasing weapons on behalf of the Afghan Mujahideen.

Gunderson said conversation during the hour-and-a-half meeting was mostly between Olberg and Riconosciuto while Osman/bin Laden "sat silent in a corner of the room." He added that he was unaware of what, if any, deal was sealed during the meeting but that he is "certain in my own mind" that arrangements were made to provide arms for bin Laden and the Arab fighters.

According to a former staffer of Republican senator David Durenberger, Olberg was a man often seen in the senator's office during the Reagan years talking about the plight of the Afghan people.

Riconosciuto, also tight with Republican bigwigs, had been involved in the development of the PROMIS software initially planned for use against criminals and terrorists.

But by the mid 1990s, the Soviets were out of Afghanistan and the Saudis were our oil friends and, except for certain counterterrorism units, little notice was taken of Osama bin Laden. The CIA, like their brethren in the FBI, apparently became somewhat complacent at the lower levels thanks to the near constant stream of tips, warnings and information. Workers not actively involved in counterterrorism took a cue from their superiors and never got too serious about terrorism.

Attorney Michael Wildes, who represented one of the Khobar Towers bombers, explained, "You see [there is a] difference between the rank-and-file counterintelligence agents, who are regarded by some as the motor pool of the FBI, who drive diplomats, and the people who are getting the shots called at the highest level of our government - it's unconscionable."

And it wasn't as if prior warnings had all proven false. Almost a year before the deadly 1998 bombings of the U.S. embassies in Kenya and Tanzania, an al-Qaeda member had warned CIA officials of the coming attacks. The informant's information was dismissed as unreliable and nothing was done.

Though admittedly vague, there was a warning in a September 1999 National Intelligence Council (NIC) report entitled "Sociology and Psychology of Terrorism: Who Becomes a Terrorist and Why?" The NIC is composed of about a dozen senior intelligence officers and is attached to the CIA.

"Suicide bomber(s) belonging to al-Qaeda's Martyrdom Battalion could crash land an aircraft packed with high explosives (C-4 and semtex) into the Pentagon, the headquarters of the Central Intelligence Agency (CIA) or the White House," stated the report, which was issued exactly two years before 9/11.

"This information was out there," noted Robert L. Worden, chief of the Federal Research Division, which prepared the report from open sources, "certainly to those who study the in-depth subject of terrorism and al-Qaeda."

In January 2000, Malaysian security agents conducted surveillance of Al-Qaeda operatives meeting in Kuala Lumpur at the behest of the CIA. One of the operatives was Khalid al-Midhar. It was determined that al-Midhar had a multiple-entry visa to the United States.

CIA agents also found that al-Midhar was traveling with a Saudi, Nawaf al-hazmi, who had already entered the United States before. Neither man was placed on the State Department "watch list" until August 23, 2001, far too late to prevent their participation in the 9/11 attacks.

Another example of CIA incompetence, if that's what it was, can be found in the case of Khalid Shaikh Mohammed, who, since the capture of Abu Zubaydah in Pakistan in the spring of 2002, is considered the highest-ranking member of the al-Qaeda network as well as a primary planner of the 9/11 attacks.

Mohammed was so highly placed in bin Laden's organization that the joint congressional committee looking into intelligence failures in the fall of 2002 took special notice of him. But they were so stymied by restrictions on classified material that they could only refer to Mohammed as a "key al-Qaeda leader," even though the man was identified as a terrorist chief as far back as 1995.

The joint committee criticized the CIA's handling of Mohammed's case, stating, "there was little analytic focus given to him and coordination amongst intelligence agencies was irregular at best." One U.S. intelligence official disputed this charge but told a *New York Times* reporter, "We had identified him as a major al-Qaeda operative before September 11."

Such controversy and contradictions continued when it was reported that Mohammed was captured on March 1, 2003 following a nighttime shootout in Rawalpindi, Pakistan. U.S. officials expressed jubilation over the arrest but their celebration faded swiftly as questions arose. Witnesses did not agree with the official account and foreign media speculated that Moahmmed may have been misidentified, killed at an earlier date or might even still be on the loose.

Mohammed Atta, the accused chief hijacker, reportedly was under surveillance by U.S. intelligence agents for nearly five months in early 2000, prior to his visit to the United States to take flying lessons.

The German magazine *Focus* reported that U.S. agents, referred to as FBI in some accounts and CIA in others, monitored Atta from January to May 2000 after he was seen buying large quantities of chemicals thought to be used for making bombs. According to the article, the U.S. agents never informed German authorities of Atta's presence or of any suspicions about him.

One of the most outrageous accounts of CIA pre-9/11 activity actually involved Osama bin Laden. One month after the attacks, the French daily *Le Figaro* reported that bin Laden had been treated at an American hospital in the Arab emirate of Dubai in July 2001, and while there was visited by a local CIA agent. According to this report, bin Laden was flown from the Quetta airport in Pakistan to Dubai, where he was admitted to the American hospital located between the Al-Garhoud and Al-Maktoum bridges. He was taken to the urology department for treatment of a kidney infection. The article stated that bin Laden had had mobile kidney dialysis equipment shipped to his hideaway in Pakistan as far back as early 2000.

It went on to say that during his stay at the hospital, between July 4 and 14, bin Laden received visits from family members and prominent Saudis and Emiratis. "During the hospital stay, the local CIA agent, known to many in Dubai, was seen taking the main elevator of the hospital to go to bin Laden's hospital room," stated the *Le Figaro* article, adding, "A few days later, the CIA man bragged to a few friends about having visited bin Laden. Authorized sources say that on July 15th, the day after bin Laden returned to Quetta, the CIA agent was called back to headquarters."

Bin Laden, with both a price on his head and eligible for execution under a last-minute order from outgoing president Bill Clinton, nevertheless was allowed without hindrance to fly from Dubai by private jet on July 14.

The article also reported that in late August, both American and French authorities were notified of the arrest of Djamel Beghal by customs agents in Dubai. Under interrogation, Beghal said he had been ordered to bomb the U.S. embassy in Paris by al-Qaeda leader Abou Zoubeida in Afghanistan. "According to Arab diplomatic sources as well as French intelligence, very specific information was transmitted to the CIA with respect to terrorist attacks against American interests around the world, including U.S. soil," stated the French piece. While this story made the rounds in the European media, nothing but a few scattered Internet reports circulated in the United States. In Europe, CIA officials denied the story.

It is either true or false. If it is false, the American public needs to know this, so that such untruths can be stopped during our "War on Terrorism." If it is true, then the American people need to know that their own CIA let the world's most wanted man walk away unmolested two months prior to the deadly 9/11 attacks. Yet no major American media apparently could spare one good reporter to travel to Dubai to check with the hospital staff and others to confirm the story.

The story of the CIA and bin Laden in Dubai is reinforced by a story in the December 23, 2001, edition of the *Washington Post* that reported that the CIA had recruited a team of Afghan agents to track bin Laden's movements in their country beginning in early 1998. This effort continued right up until September 11, 2001.

According to the paper, these agents sent the CIA daily reports on bin Laden's whereabouts but the information was often dismissed by agency officials because it sometimes conflicted with other intelligence information.

CIA foreknowledge was also obliquely admitted in April 2002 by its own Deputy director, James Pavitt. In a speech to the Duke University Law School Conference, Pavitt was simultaneously trying to excuse his agency's failure to prevent 9/11 while touting its efficiency.

"We had very, very good intelligence of the general structure and strategies of the al-Qaeda terrorist organization. We knew and we warned that al-Qaeda was planning a major strike. There is no question about that," Pavitt told his audience. His speech later was posted on the CIA's Web site.

Yet Pavitt tried to echo the administration's claim that there was not enough specific intelligence to prevent the 9/11 attacks. He added that within days of the attacks CIA operatives were "on the ground" operating in Afghanistan. "None of this came easy," he explained. "You cannot learn Pushtan overnight and you can't truly understand the complexities of tribalism, regionalism and personalism in Afghanistan by reading the newspaper or a learned book. My people learned about this by years of study and years of practice often in difficult, hostile and, yes indeed, on the ground in Afghanistan itself.

"If you hear somebody say, and I have, the CIA abandoned Afghanistan after the Soviets left and that we never paid any attention to that place until

September 11th, I would implore you to ask those people how we were able to accomplish all we did since the Soviets departed. How we knew who to approach on the ground, which operations, which warlord to support, what information to collect. Quite simply, we were there well before the 11th of September."

One of the strangest cases of apparent foreknowledge involved a man imprisoned in Canada who claimed to be an American intelligence agent who had tried to warn authorities a month or more before the 9/11 attacks.

Delmart "Mike" Vreeland claimed to be a U.S. Navy lieutenant and an agent for the Office of Naval Intelligence in 2000 when he was arrested and jailed in Canada at the behest of U.S. authorities after arriving from a trip to Russia. Canadian authorities charged Vreeland with credit card fraud and held him on an extradition warrant based on alleged credit card fraud in Michigan.

Following lengthy court hearings, all Canadian charges against Vreeland were dropped, and at this writing he had been granted political refugee status in Canada while the extradition warrant issue was resolved. According to the Canadian court records, running to some 10,000 pages, Vreeland brought back from Moscow intelligence documents in a sealed pouch in December 2000. He said he was simply a courier and was to hand over the documents to a contact in Toronto but the contact failed to arrive.

"The, uh, meeting didn't go as planned. I didn't like it, so I basically scanned and copied everything. I opened everything," Vreeland recalled in a June 5, 2002, radio interview. He said that when he returned for a second meeting he was arrested.

The documents, according to Vreeland, were written in Russian, but one contained the Arabic numerals for 9/11/01. Prior to his arrest, he said he had the documents translated and that one specifically referred to attacks in September.

"The initial strike or attack will be started at the WTC on 9/11/01 by our brothers in faith," Vreeland quoted from the documents. "Three Mile Island and Pentagon are as well the goals that we will not miss at the initial terroristic stage of our attack. If everything goes as planned, the attack with work. After Americans who undoubtedly will think that Osama is to be blamed and will start a war with his group, there stands the Russian Empire to gain the first fruit of war and money promised by the Americans."

Vreeland said while incarcerated he wrote about the warning in a letter that was opened three days after the 9/11 attacks and forwarded to authorities in Ottawa. He also said he passed this same information to Canadian authorities via his jailers about a month or more before the 9/11 attacks. "the two officers informed the United States and Ottawa immediately through the RCMP [Royal Canadian Mounted Police]..."

"The Canadians did their job. I think they were pressed down by the U.S. government. They transmitted the information just like they should. I know definitely that the [U.S.] Secret Service had it. I know the FBI had it, I know the DoD [Department of Defense] had it. I know it all went from Ontario to Ottawa, from Ottawa to the Canadian embassy in Washington, D.C., and it was just melted everywhere," he added.

The documents, entered into court records at his court hearings, apparently refer to an attack on a nuclear power plant and speak of immediate and deadly radiation within an area of four to seven miles. In a telephone interview from Canada, Vreeland said he believed that Flight 93's objective was Three Mile Island and that the jet was shot down by American fighters to prevent completion of its mission.

In another intriguing aspect to this incredible story, Vreeland's document added the cryptic line "Let one happen, stop the rest." Vreeland said this statement confirmed his belief that U.S. intelligence had penetrated the al-Qaeda network and were conducting an operation of their own.

U.S. authorities gave Vreeland's story short shrift, declaring that he was simply a petty criminal who was discharged from the navy for unsatisfactory conduct in 1986. But his records were contradictory and some appeared fabricated. Disclaiming a military operative by pronouncement and fabricated records is called "sheep dipping" and has been a common intelligence practice in the past.

A Toronto newspaper reported that Vreeland joined the U.S. Navy in 1984 and then joined a special unit operating against drug smugglers. Interestingly, an October 2, 1986, article in the *Los Angeles Times* listed Vreeland as a noncriminal witness to a major cocaine bust by LAPD officers known to have worked with U.S. intelligence agents.

"There is much about Vreeland's past that is objectionable, questionable or both," commented former LAPD officer and Internet writer Michael Ruppert. "But even in a worst-case scenario, nothing in his past explains how he was able to write a detailed warning of the attacks before they occurred and why the intelligence services of both Canada and the U.S. ignored attempts to warn them while both Vreeland and his attorneys were nagging down their doors."

Rocco Galati, one of Vreeland's attorneys fighting the extradition orders, told the *Toronto Star*, "Neither myself nor Mr. [Paul] Slansky [another Vreeland attorney] have seen anything as incomprehensibly frustrating, inexplicable and irresponsibly absurd as the RCMP's position that they are not interested in reviewing Mr. Vreeland's information."

Vreeland's story of a specific warning from Russia gained further support when it was learned that the Russian newspaper *Izvestia* reported the day of the 9/11 attacks a special messenger of the Russian Intelligence Service met with a deputy director of the CIA and delivered documents and audiotapes containing telephone conversations directly relating to terrorist attacks on Washington and New York.

One of the strangest items indicating foreknowledge of the attacks came in the form of registered Internet domain names.

Two highly suggestive domain names - attackontwintowers.com and worldtradetowerattack.com - were registered more than a year before the 9/11 attacks. Since the registration was allowed to elapse, no one knows who registered the names.

Neil Livingston, who heads Global Options LLC, a Washington-based investigation and counterterrorism firm, said, "It's unbelievable that they [the registration company whose name was withheld] would register these domain names, probably without any comment to the FBI. If they did make a comment to the FBI, it's unbelievable that the FBI didn't react to it."

Incredibly, other domain names registered prior to the 9/11 tragedy included attackamerica.com, horrorinamerica.com, horrorinnewyork.com, nycterroriststrike.com, pearlharborinmanhattan.com. terrorattack2001, worldtradecenter929.com, worldtradetowerstrike.com and wyerroristattack2001.com.

From a cursory search of September 11 reports, it would appear as though many people may have had some inkling of what was to come.

As recounted by editor Russ Kick, a veteran New York police investigator, numerous Arab-Americans in New York heard about the coming attacks. The officer said the number of leads were so overwhelming that it was difficult to tell who had heard about the attacks from a secondhand source and who had heard it from someone who may have been a participant. A Brooklyn detective was quoted as saying that "a serious and major priority" investigation was made into why so many Middle Easterners failed to show up for work at the World Trade Center on September 11.

Even certain school kids seemed to have foreknowledge, according to Kick. A Dallas suburb fifth-grader told his teacher on September 10, "Tomorrow, World War III will begin. It will begin in the United States and the United States will lose."

Another school kid in Jersey City, home of several of the accused hijackers, told friends to stay away from lower Manhattan on the morning of September 11. One week before the attacks, a Brooklyn high school freshman pointed at the WTC towers and told his class, "Do you see those two buildings? They won't be standing there next week."

There are even telltale signs that some prominent people within the United States had some warning of the September atrocities.

San Francisco mayor Willie Brown was scheduled to fly to New York on the morning of September 11, 2001. But about 10 P.M. the evening of September 10, he received a phone call at home advising him to be cautious about traveling by air. Brown would only say the call came from "my security people at the airport," but the warning was clear - don't travel by air. He said the call "didn't come in any alarming fashion, which is why I'm hesitant to make an alarming statement." Brown was preparing to leave for the airport the next morning when he joined millions of other Americans in viewing the NYC destruction on TV.

One San Francisco official noted that the FAA routinely issues security notices but added that none had been received in the days before September 11. No one discovered who sent the after-hours warning to Brown.

Newsweek magazine reported on September 24, 2001, that on September 10 "a group of top Pentagon officials suddenly canceled travel plans for the next morning, apparently because of security concerns."

On July 28, 2001, Attorney General John Ashcroft left Washington on a fishing trip to Missouri but it was not on a commercial airliner. CBS news correspondent Jim Stewart reported that Ashcroft had suddenly begun flying only on government-chartered jets in response to what an FBI spokesman called a "threat assessment" by the bureau. Ashcroft was advised to travel only by private jet for the remainder of his term under FBI guidelines.

Asked about this sudden change in policy - former Attorney General Janet Reno and all but the secretaries of interior and energy in the Bush administration had flown by commercial airliners - Ashcroft said, "I don't do threat assessments myself and I rely on those whose responsibility it is in the law enforcement community, particularly the FBI. And I try to stay within the guidelines that they've suggested I should stay within for those purposes."

But most extraordinary was a comment attributed to a member of Congress. During live coverage of the 9/11 attacks, National Public Radio congressional correspondent David Welna was describing the evacuation of the Capitol.

He reported, "I spoke with Congressman Ike Shelton - a Democrat from Missouri and a member of the Armed Services Committee - who said that just recently the director of the CIA warned that there could be an attack - an imminent attack - on the United States of this nature. So this is not entirely unexpected."

All of the above information stands in sharp contrast to Bush administration assertions that no one in government could have imagined an attack such as 9/11.

Colin Powell admitted in early October 2001 that the United States knew that terrorist attacks were coming but had no specifics. Vice President Cheney echoed Powell's comment about the warnings being vague and nonspecific.

Secretary of Defense Donald Rumsfeld also admitted "there were lots of warnings" in an interview with *Parade* magazine. A transcript of his interview was released by the Department of Defense on October 12, 2001.

Rumsfeld appeared to be laying off blame for the failure to stop the attacks on local officials when he explained, "The intelligence information that we get, it sometimes runs into the hundreds of alerts or pieces of information a week. One looks at the worldwide, it's thousands. And the task is to sort through it and see what you can find. And as you find things, the law enforcement officials who have the responsibility to deal with that type of thing - the FBI at the federal level, and although it is not, it's an investigative service as opposed to a police force, it's not a federal police force, as you know. But the state and local law enforcement officials have the responsibility for dealing with those kinds of issues."

Of course, local authorities do not normally have access to intelligence from the CIA and FBI. Furthermore, anyone who has served in the military, intelligence services or law enforcement will confirm that information only flows upward, rarely downward. Thus, lower-level agents can be forgiven their inability to see the bigger picture and connect the dots. Close scrutiny should be leveled at their superiors and, more specifically, the national leaders for whom they manage.

In July 2001, senior government officials received this report on Osama bin Laden: "Based on a review of all-source reporting over the last five months, we believe that [bin Laden] will launch a significant terrorist attack against U.S. and/or Israeli interests in the coming weeks. The attack will be spectacular and designed to inflict mass casualties against U.S. facilities or interests. Attack preparations have been made. Attack will occur with little or no warning."

On July 5, 2001, President Bush received a briefing at his Crawford, Texas, ranch that mentioned the possibility of an airline hijacking as a domestic threat. This information was not made public until nearly nine months after the attacks.

Yet, despite these warnings, when four jetliners went off course on the morning of September 11, there was little or no immediate reaction.

Inflated budgets and more manpower will add nothing to the quest for true national security until there is a commitment to such by the highest political leaders.

Selling Stocks Short Indicates Foreknowledge

What makes the information concerning foreknowledge even more ominous is the business dealings that entangle former and current American political leaders with wealthy Middle Easterners and the fact that just days after the 9/11 attacks the FBI was asked to investigate the short selling of airline and insurance stocks just prior to September 11. Just as there is growing evidence that many people had foreknowledge of these attacks, there are indications that someone used this prior knowledge for profit. And they were not members of an al-Qaeda terrorist cell.

Short selling of stocks involves the opportunity to gain large profits by passing shares to a friendly third party, then buying them back when the price falls. Historically, if this precedes a traumatic event, it is an indication of foreknowledge. It is widely known that the CIA uses the *Promis* computer software to routinely monitor stock trades as a possible warning sign of a terrorist attack or suspicious. economic behavior.

It was reported by the Interdisciplinary Center, a counterterrorism think tank involving former Israeli intelligence officers, that insiders made nearly $16 million profit by short selling shares in American and United Airlines, the two airlines that suffered hijacking, as well as the investment firm of Morgan Stanley, which occupied twenty-two floors of the WTC. According to other sources, profits from this short selling may have netted up to $15 billion worldwide.

A week after the September 11 attacks, the London *Times* reported that the CIA had asked regulators for the Financial Services Authority in London to investigate the suspicious sales of millions of shares of stock just prior to the terrorist acts. It was hoped the business paper trail might lead to the terrorists. The *Times* said market regulators in Germany, Japan and the United States all had received information concerning the short selling of insurance, airlines and arms companies stock, all of which fell sharply in the wake of the attacks.

City of London broker and analyst Richard Crossley noted that someone sold shares in unusually large quantities beginning three weeks before the assault on the WTC and Pentagon. Crossley stated that on the Friday preceding the attacks, more than 10 million shares in the U.S. investment bank Merrill Lynch were sold, compared with 4 million on a normal trade day. He said he took this as evidence that someone had insider foreknowledge of the attacks.

"What is more awful than he should aim a stiletto blow at the heart of Western financial markets?" he added. "But to profit from it. Words fail me."

Stock market regulators in Germany also reported suspicious short selling just prior to September 11.

In the United States, there was an unusually high volume of five-year U.S. Treasury note purchases made just prior to 9/11. *The Wall Street Journal* on October 2, 2001, noted, "Five-year Treasury notes are among the best investments in the event of a world crisis, especially one that hits the U.S."

"This could very well be insider trading at the worst, most horrific, most evil use you've ever seen in your entire life this would be one of the most extraordinary coincidences in the history of mankind, if it was a coincidence," said *Bloomberg Business News* writer Dylan Ratigan.

Just prior to the 9/11 attacks, there were an unusually high number of "put" options purchased for the stocks of AMR Corp. and UAL Corp., the parent firms of American and United Airlines. A put option gives the bearer the right to sell at a specified price before a certain date. Just like short selling, placing a put option is betting that the stock will fall in price.

According to Web writer and former LA policeman Michael C. Ruppert, between September 6 and 7, 2001, the Chicago Board of Options Exchange reported 4,744 put options on UAL but only 396 call options. On September 10, there were 4,516 put options placed on American Airlines compared to only 748 calls, which reflect the belief that the stock will increase in worth. American's 6,000 percent jump in put options on the day before the attacks was not matched by any other airlines.

"No similar trading in any other airlines occurred on the Chicago Exchange in the days immediately preceding Black Tuesday," Ruppert said in an

October 2001 interview. "That means that someone had advance knowledge that only the stocks of these two airlines would be adversely impacted. Had it just been an industry-wide slump, then you would have seen the same kind of activity on every airline, not just these two."

There were other questionable stock trades made just prior to 9/11. According to Ruppert, Morgan Stanley Dean Witter & Co, which occupied twenty-two floors of the WTC, witnessed the purchase of 2,157 put options during the three trading days before the 9/11 attacks as compared to 27 per day prior to September 6. Merrill Lynch & Co., which also had offices in twenty-two floors of the WTC, had 12,215 one-month put options bought during four trading days prior to 9/11 compared to the normal 252 contracts per day.

Alex Popovic, vice president of the Investment Dealers Association of Canada, in early October 2001 confirmed that the U.S. Securities and Exchange Commission had provided a list of thirty-eight companies for scrutiny but said their review need not be limited to those firms listed. "One shouldn't be wearing blinders when looking at that sort of thing," Popovic told the Associated Press.

Earlier this same commitment to an opened-ended investigation was voiced by SEC chairman Harvey Pitt, who stated his agency's "No. 1 priority" was to pursue the possible trading by people associated with the terrorists.

Interestingly enough, one of the thirty-eight companies was Vornado Realty Trust, a New Jersey based firm that earlier in 2001 lost a bid to lease the World Trade Center complex to real estate developer Larry A. Silverstein and shopping center creator Westfield America, Inc. The Silverstein Group reportedly purchased the WTC from a consortium owned by the Rockefellers about six months before the attacks. By early 2003, Silverstein was still in court fighting insurers over whether or not the two planes that struck the WTC constituted one or two separate attacks. Leaseholder Silverstein argued that there were two strikes which entitled him to a $7.1 billion total payment, $3.55 billion for each attack.

However, by year's end the story of profiting on terrorism had vanished. Apparently none of the suspicious. transactions could be traced to bin Laden so this news item quietly dropped from sight. But, if the suspicious. trading could not be linked to bin Laden, who was at the end of the investigative trail?

Many people wondered if it tracked back to American firms or intelligence agencies. This appears to be the case.

According to the *San Francisco Chronicle*, "[A] source familiar with the United trades identified Deutsche Bank Alex. Brown, the American investment banking arm of German giant Deutsche Bank, as the investment bank used to purchase at least some of these options."

Michael Ruppert said that both the International Policy Institute for Counter Terrorism, an Israeli institute located in Herzliya that studies worldwide terrorism, and European investigators tracked the UAL put options to Deutsche Bank Alex. Brown, a firm formed by the joining of the German central bank with

Alex. Brown, the United States' oldest investment banking firm.

Until 1998, the chairman of A. B. Brown was A. B. "Buzzy" Krongard, who on March 26, 2001, was appointed executive director of the CIA. Beginning in 1998, he was counselor to CIA director George Tenet.

Krongard is a man with long-standing and close ties to the financial world. Moving up through the ranks of A. B. Brown, Krongard was elected chief executive officer in 1991 and then chairman of the board in 1994. With the merging of A. B. Brown and Bankers Trust Corp. in 1997, Krongard served as vice chairman of the board until joining the CIA. Bankers Trust was acquired by Deutsche Bank in 1999, becoming the single largest bank in Europe.

Krongard also served as chairman of the Securities Industry Association. A native of Baltimore, he received degrees from Princeton University and the University of Maryland School of Law and served as an infantry officer in the marines.

"Understanding the interrelationships between CIA and the banking and brokerage world is critical to grasping the already frightening implications of [these] revelations," commented Ruppert.

Krongard indeed joined other prominent Americans connected to both the CIA and Wall Street power. These include Clark Clifford (who was a key player in gaining legitimacy for the Bank of Credit and Commerce International which collapsed in scandal), John Foster Dulles and Allen Dulles (Allen oversaw the failed Bay of Pigs invasion and sat on the Warren Commission, and both Dulles brothers were involved with the Bush-Nazi connection detailed later), William Casey (who moved to the agency after a stint as chairman of the Securities and Exchange Commission), David Doherty (former CIA general counsel, now vice president of the New York Stock Exchange), George Herbert Walker Bush (now a paid consultant to the international Carlyle Group, which lists among its clients the bin Ladens), John M. Deutch and Nora Slatkin (Deutch, a former CIA director, and his former executive director Slatkin are both now connected to Citibank and Citigroup) and Hank Greenburg (once nominated as CIA director, he is now chairman of AIG Insurance representing the third largest pool of investment capital in the world).

As detailed in *Rule by Secrecy*, the CIA historically has been top heavy with members of the Wall Street elite who desire to advance their globalist agenda. It also operates a number of front companies which themselves deal in stocks and bonds.

The CIA's *Promis* computer software to track real-time trades in world stock markets should have alerted them to all this unusual stock trading and perhaps even of the pending 9/11 attacks.

Did former FBI employee and double agent Robert Hanssen deliver an updated version of the purloined computer software *Promis* to his Russian handlers who passed it along to bin Laden, as reported by *Fox News*? Hanssen's last job before being arrested as a spy was to upgrade the FBI's intelligence computer systems.

The *Promis* software had been developed by a computer program designer named Bill Hamilton, who took his work to the federal government only to have the sophisticated software stolen by President Ronald Reagan's attorney general, Ed Meese. This software, which seemed a promising weapon in tracking criminals and illegal money, was turned into an Orwellian program that integrates databases worldwide giving its possessor nearly unlimited access to all computer records.

"One of the primary functions of the Central Intelligence Agency by virtue of its long and very close history of relationships with Wall Street has had a mandate to track, monitor, all financial markets worldwide, to look for anomalous trades, indicative of either economic warfare, or insider currency trading or speculation which might affect the U.S. Treasury, or, as in the case of the September 11 attacks, to look for trades which indicated foreknowledge of attacks like we saw," Ruppert told *OnLine Journal* on Oct. 12, 2001. "I am absolutely convinced that the Central Intelligence Agency had complete and perfect foreknowledge of the attacks, down to the date, time, place and location," he concluded.

Author Don Radlauer, who specializes in stock options and derivatives, noted the suspicious stock trading and stated, "Obviously, anyone who had detailed knowledge of the attacks before they happened was, at the very least, an accessory to their planning; and the overwhelming probability is that the trades could have been made only by the same people who masterminded the attacks themselves."

According to Chicago attorney Schippers the only attempt to track and identify the suspicious trading in the United States occurred in Chicago, where money intended for the Hamas terrorist group was stopped by a lawsuit filed by one FBI agent.

In an October 2001 interview Schippers explained, "This agent here in Chicago filed the affidavit where he laid out the whole way that the money moves, the way that it is handled, how it comes out of the Middle East into the Chicago area and into the United States, how it is covered, how the operatives are covered, how the money is transferred back and where it's kept while it's here. And that affidavit ran like thirty pages - laying it out. And he had to go through hell on earth in Washington, he had to fight like a tiger - everybody in his own bureau and in the Department of Justice was against him - and still is."

Speaking of all the warnings that had poured into government agencies, Jerry Bremer, a former State Department terrorism expert, said, "We all predicted this. We had strategic warning. This is not something the analysts missed."

Despite a barrage of information on the Internet and in the foreign press, the corporate mass media failed to respond until mid-2002, when complaints from CIA and FBI agents and certain members of Congress became too loud to ignore. Even then, they danced around the subject of all the missed clues and cues.

"Because Bush has long insisted he had no inkling of the attacks, the disclosures [in 2002] touched off a media stampede in a capital long deprived of scandal. The fact that the nation's popular war president might have been warned a little over a month before September 11 - and that the supposedly straight-talking Bushies hadn't told anyone about it - opened up a serious credibility gap for the first time in the war on terror," wrote *Newsweek* writers Michael Hirsh and Michael Isikoff.

Israeli Foreknowledge?

Since the September 11 attacks, several media pundits noted that the chief beneficiaries of the terrorism were the Bush administration and Israel. Bush gained welcome relief from bad news in the economy and his own sagging popularity while Israel found its provocation for unleashing its military against the Palestinians.

And there were indications that someone in Israel had foreknowledge of the attacks as well as questions concerning the number of Israeli citizens killed.

A major German newspaper, the *Frankfurter Allgemeine Zeitung*, reported on September 13, 2001, that German intelligence sources stated that both the American and Israeli governments received warnings of the attacks via the Echelon monitoring network. The article said information concerning a plan to hijack commercial airliners to use as weapons against the West was received at least three months prior to the attacks.

There was also a little-noticed story regarding the New York instant messaging firm, Odigo. Odigo officials confirmed soon after the attacks that two of their employees in Israel received text messages warning of the attacks two hours before planes crashed into the WTC.

Odigo's vice president of sales and marketing, Alex Diamandis, said employees in the company's research and development and international sales office in Israel received the warnings from another Odigo user unknown to them. They declined to state exactly what was in the messages or who sent them, saying the FBI was looking into the matter.

Micha Macover, Odigo's CEO, later said that while the company usually zealously protects the privacy of registered users, in this case it provided the FBI with the originating Internet Presence address of the message so the bureau could track down the Internet Service Provider and the originator of the message. There was no further word from the FBI.

Diamandis explained that Odigo offers a "People Finder" program that allows users to seek out and contact others based on common interests. He said it was possible that other Odigo members got the warnings but that the company had not heard from other recipients.

Another small item that raised eyebrows concerned a broken lease at the

World Trade Center just days before the 9/11 attacks by a company with close ties to Israel.

The *American Free Press* reported that Zim American Israeli Shipping Co. broke its lease on two floors of the WTC's north tower when it vacated the rented offices in early September 2001. The company's lease was good until the end of the year and the early pullout cost the company a reported $50,000.

The company is owned by Zim Israel Navigation Co., one of the world's largest container shipping firms. It is jointly owned by the state of Israel and Israel Corp.

Inquiries on the early withdrawal by Zim were routed to WTC owner Silverstein Properties, which in turn passed questions to its public relations firm, Howard J. Rubenstein, which also represents the nation of Israel.

A spokesman for Rubenstein said they had no information on the lease issue.

On September 12, 2001, a *Jerusalem Post* headline read "Thousands of Israelis Missing near WTC, Pentagon." The accompanying story stated, "The Foreign Ministry in Jerusalem has so far received the names of 4,000 Israelis believed to have been in the areas of the World Trade Center and the Pentagon at the time of the attacks. The list is made up of people who have not yet made contact with friends or family."

It should be noted that this 4,000 figure originated not with U.S. news media or Arabic sources but in Israel. The Arab media, however, was quick to seize on it.

A week later, a Beirut television station reported that 4,000 Israeli employees of the WTC were absent the day of the attack, suggesting foreknowledge of the attacks. This information spread across the Internet but was quickly branded a hoax.

On September 19, the *Washington Post* reported about 113 Israelis were missing at the WTC, and the next day, President Bush noted more than 130 Israelis were victims.

Finally, on September 22, the *New York Times* stated that amazingly only one Israeli was killed when the WTC towers collapsed. "There were, in fact, only three Israelis who had been confirmed as dead: two on the planes and another who had been visiting the towers on business and who was identified and buried," reported the *Times*.

But would a staunch friend of the United States like Israel conduct activities detrimental to their ally?

It might be remembered that on the day of the attacks, five Israelis were arrested for "puzzling behavior," namely shouting and dancing just after shooting video of the destruction of the World Trade Center from the roof of the New Jersey building where they worked.

The five, identified as Oded Ellner, Omer Marmari, Yaron Shmuel, Sivan and Paul Kurzberg, were seen videotaping the WTC attack by neighbors, who interpreted their shouts as jubilation and agreement with the tragedy. Police were notified and later stopped their van bearing the company name Urban Moving Systems. In their van, police found $4,000 in cash and a box cutter. One investigator told the *Bergen Record* on September 12, "There were maps of the city in the car with certain places highlighted. It looked like they're hooked in on this. It looked like they knew what was going to happen." *ABC News* quoted one of the Israelis as saying, "Our purpose was to document the event."

After the names of two of the five turned up on a CIA-FBI database of foreign intelligence nationals, Marc Perelman of *Forward* reported that the FBI launched a Foreign Counterintelligence Investigation (FCI), which is undertaken quietly at the highest levels of the bureau. One of the men's attorneys, Steven Gordon, confirmed that "counterintelligence officials from the FBI" were involved in the case.

Dominick Suter, owner of the Weehawken, New Jersey, moving company, was questioned by the FBI agents, who took documents and computer hard drives but allowed Suter to go free. A few days later, Suter left the states for Israel.

In late November, the five were quietly released and sent back to Israel, where they charged that American authorities tortured them by keeping them unclothed in solitary confinement, beatings and deprivation of food.

Irit Stoffer, a spokesperson for the Israeli Foreign Ministry, denied the men were spies and said they were deported for "only visa violations."

Chip Berlet, a senior analyst for the Political Research Associates in Boston, explained, "[There] is a backdoor agreement between allies that says that if one of your spies gets caught and didn't do too much harm, he goes home. It goes on all the time. The official reason is always a visa violation."

But was there no real harm done? This case seemed to be just another odd anomaly in the cascading news of the attacks and the subsequent bombing of Afghanistan.

But it turned out to be only the barest tip of an iceberg that was to become public in mid-2002. The story began to surface in early 2002 when a secret report by the Drug Enforcement Agency (DEA) was leaked to the European media. The report stated that most distribution of the drug Ecstasy was "controlled by organized crime figures in Western Europe, Russia and Israel." According to several reports, a DEA investigation into the Ecstasy supply uncovered a number of Israeli citizens operating in the United States.

"The report shows the clandestine network was engaged in several intelligence operations. It was a long-term project," said Guillaume Dasquie, editor of *Intelligence Online,* which broke the story in March 2002. The French Web site threatened to publish the entire DEA report if U.S. and Israeli officials continued to deny its existence. The report mentioned investigations of the spy network in Florida, Texas and California, with many of its participants posing as art students.

Beginning in early 2002, *Fox News* reporter Carl Cameron began to break the story that the U.S. government was holding more than one hundred Israeli citizens with direct links to foreign military, criminal and intelligence organizations. A bureau spokesperson would not talk about the case but did not deny it either. He referred reporters to the FBI's National Security Division.

Cameron too said he was hampered in trying to obtain information. "It's very explosive information, obviously, and there's a great deal of evidence that they say they have collected."

Cameron added that the biggest question that investigators shared with him was "How could they [the Israelis] not have known?"

By summer 2002, the estimated number of Israeli nationals being held had climbed to nearly two hundred, yet still the story went largely unreported by America's corporate mass media. One can only imagine what the newspaper headlines and TV crawl tags would look like if a gigantic Iraqi spy rung had been uncovered.

Reportedly, several of the Israelis lived in close proximity to some of the 9/11 terrorists, increasing the speculation that Israel knew more about the attacks than officially admitted. More than one-third of 120 deported Israelis lived in Florida, home to at least 10 of the 19 identified hijackers. At least 5 lived in Hollywood, Florida, home to Mohammed Atta and three other hijackers. Two others lived near Delray Beach, where other hijackers temporarily stayed. Six of the Israelis used cell phones purchased by a former Israeli vice consul in the United States, reported *Le Monde.*

Furthermore, several of the persons involved in this "art student scandal" were observed taking pictures and reconnoitering U.S. military bases and the homes of government officials.

In March 2001, the National Counterintelligence Center (NCIC) issued a warning that "in the past six weeks, employees in federal office buildings have reported suspicious activities concerning individuals representing themselves as foreign students selling artwork."

Paul Rodriguez with *Insight* magazine reported, "Besides federal law enforcement incidents, DEA's I[nternal] S[ecurity] unit found that several military bases also had experienced unauthorized entries by some of the students including two bases from which Stealth aircraft and other supersecret military units operate. Unauthorized photographing of military sites and civilian industrial complexes, such as petroleum storage facilities, also was reported to the DEA, the documents show and interviews confirm."

Many of these young men and women had known connections to Israeli military, intelligence or even criminal organizations. Some even worked in electronic signal intercept units in the Israeli army.

Most claimed to be art students from Israel's Bezalel Academy or the University of Jerusalem. The Jerusalem university does not exist, and officials with Bezalel Academy said none of the "art students" turned up in the school's data bank.

According to the prestigious French newspaper *Le Monde*, student art sales were merely a cover for a vast Israeli spy ring whose primary purpose was to track al-Qaeda in the United States without informing American authorities. The paper said this was the biggest Israeli spy case in the United States since 1984, when naval intelligence officer Jonathan Pollard, an American Jew, was caught giving military secrets to Israel.

The German newspaper *Die Zeit* reported in late 2002 that the CIA was given a detailed report on the actions of terrorists within the United States by the Mossad but failed to act on the information. According to *BBC News*, "The paper has uncovered details of a major Israeli spy ring involving some 120 agents for the intelligence service Mossad operation across America and some masquerading as art students. The ring was reportedly hard on the heels of at least four members of the hijack gang, including its leader Mohammed Atta. But the Israeli agents were detected by their American counterparts and thrown out of the country. The U.S. authorities said then that they were students whose visas had expired."

The paper also said that had the CIA notified German authorities that Ramzi Binalshibh, a key logistician for the attacks, had attended the meeting of al-Qaeda members in Malaysia more than eighteen months prior to 9/11, the Germans could have prevented him from entering Germany and making contact with the Hamburg cell that planned the 9/11 atrocities.

Central to this tale of spies infiltrating the United States is the fact that the people taken by the FBI in connection with the spy ring included employees of two Israeli-owned high-tech companies that currently perform nearly all official wiretaps in the United States.

Such wiretaps are authorized by the Communications Assistance for Law Enforcement Act (CALEA). Actually wiretaps is a misnomer, because today's communications systems may be accessed by electronic signals rather than physical "taps," but the end result is the same - eavesdropping.

Two firms that handle most of this wiretapping are Amdocs, Ltd. and Comverse Infosys, both identified by *Fox News* as Israeli telecommunications companies. Amdocs reportedly keeps records of virtually every call made in the United States, although not the content of the calls. Comverse provided custom computers and software that allowed U.S. investigators to intercept, record, store and receive data from the U.S. phone system.

According to *NewsMax.com* reporter Charles R. Smith, "The spy ring enabled criminals to use reverse wiretaps against U.S. intelligence and law enforcement operations. The [spy ring's] illegal monitoring may have resulted in the deaths of several informants and reportedly spoiled planned anti-drug raids on crime syndicates."

Officials at both Amdocs and Comverse denied any knowledge of the Israeli spy ring. Comverse spokesman Paul Baker stated, "In full compliance with the U.S. Department of Defense regulations, this subsidiary's operations are completely segregated from all other Comverse businesses and are insulated from any foreign influence."

The official response to the allegations of widespread spying and even foreknowledge of the 9/11 attacks has prompted overly strenuous denials from U.S. officials and even attacks in the major media. Daniel Pipes in an article for *Jewish World Review*, which was then published as an op-ed piece in the *New York Post*, decried the spy ring story as "conspiracy theories" based on a "crazy-quilt of unsourced allegations, drive-by innuendoes and incoherent obscurities, but no hard facts." Pipes, director of the Middle East Forum and the author of *Conspiracy, How the Paranoid Style Flourishes and Where It Comes From*, is trotted out from time to time to dispel what he considers conspiracy theories. usually, no one mentions that Pipes also is a member of the Council on Foreign Relations.

If the major news media is cowed about negative reporting on Israel, U.S. government officials may be worse. *Insight* magazine reporter Paul Rodriguez said one Justice Department official told him, "We think there is something quite sinister here but are unable at this time to put our finger on it." Another official flatly stated, "The higher ups don't want to deal with this and neither does the FBI because it involves Israel." *Fox News* reported that "investigators within the DEA, INS and FBI have all told *Fox News* that to pursue or even suggest Israel is spying through Comverse is considered career suicide."

Critics have voiced opposition to the wiretapping system. "From the beginning, both the political right and left warned Congress and the FBI that they were making a huge mistake by implementing CALEA, that it would jeopardize the security of private communications, whether it's between a mother and her son or between government officials," said Lisa Dean, vice president for technology policy at the Free Congress Foundation. The foundation's Brad Jansen added, "The CALEA form of massive surveillance is a poor substitute for real law enforcement and intelligence work. Massive wiretapping does not equal security. Instead, we have elected to jeopardize our national security in exchange for poor law enforcement. The current mentality of law enforcement is what failed to protect U.S. from 9/11. CALEA wiretaps will not protect us from terror attacks in the future. The system does not provide better intelligence information. It actually leads to less security and more crime. We get the worst of both worlds."

Some observers of today's geopolitical scene, especially perennial presidential candidate Lyndon LaRouche, believe that the 9/11 attacks provided a pretext to implement a plan to strengthen Israel, as articulated in a 1996 paper prepared by an Israeli think tank. This plan was pushed throughout the Clinton administration.

The leader of the study group that produced this paper was Richard

Perle. In 2002, Perle was chairman of Bush's Defense Policy Board, which reported to Deputy Defense Secretary Paul Wolfowitz. Perle is a ranking member of the Council on Foreign Relations.

Perle's 1996 paper, entitled "A Clean Break: A New Strategy for Securing the Realm," was prepared for the Institute for Advanced Strategic and Political Studies (IASPS), a Jerusalem-based think tank with an affiliated office in Washington. The institute, along with issuing policy studies, trains Israeli university graduates in "economic and strategic studies" and helps them become "research aides in the Israeli Parliament (Knesset) and the U.S. Congress."

The "Clean Break" paper, prepared by IASPS consultants - two of whom also were members of the CFR, stated in 1996 that Israel had an opportunity to make a "clean break" with past policies and formulate "a new strategy to seize the initiative." The paper urged Israeli leaders to "work closely with Turkey and Jordan to contain, destabilize, and roll-back some of its most dangerous threats. This implies a clean break from the slogan 'comprehensive peace' to a traditional concept of strategy based on balance of power." This would mean, as the paper goes on to explain, that "Israel can shape its strategic environment, in cooperation with Turkey and Jordan, by weakening, containing, and even rolling back Syria. This effort can focus on removing Saddam Hussein from power in Iraq - an important Israeli strategic objective in its own right - as a means of foiling Syria's regional ambitions."

Perle's paper also calls for changing "the nature of [Israel's] relations with the Palestinians, including the right of hot pursuit for self defense into all Palestinian areas and nurturing alternatives to Arafat's exclusive grip on Palestinian society."

"The ongoing drive to induce President George W. Bush to launch a war against Iraq, is a 1996 Israeli government policy that is being foisted on the President by a nest of Israeli agents inside the U.S. government," declared LaRouche in campaign literature. "This Israeli spy network inside the United States was unable to achieve their objective until President Bush was entrapped by the events of September 11, 2001, and the falsified account of those events provided by this foreign intelligence apparatus and lured over their policies.

"On Feb. 19, 1998, Richard Perle and former congressman Stephen Solarz released an 'Open Letter to the President,' demanding a full-scale U.S.-led drive for 'regime change' in Baghdad. Among the signers of the original Perle-Solarz letter were the following current Bush Administration officials: Elliot Abrams (National Security Council), Richard Armitage (State Department), John Bolton (State Department), Doug Feith (Defense Department), Fred Ikle (Defense Policy Board) Zalmay Khalilzad (White House), Peter Rodman (Defense Department), Donald Rumsfeld (Secretary of Defense), Paul Wolfowitz (Defense Department), David Wurmser (State Department) and Dov Zakheim (Defense Department)."

Shortly after the invasion of Iraq began in late March 2003, Perle resigned as chairman of the Bush administration's Defense Policy Board amid charges of conflict of interest. *New Yorker* magazine investigative writer Seymour Hersh reported that Perle had met in France with a Saudi arms dealer while soliciting investments for Trireme Partners, a firm he helped create and that planned to profit from homeland security activities. Perle threatened to sue Hersh and called him "the closest thing American journalism has to a terrorist" shortly before resigning.

LaRouche concluded that "President Bush is being pressured - from inside his own national security apparatus - to adopt an Israeli Likud foreign policy! This is a scandalous hoax, far worse than the Gulf of Tonkin affair of the late 1960s."

At least that's LaRouche's view of it. Considering that seven of the eleven men listed above are members of the Council on Foreign Relations, this plan could also be viewed as advancing stated CFR policy.

It should be remembered that it was the Rothschild banking dynasty that helped create the state of Israel. And the British Rothschilds aided African diamond magnate Cecil Rhodes in creating what was to become the Council on Foreign Relations.

The 2nd Lord Lionel Walter Rothschild served as a member of the British Parliament during World War I. He was the eldest son of Nathan Rothschild, who dominated the Bank of England for so many years. Under the Rothschild's policy of "primogenitude," which stated the eldest son controlled the family fortune, Lionel inherited both Nathan's money and title after his death in 1915.

In 1917, Lionel Rothschild, a dedicated Zionist, received a letter from British foreign secretary Arthur Balfour expressing approval for the establishment of a home for Jews in Palestine. Both Rothschild and Balfour were members of a secret society founded by Rhodes known as the Round Table Group, a forerunner of the present Council on Foreign Relations. It has been speculated that the Balfour letter was agreed to jointly by these two fellow secret-society members.

This letter later became known as the Balfour Declaration. In 1922, the League of Nations, rife with secret-society men, approved the Balfour mandate in Palestine, thus paving the way for the later creation of Israel. Baron Edmond de Rothschild, who built the first pipeline from the Red Sea to the Mediterranean to bring Iranian oil to Israel and founded the Israel General Bank, has been called "the father of modern Israel."

Several writers and researchers have even suggested that the suicide hijackers were not Arabs at all, but Israelis determined to instigate an all-out war between the United States and the Arab world. While this undoubtedly will be proclaimed a monstrous lie by the corporate mass media, almost unanimously pro-Israel, there are tantalizing facts that support such a theory.

The obvious involvement of Israel in the events of 9/11 has already been noted. It has long been recognized in intelligence circles that Israelis received lengthy and extensive training in order to pass as Arabs. Some even go so far as to marry Arab women and raise families.

Columnist Jack Anderson wrote in 1972 that "Israeli agents - immigrants whose families had lived in Arab lands for generations - have a perfect knowledge of Arab dialects and customs. They have been able to infiltrate Arab governments with ease."

The idea that the 9/11 attacks were actually contrived by Israel is one that was mentioned soon afterward by Internet commentator Dick Eastman, who pointed to two separate investigations that may have been sabotaged by the WTC destruction.

One dealt with a probe into drug running between Afghanistan's Northern Alliance and China with the possible involvement of American businessmen, and the other had to do with a lawsuit being prepared against prominent financial figures and institutions alleging price fixing on the price of gold.

According to Eastman, all of the case files were stored in the FBI offices in the World Trade Center.

"'China white' heroin distributed by [China's] People's Liberation Army, made from Afghan opium links all bankers and oilmen to the corrupt and renegade secret state agencies, CIA, FBI, Mossad - renegade agents of either agency may have seen this opportunity for mutual gain and found the way - having profiles of each of the players to propose the crash bombing frame-up as the best 'solution' to each of the players' most troublesome problems, while making enormous profits besides," wrote Eastman.

"The getting and conditioning/deceiving of hijackers is an easy affair. Mossad has infiltrated bin Laden's forces in Central Asia and the Mideast a radically decentralized organization (as it must be to remain viable) and so it was an easy matter for this 'dark side' Mossad to trick some very angry and vengeful Arabs into thinking they were doing bin Laden's [will]. When the crashes take place, word merely has to be put out by those involved (the CIA, Mossad, [Israel's] Sharon and those complicit in the administration, to push the theme that bin Laden was responsible and that this aggressive war to overthrow the Taliban is the only immediate appropriate response," he added. Eastman noted that whatever "proofs" America had to support the idea of bin Laden's guilt "has come exclusively through Sharon via Mossad." "The 'evidence' comes exclusively from the prime 'frame-up' suspect."

General Hameed Gul, former director general of the Pakistani intelligence services, who worked closely with the CIA during the years of fighting against the Soviets in Afghanistan, said in an interview with UPI news service it was his belief that the Israeli Mossad orchestrated the 9/11 attacks with the support of its own assets already within the United States.

While obviously anti-Israel, Gul nevertheless was in an insider's position. His views should be considered when he explained how there was little or no response from security forces on the morning of 9/11. "This was clearly an inside job," Gul said. "Bush was afraid and rushed to the shelter of a nuclear bunker. He clearly feared a nuclear situation."

"Who could that have been?" Gul asked rhetorically, alluding to Israel's nuclear capability.

Gul went on to explain that Israel had grown to detest both President Bush and his father because they are considered "too close to oil interests and the Gulf countries." He noted that Arab sources, through American conduits and "soft money," poured some $150 million into Bush's 2000 campaign, another danger signal to Israeli hardliners.

"Bush conveniently overlooks - or is not told - the fact that Islamic fundamentalists got their big boost in the modern age as CIA assets in the covert campaign to force the Soviets out of Afghanistan.

"All summer long [2001] we heard about America's shrinking surplus and that the Pentagon would not have sufficient funds to modernize for the 21st century. And now, all of a sudden, the Pentagon can get what it wants without any Democratic Party opposition. How very convenient.

"Even [America's] cherished civil liberties can now be abridged with impunity to protect the expansion of the hegemony of transnational capitalism. There is now a new excuse to crush anti-globalization protests. And now the Israelis have given the U.S. the pretext for further expansion into an area that will be critical in the next 25 years - the Caspian basin," Gul stated.

Lest one think that Gul had his own agenda for making such statements, similar ideas were expressed by two former German intelligence chiefs. Ekehardt Werthebach, former president of Germany's domestic intelligence service, *Verfassungsschutz*, and Andreas von Buelow, who served on a parliamentary commission with oversight over Germany's secret service, both said the 9/11 attacks gave every evidence of being a state-sponsored event. Recall that U.S. Attorney General Ashcroft soon after 9/11 announced that at least three of the hijackers were traced to a terrorist cell that had operated out of Hamburg, Germany, since at least 1999.

Werthebach said a sophisticated operation such as displayed on 9/11 would require a state intelligence service behind it, totally unlike the "loose group" of terrorists reportedly led by Mohammed Atta.

Von Buelow said the 9/11 planner used mercenaries or "guns for hire," such as Palestinian terrorist leader Abu Nidal, whom von Buelow described as an "instrument of the Mossad." Such people as Nidal and other Arab mercenaries are the "working level," according to von Buelow, pointing out the problems with such low-level agents.

He said they were "like assailants who, in their preparations, leave tracks behind them like a herd of stampeding elephants. They made payments with credit cards with their own names; they reported to their flight instructors with their own names. They left behind rented cars with flight manuals in Arabic for jumbo jets. They took with them, on their suicide trip, tills and farewell letters, which fall into the hands of the FBI, because they were stored in the wrong place and wrongly addressed. Clues were left behind like in a child's game of hide-and-seek, which were to be followed!"

He said such an operation is carefully conducted with an eye toward deception that is widely propagated in the mainstream media, creating an accepted version of events.

"Journalists don't even raise the simplest questions," he added. "Those who differ are labeled as crazy."

Von Buelow specified Israel as the most likely sponsor and said that the attacks were designed to turn public opinion against Arabs while boosting military and security spending.

Interestingly enough, the day before the 9/11 attacks, the *Washington Times* ran a story quoting members of the U.S. Army's School of Advanced Military Studies (SAMS). Speaking about the capability of Israel, the paper noted, "Of the Mossad, the Israeli intelligence service, the SAMS officers say: 'Wildcard. Ruthless and cunning. Has capability to target U.S. forces and make it look like a Palestinian/Arab act.'"

Remote Controlled Aircraft A Reality

On October 7, 2001, the first operational deployment of Global Hawk led the first of the American air and missile strikes on Afghanistan.

Global Hawk is the name of the latest version of a high-altitude, long-endurance unmanned air vehicle (UAV); in other words, an unarmed pilotless drone plane that can take off, conduct missions such as photographing battlefields and land by remote electronic control. Armed versions are in the works. The jet aircraft, equivalent in wing size to a Boeing 737 commercial airliner, has a publicly announced range of 14,000 nautical miles (about halfway around the world) and can fly at altitudes of 65,000 feet for about forty hours.

"Working alongside other UAV reconnaissance assets, at least one Global Hawk was used to provide reconnaissance prior to the [Afghanistan] strikes and for successive post-strike battle damage assessment," reported *Jane's Aerospace* on October 8.

This Buck Rogers equipment had been developed in the 1970s and, by several credible accounts, was operational in the 1980s. By the spring of 2001, this unmanned drone, designated the RQ-4A Global Hawk UAV, was capable of flying a mission to Australia.

"On 23 April 2001," according to Australia's Defence Science and Technology Organization (DSTO), "Global Hawk flew non-stop from Edwards Air Force Base, California, to Edinburgh Air Force Base, South Australia, where it was based for nearly two months undergoing a series of demonstration flights.

Global Hawk returned to the U.S. on 7 June 2001."

Dr. Brendan Nelson, Australia's parliamentary secretary to the minister of defense, said Global Hawk made aviation history when it became the first unmanned aircraft to fly nonstop across the Pacific Ocean in twenty-three hours and twenty minutes. The previous record had stood for twenty-six years.

During its six weeks of demonstrations in Australia, Global Hawk undertook eleven missions with crews from both the U.S. Air Force and the Royal Australian Air Force. It was the first time the United States had operated Global Hawk with another nation.

According to the Defense Advanced Projects Agency (DARPA), a newly designed Global Hawk aircraft was first flown at Edwards AFB on Feburary 28, 1998. A Defense Department news release said, "The entire mission, including take-off and landing, was performed autonomously by the aircraft based on its mission plan." The craft's ground controllers monitored the status of the flight.

The Global Hawk program is managed by DARPA for the Defense Airborne Reconnaissance Office. The primary contractor is Teledyne Ryan Aeronautical and the principal suppliers are Raytheon Systems, Allison Engine Co., Boeing North American and L3 Com.

So what does this unmanned flight system have to do with September 11?

Former German secretary of defense Andreas von Buelow, in a January 13, 2002, interview with the newspaper *Tagesspiegel* in speaking about the 9/11 attacks, noted, "There is also the theory of one British flight engineer [and] according to this, the steering of the planes was perhaps taken out of the pilots' hands from outside. The Americans had developed a method in the 1970s whereby they could rescue hijacked planes by intervening into the computer piloting [the electronic flight system]. This theory says this technique was abused in this case;" Von Buelow could well have knowledge of this technology as several researchers and Web sites have stated that Lufthansa, Germany's national airline, was aware of the possibility of electronic capture and had quietly stripped the flight control systems out of American-built jetliners in the early 1990s.

The British flight engineer Von Buelow mentioned is Joe Vialls, a journalist, author, private investigator and former member of the Society of Licenced Aeronautical Engineers and Technologists in London. In an article published on several Web sites, Vialls claimed, "[T]wo American multinationals collaborated with the Defense Advanced Projects Agency (DARPA) on a project designed to facilitate the remote recovery of hijacked American aircraft. Brilliant both in concept and operation, 'Home Run' [Vialls' designation, not its real code name] allowed specialist ground controllers to listen in to cockpit conversations on the target aircraft, then take absolute control of its computerized flight control system by remote means.

"From that point onwards, regardless of the wishes of the hijackers or flight deck crew, the hijacked aircraft could be recovered and landed automatically at an airport of choice, with no more difficulty than flying a radio-controlled model airplane. The engineers had no idea that almost 30 years after its initial design, Home Run's top secret computer codes would be broken [or passed to unauthorized personnel] and the system used to facilitate direct ground control of four aircraft used in the high-profile attacks in New York and Washington on 11th September, 2001."

Even when news of Global Hawk and its remote controlled capability was first released, there was speculation that UAV technology might be used to thwart airline hijackings. Once a hijacking took place, the Global Hawk flight technology would be triggered and the electronically captured plane flown to a landing at a safe location regardless of the actions of the flight crew or the hijackers.

The seemingly outlandish suggestion that remote-controlled planes were crashed into American targets is backed by several intriguing facts, beginning with a little-noticed item in the September 28, 2001, edition of the *New York Times* in which President Bush announced his plans to protect air passengers. Along with the usual proposals, such as strengthening cockpit doors and transponders that cannot be turned off, he mentioned "new technology, probably far in the future, allowing air traffic controllers to land distressed planes by remote control." Apparently, Bush was familiar with the Global Hawk technology but chose to present it as technology not yet available. Yet earlier that year, a former chief of British Airways suggested that such technology could be used to commandeer an aircraft from the ground and control it remotely in the event of a hijacking.

After the 2001 attacks, many Web sites speculated that perhaps Global Hawk's first true operational use might have been conducted on September 11. After all, as all experienced aviation and military persons well know, if a technology such as Global Hawk is publicly revealed, it most probably has been in secret use for many years.

According to aviation insiders, while it may indeed be years before air traffic controllers can take control of flying airliners, such technology already exists in certain modern jumbo jets equipped with electronic flight control systems, such as the Boeing 757 and 767, both of which were involved in the 9/11 attacks.

This assertion seemed to be confirmed by a technical and operational analysis white paper published shortly after the 9/11 attacks by two Arizona technology companies, KinetX, Inc. of Tempe and Cogitek Corp. of Chandler.

These firms were trying to market their version of Global Hawk as an anti-hijacker system. "The National Flight Emergency Response System (NFERS) was developed to prevent the terrorist incident of 9/11 from ever happening again," stated the companies' white paper. "This system will protect passenger and cargo aircraft from being used as terrorist weapons. NFERS is essentially the integration of *existing technology* [emphasis added] for the

-65-

purpose of transferring cockpit operations to a secure ground station in case of an emergency. It is important to note that the essential technology exists now."

The two Arizona companies reported that they could have a prototype system ready for use in twelve months. If independent firms could manage a prototype that soon, it is clear that the government most probably has the same technology operational.

Under such a system, a computer command ground station could electronically capture a plane equipped with such technology and direct it wherever the controllers wished it to go. Some experts contended that flying electronic command centers - Airborne Warning and Control System (AWAC) aircraft - can perform the same function as a ground station.

Other news items that reinforce the idea that electronically captured planes were used on 9/11 include the tape of Osama bin Laden made public by the CIA in late 2001, in which he revealed that some, if not all, of the hijackers did not realize they were on a suicide mission.

This could explain the Boston reports that the hijackers spent their last night drinking heavily and looking for hookers.

Speaking about Flight 77, which reportedly struck the Pentagon, the *Washington Post* noted, "Aviation sources said that the plane was flown with extraordinary skill, making it highly likely that a trained pilot was at the helm, possibly one of the hijackers. Someone even knew how to turn off the transponder, a move that is considerably less the obvious."

This same story noted, "But just as the plane seemed to be on a suicide mission into the White House, the unidentified pilot executed a pivot so tight that it reminded observers of a fighter jet maneuver. The plane circled 270 degrees from the right to approach the Pentagon from the west, whereupon Flight 77 fell below radar level, vanishing from the controller's screens, the sources said."

One Internet source said this was proof that the plane had been electronically captured because software with built-in safety programs would not have allowed such a maneuver. But the software could have been overridden if the craft was taken over electronically as the outside capture would have negated the airliner's safety software.

According to news reports, the suspected pilot of Flight 77 was Hani Hanjour, who trained at the Bowie Maryland Freeway Airport. Instructors there evaluated Hanjour when he attempted to rent a plane. He took three flights with the instructors in the second week of August 2001, but flew so poorly he was rejected for the rental, said Marcel Bernard, chief flight instructor at Freeway. The news article also pointed out that Hanjour trained for a few months in Scottsdale, Arizona, but did not finish the course "because instructors felt he was not capable."

Mohammed Atta and Marwan-al-Shehhi, the other suspected hijackers, also were reported to be mediocre to poor pilots. One flight instructor said neither man was able to pass a Stage 1 rating test.

Suspected hijackers Nawaf al-Hazmi and Khalid al-Midhar both were sent packing from Sorbi's Flying Club in San Diego. "Their English was horrible and their mechanical skills were even worse," commented one flight instructor. "It was like they had hardly even ever driven a car."

Could a capture by Global Hawk and NFERS technology explain why none of the recordings from either air traffic controllers or the cockpit recorders have been made available to the public? Some reports claimed the tapes were blank.

According to some, an electronic capture of the flight control systems would have prevented any normal recordings. Others argue that the recordings were sequestered to prevent the public from hearing how the crews were unable to control their planes.

Investigator Vialls offered this explanation of why the cockpit voice recorder did not send a warning of the hijacking, their transponders. "Technically, a transponder is a combined radio transmitter and receiver which operates automatically, in this case relaying data between the four aircraft and air traffic control on the ground. The signals sent provide a unique 'identity' for each aircraft, essential in crowded airspace to avoid mid-air collisions, and equally essential for Home Run controllers trying to lock onto the correct aircraft.

"Once it has located the correct aircraft, Home Run 'piggy backs' a data transmission onto the transponder channel and takes direct control from the ground. This explains why none of the aircraft sent a special 'I have been hijacked' transponder code. This was the first hard proof that the target aircraft had been hijacked electronically from the ground."

In an effort to explain the reported cell phone calls from passengers on the flights, Vialls stated his belief that many of the calls were concocted after the fact. "There are no records of any such calls," he said. "We had the media's invisible 'contact' at an airline who 'said' a hostess called to report a hijacking and we had a priest who 'said' he received a call from a man asking him in turn to call his wife and tell her he loved her."

Vialls said one big reason why electronic capture of jetliners cannot be admitted is the billions of dollars required to replace the flight control systems, an expense the already hard-pressed airlines cannot afford.

"The most innovative anti-hijacking tool in the American arsenal has now become the biggest known threat to American national security," he lamented.

Vialls's thoughts were echoed by Donn de Grand Pre, a retired U.S. Army colonel and author of *Barbarians Inside the Gates.* Shortly after the 9/11 attacks, Grand Pre, along with several commercial and military pilots, participated in a marathon discussion of the events. He acknowledged that the USA, Russia, China and Israel all possess AWACS aircraft that "have the capability to utilize electro-magnetic pulsing [EMP] to knock out on-board flight controls and communications of targeted aircraft, and then, fly them by remote control.

"The 9/11 activity and horrific destruction of U.S. property and lives was intentionally meant to trigger a psychological and patriotic reaction on the part of the U.S. citizens, which is paving the way for 'combined UN activity' (using the fig leaf of NATO) for striking key targets in both the Middle East/South Asia and the Balkans.

"The goal continues to be the ultimate destruction of all national sovereignty and establishment of a global government," he said.

It is indeed difficult for many people to believe that four jetliners with crews trained in detecting and deflecting a hijacking attempt could all be taken at the same time by a handful of men armed only with knives (some reports said plastic knives) and "box cutters." It is more believable to think that the four craft were captured by electronic technology such as that used on Global Hawk.

One tape, whose authenticity could not be established, was sent through the Internet in the early fall of 2002. It was said to be between air traffic controllers and Flight 93. In this tape, controllers and other nearby flights heard a male voice speak of a bomb onboard and hostage conditions. Other pilots reported seeing a black plume of smoke coming from the doomed flight.

One Internet user, who only identified himself as "Snake Plissken," offered his "bumble bee" theory:

The masterminds of the 9/11 attacks kept the airliner passengers artificially low by hacking and manipulating the airlines' computer systems. Once in the air, the pilots were told by radio that an attack on America has taken place and ordered them to turn off their transponders and land at a designated military air base, which they did. The planes are still visible on radar but cannot be identified.

Duplicate jets with remote-control technology have already been sent aloft by the 9/11 masterminds and reach similar altitudes and coordinates and are picked up by air traffic controllers while the original flights descend below radar to the military base.

Once all are on the ground, all passengers are transferred to Flight 93, which is soon airborne under Global Hawk remote control. Duplicate flights 11, 175 and 77 are flown to their targets while original Flight 93 is shot down over Pennsylvania silencing all witnesses.

While this outlandish theory sounds more like a script from the old *Mission Impossible* series than reality, it is an object lesson in turning an event around and looking at it from different angles. This theory also does account for many of the unexplained facts of that day. For example, it would explain the extraordinary piloting by the Arab hijackers who, according to their flight instructors, could barely locate the landing gear; the absence of any recordings on flight data systems and the fact that transponders were turned off. The inability to control the aircraft might also explain why apparently none of the crews or passengers on the hijacked craft tried to overcome their ill-armed captors, except for Flight 93. And there is an intriguing theory, backed by solid evidence, regarding that doomed flight.

After learning of the WTC and Pentagon attacks and the news that a fourth jetliner was in the air and that fighter jets had been scrambled, many people's first thought upon learning of the Flight 93 crash was that it had been shot down.

The government quickly denied this and, instead, built up the legend of the courageous passengers deciding to attack their captors. This, of course, provided a foundation for the story that the jet crashed during a ferocious battle onboard.

However, the last cell phone call received from the doomed flight came from an unidentified male passenger who called the 911 emergency number about eight minutes before the plane crashed. Operator Glen Cramer told the *Associated Press* on September 11 that the man said he had locked himself in a toilet. "We're being hijacked! We're being hijacked!" the man screamed into his phone.

"We confirmed that with him several times," said Cramer, "and we asked him to repeat what he had said. He was very distraught. He said he believed the plane was going down. He did hear some sort of an explosion and saw white smoke coming from the wing, but he didn't know where. And then we lost contact with him."

The FBI confiscated Cramer's tape and ordered him not to discuss the matter further. No explanation of this cell phone conversation has been offered.

According to an Internet posting by Robb Magley, an earthquake monitoring station in southern Pennsylvania registered a seismic signature somewhat characteristic of a sonic boom at 9:22 A.M. on September 11, 2001. Sonic booms are created by aircraft exceeding the speed of sound. Jumbo airliners do not exceed the speed of sound but supersonic jet fighters do.

This seismic evidence was thought to suggest that a supersonic jet was in the area just prior to the crash of Flight 93 and added support to a growing suspicion that the airliner was shot down by the U.S. military. After conferring with a NASA scientist, Magley became convinced that the seismic spike was not a sonic boom but perhaps an explosion from a nearby rock quarry. Later, Magley's attention turned to the possibility that Flight 93 may have been the victim of a high-powered microwave (HPM) device rather than an aircraft.

Supporting Magley's original theory of a shoot down was a statement by top government officials that President Bush had authorized the use of military force on the morning of September 11.

Speaking on NBC's *Meet the Press* less than a week after the attacks, Vice President Cheney said Bush "made the decision that if the plane [Flight 77, which reportedly struck the Pentagon] would not divert, if they wouldn't pay any attention to instructions to move away from the city, as a last resort, our pilots were authorized to take them out."

Deputy Defense Secretary Paul Wolfowitz acknowledged that the military was closing on Flight 93. "We responded awfully quickly, I might say, on Tuesday," he said in a PBS interview. "And in fact, we were already tracking in on that plane that crashed in Pennsylvania. I think it was the heroism of the passengers on board that brought it down, but the Air Force was in a position to do so if we had had to."

General Richard Myers, chairman of the Joint Chiefs of Staff, also confirmed that fighters approached Flight 93, but denied that they fired on the craft.

Several ground witnesses reported sighting a small aircraft circling the area at the time of the Flight 93 crash. Later, the FBI explained that it was a business jet that had been requested by authorities to descend and provide the location of the crash.

This explanation is wanting due to the fact that by then all air traffic had been grounded, the plume of smoke from the wreckage plus numerous calls to 911 would have provided a sufficient location bearing, and the FBI has failed to provide any information concerning this aircraft or its passengers, none of whom have come forward to give their account.

One craft that was in the area was a single-engine Piper piloted by Bill Wright. Wright said he was within sight of Flight 93, in fact so close he could see its United markings. He said he suddenly received orders to get away from the airline and land immediately. "That's one of the first things that went through my mind when they told us to get as far away from it as fast as we could, that either they were expecting it to blow up or they were going to shoot it down," Wright told newsmen.

There is also a question concerning the wreckage. According to the official story, Flight 93 barreled into the ground at close to five hundred miles per hour. Yet, wreckage was strewn for up to eight miles, including paper mail the plane was carrying. One engine, which weighs in excess of one thousand pounds, was found more than two thousand yards from the crash scene; indicating it came loose prior to ground impact.

Wally Miller was the local coroner at the time of the crash and was required by law to establish the cause of death of the victims. "I put down 'murdered' for the 40 passengers and crew; 'suicide' for the four terrorists," Miller told a reporter, adding significantly that he could not prove what actually happened.

Subsequent actions by government authorities did little to dissuade conspiracy theorists. They didn't make public the flight data recordings until April 18, 2002, and then played edited excerpts to the victims' family members, who were ordered not to discuss what they heard. Even then, at least one person said he learned things he hadn't known before. Bureau agents also muzzled Cleveland air traffic controllers involved in the last moments of the flight, ordering them not to speak about what they saw on their radar screens.

Amidst near-hysterical cries of national security, the public was once again asked to blindly accept official pronouncements backed by little, no, or even contradictory evidence. With all hard evidence locked away by the government, speculation has run rampant on the true cause of Flight 93's demise. Countering the official story of the crash occurring during a heroic battle with the hijackers are other equally credible theories.

The most prevalent theory is that a U.S. fighter downed the craft with missile and/or cannon fire, a suspicion firmly supported by all the available evidence. Another theory holds that, since one unauthenticated air traffic controller tape available on the Internet speaks of a bomb onboard, one of the hijackers may have detonated such a device in the air.

A more fanciful theory, though backed by solid science, was offered by researchers citing Harvard academic Elaine Scarry. Scarry, in a series of articles and books, postulated that some recent airline crashes were caused by a high-tech military "electronic warfare" weaponry akin to Global Hawk technology and capable of disrupting an aircraft's control system,. The FBI did confirm that a C-130 military plane was within twenty-five miles of Flight 93, and since 1995 the air force has installed "electronic suites" in twenty-eight of its C-130 aircraft.

This Scarry scenario leads to yet another theory that posits that the plane's passengers were successful in their attempt to regain control of the craft but then found they could not control the plane due to electronic seizure.

Under the theory that all the aircraft were captured and flown remotely using Global Hawk technology, the masterminds behind such a scheme could not possibly allow Flight 93 to land safely and give away the game. Since both the shoot-down orders and the fighters were in place, it would be simply a matter of giving the go-ahead and then sweeping it all under the rug of "national security."

But regardless of what truly happened to Flight 93 or how the hijacked planes were controlled, it is clear that whoever was behind the attacks had information, if not help, from inside the government.

One key question is how at least nineteen foreign terrorists were able to separately evade standard airport security precautions and simultaneously hijack four commercial airliners using only box cutters.

As Internet pundit Gary North stated, "We need a theory of the coordinated hijackings that rests on a plausible cause-and-effect sequence that does not assume the complete failure of both check-in procedures and the on-board seating procedures on four separate flights on two separate airlines. I don't see how anyone can make an accurate judgment about who was behind the attacks until he has a plausible explanation of how hijackers got onto the planes and were not removed."

These terrorists were then able to divert four scheduled flights, all under the nose of air traffic controllers, and there was no immediate response despite the standard response procedures in place. By 8:15 A.M., at the latest, on the morning of September 11, air traffic controllers knew that Flights 11 and 175 were badly off course and probably hijacked. Yet by 8:45 A.M., according to NORAD, fighters were still on the ground. When they did become airborne, standard procedures were ignored.

It was established that the person who called the warning to the White House had access to top-secret government codes, and to many knowledgeable persons the lack of rapid response by the U.S. defense establishment is simply inconceivable.

Military forces had been on a heightened state of alert for several days before the attack and a FEMA emergency response team arrived in NYC on September 10. The National Reconnaissance Office had scheduled a training simulation of a jet crashing into a government building the morning of September 11, 2001.

Yet the U.S. continental defense system consistently failed. Something was very wrong.

If even half of the information outlined in the above section is proven in error, the remainder is a damning indictment of official malfeasance. It's much worse than what *Newsweek* termed "a whole summer of missed clues." The totality of the information available today can only lead to two inescapable conclusions: either the highest leadership of the United States is composed of imbeciles and incompetent blunderers or they are criminally negligent accessories to the crimes, if not worse.

Either way, it is clear that such leadership must be changed and soon if the traditional standards of freedom and democracy in the United States are to be retained.

Remote Viewers Look At 9/11

Several experienced remote viewers were commissioned to take a mental look at the people and circumstances surrounding the 9/11 attacks.

One of the viewers who agreed to participate in this study was Lyn Buchanan, formerly the trainer of the U.S. Army's then top secret Grillflame and Stargate remote viewing programs. This technique for viewing persons, places and things by means other than the normal five senses has been known as clairvoyance. The term "remote viewing" was substituted to avoid the ongoing arguments over psychic phenomena and is used to describe the controlled use of psychic abilities.

Remote viewing was extensively studied in the 1960s, '70s, and '80s, first by the CIA, followed by the U.S. Army, Defense Intelligence Agency and National Security Agency. This secret program was funded through six administrations, both Republican and Democrat, for more than a quarter of a century. All of the world's religions, from the Bible to the Koran to Oriental mysticism, contain a wealth of stories involving prophecy, visions and spiritual instruction. And all seem to involve visual input.

The Bible's book of Isaiah opens with the statement, "These are the messages that came to Isaiah, son of Amoz, in the visions he saw during the reigns of King Uzziah, King Jotham, King Ahaz and King Hezakiah - all kings of Judah."

Biblical prophecy was not limited to men. In the Old Testament book of Judges, we find that a "prophetess" named Deborah provided the Israelite leader Barak with information about the military disposition of Sisera, the commander of the forces of Jabin, the King of Canaan. Sisera's forces were routed and thus Deborah, using psychic intelligence, played a pivotal role in the conquest of the Promised Land. She might rightly be called the world's first military remote viewer.

Even in the New Testament, prophecy and visions played an important role as the messianic plan unfolded. St. Paul offered some advice on remote viewing that modern people might well take to heart. "Do not scoff at those who prophesy, but test everything that is said to be sure if it is true, and if it is, then accept it," he wrote to church members in Thessalonica.

Throughout the ages, men and women have practiced "spiritualism" to include versions of remote viewing, but it was never accepted by the mainstream public because modern science, while able to demonstrate that some phenomenon was occurring in laboratory experiments, could never quite get a handle on the how and why of it.

But after reports leaked out from behind the Iron Curtain in the early 1970s that Soviet Russia and its Eastern European allies were experimenting with psychics, the American intelligence establishment felt the need to join in the pursuit of psychic spies. Beginning in 1972, the CIA began funding scientific studies into psychic phenomena at California's Stanford Research Institute (SRI). According to former Jack Anderson investigator and author Ron McRae, it was "the most severely monitored scientific experiment in history." And it got results. By 1976, the remote viewing program had left the CIA and by 1977 was under the U.S. Army's newly formed Intelligence and Security Command (INSCOM). Soon a full-time operational unit, code-named Grill Flame, was under way and producing remarkable results from about a dozen remote viewers. In 1985, the unit was placed within the secretive Defense Intelligence Agency (DIA).

Some people have argued that the use of psychic spies by both sides may have ended the Cold War, which was based primarily on secrecy. Once this secrecy was penetrated by remote viewers, the impasse between the USA and Russia fell apart. In 1995, the story of remote viewing broke in the *Washington Post* and the *New York Times* after the CIA issued a press release acknowledging the psychic program. The story never really reached the American heartland and many people are still unaware of this most significant issue.

According to several sources, remote viewing continues to be used within both the military and intelligence communities. Military-trained remote viewers have been used in the search for Osama bin Laden and also to help identify and locate the sniper around Washington in October 2002, according to several news reports.

In a specially commissioned study, eleven remote viewers with extensive track records took a psychic look at the events of September 11, 2001. Several of the viewers involved asked not to be identified. Among those who agreed to be identified were Buchanan, who now heads up Problems Solutions Innovations of Alamogordo, New Mexico; Prudence Calabrese, director of TransDimensional Systems of Carlsbad, California; Ericca Cordier, director of the Texas Research & Information Bureau, and Gail Ferguson, author of *Cracking the Intuition Code*.

These viewers gave yes-or-no answers to questions. The answers below reflect the majority of the viewers' responses:

> Did President George Bush have foreknowledge of the 9/11 attacks? No.
> Did George Bush, Sr. have foreknowledge of the 9/11 attacks? Yes.
> Did Dick Cheney have foreknowledge of the 9/11 attacks? Yes.
> Did the Israeli Mossad have foreknowledge of the 9/11 attacks? Possibly.
> Did Osama bin Laden have foreknowledge of the 9/11 attacks? Yes.
> Were the planes that crashed into the WTC controlled from the planes' cockpits? No.
> Was the collapse of the WTC towers caused only by the planes striking the buildings? Probably.
> Was any U.S. intelligence agency involved in the 9/11 attacks? Yes.
> Were any members of the Trilateral Commission, Council on Foreign Relations or Bilderberger group responsible for the 9/11 attacks? Yes.
> Was United Airlines Flight 93 shot down? Yes.

Since the answers to most of these questions would seem provocative to many people, it should be pointed out that remote viewing, despite extensive and careful laboratory experiments, is more of an art than a science. It also should be noted that none of the remote viewers knew the questions before their session.

They were simply given a ten-digit set of coordinates that represented each question. For example, the question concerning President Bush was "48965-74123." Those numerals were the extent of information given to the viewers, yet there was a certain consistency in their answers, with the exception of one question that was nearly a tie. Some of the answers were obvious. For example, the question if the WTC planes were controlled from the cockpits of the craft resulted in seven nos, only three yeses and one "no answer." No answer responses resulted from either no data returned or no answer given due to an inconclusive session.

Other answers were much closer. The question concerning the involvement of the Israeli Mossad prompted an almost even split, with six yeses compared to five nos. The question regarding President Bush's foreknowledge yielded seven nos to four yeses while the same question regarding his father resulted in the opposite, seven yeses to three nos with one no answer.

Another near tie was the question that asked if the planes alone were responsible for the collapse of the WTC towers. This query brought five yes responses to four nos with two no answer". The question regarding the involvement of secret society members also was a near tie, with five answering yes, four no and two no answer.

While this one small remote viewing study cannot be taken by anyone as ground truth, based on the remarkable track record of the U.S. government's operational use of this mental technology, it certainly should be the cause for sober reflection and further investigation.

Part II – War For Oil And Drugs

"We haven't heard from [Osama bin Laden] in a long time. I truly am not that concerned about him."
- President George W. Bush, news conference, March 13, 2002

The high plateau of Iran curves along the southern shore of the Caspian Sea. In ancient times, this area was known as Persia and was the spawning ground of several great civilizations. It was also the home of the "eternal pillars of fire" worshiped by the followers of Zoroaster, a sixth-century B.C. sage who added monotheism to an even older Aryan creed. Today, most believe that the pillars of fire were flaming petroleum gas escaping through holes in the local limestone. Marco Polo wrote of springs in the area that produced water that was undrinkable but burned well and removed mange from camels. It was not until the modern era that man found a practical use for liquid petroleum - fuel for transportation and the machines of war.

In 1873, Robert and Ludwig Nobel, sons of the famed inventor of dynamite, Alfred Nobel, came to the Baku area on the western shore of the Caspian Sea and soon were supplying half of the world's petroleum supply. The Swedish Nobel brothers were soon in competition with the French branch of the powerful Rothschild banking family. At the same time, John D. Rockefeller's Standard Oil was becoming a major force in the burgeoning oil industry and also coveted the Caspian Sea oil. With the help of their respective governments, these powerful families competed for control over the Caspian Sea oil for many years. This struggle became known as "the Great Game."

Petroleum has been behind all recent wars, beginning in the early 1940s, when a mostly rural and isolationist America was suddenly thrown into a world war as a reaction to the Japanese attack on Pearl Harbor. Americans mourned the loss of some three thousand soldiers and civilians in Hawaii and, in righteous indignation, allowed their country to be turned into a giant military camp. The federal government, which had consolidated so much power unto itself under the Depression-busting policies of President Franklin Delano Roosevelt, grew even stronger and more centralized under the aegis of "national security." It all seemed quite natural and necessary at the time.

But serious students of history now know that even that "good war" was the result of machinations by a handful of wealthy and powerful men. By closing off Japan's oil supplies in the summer of 1941, Roosevelt, closely connected to

Wall Street power, ensured an eventual attack on the United States. It has now been well established that Roosevelt and a few close advisers knew full well that Pearl Harbor would be attacked on December 7, 1941, but chose to allow it to happen to further their agenda for dragging the isolationist American population into war.

In an odd addendum, the 9/11 attacks apparently blocked an effort to bring the truth concerning foreknowledge of the Pearl Harbor attack to the American public.

Ever since the war, efforts have been mounted to exonerate the two military commanders who were initially blamed as being unprepared for the attack on Pearl Harbor. The latest attempt, aided by Delaware Representative Michael Castle, was stopped when White House Chief of Staff Andrew Card refused to pass along a plea for exoneration to President Bush despite the admission that Rear Admiral Husband Kimmel and Major General Walter Short "were, without question, honorable and patriotic Americans who served our country with bravery and dedication." Furthermore, *White House Weekly,* in reporting this effort, declared, "Subsequent investigations by those inside and outside the military proved that Washington knew the Japanese were on the move but never told Hawaii."

According to reporter James P. Tucker, Jr. the rationale for not forwarding the plea from the officers' families to Bush was that the White House considered the issue too explosive in light of the questions being raised regarding the Bush administration's foreknowledge of the 9/11 attacks.

During World War II, Hitler's Army Group South rampaged through the Ukraine of Russia and moved inexorably toward Baku and the rich Caucasian oil fields. With these oil reserves in hand, Hitler planned to turn south and capture the oil of the Middle East in a combined operation with Field Marshal Erwin Rommel's famed Afrika Korps' assault from North Africa. This scheme was thwarted by Rommel's defeat at El Alamein and the eventual destruction of the German Sixth Army at Stalingrad.

The Vietnam War was about the oil and mineral wealth of Southeast Asia and was prosecuted by men who had been close to Roosevelt and the secretive Council on Foreign Relations. The CFR position papers had long voiced a desire for the United States to gain control over Indochina's oil, magnesium and rubber assets.

Again a provocation was created. In August 1964, President Lyndon Johnson whipped Congress into a frenzy claiming that North Vietnamese gunboats had attacked the U.S. Sixth Fleet in the Gulf of Tonkin off the coast of Vietnam. "Our boys are floating in the water," he cried. Congress responded by passing the Gulf of Tonkin Resolution, which bypassed the Constitution and gave Johnson the power to wage war to stop attacks on Americans. Soon after this, ground combat troops augmented American military advisers there. It was the beginning of the real shooting in the Vietnam War.

But the attack was all a lie. No evidence has ever been brought forward that such an attack ever took place. In fact, editors for *U.S. News & World Report* (July 23, 1984) called it "The 'Phantom Battle' That Led to War."

While America was waging war against North Vietnam, which we were told was merely a puppet of communist Russia and China, Johnson was encouraged by his CFR advisers to grant the Soviet Union loans at higher levels than offered during World War II, when they were our ally. U.S.-backed loans provided Russia with funds to build facilities that turned out war materials that were then sent to North Vietnam for use against American troops. This was a prime example of the duplicity of the men behind our modern wars.

Everyone understood that the Persian Gulf War of 1991, as with most Middle-East conflicts, was a war for oil that ended with its cause celebre, Saddam Hussein, the "new Hitler," still in power.

Stock purchases, oil and grain deals, arms sales, loans and guarantees, the weakening of the Arabs to benefit Israel, the movement toward a global army and government created a mind-numbing entanglement. "It is doubtful whether the 'real' reasons why the United States went to war in the Persian Gulf will ever emerge," wrote authors Jonathan Vankin and John Whalen. "Unlike in Vietnam, where the ambiguous outcome elicited natural suspicions, in the Gulf the decisiveness of victory has buried the reality deeper than any Iraqi or American soldier who went to a sandy grave."

The Central Asian Gas Pipeline

Oil continued to drive the politics of Central Asia when in the late 1970's, the Soviet Union discovered further untapped oil in the southern republic of Chechnya. The region was ripe for exploitation but control over Afghanistan was needed to ensure the safety of a pipeline to bring the oil to world markets.

With the withdrawal of the Soviets, international bankers and oilmen gained a foothold in cash-strapped Russia and the estimated $3 trillion in Caspian Sea oil was once again attracting serious attention. In 1997, six international companies and the government of Turkmenistan formed Central Asian Gas Pipeline, Ltd. (CentGas) to build a 790-mile-long pipeline to link Turkmenistan's natural gas reserves with Pakistan and perhaps on to the New Delhi area of India.

Leading this consortium was America's Unocal Corporation, whose president, John F. Imle Jr., said the project would be "the foundation for a new commerce corridor for the region often referred to as the Silk Road for the 21st Century."

Also involved were these companies: Delta Oil Company Limited of Saudi Arabia, Indonesia Petroleum Ltd. of Japan, ITOCHU Oil Exploration Co.

Ltd. of Japan, Hyundai Engineering & Construction Co., Ltd. of Korea, and the Crescent Group of Pakistan. RAO Gazprom of Russia also was interested in joining the consortium.

But problems developed with the fundamentalist Muslim government in Afghanistan, not the least of which was the Taliban government's treatment of women, which prompted feminist demonstrations against firms seeking to do business there. Additionally, the Taliban regime was creating chaotic conditions by pitting the various Islamic sects against each other in order to maintain control. In early December 1998, Unocal withdrew from the pipeline consortium, citing the hazardous political situation, and the project languished.

Was some event, some provocation, required to propel the normally disinterested American public into a war as in the past?

Many people have noticed that in President Bush's declaration of war on terrorism, he never mentioned terrorists in Northern Ireland or the Palestinian suicide bombers. Attention was only focused on Afghanistan, the one nation necessary to complete the lucrative pipeline. It should also be noted that Vice President Dick Cheney has been heavily involved in the oil industry. He headed the giant oil industry service company Halliburton and is generally thought to wield more power than the president. Halliburton had a major stake in the central Asian pipeline project as it would gain lucrative service contracts.

Despite Unocal's public announcement that it was withdrawing from the CentGas project, industry insiders said the firm never completely abandoned hopes for the project. The Texas-based Unocal never actually dropped plans for a trans-Afghanistan oil pipeline, which it considered a separate venture, and even held discussions on worker safety with the Taliban regime in March 2000.

With the shooting all but stopped in Afghanistan by mid-2002, the gas pipeline project was back on a front burner. *BBC News* reported on May 13 that interim leader Hamid Karzai was to hold talks with Pakistan and Turkmenistan officials to revive the $2 billion pipeline. Karzai, according to European news reports, formerly worked for Unocal, as did U.S. envoy John J. Maresca. "The work on the project will start after an agreement is expected to be struck at the coming summit," said Mohammad Alim Razim, minister for Mines and Industries.

Mr. Razim stated Unocal was the "lead company" among those that would build the pipeline. He added that the pipeline is expected to be built with funds from donor countries earmarked for the reconstruction of Afghanistan.

A mere nine days after the new interim government of Hamid Karzai took power in Afghanistan, President Bush appointed National Security Council official Zalmay Khalilzad his special envoy. Unsurprisingly, Khalilzad, an American born in Afghanistan, had been employed by the oil giant Unocal.

Khalilzad grew up in Kabul, where he attended an English-language school. "Zal," as he is known to friends, left Afghanistan in the 1970s after obtaining a scholarship to the American University of Beirut. He did graduate work at the University of Chicago, where he received his Ph.D. in 1979. In the early 1980s, he taught political science at Columbia, where he worked with Zbigniew Brzezinski. In 1984, Khalilzad, who had by then become an American citizen, joined the State Department on a one-year fellowship.

During the conflict in his home country with the Soviet occupation, Khalilzad's expertise and high-level contacts gained him a permanent position on the State Department's Policy Planning Council, where he served under Paul Wolfowitz, then director of policy planning for the Reagan administration. The two have been allies ever since. Khalilzad was a longtime supporter of the Taliban. "The Taliban does not practice the anti-U.S. style of fundamentalism practiced by Iran," he wrote in the *Washington Post* in 1998. His support for the Taliban waned in August of that same year when President Clinton ordered fifty-eight cruise missiles fired into Afghanistan in retribution for bombings at the U.S. embassies in Kenya and Tanzania. At the same time, Khalilzad has been a longtime advocate of U.S. action against Iraq, and in 1998 he joined Wolfowitz and others in signing an open letter to the Clinton administration arguing for a policy of overthrowing Saddam. During the elder Bush's administration, Khalilzad's anti-Iraq attitudes had hardened. He worked with both Wolfowitz and Dick Cheney during and after the Persian Gulf War as deputy undersecretary of defense.

When George W. was appointed president, Khalilzad was selected by Cheney to head the Bush transition team in the area of defense. In the spring of 2002, he was appointed by Bush as the chief National Security Council official working under National Security Adviser Condoleezza Rice, dealing with issues pertaining to the Persian Gulf and Central Asia. According to BBC reporter Mike Fox, Khalilzad "played an important part in developing the defense strategy of the Bus.h administration, both before and after the September the eleventh attacks."

FBI deputy director John O'Neill said in an interview with French authors Jean Charles Brisard and Guillaume Dasquie, "(T)he main obstacles to investigate Islamic terrorism were U.S. oil corporate interests and the role played by Saudi Arabia in it." Early in 2002, the former oil minister of Saudi Arabia, Ahmad Zaki al-Yamani, put it bluntly when he stated, "[The] U.S. has a strategic objective, which is to control the oil of the Caspian Sea and [thereby] to end dependence on the oil of the [Persian] Gulf."

One of the primary arguments to this attempt to secure oil and gas reserves for the United States is that we really don't need it.

Harry Braun, chairman of the Hydrogen Political Action Committee, summed up the case against petroleum when he said, "According to a recent poll by the *New York Times* and CBS *News,* both political parties lack a clear vision for the country. While the Bush administration seeks to secure the oil in Iraq and recover the remaining reserves in sensitive offshore or wilderness areas, the Democratic leadership is focused on conserving the remaining oil by getting American consumers to give up their SUVs. Given the exponential nature of the global energy and environmental crisis, these policies have been characterized as rearranging the deck chairs on the *Titanic.*

"The focus needs to be on shifting from oil to hydrogen because it is the only inexhaustible and pollution-free fuel that can make the U.S. energy-independent of not only Middle East oil, but of all fossil and nuclear fuels, and the staggering environmental problems they create. Indeed, it is because of the exponential nature of the interrelated energy and environmental problems that the transition to a 'hydrogen economy' needs to be undertaken with wartime speed.

"Fortunately, wind and other solar technologies can be rapidly mass-produced to economically manufacture hydrogen on a scale to displace all fossil and nuclear fuels. Millions of Americans will be employed as the U.S. is transformed into a Saudi Arabia class energy exporter and every existing vehicle is modified to use hydrogen, the only 'universal fuel' that can power any existing vehicle or appliance, from a Model T Ford to the Space Shuttle or a Coleman stove on a mountain-top."

Of course, to challenge the oil and gas monopoly is to challenge the inner core leadership of Wall Street, the Council on Foreign Relations and other powerful interests, who have owned or controlled the federal government since before World War II. Until the American people gather the will to wean politicians off the oil spigot, this nation will continue to pursue a petroleum-based energy policy. With $3 trillion in Caspian Sea oil as the prize, it can be demonstrated now that military action against Afghanistan has been in the works long before the September 11 attacks.

Afghan Action Planned Long Ago

Shortly after Bush was selected for the presidency in late 2000, S. Frederick Starr, head of the Central Asia Institute at Johns Hopkins University, stated in the *Washington Post,* "The U.S. has quietly begun to align itself with those in the Russian government calling for military action against Afghanistan and has toyed with the idea of a new raid to wipe out bin Laden."

Others in that area were gearing up for an armed attempt to oust the Taliban.

"Indian officials say that India and Iran will only play the role of 'facilitator' while the U.S. and Russia will combat the Taliban from the front with the help of two Central Asian countries, Tajikistan and Uzbekistan, to push the Taliban lines back to the 1998 position."

Thus began a detailed story concerning American-led military operations against Afghanistan published on NewsInsight.net compiled from the Indian

News Agency. It was published on June 26, 2001, more than two months prior to the attacks on the World Trade Center and the Pentagon.

The article noted, "Military action will be the last option though it now seems scarcely avoidable with the UN banned from Taliban-controlled areas. Diplomats say that the anti-Taliban move followed a meeting between U.S. secretary of state Colin Powell and Russian foreign minister Igor Ivanov and later between Powell and Indian Foreign Minister Jaswant Singh in Washington." It was added that "the Northern Alliance requires a 'clean up' operation to reduce Taliban's war-fighting machinery to launch an attack against the Taliban advance to the Tajik-Afghan border. This 'clean up' action is being planned by the U.S. and Russia since the Taliban shows no 'sign of reconciliation.'"

This article also presented a basic rationale for opposition to the Taliban government, stating, "Such Central Asian countries as Uzbekistan, Tajikistan, Kazakhstan and Turkmenistan are threatened by the Taliban that is aiming to control their vast oil, gas and other resources by bringing Islamic fundamentalism into power."

As reported by BBC's George Arney, former Pakistani foreign secretary Niaz Naik was alerted by American officials in mid-July that military action against Afghanistan would be launched by mid-October. At a UN-sponsored meeting in Berlin concerning Afghanistan, Naik was informed that unless bin Laden was handed over, America would take military action either to kill or capture both him and Taliban leader Mullah Omar as the initial step in installing a new government there.

In other words, contrary to the words of America's leadership, who proclaimed that "everything has changed" because of the 9/11 attacks, U.S. foreign policy stayed right on track, right down to the October date given out in the summer for military action in Afghanistan.

However, it should be noted that American intervention in Afghanistan began years ago, at least six months prior to the Soviet invasion in December 1979.

In a 1998 interview with former national security adviser Zbigniew Brzezinski in the French publication *Le Nouvel Observateur*, he admitted that American activities in Afghanistan actually began six months prior to the 1979 Soviet invasion.

Brzezinski, Jimmy Carter's national security adviser, said the Carter administration began secretly funding anti-Soviet rebels in July 1979 with the full knowledge such action might provoke a Soviet invasion. Soviet leaders at the time argued the invasion was necessary to thwart American aggression in Afghanistan.

Brzezinski told French interviewers, "According to the official version of history, CIA aid to the Mujahideen began during 1980, that is to say, after the Soviet army invaded Afghanistan, 24 December, 1979. But the reality, secretly guarded until now, is completely otherwise. Indeed, it was July 3, 1979, that President Carter signed the first directive for secret aid to the opponents of the pro-Soviet regime in Kabul."

Based upon this admission, it would appear that the Soviets were speaking the truth when they told the world they were forced to move Russian troops into that nation to prevent a secret American takeover.

Brzezinski expressed no regret at this secret provocation, stating, "That secret operation was an excellent idea. It brought about the demoralization and finally the breakup of the Soviet empire." It also led to the creation of the Taliban regime as well as Osama bin Laden.

But after almost ten years of brutal, no-quarter fighting against Afghans and Arab mercenaries backed by the United States, including Osama bin Laden, the Soviets were forced to withdraw. The economic stress of this Russo-Afghan War was enough to help topple communism in the early 1990s. Brzezinski was happy enough to take full credit for this even though it resulted in introducing militant Muslim theology into that volatile region.

Asked if he regretted such activities, Brzezinski replied, "What is most important to the history of the world? The Taliban or the collapse of the Soviet Empire? Some stirred up Moslems or the liberation of Central Europe and the end of the cold war?"

It is pertinent to note three things about the Brzezinski interview: one is that he is a leading luminary of the Council on Foreign Relations as well as a founder of the Trilateral Commission; second, that with the apparent exception of a copy in the Library of Congress, his interview was not included in a truncated version of the article circulated in the United States; and third, no one in 1979 could have foreseen the collapse of communism, with or without the Afghan incursion.

In a 1997 Council on Foreign Relations study entitled *The Grand Chessboard: American Primacy and its Geostatic Imperatives*, Brzezinski clearly showed why he and his fellow CFR members believed it necessary for the United States to maintain a military presence in the Near East. "[A]s America becomes an increasingly multicultural society, it may find it more difficult to fashion a consensus on foreign policy issues," he wrote, "except in the circumstance of a truly massive and widely perceived direct external threat."

Shortly after 9/11, the *Guardian*, a British newspaper, conducted its own investigation and concluded that both Osama bin Laden and the Taliban received threats of possible American military attacks on them two months before 9/11. According to "senior diplomatic sources," the threats were passed along by the Pakistani government.

The newspaper elaborated on BBC reporter Arney's report of the preattack warnings by stating that the warning to the Taliban originated at a four-day meeting of senior Americans, Russians, Iranians and Pakistanis at a hotel in

Berlin in mid-July 2001. The conference, the third in a series dubbed "brainstorming on Afghanistan", was part of a classic diplomatic device known as "track two," a method whereby governments can pass messages to each other. "The Americans indicated to us that in case the Taliban does not behave and in case Pakistan also doesn't help us to influence the Taliban, then the United States would be left with no option but to take an overt action against Afghanistan," said Niaz Naik, former foreign minister of Pakistan, who attended the Berlin meeting.

Many Internet sources have quoted from an interview with French authors Jean Charles Brisard and Guillaume Dasquie that reported U.S. representatives threatened, "Either you accept our offer of a carpet of gold, or we bury you under a carpet of bombs." However, no other source, including Naik, has confirmed this quote.

Naik did say he was told that unless bin Laden was handed over quickly America would take military action to kill or capture not only bin Laden but also Taliban leader Mullah Omar. He added that he was informed that the broader objective was to end the Taliban regime and install a transitional government in Afghanistan, presumably one less intransigent on the oil pipeline negotiations.

The former Pakistani diplomat was further informed that if such military action were to commence, it would happen before the first snows in Afghanistan, no later than the middle of October. Naik's prophetic words were reported on September 18, 2001, almost three weeks before the start of the U.S. bombing campaign.

According to the *Guardian* article, the American representatives at the Berlin meeting were Tom Simons, a former U.S. ambassador to Pakistan, Karl "Rick" Inderfurth, a former assistant secretary of state for South Asian affairs, and Lee Coldren, who headed the office of Pakistan, Afghan and Bangladesh affairs in the State Department until 1997.

Naik was quoted as saying that he specifically asked Simons why such an attack would be more successful than President Clinton's missile strikes against Afghanistan in 1998. That attack killed twenty persons but missed bin Laden.

"He said this time they were very sure. They had all the intelligence and would not miss him this time. It would be aerial action, maybe helicopter gunships;" Naik said, adding, "What the Americans indicated to us was perhaps based on official instructions. They were very senior people. Even in 'track two' people are very careful about what they say and don't say."

No representative from the Taliban was present but Naik, representing one of only three governments that recognized the Taliban, said he passed the warning along to the Afghan authorities.

Coldren told the British paper, "I think there was some discussion of the fact that the United States was so disgusted with the Taliban that they might be considering some military action." But he added that it was not an agenda item at the meeting.

According to the article, Nikolai Kozyrev, Moscow's former special envoy on Afghanistan and one of the Russians in Berlin, would not confirm the contents of the U.S. conversations, but said: "Maybe they had some discussions in the corridor. I don't exclude such a possibility."

Naik's recollection is that "we had the impression Russians were trying to tell the Americans that the threat of the use of force is sometimes more effective than force itself."

Simons denied having said anything about detailed operations and Inderfurth told the *Guardian,* "There was no suggestion for military force to be used. What we discussed was the need for a comprehensive political settlement to bring an end to the war in Afghanistan that has been going on for two decades and has been doing so much damage."

Told the American participants were denying the preattack warnings, Mr. Naik was quoted as saying, "I'm a little surprised but maybe they feel they shouldn't have told us anything in advance now we have had these tragic events".

Perhaps the reason that no one in the American delegation wanted to admit the pre-attack threats was presented by the *Guardian* writers. They speculated, "The Taliban refused to comply but the serious nature of what they were told raises the possibility that bin Laden, far from launching the attacks on the World Trade Center in New York and the Pentagon out of the blue ten days ago, was launching a pre-emptive strike in response to what he saw as U.S. threats."

A pre-emptive strike? No one mentioned that in the major corporate media.

The destruction of the Taliban actually was the object of several diplomatic discussions months before the events of 9/11, including a May 2001 meeting between the State Department and officials from Iran, Germany and Italy. The talks centered around replacing the Taliban with a "broad-based government." This same topic was raised at the Group of Eight (G-8) talks in Genoa, Italy, in July 2001.

Many people have questioned why we bombed Afghanistan when apparently none of the listed hijackers was an Afghan, but instead were Arabs from various Middle Eastern nations. Since Iraq was implicated in the 1993 WTC attack, why are we not bombing that "rogue" nation? Better yet, since Attorney General John Ashcroft announced soon after 911 that the "masterminds" of the attacks were operating out of Hamburg, Germany, why not bomb Germany?

Such questions grew as American troops moved into Afghanistan. Sources in the oil industry reported that with the American military incursion into Afghanistan came the troubling news that the country might prove to be a dry hole. Once old seismic data was coupled with actual drilling, it was learned that the Caspian Sea oil was in concentrated in small pools rather than in large deep reserves. Another source of plentiful oil was needed.

That source may have become known to the public in late 2002, when the Bush administration appeared hell-bent on attacking Iraq despite howls of protest from other Middle East nations, many Americans and other NATO countries. Most Americans got the idea that the underlying motive for the invasion of Iraq was to gain control over its oil reserves.

However, it should be remembered that no matter how one viewed Saddam Hussein, he nevertheless was a member of the Organization of Petroleum Exporting Countries (OPEC) and Iraqi oil continued to flow to the United States right up until the time of the invasion. Furthermore, Iraqi oil made up only about 16 percent of America's requirements.

Something else appeared to be behind the push for war in Iraq and, in fact, plans to conquer Iraq had been laid quite some time before.

A once-secret conservative think tank paper written in September 2002, details how future members of the Bush administration were contemplating military action in the Middle East long before the 9/11 attacks.

The report, entitled "Rebuilding America's Defenses: Strategies, Forces And Resources for a New Century," was drafted by the Project for the New American Century (PNAC), a nonprofit educational organization dedicated to "a few fundamental propositions: that American leadership is good both for America and for the world; that such leadership requires military strength, diplomatic energy and commitment to moral principle; and that too few political leaders today are making the case for global leadership."

In this document, which drew heavily from a Defense Guidance position paper issued in 1992 during Vice President Dick Cheney's stint as secretary of defense in the previous Bush administration, it states, "The United States has for decades sought to play a more permanent role in Gulf security. While the unresolved conflict with Iraq provides the immediate justification, the need for a substantial American force in the Gulf transcends the issue of the regime of Saddam Hussein."

The paper explained that when this view of a "Pax Americana" throughout the world was proposed in 1992, its authors were seen as "cold warriors" seeking to increase the defense budget and the plan was shelved by the Clinton administration.

With many of the same players back in power Cheney, Rumsfeld, Wolfowitz, etc., this "blueprint for maintaining U.S. preeminence" has been pulled out of mothballs. It describes "four core missions" for the U.S. military: to defend the American homeland; fight and decisively win multiple simultaneous major theater wars; perform the "constabulary" duties associated with shaping the security environment in critical regions, and to transform U.S. forces to exploit the "revolution in military affairs."

This "revolution," according to this paper, includes the control of "cyberspace" or the Internet as well as outer space with the creation of a new military service, the "U.S. Space Force."

U.S. News & World Report writer Jay Tolson noted that the plan for U.S. hegemony over the world was rejected by President G. H. W. Bush after an outcry in Washington. "Today, though, with Wolfowitz back at the Pentagon, that blueprint shapes the doctrine of preeemption that the younger Bush recently presented to Congress. And even before he did, other nations charged that America was disregarding the international system that it had helped build."

It should be pointed out that at least eight of the participants in the 2000 position paper are members of the secret societies the Council on Foreign Relations, the Bilderbergers or both.

Only three days after the U.S. began bombing Afghanistan, American firepower was being used against nonmilitary targets in violation of international conventions. In that nation's capital, Radio Kabul was knocked off the air by U.S. bombs, silencing the voice of the Taliban. Farhad Azad of Afghanmagazine.com reported that the station's stored musical library was lost. "The Taliban made music illegal, but it was U.S. bombs that physically destroyed the hidden archive," he said. But more suspiciously, a month later the satellite television station Al-Jazeera, which sat in the middle of a residential neighborhood, was struck by two five hundred-pound bombs.

Colonel Brian Hoey, a spokesman for the U.S. Central Command, confirmed that the United States had bombed the building but stated, "the indications we had was that this was not an Al-Jazeera office."

Al-Jazeera had already come under figurative fire from U.S. authorities for broadcasting interviews with Osama bin Laden. The station also had aired interviews with Donald Rumsfeld and National Security Adviser Condoleezza Rice.

The military action against a civilian TV station "could prove to be a public relations fiasco for the U.S. government," noted the *Washington Post* at the time. But this could only occur if the American people were told about it. In fact, little or no reporting on this incident reached the public.

The evidence now available that operations against Afghanistan were planned long before the 9/11 attacks prompted author Gore Vidal to remark, "With that background, it now becomes explicable why the first thing Bush did after we were hit was to get Senator Daschle and beg him not to hold an investigation of the sort any normal country would have done. When Pearl Harbor was struck, within twenty minutes the Senate and the House had a joint committee ready. Roosevelt beat them to it, because he knew why we had been hit, so he set up his own committee. But none of this was to come out and it hasn't come out."

Since it is now plain that military operations against Afghanistan were in the planning stages months before 9/11, the question must be asked why there was no buildup of propaganda in the American media. Before every military action, the reasons and rationales must be placed before the public to accustom them to the idea and gain their support. Yet, while both diplomatic and military preparations were being made for war against Afghanistan, the American public remained ignorant and contented. Some researchers contend this is an indication that national leaders knew such a propaganda campaign would be unnecessary because a surprise attack would do the job.

Wag The Dog In Iraq?

Just such a propaganda campaign was in progress prior to the invasion of Iraq in March 2003. President Bush told Americans that Saddam Hussein was preparing weapons of mass destruction that demanded a preemptive strike.

There was little mention of other nations who also have weapons of mass destruction, such as India, Pakistan, France, Israel, Russia and China. India and Pakistan seem frighteningly determined to use theirs.

In fact, it was later announced that the Bush administration had been informed as early as October 3, 2002, that North Korea, a military power more than twice the size of Iraq, had developed nuclear capability as well as even "more powerful" chemical or biological weapons. Yet no mention of this "Axis of Evil" nation was made during the remainder of the month when Bush sought and won a congressional resolution approving an attack on Iraq. Democrats, especially in the Senate, fumed because Bush officials kept them in the dark about North Korea's plans just as they were deliberating the Iraqi resolution. Common people snickered that, of course, North Korea has no oil to covet.

Also missing amongst the press coverage of North Korean's nuclear development plans was the fact that the funds needed to produce weapons-grade plutonium in their nuclear reactors came from U.S. taxpayers, approved by President Bush in the spring 2002.

In early April, Bush released about $94 million to North Korea as part of the 1994 Agreed Framework agreement to replace older nuclear reactors despite suspicions that the nuclear project was being used to produce weapons and that nation's refusal to allow UN inspections. According to *BBC News*, Bush argued that his decision was "vital to the national security interests of the United States." And prominently missing from the crescendo of corporate mass media pieces on the need to attack Iraq were the names and arguments of many prominent persons who counseled caution. Eighteen former high-ranking U.S. military leaders, intelligence analysts, diplomats and academics in early 2002 sent President Bush a letter urging him to "resist military actions against Iraq and focus on capturing the terrorists responsible for the September 11 attacks."

Among those who signed the letter were retired navy admiral Eugene Carroll, former CIA national intelligence officer William Christison, former chief of mission to Iraq Ed Peck, former ambassador to Saudi Arabia James Atkins, and former senator George McGovern.

The story of this letter was featured in China's official news agency Xinhau but received little attention at home.

Democratic senator Robert Byrd of West Virginia claimed Bush's effort to start a war with Iraq was nothing more than a conscious effort to distract public attention from domestic problems. "This administration, all of a sudden, wants to go to war with Iraq," Byrd said. "The polls are dropping, the domestic situation has problems. All of a sudden we have this war talk, war fervor, the bugles of war, drums of war, clouds of war. Don't tell me that things suddenly went wrong." Byrd said his allegiance to the Constitution prevented him from voting for Bush's war resolution. "But I am finding that the Constitution is irrelevant to people of this administration."

And again, it seems as though the impetus for war against Iraq came just hours following the 9/11 attacks, at a time when there was no evidence indicating Iraqi involvement. According to CBS Correspondent David Martin, notes taken by aides just five hours after the attacks show Secretary of Defense Rumsfeld ordered up plans for a strike against Iraq. According to notes made at the time, Rumsfeld ordered, "Go massive; sweep it all up; destroy it all...Things related and not, it doesn't matter."

By mid-2002, the push for war against Iraq was continuing within the Bush administration despite lack of any real proof that Saddam represented a threat to the United States In fact, some of the proof that was presented proved dubious.

On September 7, 2002, President Bush was trying to summon support for an attack on Iraq. In a news conference with British prime minister Tony Blair, Bush announced, "I would remind you that when the inspectors first went into Iraq and were denied finally denied access, a report came out of the Atomic the IAEA [International Atomic Energy Agency] that they were six months away from developing a weapon; I don't know what more evidence we need."

However, Mark Gwozdecky, chief spokesman for the IAEA, stated days later, "There's never been a report like that issued from this agency. We have never put a time frame on how long it might take Iraq to construct a nuclear weapon."

Bush and Blair also cited an IAEA report claiming satellite photography had revealed that the Iraqis were starting construction at several nuclear-related sites. Again, the IAEA, the agency charged with assessing Iraq's nuclear capability for the UN, denied any such report. When asked about the contradictions, Bush White House Deputy Press secretary Scott McClellan said, he's referring to 1991 there. In '91, there was a report saying that after the war they found out they were about six months away."

Gwozdecky, speaking from IAEA headquarters in Vienna, said there was no such report issued in 1991 either. In fact, in an October 1998 report to the UN secretary-general, IAEA director-general Mohamed Elbaradei stated, "There are no indications that there remain in Iraq any physical capability for the production of weapon-usable nuclear material of any practical significance."

Gwozdecky told one reporter, "There is no evidence in our view that can be substantiated on Iraq's nuclear weapons program. If anybody tells you they know the nuclear situation in Iraq right now, in the absence of four years of inspections, I would say they're misleading you because there isn't solid evidence out there."

"It is ironic to me that we can commit a nation to war, even world war, on less evidence than it takes to convict someone for smoking a joint in downtown Manhattan," commented defense attorney Ron Kuby on Fox News.

The chief UN weapons inspector Hans Blix in April 2003 confirmed that plans to attack Iraq were longstanding and had little to do with weapons of mass destruction. "There is evidence that this war was planned well in advance," Blix stated in an interview with the Spanish daily *El Pais*. Blix said that despite assurances from President Bush in late 2002 that he supported the UN's efforts to determine if Iraq had any biological, chemical or nuclear weapons, "I now believe that finding weapons of mass destruction has been relegated, I would say, to fourth place...Today, the main aim is to change the dictatorial regime of Saddam Hussein."

A survey conducted in both the states and in Europe was published in London's *Financial Times* on September 4, 2002. It found 50 percent of respondents from six European nations agreed that U.S. foreign policy had contributed to the attitudes resulting in the 2001 attacks.

In spite of this acknowledgment that foreign policy had created the atmosphere of fear and hatred toward the United States, this same survey indicated that 75 percent of American respondents remained in support of the use of military force against Iraq and its leader, although 60 percent of Europeans and 65 percent of Americans wanted allied support and approval for such action. Only 10 percent of Europeans surveyed indicated they would support U.S. military action in Iraq without support from its allies.

Interestingly enough, this poll of 9,000 Americans and Europeans concerning U.S. foreign policy was conducted by a branch of the same folks that had dictated that foreign policy, the Chicago Council on Foreign Relations (CCFR) in association with the German Marshall Fund of the United States (GMF). Branches of the original Council on Foreign Relations were established beginning in the early 1970s to extend the secret society's influence beyond the eastern seaboard. The CCFR is one such branch.

On February 5, 2003, Secretary of State Colin Powell stood before the United Nations and presented a scathing indictment of Iraq's transgressions and called for a coalition to oust the regime of Saddam Hussein. "My colleagues, every statement I make today is backed up by sources, solid sources. These are not assertions. What we're giving you are facts and conclusions based on solid intelligence," Powell told his audience.

It was later learned and widely reported in Europe that Powell's presentation was based on a British government dossier which had plagiarized the work of a California graduate student named Ibrahim al-Marashi. Large portions of al-Marashi's essay had been taken by British intelligence and, in some cases, altered in a manner damaging to Iraq. The essay had been published in September 2002 in a small journal entitled the *Middle East Review of International Affairs.*

If this wasn't problem enough to the hawks pushing for war in Iraq, Powell also produced for the UN a satellite photo of a northern Iraqi installation said to be producing chemical weapons for both Saddam Hussein and the al-Qaeda network. Somes days later when news reporters actually toured the camp they found nothing but a bunch of dilapidated huts with no indoor plumbing or the electrical capability to produce such weapons.

Such problems with the rationales given for war prompted one Democratic congressman to state that President Bush would lie to provoke war with Iraq.

Jim McDermott of Washington State in an ABC interview pointed out that in fall 2002, the Iraqis had pledged to allow unrestricted inspections within their country. "They should be given a chance," said McDermott, who voted against war with Iraq in 1991, "otherwise we're trying to provoke them into war." Following a visit to Iraq, McDermott said he believed Bush "would mislead the American people" to go to war with Iraq.

Another congressman on the visit to Baghdad, Michigan Democrat David Bonior, said a renewed war with Iraq would bring further suffering to the Iraqi people, especially children suffering from cancers caused by the U.S. use of depleted uranium shells, which he described as "horrific and barbaric."

Apparently lacking the spirit of American freedom of speech, Senate Minority Leader Trent Lott referred to McDermott saying, "He needs to come home and keep his mouth shut."

Even former president Clinton weighed in by urging the Bush administration to finish the job with Osama bin Laden before taking on Iraq. Speaking at a Democratic Party fund-raiser in early September 2002, Clinton undoubtedly spoke for millions of Americans when he said, "Saddam Hussein didn't kill 3,100 people on September 11. Bin Laden did, and as far as we know he's still alive. I also believe we might do more good for American security in the short run at far less cost by beefing up our efforts in Afghanistan, Pakistan and elsewhere to flush out the entire network."

One pivotal Democrat who spoke out against war with Iraq was Minnesota Senator Paul Wellstone, who also was one of the few congressmen calling for an independent investigation of the 9/11 attacks. Wellstone, who according to supporters worked for the benefit of all his constituents including workers, unionists and the needy, in late October 2002 was in a tough political fight against a Republican challenger backed by both GOP money and the Bush White House. Wellstone's seat could have tipped the entire Senate into the Republican camp, giving Bush a majority in Congress.

But the question of whether Wellstone might have won his battle will never be answered. He, his wife and daughter, three staffers and two pilots were killed in a private plane crash on October 25, 2002. It was reminiscent of the many plane crashes that have taken so many members of Congress, especially during the Reagan administration. In fact, well into 2003, questions were being raised about the cause of Wellstone's fatal crash.

Texas representative Ron Paul even noted that his challenge to the constitutionality of a war with Iraq was blocked on live TV and prompted the chairman of one congressional committee to openly declare that the U.S. Constitution is no longer relevant. In a late 2002 newsletter to his constituents, Paul wrote that during hearings on the Iraqi war resolution before the International Relations Committee being televised live by C-SPAN, he tried to bring up the issue that declaring war was a power granted only to Congress by the Constitution, but the ranking minority member called his attempt to add an amendment declaring war "frivolous and mischievous". "The proposed resolution on the use of force mentioned the United Nations twenty-five times. That was considered safe. Not once did it mention the Constitution. I do not look to the UN to find the authority for this sovereign nation to defend herself," stated Paul. "It was almost noon on October 3, the second day of the hearings, when my turn came [after offering his war amendment] I reminded the committee of the words of James Madison, who in 1798 said, 'The Constitution supposes what the history of all governments demonstrates, that the Executive is the branch of power most interested in war and most prone to it. It has accordingly, with studied care, vested the question of war in the legislature.' The Chair[man, Illinois Republican Henry J. Hyde] went on to say that the Constitution has been 'overtaken by events, time' and is 'no longer relevant.' At least it was out in the open. Now surely the display of such disdain for their oath to 'support and defend the Constitution' would light up Capitol Hill switchboards with angry callers!

"Little did I know that no one watching the hearings over C-SPAN not one single person of what statistically is an audience of several million Americans even heard those inflammatory comments. When my staff called C-SPAN to get a copy of the video record to document these outrageous statements, we were told 'technical difficulties' prevented that portion of the proceedings from being recorded and that same portion of the proceedings was also the only part missing on the internal record the House makes of such official hearings. It was as though it never happened."

Another Democrat who dared to simply raise questions about the War on Terrorism lost her seat in congress. Representative Cynthia McKinney represented the 4th District of Georgia, which includes Decatur, just outside Atlanta. This was the district that sent Newt Gingrich to Washington. McKinney had three strikes against her in this Dixie district — she was a woman, black and a Democrat. The forty-seven-year-old former college professor was also quite outspoken.

At a peace rally in Washington on April 20, 2002, Rep. McKinney told the crowd, "despite our differences, we are here today one community with one thing in common: a desire to see the restoration of the true ideals of America. America- where the fundamental rights to vote, speak and practice religion mean something. But America today is still a far cry from the noble Republic founded upon these words: All men are created equal." She then declared, "Sadly, nor is ours a democratic society. In November 2000, the Republicans stole from America our most precious right of all: the right to free and fair elections.

"Florida governor Jeb Bush and his secretary of state, Katherine Harris, created a phony list of convicted felons 57,700 to be exact to 'scrub' thousands of innocent people from the state's voter rolls. Of the thousands who ultimately lost their vote through this scrub of voters, 80 percent were African-Americans, mostly Democratic Party voters. Had they voted, the course of history would have changed. Instead, however, Harris declared Bush the victor by only 537 votes.

"Now President Bush occupies the White House, but with questionable legitimacy. But, however he got there, his Administration is now free to spend one to four billion dollars a month on the war in Afghanistan; free to cut the high deployment overtime pay of our young service men and women fighting in that war; free to propose drilling in the Arctic National Wildlife Reserve National Park; free to stonewall on the Enron and Energy Task Force investigations; free to revoke the rules that keep our drinking water free of arsenic; free to get caught in Venezuela and free to propose laws that deny our citizens sacred freedoms cherished under the Constitution.

"We must dare to remember all of this. We must dare to debate and challenge all of this."

Some time later, McKinney drew the ire of Washington insiders when she dared to suggest that Bush administration officials may have ignored warnings of the terrorist attack to further their political agenda and that they and their cronies were profiting from the War on Terrorism. The war-for-profit argument has much objective data to support it, as will be seen later. McKinney certainly spoke for many when she said that the Bush administration has created a climate in which elected officials must censor themselves or be branded as less than patriotic.

McKinney also suggested that the terrorism war has benefited the Washington based Carlyle Group investment firm, which employs a number of former high-ranking government officials, including former president George H. W. Bush.

A Carlyle Group spokesman, while not addressing McKinney's facts, nevertheless asked, "Did she say these things while standing on a grassy knoll in Roswell, New Mexico?" It was truly ironic that such dismissive tactics should come at a time when national polls show a growing number of persons believe there was a conspiracy to kill President Kennedy and a willingness to consider that there may be substance to the claims of a UFO crash near Roswell in 1947.

Typical of the diatribes against McKinney to be found in the mainstream corporate media were the remarks of *Orlando Sentinel* columnist Kathleen Parker, who described the congresswoman as "a delusional paranoiac" and called for an investigation of the woman "as passionately as she demands we investigate Bush's 'involvement' in the 9/11 terror attacks." Parker added, "we no longer can afford to tolerate people like McKinney, who should never be taken seriously."

Parker's stance was echoed throughout the mass media, which called attention to the fact that McKinney had accepted, long before 9/11, campaign contributions from Abdurrahman Alamoudi, founder of the American Muslim Council, and a man who has voiced support for terrorist organizations such as Hamas and Hezbollah.

Naturally, no one in the mainstream media called attention to the fact that the Bush administration blocked a number of investigations into their connections with terrorist groups or that the family has been longtime friends with the Saudi royalty, made up of mostly hard-line Muslims.

For example, about a week after McKinney's defeat, President Bush telephoned Saudi crown prince Abdullah and praised "eternal friendship" between the United States and Saudi Arabia. The president then retired to his Crawford, Texas, ranch for some private time with Saudi ambassador Prince Bandar bin Sultan and his family. The visit was styled as a family trip and a casual get-together. No cameras were allowed and neither Bush nor his royal guest would agree to be interviewed.

Also the media failed to mention that, according to British publications, the Republican Party had been receiving sizeable contributions from the Arabic Safa trust, which at the same time was funneling money to terrorist groups.

All of this came about shortly after a Rand Corporation analyst briefed a Pentagon advisory panel, stating, "The Saudis are active at every level of the terror chain, from planners to financiers, from cadre to foot soldier, from ideologist to cheerleader. Saudi Arabia supports our enemies and attacks our allies."

It must be noted that no one disputes the fact that fifteen of the nineteen 9/11 hijackers named by the FBI were Saudis and that nine hundred families of 9/11 victims of the attacks filed a trillion-dollar lawsuit against Saudi officials, including members of the royal family, contending complicity in the terror attacks.

It is also interesting that some media lose enthusiasm for polling when the outcome deviates from the desired results. For example, the *Atlanta Journal-Constitution* placed a poll on its Web site asking, "Are you satisfied the Bush administration had no warning of the September 11 attacks?" Visitors could vote "Yes," "No, I think officials knew it was coming" or "Not sure." The vote seesawed back and forth for one day. When the final count of 23,145 voters showed 52 percent for Yes, 46 percent No and only 1 percent not sure, the poll was suddenly pulled with no real explanation.

Anyone who has visited Israel can confirm that among that nation's Jewish inhabitants there are ongoing and strenuous deliberations over policy, yet no one calls dissenters there anti-Semites. Rather, it is properly seen as free political discussion.

Yet in the United States the mass media gave scant attention to those who spoke out in support of McKinney. It has regularly characterized any opposition to the official party line as somehow unpatriotic, ignoring the fact that this county was founded on dissent. One supporter of McKinney stated, "Some clear-eyed citizens see this woman as an astute observer of the national scene, and as one who has bravely stepped forward to voice the opinion of millions of us who have been denied a voice since President Bush's selection". Another McKinney constituent, Decatur landscaper David Hernandez, said, "She'll stand up and say it. I like that. She's coming out with hidden secrets about the government that everybody should know."

The Associated Press in the late spring predicted McKinney would win the Democratic primary by a wide margin. However, in the August 22, 2002, primary election McKinney was defeated.

Stephen Zunes, an associate professor of politics at the University of San Francisco, suggested the outspoken Georgia congresswoman was beaten more by crossover voting of Republicans than by pro-Israel political action committees (PAC) that poured money into her opponent, former Georgia state judge Denise Majette.

"In a district where barely half of all registered voters were Democrats, fourteen out of fifteen primary ballots were cast in the Democratic Party," Zunes noted. "In short, thousands of conservative Republicans without a similarly significant primary race in their own party voted in the Democratic primary for the sole purpose of defeating one of Congress' most outspoken defenders of civil rights, labor and the environment and one of the most vocal critics of President George W. Bush."

Consideration might be given to the fact that McKinney's public statements were made beginning in late 2001, when emotions still clouded any objective view of the recent attacks. By the time of her primary defeat many Americans were becoming aware of the many and early warnings that went to the administration throughout 2001. Likewise, there is now abundant evidence that Bush and his friends have profited mightily from the War on Terror. But apparently it was too late for these revelations to seep into the consciousness of the voters in Georgia's 4th District.

The controversy over war with Iraq did nothing to stop a cowed and compliant Congress from voting overwhelmingly in October 2002 to authorize Bush to launch his war whenever he desired. Once again the ugliest side of politics revealed itself. The people in Congress knew that if Bush's action in Iraq proves successful, they can share the credit and glory come the next elections. If it proves to be an unwise decision, they can shift the blame to the president. So, an affirmative vote was much safer than to stand among the few for honesty and integrity.

The irony of Bush urging war with Iraq because of Saddam Hussein's actions was not lost on commentators in other parts of the world. "There is something almost comical about the prospect of George Bush waging war on another nation because that nation has defied international law," wrote George Monbiot of London's *Guardian*. "Since Bush came to office, the United States government has torn up more international treaties and disregarded more UN conventions than the rest of the world has in twenty years."

While vigorous debates between antiwar activists and Bush supporters might otherwise be seen as just another political battle between liberals and conservatives, there was a worrisome aspect to it all.

When an administration that arrived in office under a cloud of controversy and suspicion of election fraud can trigger such attacks upon persons who only speak their minds and publicly ask questions that deserve to be answered, thoughtful persons should become concerned over basic First Amendment rights.

But such lofty ideals as the First Amendment come second when compared to the evidence that some top U.S. officials have exhibited hypocrisy in the debate over Iraq.

There were profits to be made even before the propaganda war against Iraq ramped up in 2002. Vice President Dick Cheney, already under attack for his involvement in profiting from doing business in Iraq despite U.S. sanctions in place since the Gulf War, was pinpointed as one whose business interests profited from the 9/11 attacks.

"Under the guidance of Richard Cheney, a get-the-government-out-of-my-face conservative, Halliburton Company over the past five years [1995~2000] has emerged as a corporate welfare hog, benefiting from at least

$3.8 billion in federal contracts and taxpayer-insured loans," stated a report by the Washington-based Center for Public Integrity.

It was Cheney who led the effort to wage yet another war on Iraq. "But Cheney isn't just selling the policy. He is on the inside making it," noted Kenneth T. Walsh of *U.S. News & World Report.* "In fact, to understand the Bush presidency, it is necessary to understand how central Cheney's role actually is and how his innate conservatism is an anchor for administration policy not just on Iraq but across the board."

In 1991, the elder President Bush awarded Cheney the Presidential Medal of Freedom. Cheney, age sixty-one in 2002, was an important choice for Bush Jr. in the election year of 2000. Cheney had promised the nation "light at the end of the tunnel" in Vietnam during his stint with the Nixon administration. He had vouched for the need of a fifty-five-mile-per-hour national speed limit during the short-lived gas shortage while serving with President Ford and he promised more freedom when he supported the Contras as well as the Afghan Majuhideen during his congressional service under the Reagan administration. He then oversaw the 1989 invasion of Panama and the destruction of Saddam Hussein's war machine while serving as secretary of defense during the Gulf War under the previous Bush administration.

Following the defeat of Bush Sr. in 1992, Cheney entered the world of corporate business and by 1995 became president and chief executive officer of the Halliburton Company of Dallas. Halliburton is the world's largest oil service firm and, according to *Oil & Gas Journal*, the company ranks twenty-fourth in the top energy corporations in the world, with a market value of $18.2 billion. The company employs about 100,000 people in 120 countries. Cheney also happened to be the largest stock holder.

Cheney's firm, through a subsidiary, certainly gained a lion's share of the $30 billion in emergency funds appropriated by Congress in the War on Terrorism.

"From building cells for detainees at Guantanamo Bay in Cuba to feeding American troops in Uzbekistan, the Pentagon is increasingly relying on a unit of Halliburton called KBR, sometimes referred to as Kellogg Brown & Root," reported Jeff Gerth and Don Van Natta Jr. of the *New York Times.* "Although the unit has been building projects all over the world for the federal government for decades, the attacks of September 11 have led to significant additional business. KBR is the exclusive logistics supplier for both the Navy and the Army, providing services like cooking, construction, power generation and fuel transportation. The contract recently won from the Army is for 10 years and has no lid on costs, the only logistical arrangement by the Army without an estimated cost."

George and Herman Brown, who created the construction firm back in the late 1930s, put Lyndon B. Johnson in Congress and benefitted from prime government contracts ever since, beginning with a large naval base in Corpus Christi, Texas, and later in South Vietnam. After merging with Halliburton, the company provided logistical support for the Pentagon in Haiti, Somalia, the Balkans and more recently, in Afghanistan.

Halliburton officials denied that Chaney played any role in assisting KBR in obtaining government contracts but did admit that the senior vice president responsible for the lucrative KBR contracts, former four-star navy admiral Joe Lopez, was hired in 1999 on the recommendation of Cheney. There have been a number of other accusations made against Halliburton during Cheney's stint as CEO. According to the Environmental Rights Action (ERA) group, Halliburton ordered Nigerian Mobile Police officers to shoot youthful demonstrators protesting what they perceived as environmental damage caused by Chevron Oil, which had contracted for Halliburton's services. One youth, Gidikumo Sule, was killed, and others claimed to have been beaten. The oil companies countered this charge by claiming the youth was killed during an attempt to rescue officers who had been detained and disarmed by the youths.

In fact, various environmental groups were upset with Halliburton in general and Cheney in particular, especially after he cosponsored legislation to open the Artic Wildlife Refuge in Alaska to oil drilling and voted against the Clean Water Act while serving as a representative from Wyoming. Halliburton's Duncan, Oklahoma, facility was identified by the Environmental Protection Agency in 1997 as one of the top 20 percent of polluting companies in the nation.

Aspersions were made about the fact that Halliburton has joined Bush's Harken Energy in maintaining offshore subsidiaries in the Cayman Island's, the favorite site for tax dodgers, such as Enron, which had 692 subsidiaries of its own there.

Under Cheney's leadership, Halliburton's subsidiaries in tax havens grew from nine in 1995 to forty-four in 1999. This coincided with a drop in Halliburton's federal taxes from $302 million in 1998 to an $85 million tax refund in 1999.

But the real criticism of Cheney came from his company's dealings in Iraq and his role in the Enron scandal.

In 1998, the UN passed a resolution permitting Iraq to purchase material to repair and maintain its oil industry, which had become dilapidated following the country's defeat in the Gulf War.

Immediately, U.S. companies, including Halliburton, Baker Hughes, Schlumberger, Flowserve, Fisher-Rosemount and others, moved surreptitiously to get a part of this lucrative business.

These firms used European subsidies to front for multimillion-dollar business deals. "It is a wonderful example of how ludicrous sanctions have become," noted Raad Alkadiri, an analyst for Petroleum Finance Company, a Washington consulting firm.

Furthermore, Halliburton brought in substantial business by hiding behind other business entities. Reporter Carola Hoyos noted, "From September 1998, until it sold its stake last February [2000], Halliburton owned fifty-one percent of Dresser-Rand. It also owned forty-nine percent of Ingersoll-Dresser Pump, until its sale in December 1999. During the time of the joint ventures, Dresser-Rand and Ingersoll-Dresser Pump submitted more than $23.8 million worth of contracts for the sale of oil industry parts and equipment to Iraq. Their combined total amounted to more than any other U.S. company; the vast majority was approved by the sanctions committee."

There was no outcry from the Democrats because John Deutch, President Clinton's CIA chief in the mid-1990s, served on the board of Schlumberger, another firm that did business with Iraq through subsidiaries.

Cheney also came under fire for Enron-like accounting practices. According to Judicial Watch, which in 2002 filed a lawsuit in Dallas, Texas, against Cheney on behalf of Halliburton shareholders, he artificially boosted the share price of Halliburton stock while he was CEO. The suit charges that Cheney overstated profits by $445 million between 1999 and 2001, resulting in "huge losses" for some investors.

Ironically enough, Cheney in 1996 was featured in a promotional video for the now disgraced accounting firm of Arthur Andersen, convicted in 2002 of shredding documents relating to failed energy giant Enron. Perhaps that tainted accounting firm handled some of Cheney's $20 million-plus severance money from Halliburton.

In early 2002, Cheney was considered as the object of an unprecedented lawsuit by the General Accounting Office for his failure to give congressional investigators documents relating to the formulation of energy plans by the energy task force he once headed. Cheney claimed the GAO did not have the authority to demand the information, despite the fact that the Bush administration task force was funded by public money. The task force's energy proposals carried many provisions sought at the time by the energy giant Enron. In early 2003, the GAO, under pressure from Republicans who threatened to cut its budget, quietly dropped the matter.

During the 2000 campaign, Cheney told audiences that since leaving government under the original Bush administration, he had been "out in the private sector creating jobs." He did not mention that just after Halliburton absorbed Dresser, Cheney laid off ten thousand workers.

Meanwhile, Halliburton announced in May 2002 that the Securities and Exchange Commission was investigating the company for accounting practices related to how it reported cost overruns on construction projects. No charges were immediately filed.

Many researchers and even more knowledgeable members of the public have questioned the hypocrisy of Cheney, the man who oversaw $23.8 million in business to Iraq during the time of sanctions against that nation while chief of Halliburton, leading the voices to put an end to the "murderous dictator."

Some wags even suggested that Cheney's desire to bomb Iraq might be motivated less by the desire to make money for his former company than by the desire to obliterate documentation of his business dealings there as well as connections between the senior Bush, the CIA and Saddam Hussein prior to the Gulf War.

Despite a loud silence by the mainstream media, many alternative articles as well as the report of Oklahoma senator Charles Key have pointed to the involvement of Iraqis in the April 19, 1995, bombing of the Alfred P. Murrah Federal Building in Oklahoma City.

So much evidence is available pointing to Iraqi complicity in that terrorism act that Judicial Watch has filed suit against the Republic of Iraq on behalf of fourteen survivors of the bombing. The complaint, filed in the U.S. District Court for the District of Columbia, is brought against Iraq, as a State Department-designated terrorism sponsor, under the provisions of the Antiterrorism and Effective Death Penalty Act of 1996.

According to court papers, the bombing of the Murrah Federal Building "was not as simple as has been portrayed by the United States Government. The entire plot was, in whole or in part, orchestrated, assisted technically and/or financially and directly aided by agents of the Republic of Iraq."

The suit also charges that Iraq knew in advance of the 9/11 attacks and that there was wrongdoing in both the Clinton and Bush administrations.

A portion of the evidence concerning foreknowledge of 9/11 involve's an Iraqi newspaper column published on July 21, 2001, in which it stated that Osama bin Laden was thinking "seriously, with the seriousness of the Bedouin of the desert, about the way he will try to bomb the Pentagon after he destroys the White House." The column also mentioned that bin Laden was "insisting very convincingly that he will strike America on the arm that is already hurting," an apparent reference to the 1993 World Trade Center bombing.

Jim Kreindler, one of the lawyers pursuing the suit, said the columnist, Naeem Abd Muhalhal, had advance knowledge of bin Laden's plans and that "Iraqi officials were aware of plans to attack American landmarks." He added, "Further, we have evidence that Iraq provided support for bin Laden and his al Qaeda terror organization for nearly a decade."

This charge was supported by Craig Roberts, a former Oklahoma policeman and National Guard officer, who said, "At the end of the Gulf War, over 5,000 former Iraqi soldiers (mainly consisting of officers) were transported (illegally) to this country by the administration for 'humanitarian purposes' and resettled at taxpayer expense. This created a massive stir in the veterans organizations, who remembered how many American POWs had been abandoned by our government in past wars, but was only publicized in their magazines."

Roberts, a Vietnam veteran and author who participated in the official Oklahoma City investigation of the Murrah Building bombing, said these Iraqi officers had worked with the CIA during the eight-year war between Iraq and Iran. They feared Saddam's wrath after losing the Gulf War. Within this group were many men who joined various Muslim extremist groups, such as Hamas and the Islamic Jihad, after arriving in the U.S.A, according to Israeli intelligence.

Despite a rush to judgment by the federal authorities that only one man Timothy McVeigh bombed the Murrah Federal Building, controversy continues today over the facts of the tragedy. Oklahoma City has been added to the list of controversial and never properly investigated American tragedies beginning with the assassinations of President John F. Kennedy, Martin Luther King, Robert Kennedy, and the killings at Ruby Ridge, Idaho, and Waco, Texas.

Oklahoma representative Charles Key in 1997 tried to bring facts concerning the Muslim connection in the Oklahoma City bombing to the public and finally produced a five hundred-page report released in 2001.

As far back as 1997, Key and many others had raised questions about McVeigh's contacts prior to the bombing that killed 161 men, women and children.

Many still recall the FBI bulletins issued immediately after the bombing seeking several Middle Eastern men reportedly driving a brown pickup truck. Other Arabic men dressed in blue coveralls were seen in the vicinity of the federal building shortly before the explosions.

As in the case of District Attorney Jim Garrison attempting to question the official verdict of the Kennedy assassination, Key was raked over the coals by the mainstream media and accused of "howling at the moon" by Oklahoma governor Frank Keating, a former FBI agent.

"Why was there such extreme opposition?" Key wrote in a letter to constituents. "I believe the answer is because some in our federal law enforcement agencies (i.e., ATF and FBI) had prior knowledge that certain individuals were planning to bomb the Murrah Federal Building! I believe that because of at least four reasons:

"1. Six different individuals have come forward and reported seeing the bomb squad in the immediate vicinity of the Murrah Building early on the morning of the bombing.

"2. The Oklahoma City Fire Department received a call from the FBI the Friday before the bombing and was told to be on the alert for a possible terrorist attack on a government building.

"3. Bruce Shaw, who had frantically come to look for his wife inside the smoldering building, was told by an ATF agent, 'You won't find any ATF agents in the building because they were warned on their pagers not to come in this morning and they're now in debriefing.' This conversation was corroborated by his boss, who accompanied Bruce to help him find his wife.

"4. Carol Howe, a paid informant for the ATF, has recently come forward to confirm that she informed the ATF that two individuals, Dennis Mahon and Andreas Strassmier, were planning to bomb the federal building in Oklahoma City. She also said that the likely date for the bombing was April 19!"

In addition to the suppressed information concerning the Middle East connection to the federal building bombing, at least one Oklahoma City investigative reporter claimed to have gathered evidence that Osama bin Laden was involved. Jayna Davis, former news reporter for the NBC affiliate in Oklahoma City, KFOR-TV, tried to make public this information several months prior to 9/11.

Davis said she developed information that a Middle Eastern terrorist cell was operating only blocks from the Murrah Building and that Timothy McVeigh on the day of the bombing was in contact with an Iraqi who had served in Saddam Hussein's Republican Guard. This man was the object of an "all-points" bulletin immediately after the bombing that was inexplicably withdrawn.

Davis said her evidence led her to believe that McVeigh, along with Terry Nichols (now serving a life sentence as an accomplice in the bombing) and at least seven men of Middle Eastern ethnic backgrounds were involved in a conspiracy masterminded by bin Laden.

The reporter said she took her evidence, composed of hundreds of court records, twenty sworn witness affidavits and reports from law enforcement, intelligence and terrorist experts, to the FBI but bureau officials refused even to accept the material.

Further clouding the issue of why the FBI refused to even look at the evidence that refuted the Clinton administration's assurance that the bombing was the work of one lone man, McVeigh, plus a friend, was evidence showing that the FBI top counterterrorism expert checked into an Oklahoma City hotel just after midnight on the morning the federal building was destroyed.

Danny Coulson, then director of the FBI's Terrorist Task Force, checked into the Embassy Suites Hotel at 12:20 a.m., about nine hours prior to the bombing, according to a hotel receipt obtained by WorldNetDaily. The hotel receipt showed Coulson checked out of the hotel on April 27.

Coulson, in a book published in 1999, claimed he was in Fort Worth when he received a call from John O'Neill, the FBI counterterrorism expert, informing him of the Murrah Building bombing.

The discrepancy of these stories adds support to those who claim the FBI was involved in the case well before the explosion.

The lawsuit alleged that Ramzi Yousef, convicted in the 1993 World Trade Center bombing, was an Iraqi government agent who, prior to his arrest, went to the Philippines, where he recruited Terry Nichols, McVeigh's accomplice in Oklahoma, to join in a plot to blow up several U.S.-bound airliners.

Further evidence of a connection between McVeigh and the bin Laden network, over and beyond the Philippines meeting involving Nichols, is the testimony of witnesses at a small motel outside Oklahoma.

A co-owner of the motel, who asked for anonymity, told reporter Jim Crogan of *LA Weekly* that he distinctly recalled terrorist leader Mohammed Atta at his motel with Zacarias Moussaoui, the infamous "twentieth hijacker," about August 1, 2001, just six weeks prior to the 9/11 attacks. He identified a third man as Marwan al-Shehhi, reportedly one of the terrorists that was aboard Flight 175.

He said the men asked for a weekly rate on some rooms at the motel but they were told the rooms were all occupied. He said all three men were friendly but that Atta did most of the talking.

"I asked him what they were doing here in the area," the owner said. "And Atta told me they were going to flight school. I thought he meant training in Oklahoma City. But Atta told me no, they were taking flight training in Norman.

"I said I didn't understand why they would want to rent one of my rooms, since we were about twenty-eight miles from Norman and there are a lot of reasonably priced motels a lot closer. But he said they had heard good things about my place and wanted to stay there."

The man explained that there were no weekly rooms available and the trio left. Later, following the 9/11 attacks, the motel owner saw their pictures on the news and called the FBI. But there was never any significant follow-up to his report.

One law enforcement source said he considered the motel owner's story credible and took the information to the FBI but was told, "it probably would go nowhere." "They were afraid the whole Oklahoma City bombing can of worms would be opened up and the FBI would have to explain why they didn't investigate this material before," the officer told a reporter.

"One reason for the FBI's apparent lack of interest might be this motel's alleged connection to Timothy McVeigh and a group of Iraqis who worked in Oklahoma City," noted reporter Crogan. "According to the motel owner and other witnesses and investigators interviewed by the *Weekly*, McVeigh and several of these Iraqis were motel guests in the months preceding the 1995 bombing. Witnesses also claimed they saw several of the Iraqis moving barrels of material around on the bed of a truck. The motel owner said the material smelled of diesel fuel and he had to clean up a spill. Diesel fuel was a key component of the truck bomb that blew up the Federal Building."

The motel owner was interviewed by the FBI on several occasions but there was no indication that prosecutors in the case of Moussaoui were even notified of the Moussaoui-Atta connection, who was arrested prior to 9/11, has been characterized as a marginal figure in the plot. But if he was connected to Atta, it makes him much more of a participant than previously thought.

Reporter Crogan wrote, "If this recollection is correct, the entire incident, and its absence from the public record, raises new questions about the FBI investigation of Moussaoui and the 1995 destruction of the Federal Building in Oklahoma City."

There were so many leads and bits of information about the cover-up in the Oklahoma City bombing that it occasionally slipped into the mainstream media.

According to a report in *U.S. News & World Report* in late 2001, McVeigh possessed several Iraqi telephone numbers, which prompted Pentagon officials to suspect that he was some sort of Iraqi agent. Writer Paul Bedard wrote, "Why haven't we heard this before about the case of the executed McVeigh? Conspiracy theorists in the Pentagon think it's part of a coverup."

Plagiarized papers, secret pre-planning for invasion, distortion of evidence and outright lies permeate the effort to win support for the invasion of Iraq. No wonder so many other nations declined to support the U.S. effort.

There may even be more reasons that most people realize that prompt U.S. leaders with secret-society connections to send troops into Iraq.

According to ABC News, nearly four hundred ancient Sumerian artifacts were discovered in Iraq in 1999 in the southern Iraqi town of Basmyiah, about one hundred miles south of Baghdad. The Iraqi News Agency said the objects ranged from animal and human-shaped "toys" to cuneiform tablets and even "ancient weapons." At least one cylinder seal depicted a tall person thought to represent the ancient king Gilgamesh. The antiquities were dated to about 2500 *B.C.*, said excavation team leader Riyadh al-Douri.

Iraqi archeologists made the discoveries in late 1999 and said the artifacts would be brought to the Iraqi Museum in Baghdad, which has been closed to the public since the Gulf War. Reportedly, other astonishing finds were being made during this time by a German archaeological team given permission to excavate by Saddam Hussein.

McGuire Gibson, with the Oriental Institute of the University of Chicago and president of the American Association for Research in Baghdad, already had lamented the loss of ancient artifacts and writings because of the Gulf War and subsequent embargo of Iraq.

"The aftermath of the war witnessed the looting and sometimes the burning of nine regional museums and the loss of more than 3,000 artifacts, only a few of which have been recovered," wrote Gibson. "The loss of the objects, although grave, was not as destructive as the change that the attacks on the museums will have on the future relationship of museums to the people of Iraq. It is unlikely that there will ever again be an effort at public education about archeology on the scale that was represented by those regional museums."

In addition to the destruction of historical artifacts, such as the American bombing of the giant ziggurat at Ur and the losses due to construction by U.S. troops at Tell al-Lahm, economic conditions caused by the American embargo have caused an increase in the illegal trading of Iraqi artifacts. Gibson added that almost all archeological research in Iraq came to a halt because of the war and embargo.

The problem was exacerbated in late April 2003 when at least 50,000 priceless artifacts and tablets were taken from the Baghdad museum by what appeared to be organized looters.

Despite prior attempts to alert American military officers of the danger of losing artifacts dating back 7,000 years, American authorities failed to prevent the wholesale looting of humankind's most ancient treasures.

"It was my impression that the Department of Defense had made provisions for the safeguarding of monuments and museums," lamented Maxwell Anderson, president of the Association of Art Museum Directors. Anderson was among a group that in January 2003 alerted Pentagon and State Department officials to the importance of these antiquities.

Furthermore, according to an *Associated Press* report, the thieves had keys to the museum and its vaults. Gibson said what appeared to be random looting actually was a carefully planned theft. "It looks as if part of the theft was a very, very deliberate, planned action," he said. "They were able to obtain keys from somewhere for the vaults and were able to take out the very important, the very best material. I have a suspicion it was organized outside the country. In fact, I'm pretty sure it was."

"Glass cutters not available in Iraq were found in the museum and a huge bronze bust weighing hundreds of pounds...would have required a fork lift to remove it indicate that well organized professional cultural thieves were mixed in with the mob," noted Christopher Bollyn of the *American Free Press.*

The fact that some display cases were empty without being broken indicated that some of the precious materials may have been taken out prior to the arrival of the looters. A thorough investigation of this grand theft should be instigated, but mostly probably interest in this issue will quickly fade from the public consciousness.

When the looting began on April 17, 2003, one Iraqi archaeologist summoned U.S. troops to protect the national museum. Five Marines accompanied the man to the museum and chased out the thieves by firing shots over their heads. However, after about 30 minutes, the soldiers were ordered to withdraw and the looters soon returned.

"Not since the Taliban embarked on their orgy of destruction against the Buddhas of Bamiyan and the statutes in the museum of Kabul - perhaps not since

World War II - have so many archaeological treasures been wantonly and systematically smashed to pieces," reported British newsman Robert Fisk, who toured the museum shortly after the incident.

The preventable looting prompted three members of the White House Cultural Property Advisory Committee to resign, disgusted that the alerted American military had failed to protect the Mesopotamian treasures. "This tragedy was not prevented, due to our nation's inaction," wrote committee chairman Martin E. Sullivan in his resignation letter.

It has been widely reported that Saddam Hussein believes himself to be the reincarnation of the King Nebuchadnezzar, who performed wondrous achievements in construction, including the Hanging Gardens of Babylon, in an attempt to communicate with ancient Mesopotamian gods from the heavens. Could the rush to war with Iraq have something to do with gaining control over recently-discovered knowledge, and perhaps even technology, which might undo modern monopolies in religion and science?

Recent scientific studies into heretofore unknown monatomic elements have linked this discovery to ancient writings from Mesopotamia and Egypt. Scientists claim such elements may hold the key to unlocking the secrets of limitless free energy, faster-than light propulsion systems, teleportation and even the possibility of inter-dimensional and time travel.

It is most intriguing to some researchers to realize that Iraq, most probably the cradle of human civilization if not the starting point for all humanity, is today just about the only place on the planet that the free people of America cannot visit. (See *Rule by Secrecy* for further information concerning the significance of these ancient Mesopotamian artifacts.)

As the year 2002 drew to a close, there were demonstrations in both America and other nations against a war with Iraq. Protest rallies took place in Mexico, Japan, Germany, South Korea, Belgium and Australia, but most were ignored by the corporate mass media in the United States.

There was scant coverage of the 100,000 to 150,000 that marched in Washington on Sunday, October 27. Led by celebrities such as musician Patti Smith and actress Susan Sarandon, the protests were hailed as some of the largest in the nation since the Vietnam War. Jesse Jackson told a crowd gathered by the Vietnam Veterans Memorial, "If we launch a pre-emptive strike, we will lose all moral authority we must have a higher order than a one-bullet diplomacy."

The protest marches came following a poll conducted for the *New York Times* and CNN that showed half of those queried were uneasy at the prospect of war with Iraq.

None of this seemed to sway President Bush, who declared, "If the UN won't act, if Saddam won't disarm, we will lead a coalition to disarm him." On March 20, 2003, Bush made good on these words by launching U.S. forces across Iraqi's borders.

Destroyed Crops Impact World Drug Trade

The current War on Drugs has been going on for so long that most people have forgotten when it began. Most authorities trace this failed but ongoing war to President Richard Nixon who, in 1970, established the National Commission on Marijuana and Drug Abuse. The commission, under the chairmanship of Raymond P. Schafer, former governor of Pennsylvania, began work the following year.

According to the commission's report, *Marihuana, A signal of Misunderstanding*, "Soon after funds became available on March 22, 1971, we commissioned more than fifty projects, ranging from a study of the effects of marihuana on man to a field survey of enforcement of the marihuana laws in six metropolitan jurisdictions. Of particular importance in our fact-finding effort were the opinions and attitudes of all groups in our society."

In other words, this was a genuine, objective report. Its conclusions?

After dismissing public approval of recreational drug use as counter to the benefit of society, the commission likewise opposed the option of using criminal penalties to eliminate drug use, stating, "Marihuana's relative potential for harm to the vast majority of individual users and its actual impact on society does not justify a social policy designed to seek out and firmly punish those who use it."

Commission members pointed out that "even during Prohibition, when many people were concerned about the evils associated with excessive use of alcohol, possession for personal use was never outlawed federally and was made illegal in only five States."

The report also stated, "There is a legitimate concern about what the majority of the non-using population thinks about marihuana use and what the drug represents in the public mind. The question is appropriately asked if we are suggesting that the majority in a free society may impose its will on an unwilling minority even though, as it is claimed, uncertainty, speculation, and a large degree of misinformation form the basis of the predominant opinion. If we have nothing more substantial than this, the argument goes, society should remain neutral."

The commission concluded, "We recommend to the public and its policy-makers a social control policy seeking to discourage Marihuana use, while concentrating primarily on the prevention of heavy and very heavy use."

Nixon said he disagreed with the report and launched the first of many wars on drugs. But then again, it has been firmly established that Nixon had many close associations with organized crime figures, so perhaps his friends did not want the cost of drugs to fall due to legalization, no matter how limited.

Today the number of U.S. prison inmates held on drug charges is about half a million, greater than the entire jail population of Western Europe. And most of these are persons of color who lived below the poverty line.

Another possible explanation for the never-ending War on Drugs came when Senator Carl Levin, a Michigan Democrat, documented how more than $300 billion in drug money moves yearly through the U.S. banking system.

Levin's estimate, based on a staff investigation lasting more than a year, was augmented by the Brookings Institution in 2001. Brookings spokesman Raymond Baker reported that despite the strictest money-laundering laws in the world, U.S. banks still held an estimated $500 billion a year in money from drug dealers and terrorists.

In one sting operation by U.S. Customs, $7.7 million was deposited in the Citibank account of a Cayman Islands bank. When the money was transferred to M. A. Bank, it turned out to be a shell company without any physical office.

In the more naive times of the early 1970s, no one foresaw the advent of synthetic cocaine, adulterated hash, rock cocaine, PCP and the recent designer drugs such as Ecstasy. Then, the greatest drug bugaboo was heroin, the drug that placed a "monkey on your back." Interestingly enough, heroin use in the 1970s was reported at about 2 percent of the drug-taking population, a percentage that has remained remarkably stable up until this day.

Everyone knowledgeable of the world drug trade knows that the two primary sources of poppies, the flower from which heroin is made, are the Golden Triangle in Southeast Asia and Afghanistan.

The modern afghan drug industry began with U.S. involvement in Afghanistan at the time of the Soviet invasion, as recounted by Alfred McCoy, author of the respected *The Politics of Heroin in Southeast Asia*:

"CIA assets again controlled this heroin trade. As the Mujahideen guerrillas seized territory inside Afghanistan, they ordered peasants to plant opium as a revolutionary tax. Across the border in Pakistan, Afghan leaders and local syndicates under the protection of Pakistan Intelligence operated hundreds of heroin laboratories. During this decade of wide-open drug-dealing, the U.S. Drug Enforcement Agency in Islamabad failed to instigate major seizures or arrests. U.S. officials had refused to investigate charges of heroin dealing by its Afghan allies 'because U.S. narcotics policy in Afghanistan has been subordinated to the war against Soviet influence there.'

"In 1995, the former CIA director of the Afghan operation, Charles Cogan, admitted the CIA had indeed sacrificed the drug war to fight the Cold War. 'Our main mission was to do as much damage as possible to the Soviets. We didn't really have the resources or the time to devote to an investigation of the drug trade, I don't think that we need to apologize for this. Every situation has its fallout.... There was fallout in terms of drugs, yes. But the main objective was accomplished. The Soviets left Afghanistan.'"

The Taliban were not so lenient on the opium trade.

It was reliably reported that zealous Muslims within the Taliban government had banned the growth of poppies and had succeeded in destroying nearly 95 percent of the crop by the spring of 2001. Britain's *Financial Times* early in 2002 reported, "The Taliban's ban on opium poppy two years ago was 'enormously effective' in reducing poppy crops almost entirely in areas under the regime's control. The U.S. estimates that Afghanistan produced 74 tons of opium last year, compared to 3,656 tons the previous year." Anti-Taliban hard-liners in the United States believed this reduction of the poppy crop was merely a "business decision" designed to drive prices up and ensure higher profits to the Taliban. More knowledgeable drug experts have pointed out that the Taliban are not peddling heroin on the streets of LA or New York and that powerful drug distributors must have viewed the poppy loss as a business disaster.

After the U.S. invasion of Afghanistan, opium production soared. Under the Taliban no more than 185 tons of opium was produced. By the end of 2002, that figure had risen to an estimated 3,400 tons, according to BBC's Central Asian analyst Pam O'Toole. This means that Afghanistan is back to late-1990s levels, when the country produced 70 percent of the world's illicit opium.

To fully explain the politics of drugs would require a separate book, but it must be understood that drugs, particularly opium-based drugs such as heroin, have been the basis for both social control and wealth for many centuries.

In 1799, China banned opium. However, following a series of Opium Wars in China during the early 1800s, treaties signed in 1858 by Britain, France, Russia and the United States legalized the drug trade. General William Huntington Russell, founder of the Skull and Bones Order at Yale, was a member of the Connecticut legislature. His family was at the center of Russell and Company, a firm controlled by some of Boston's finest blue blood families that were enriched first by the slave trade and then by opium smuggling in the early 1800s.

Other Boston families integrated Russell's firm into an opium syndicate created by Thomas Handasyd Perkins of Newburyport, Massachusetts, including the Cabots, Lowells, Higginsons, Forbeses, Cushings and Sturgises.

It has been charged ever since the Vietnam War that the CIA has imported drugs to support its clandestine operations. Mounds of court papers and news stories attest to this criminal activity yet no one in high authority seems capable of doing anything about it. One former British commando who operated in Afghanistan during the Soviet occupation has stated that both American and British military officers tolerated opium smuggling by the Mujahideen as the profits were used to support their actions against the Russians.

Tom Carew, who retired from the British army in 1992, told the *Sunday Times* how both British and American officers worked together with China in both Afghanistan and Pakistan. "I also took orders from Col. John Miley of the

U.S. Defense Intelligence Agency," Carew reported. These same authorities helped create the Mujahideen in Afghanistan to fight the Russian invaders.

"The somewhat dubious legacy of our intervention is evident in international drug smuggling and terrorism today," he said, adding that after two British officers were killed by the Russians, allied authorities, fearful that their role might be uncovered, sent their Afghan fighters to Scotland for training by his unit, the 22nd Special Air Service Regiment.

Carew said after debriefing sessions in both London and Washington, he quickly became aware that both British and American authorities turned a blind eye to the Mujahideen drug smuggling.

What becomes clear in all this is that anyone desiring to profit from the drug trade would be opposed to the destruction of the poppy crop.

At least five books and many Web sites have connected both President George W. Bush and his father with the drug trade.

The most prominent anecdote involves a colorful assassinated drug dealer and DEA informant named Barry Seal. Daniel Hopsicker, formerly executive producer of a business news television show aired on NBC, published a book on Seal in 2001 entitled *Barry & 'the boys': The CIA, The Mob and America's Secret History.*

In this book, Hopsicker details how Seal, who was at the same time one of America's most successful drug smugglers and a CIA agent, became angry at George H. W. Bush when he was Reagan's vice president. Seal felt Bush had betrayed him by not getting him out of legal problems concerning drugs. Seal had been implicated in the CIA drug smuggling connected to the airport at Mena, Arkansas. In retaliation, Seal reportedly arranged for a DEA "sting" at a Florida airport in 1985 that instead of nabbing ordinary drug dealers caught Bush's sons, Jeb and George W., accepting a shipment of cocaine. Both were already prominent political leaders at time. According to Hopsicker, "Seal then stepped in and 'took care' of things. The Bushies were now supposedly in his debt. Plus he hung on to the videotape shot of the sting for insurance."

This same story was echoed in a book by former air force intelligence officer and CIA asset Terry Reed, along with former *Newsday* prize-winning investigative reporter John Cummings. In *Compromised*, Reed asserts that Seal told him, "It seems some of George Bush's kids just can't say no ta drugs, ha, ha, ha, ha.Well, ya can imagine how valuable information like that would be, can't ya? That could get you out of almost any jam it's like a get-out-of-jail-free card. I even got surveillance videos catchin' the Bush boys redhanded. I consider this stuff my insurance policy."

Seal's "insurance policy" lapsed quickly. He was machine-gunned in Baton Rouge, Louisiana, on February 19, 1986, less than a year later.

His death inspired a lengthy letter to then, attorney general Ed Meese from the Lousiana attorney general, William J. Guste Jr., stating, "I, for one, was shocked when I learned of his death. In October, as chairman of the Subcommittee on Narcotics and Drug Interdiction of the President's Commission on Organized Crime, I had presided over a seminar at which Barry Seal had testified. His purpose there was to inform the commission and top United States officials of the methods and equipment used by drug smugglers."

According to investigator Hopsicker, three boxes of documents, including audio/videotapes, which Seal had kept with him at all times, were taken from the scene of his murder by the FBI special agent of the Baton Rouge office. The agent arrived at the crime scene less than ten minutes after the shooting.

Was Barry Seal's murder just another drug-related street shooting or did someone not want him to reveal what he knew? Hopsicker did discover that the very plane Seal claimed was used to fly cocaine to the 1985 sting ended up as the property of George W. Bush sometime after Seal's death . The writer also found in tracing the ownership of the turboprop King Air 200 that the trail led to several persons connected to either the IranContra or the savings and loan scandals of the 1980s. Hopsicker also found FAA records that showed that Seal had flown aircraft connected through a Phoenix firm to Southern Air Transport, a known CIA proprietary company.

Voters might recall that the younger Bush never actually denied using cocaine when the issue came up in his 2000 campaign for president. He simply brushed the allegation aside with a claim of youthful foolishness. Some of the thousands still serving prison sentences for possession of cocaine must wish their convictions could be overturned and excused as the foolishness of youth.

Cheney also has had questions raised about drug running through Halliburton's subsidiary Kellogg Brown & Root as well as the firm's connection to a suspect Russian oil company.

At least one of the fat loans given by the U.S. Export-Import Bank in 2000 after being lobbied by Halliburton was to the Tyumen Oil Co., controlled by the Alfa Group conglomerate. The loan was approved in April 2002. A Center for Public Integrity investigative report stated, "It guaranteed $489 million in credits to a Russian oil company whose roots are imbedded in a legacy of KGB and Communist Party corruption, as well as drug trafficking and organized crime funds, according to Russian and U.S. sources and documents."

In 1997, the Russian equivalent of our FBI presented Russia's lower House of Parliament a report alleging both organized crime and drug running involving Tyumen's parent company, the Alfa Group. The report stated that two Alfa entities, Alfa Bank and the trading company Alfa Eko, in the early 1990s were deeply involved in laundering both Russian and Colombian drug money and in importing drugs from the Far East into Europe. A former KGB officer said Alfa Bank was founded with Communist Party and KGB funds and utilized former government agents who had served in anti~organized crime units under the communist regime. He said heroin was often disguised as flour and sugar shipments bound for Germany.

Russian reports showed that in 1995 a Siberian railroad worker stole a sack of sugar from a rail car leased to Alfa Eko and that shortly afterward many people in his town became "poisoned" after eating the heroin-laced sugar. This incident prompted official raids on Alfa Eko that turned up "drugs and other compromising documentation."

Even Alfa Group's 1998 takeover of Tyumen Oil prompted allegations of impropriety and connections to Moscow's Solntsevo crime family. Despite all this, Cheney's Halliburton prevailed and the U.S. taxpayer backed loans went through.

More heavy political pressure may have come from Tyumen's lead attorney, James C. Langdon Jr., a managing partner of the worldwide law firm of Akin Gump Straus's Hauer & Feld. Langdon was one of George W. Bush's "Pioneers," a group of fund-raisers that gathered at least $100,000 each for the 2000 campaign. Another helpful person was Halliburton's top lobbyist, Dave Gribbin, who served as Cheney's chief of staff when he headed the Pentagon under the elder Bush.

Drugs, oil, shady and complicated business dealings all found a focal point in 2001. It was in the wayward son of a prominent Saudi family Osama bin Laden.

Who and Where Is Bin Laden?

As in the JFK assassination, authorities on the day of the 9/11 attacks had a suspect even before anyone knew for certain what had happened. He was identified as Osama bin Laden, the son of a wealthy Saudi Arabian oil family and a man who during the Russo-Afghan War of the 1980s received arms and financing from the U.S. government.

Despite the fact that bin Laden repeatedly denied knowledge of the attacks, he was presumed guilty by both the government and the press. No other interpretation of the attack was allowed in the corporate mass media. Bin Laden is a made-to-order enemy. He is the man blamed for the 1993 WTC attack and had been a fugitive from U.S. Justice for more than a decade, and nobody might have ever heard of Osama bin Laden if President Bill Clinton had not fired missiles indiscriminately into Afghanistan in an attempt to kill him in 1998.

Bin Laden's history is relatively nondescript yet fascinating as an example of a pious religious man being drawn into a world of geopolitics and murder.

A lengthy biography of bin Laden was presented recently by PBS's *Frontline*. The show's editors said the document came from an anonymous source close to bin Laden. They added that while some of the information could not be independently verified and even ran contrary to other sources, the document nevertheless was "a very useful source of information." The document seemed to be a fairly accurate and somewhat sympathetic biography of bin Laden.

According to this document, bin Laden was born in 1957 to a Syrian mother. He was the seventh son of more than fifty brothers and sisters. His father, Mohammed Awad bin Laden, had immigrated to Saudi Arabia about 1930, where he worked as a laborer in the port city of Jeddah on the Red Sea. During the post~World War II reign of King Ibn Saud, the founder of modern Saudi Arabia, the elder bin Laden gained a fortune by constructing the king's palaces. He impressed the king and began to build good relations with the royal family, especially Faisal, who took the throne when his brother, King Saud IV, was forced to abdicate in 1964. The elder bin Laden reportedly played a role in convincing Saud IV to step down in favor of Faisal. For his trouble, Faisal issued a decree that all construction projects would go to bin Laden.

According to the PBS document, the elder bin Laden was a stern disciplinarian who kept his children in one location and instilled in them strict business and religious mores. To his credit, the father reportedly showed no difference in the treatment of his vast brood. During the Haji holy season, the elder bin Laden spent his construction company wealth on funding the travels of many Islamic leaders and scholars. Through the father's generosity, the son made many long-lasting friendships.

Mohammed Awad bin Laden died in a 1968 plane crash when Osama bin Laden was still a teenager. By age seventeen, bin Laden had married a young Syrian relative and had completed his early education. In 1981, he received a degree in public administration from the King Abdul-Aziz University in Jeddah. During this time, bin Laden joined many other educated Arabs in joining the Muslim Brotherhood. As early as the first two weeks of the Soviet invasion of Afghanistan in December 1979, bin Laden was taken to Pakistan to meet leaders of the anti-Soviet forces and to witness the pitiful columns of refugees. Returning to Saudi Arabia, he began collecting for the Afghan cause. He made several short trips to Pakistan during the next couple of years, taking with him an immense amount of money and materials.

In 1982, bin Laden finally entered Afghanistan to meet with the Mujahideen fighters, taking along construction machinery and even a few of the bin Laden construction workers. He also reportedly established a "Guest House" in Peshawar on the Afghan-Pakistan border that became a way station for Arab fighters, sent by him to various Afghan factions fighting the Soviets. By 1988, he had established more than six camps of his own in Afghanistan and his own force, the Maktab al-Khidimat (MAK), which soon was engaging the Soviets. Composed primarily of devout Muslims, these fighters came from Egypt, Lebanon, Syria, Turkey, Saudi Arabia and other Middle Eastern nations.

From 1984 through 1989, he spent more than eight months out of each year in Afghanistan, where he participated in several major battles and numerous smaller skirmishes. His relations with the Taliban were warm because they both saw themselves as devout practitioners of Islam. Theirs was a bonding of religion, not of politics.

Returning to Saudi Arabia in late 1989 as the Soviets were withdrawing from Afghanistan, bin Laden found himself trapped by a royal ban on his travels. He had angered the Saudi royals by announcing his intention of spreading his holy war into South Yemen and warning of invasion by Saddam Hussein, who then had warm relations with the Saudis. When Saddam Hussein invaded Kuwait in 1991, he saw it as a sign of his prophecy come true and proposed to the Saudis that he bring in his Arab Mujahideen to protect the kingdom. Before a decision was made on his suggestion, bin Laden was shocked to learn that American troops had arrived in Saudi Arabia. It was a transforming moment, as the presence of any foreign troops on Saudi soil was considered intolerable by many Muslims. He had much earlier stated that the next great battle would be against America. His virtual house arrest in Jeddah and an armed raid on his suburban farm by the national guard caused his relations with the Saudis to sour. Bin Laden convinced a brother to arrange for him to visit Pakistan on business, but once he arrived there in the spring of 1991 he sent back a letter stating he would not return and apologized for his perfidy.

Heading immediately for Afghanistan, he tried unsuccessfully to mediate between the various factions there. His devout demeanor endeared bin Laden to fellow Muslims. He was considered a truthful person, a simple person with good manners and a humble and generous personality. Despite his frail appearance and bland speeches, his followers saw him as an inspirational leader and showed him great respect. He also evinced a cunning caution, to the point of avoiding electronic devices, including wristwatches, which he believed might be used to track him.

During his stay and later in Sudan, the Saudis with the aid of Pakistani intelligence and perhaps their close associates, the CIA, reportedly tried to kill him but his many friends within the Pakistani establishment tipped him off each time. Apparently, the forces of the status quo desired to eliminate this religious fanatic who heeded neither bribes nor Western reasoning. By 1994, the Saudis publicly renounced bin Laden, withdrawing his citizenship and freezing his assets, estimated at between $200 million and $300 million. But this was only money traceable to him through the Bin Laden Group. Millions more are tied up in bin Laden family money and their complex joint ventures with the royal Saudi family, including King Fahad.

While visiting in Sudan, there were anti-American incidents in Somalia and South Yemen, followed in 1995 by a car bombing in the Saudi capital of Riyadh. Although bin Laden was blamed in each of these incidents, the PBS document claimed he had no direct knowledge of them. They reportedly were carried out by Arabs who had trained with bin Laden in Afghanistan and had been imbued with anti-American feelings. There was no indication of who truly was behind them and the perpetrators themselves may not have known.

Sought by both the Americans and the Saudis, bin Laden returned to Afghanistan, where he was granted sanctuary by the ruling Taliban. Shortly after arriving back there in mid-1996, the Khobar Towers on an American base in Saudi Arabia was bombed, killing nineteen American soldiers. Although no one claimed responsibility for the attack, once again Arab Afghan fighters who had been connected to bin Laden were blamed.

But no one was paying much attention to the diminutive "freedom fighter," so bin Laden issued what may have been his first public anti-American message, a twelve-page declaration of war against America. At that time his only demands were that American troops leave Saudi Arabia.

Reportedly, American Special Forces planned to attack his residence in 1997 but canceled the plan when an Arab newspaper in London published a report on the operation, again apparently provided by leaks from the sympathetic Pakistani military and intelligence personnel. By now, bin Laden was completely caught up in his own war against what he considered "infidels." He utilized every resource at his command, including the media. He even allowed an ABC television interview in April 1998, warning at that time that attacks would come within weeks.

An attack was expected inside Saudi Arabia. Instead American embassies in Kenya and Tanzania were bombed on August 7, 1998, provoking outrage all around the world.

President Clinton responded by ordering missiles fired at bin Laden's Afghan camp in Khost. About 250 Arabs were killed but bin Laden was not there. A plant in the Sudan, suspected of producing chemical weapons, also was targeted by sixteen Cruise missiles. Later it was found that the plant, owned by Saudi businessman Saleh Idris, actually was producing medicine, not chemical weapons.

The Taliban government of Afghanistan offered to put bin Laden on trial provided the U.S. government provided sufficient evidence of his guilt in the bombings. Nothing came of this offer. By then, some members of the U.S. intelligence establishment were saying that bin Laden was training Islamic fighters for action in Chechnya and other areas of Russia. In fact, the al-Qaeda network is quite different from World War II "fifth columnists" and traditional insurgent movements in that it is not closely connected and does not have a clear command structure. It is a loose conglomeration of groups operating across continents. Such an organization would be susceptible to penetration by any number of national security forces, in fact, almost anyone.

The PBS document stated that bin Laden's followers are not mercenaries but religious zealots who do not require much money. "Explosives and weapons are very cheap in some parts of the world," it read. "In Somalia, TNT, for example, is cheaper than sugar. In Yemen, you can buy an RPG [Rocket Propelled Grenade] for less than a TV set. The role of money here is over-exaggerated by many writers."

According to this document, bin Laden was nearly forgotten by his Arab followers until the African bombings that killed twelve Americans, about three hundred Kenyans and Tanzanians and wounded five thousand. President Clinton told the public, "Our target was terror. There is convincing evidence from our intelligence community that the bin Laden terrorist network was responsible for these bombings. Based on this information, we have high confidence that these bombings were planned, financed and carried out by the organization bin Laden leads."

With bin Laden's name bantered about by the news media, his notoriety rose once again. The PBS document stated, "People's reaction, however, was mixed. While many felt triumph for scaring the Americans, many others felt upset by the picture of hundreds of civilians killed and injured in the attack. They felt this can never be justified

"After the American [missile] attack on Sudan and Afghanistan, it became almost shameful to criticize bin Laden. The American strike with associated remarks by Clinton and American officials proved that bin Laden is a big challenge to America. In the minds of the average Arab and Muslim, bin Laden appeared as the man who was able to drive Americans so crazy that it started shooting haphazardly at unjustified targets. Their view was that while bin Laden or others can make 'executive' mistakes because of their difficult circumstances, logistics and communication, America is not supposed to [make] mistakes unless it is done on purpose."

Bin Laden Replies

What did the primary suspect have to say about the 9/11 attacks?

First off, the Bush administration asked the major news media not to report on what bin Laden had to say, arguing that he might use the opportunity to pass secret messages along to his al-Qaeda network. Next, White House spokesman Ari Fleischer instructed the press to censor any future tape-recorded messages from bin Laden, although he didn't actually use the word "censor". Fleischer spent some time arguing with the media representatives, saying only, "we have the power but this is only a request." In the end, the sycophantic media agreed to self-censor any word from bin Laden. However, the European media and alternative outlets in America, especially on the Internet, made no such agreement.

In an interview on September 28, according to the Pakistani newspaper *Ummat*, bin Laden stated, "I have already said that I am not involved in the 11 September attacks in the United States. As a Muslim, I try my best to avoid telling a lie. I had no knowledge of these attacks, nor do I consider the killing of innocent women, children and other humans as an appreciable act. Islam strictly forbids causing harm to innocent women, children and other people. Such a practice is forbidden even in the course of battle. It is the United States, which is perpetrating every maltreatment on women, children and common people."

In this interview, largely unreported in the United States, bin Laden unsurprisingly blamed the attacks on Israel, claiming, "All that is going on in Palestine for the last eleven months is sufficient to call the wrath of God upon the United States and Israel, (and) what had earlier been done to the innocent people of Iraq, Chechnya and Bosnia."

Bin Laden went on to state, "we are not hostile to the United States. We are against the [U.S. government] system which makes other nations slaves to the United States or forces them to mortgage their political and economic freedom."

One cannot, of course, take bin Laden at face value, but then the same could be said for the U.S. government, which in the past has been caught in so many lies and deceit that it is surprising that anyone pays serious attention to official pronouncements.

In the late fall of 2001, a videotape of Osama bin Laden was offered to the public by the CIA and proclaimed by President Bush as a smoking gun, "a devastating declaration of guilt" in the 9/11 tragedies.

Immediately, voices rose criticizing the tape. Bin Laden's mother, Alia Ghanem, told a British newspaper, "There are too many gaps and the statements are very unlike him. Osama is too good a Muslim and too good a person to say or do what the script of the video suggests." Ghanem, who still lives in Saudi Arabia, said the tape was "doctored." Ghanem also denied reports that her son had called her prior to September 11 and told her he would be out of touch for some time because something big was about to happen. Some days later, his mother's claim was supported by Arabic language experts, who claimed that the Pentagon's translation of the tape was incorrect, taken out of context and that incriminating words had been put in bin Laden's mouth.

Two independent translators and an expert on Arabic culture reported their findings on the German state television program *Monitor*, which broadcast on December 20, 2001, over Germany's Channel One, *Das Erst*, often compared to NBC or the BBC. Dr. Abdel El M. Husseini stated, "I have carefully examined the Pentagon's translation. This translation is very problematic. At the most important places which have been presented as proof of bin Laden's guilt, it is not identical with the Arabic."

In the Pentagon translation given great publicity by the United States corporate media, bin Laden was quoted as saying, "We calculated in advance the number of casualties from the enemy." But, according to Dr. Murad Alami, "The words 'in advance' are not even head on the tapes. This translation is wrong. When we take the original Arabic from the tape there are no misunderstandings which would allow for us to read this into the original."

At another point in the Pentagon translation, bin Laden was reported saying, "We had notification since the previous Thursday that the event would take place that day." But Alami stated, "'Previous' is never said. The following sentence that the event would take place on that day is not heard in the original Arabic." Alami said the sentence "We ordered each of them to go to America" was in the active voice while the original Arabic was in the passive voice, "they were ordered to go to America." He added the translation with the word "we" was simply wrong. The expert said the sentence translated by the Pentagon as "they didn't know anything about the operation" is not understandable on the original tape.

Another of the experts interviewed, Gernot Rotter, a professor of Islamic and Arabic studies at the University of Hamburg, after studying the Pentagon's translations, stated, "The American translators who listened and transcribed the tapes have apparently written a lot of things into the text that they wanted to hear, which are actually not heard on the tape no matter how many times you listen to it."

This was somewhat supported by a December 20, 2001 *U.S.A Today* article that described how the tape was hurriedly translated in twelve hours by a Lebanese and an Egyptian who "had difficulties with the Saudi dialect bin Laden and his guest used in the tape. Regardless of whether bin Laden or his organization was involved in the attacks or not, this tape is of such bad quality, in some places it cannot be understood at all, and those parts which can be understood are torn out of context so that the tape cannot be used as evidence to prove anything."

Bin Laden Family And Friends

Media reports to the contrary, Osama bin Laden still receives financial support from his family even if they do not agree with his views and actions.

According to the PBS biography, most of the bin Ladens are faithful Muslims, who are taught that it is a sin to keep something that is not rightfully yours. Whether they agree with their sibling or not, they sincerely believe that bin Laden's share of the family fortune rightfully belongs to him and they see that he receives his due.

So, while the bin Laden assets are held by other family members, who can rightfully argue that bin Laden owns none of it, his share of the profits continue to go to him. Some family members support bin Laden because they feel it is their religious duty. Others are more circumspect, not wishing to offend the Saudi royals, while others still make no effort to hide the fact that they send bin Laden money.

Of all the nations that are the most probable sponsors of bin Laden, first place must go to Saudi Arabia, home of bin Laden, militant Muslims and the business partners of the Bush family, which goes far in explaining the dearth of reporting on the Saudis in the mainstream media.

Defense Secretary Donald Rumsfeld tried to suppress a mid-2002 special report by the Defense Department naming Saudi Arabia as the "kernel of evil" and stating that Saudi funds support most of the Middle East's terrorist groups because the Saudis have a vested interest in perpetuating tension in the region. According to federal whistle-blower Al Martin, "It has always been a guideline of Republican administrations, starting with Richard Nixon, to suppress the truth about Saudi Arabia."

Saudi Arabia profited most from the 1991 Gulf War. According to London's *Financial Times*, "Saudi Arabia oil revenues have tripled since mid-1990 because of the closure of production in Iraq and Kuwait."

Interestingly enough, it was the elder Bush's own former secret society - the Council on Foreign Relations (CFR) - that blew the whistle on his business partners and friends in Saudi Arabia. In a report issued in October 2002, a CFR task force reported that Saudi Arabian officials for years have ignored countrymen and Muslim charities that were the main sources of funding for the al-Qaeda network and that U.S. officials have systematically refused to acknowledge this connection.

"Saudi nationals have always constituted a disproportionate percentage of al-Qaeda's own membership; and al-Qaeda's political message has long focused on issues of particular interest to Saudi nationals, especially those who are disenchanted with their own government," stated the CFR report. Such connections are so numerous and documented that by late 2002 even the mass media began to question the Saudi role.

Individual Saudis also became the defendants of a $1 trillion lawsuit filed on behalf of more than six hundred families of 9/11 victims in 2002. The suit was filed by attorney Ron Motley of Charleston, South Carolina, best known for his landmark $350 billion settlement from the tobacco industry in the late 1990s.

"This has become a true mission for me," said Motley. "The individuals that we've sued facilitated the events of September 11." Liz Alderman of Armonk, New York, whose son Peter died in the WTC attack, said she joined the suit because "there is no other way for the truth to come out. I've learned and I believe that an awful lot of the funding that enabled the terrorists to attack America was provided by Saudi Arabia," she said.

Two of the most prominent Saudis named in the suit were Prince Sultan bin Abdul Aziz al-Saud, Saudi Arabia's defense minister, and Prince Turki bin

Faisal, a former intelligence chief and ambassador to Britain. The Saudi embassy in Washington had no comment on the suit but, according to the *New York Times*, a State Department source said, "The Saudis have made their concerns known at a senior level [of the U.S. government]."

The *Times* also reported that the Bush administration might well move to dismiss or delay the suit because it might damage the already strained relationship between the two countries. The paper made no mention of the close business relationships between the Saudis and the Bush family nor the fact that victim's families have implored Bush not to block the suit.

Saudi Arabia is not only in conflict over the politics but there are serious schisms within its religious community too. There is a serious division in the Muslim faith between the followers of the prophet Mohammed and its most extreme sect, the Wahabbi. The Wahabbis are taught that Jews are subhumans who should be killed, while Muslims who have studied the Hadith, or Traditions, know that Mohammed married a Jewish woman and stated that faithful Jews would join Muslims in Paradise.

The most vicious opponents of Israel are the Wahabbis and there is one very good reason for their fear and anger.The statistics tell the tale. Literacy in the Arab world is below 50 percent. "Wahabbis are functionally illiterate, they cannot read about this conflict on their own. Typically, they memorize a few passages of the Koran taken out of context, and never read the accompanying Hadith for explanation," noted attorney and author John Loftus in a widely distributed e-mail in spring 2002.

"The Muslim faith envisioned by the Prophet in the Koran and recorded by his contemporaries in the Hadith is a religion that practices tolerance toward all races and religions, stresses the extreme importance of literacy and education and elevates the status of women to unprecedented levels in many societies," Loftus wrote. "This is the gentle, peaceful Muslim faith practiced everywhere in the world, except in Saudi Arabia and the Taliban provinces of Afghanistan and Pakistan."

The word "Islam" means "submission" (to God), and over many centuries followers of Muhammed have made many constructive contributions to philosophy, culture, art and science. This praiseworthy heritage is mocked by terrorists who claim to act in its name.

Loftus said Muslim scholars and leaders do not speak out against the "primitive Wahabbi apostasy" because most Muslim mosques are impoverished and depend on Saudi subsidies. To the Saudi royalty, literacy and knowledge would mean an end to their domination, so, according to Loftus, for years they have funded anyone who might aid their cause, which is two fold: the destruction of Israel and the prevention of an independent Palestinian state.

Why? Israel's literacy rate is 97 percent and it is the only nation in the Middle East that allows Arab women to vote. "To the Saudis, a democratic

Palestinian nation would be a cancer in the Arab world, a destabilizing example of freedom that would threaten Arab dictators everywhere," explained Loftus, who has represented a number of federal whistle-blowers within the U.S. intelligence community.

As information slowly leaked to the public during 2002, more and more attention was drawn to the role of the Saudis in supporting terrorism. In early October, the congressional committee investigating the 9/11 attacks was shocked to hear testimony from FBI special agent Steven Butler concerning the bureau's knowledge of Saudi money going directly to two of the accused hijackers.

Butler said one of his confidential informants, Abdussattar Shaikh, rented rooms in San Diego to Khalid al-Midhar and Nawaf al-Hazmi, both accused of hijacking American Airlines Flight 77. Two other Saudi nationals, Osama Basnan and Omar alBayoumi, also aided the hijackers by paying their rent, helping to open a bank account and arranging flight training, despite the fact that both had been charged with visa fraud.

Agent Butler also said he alerted his superiors in the FBI about this money flow but it went nowhere. Perhaps this inaction was due to evidence that at least some of the funding of the two terrorists came from the Saudi embassy. It was reported that Princess Haifa bint Faisal, wife of the Saudi ambassador, wrote cashier checks to Bayoumi, which were believed passed along to the hijackers al-Midhar and al-Hazmi.

The worldwide banking connections- including banks controlled by globalists - of the Saudis make untangling their finances difficult. For example, The National Commerce Bank in Saudi Arabia maintains a correspondent bank relationship with JP Morgan Chase as well as the Bank of America, according to the worldwide bank database, bankersalmanac.com. Correspondent banks act like branch banks, offering a variety of services including payments, wire transfers and stock trades. U.S. officials charged that National Commerce Bank was used by wealthy Saudi businessman Yasin al-Qadi to funnel money to the al-Qaeda network through a charity called the Muwafaq Foundation.

Jeff Hershberger, a spokesman for Bank of America, declined to say if the bank had a relationship with the Saudi bank but Kristin Lemkau, speaking on behalf of JP Morgan, confirmed that her bank had a correspondent relationship with the Saudi bank. Some bank officials have noted that the new antiterrorist legislation gives the government too much discretion in deciding which banks are blacklisted. It has been said that the government apparently has spent more time and money chasing Microsoft's Bill Gates than in capturing bin Laden. This may well be due to the business connections between the Saudis and American businessmen, including the Bushes.

"the famous Saudi family [bin Laden] and the Bushes of Texas moved in similar financial circles down in Houston," noted the *Austin American-Statesman* in late 2001. In 1973, the oldest son of the bin Laden clan, Salem bin Laden -

though at the time he spelled it Binladen or Binladin - came to Texas to recruit his father's former pilot to fly the family's corporate jet. Soon, Salem became involved in a number of Texas businesses, including ownership of a small Houston airport, a San Antonio aviation services company and a home in a San Antonio suburb called Enchanted Valley.

Under a policy of primogenitude, only the oldest bin Laden son has control of the family fortune. This is the same method with which the European Rothschilds have managed to maintain their immense wealth over the centuries. When Salem found that his father's old pilot, Gerald Auerbach of San Antonio, did not want to leave Texas, he established Binladen Aviation at San Antonio International Airport and put Auerbach in charge. Salem also purchased a lot from Auerbach in Kingsland, Texas, and built a house there. "I had owned [the lot] for several years, but I couldn't afford to build a House myself," Auerbach told a news reporter. "I really think he did it for me. He let us use it when he wasn't there." He added that Salem would jet into Texas for brief stays two or three times a year.

Today, just up the road from the house once used by Salem bin Laden, there are clumps of American flags with a sign reading Bomb bin Laden!

According to the Texas news article, "Had it not been played out in the Middle East, the bin Laden family story could have been pure Texas - a business dynasty linked to power, politics and big money. Besides its business ties to the Lone Star state, the family acquired holdings that range from waterfront condos in Boston to property in California to holdings in medical research firms and a U.S. private investment firm to which former President Bush serves as an adviser [the Carlyle Group].

"The family's high-level connections were longstanding and well-known: The former President visited the bin Laden family in Saudi Arabia in 1998 and 2000." According to several published reports, Bush family friend James R. Bath used money from Osama bin Laden's brother to open a partnership with George W. Bush in Arbusto Energy, a West Texas drilling company.

Bath and the younger Bush had served together in the Texas Air National Guard. Later, according to *The Houston Chronicle*, Salem bin Laden named Bath his business representative in Texas shortly after the senior Bush was named CIA director by appointed President Gerald Ford in 1975. According to Texas court and financial records, Bath, a Houston entrepreneur, represented Salem bin Laden in such business deals as the $92 million customization of a Boeing 747 jet for use by the Saudi royal family and the purchase of the single-runway Houston Gulf Airport.

In 1992, Bath came under investigation by federal authorities for lobbying illegally for Saudi interests but nothing came of the inquiry. But, in sworn depositions, Bath acknowledged he represented four prominent Saudis, including Salem, as a trustee and used his name on their investments in return for a 5 percent commission on each deal. Bath, whose resume stated he handled all North American investments and operations for Sheikh Salem bin Laden, has consistently declined to discuss his business dealings for the record.

"Throughout Salem bin Laden's dealings in Texas, he cloaked himself in third parties and offshore companies that gave few clues to his identity," wrote Mike Ward of the *Austin American-Statesman*. "Other Texas investments were listed in the names of trustees, not Salem." Documents that are normally public, such as aviation, registration and other records that might provide more detail about the bin Laden family connections in Texas, have been denied to the public on the orders of Attorney General John Ashcroft in the wake of 9/11.

Salem bin Laden had a keen interest in aviation and it proved his undoing. On May 29, 1988, the forty-two-year-old flying enthusiast went up in an ultra-light craft that suddenly and inexplicably veered into power lines. He was pronounced dead after being rushed to San Antonio's Brooke Army Medical Center.

Another prominent Saudi represented by Bath was Sheikh Khalid bin Mahfouz, former CEO of National Commerce Bank, Saudi Arabia's largest bank and the one most closely associated with the royal family. It is also one that U.S. authorities have identified as a conduit to the al-Qaeda terrorist network.

Sheikh Khalid bin Mahfouz was one of several Saudi defendants named in a one trillion lawsuit filed in 2002 by attorney Ronald Motley, representing more than six hundred families of 9/11 victims.

Mahfouz was described by author J. H. Hatfield as a "deal broker whose alleged associations run from the CIA to a major shareholder and director of the Bank of Credit & Commerce International (BCCI). BCCI was closed down in July 1991, amid charges of multibillion-dollar fraud and worldwide news reports that the institution had been involved in covert intelligence work, drug money laundering, arms brokering, bribery of government officials and aid to terrorists."

The wealthy Saudi also reportedly paid $200 million for Dallas's Texas Commerce Bank Tower in 1985, which cost only $140 million to build. This deal not only helped cash-strapped Texas oilmen at the time but also benefited the founders of Texas Commerce Bank, the family of James Baker, former secretary of state under George Bush Sr. Mahfouz, Bath and former Texas governor John Connally were partners in Houston's Main Bank, according to *Time* magazine reporter Jonathan Beaty.

In the early 1980s, Bath was listed as a $50,000, 5 percent investor in two limited oil exploration partnerships controlled by George W. Bush. This venture, Arbusto Energy, evolved into Harken Energy. The Bush White House has consistently argued that the money invested in Arbusto Energy belonged to Bath, not bin Laden. However, several researchers have maintained that Bath at the time did not have this kind of money to invest. This was supported by Bath's former business partner, Charles W. "Bill" White of Houston.

White said, based on his knowledge of Bath's finances at the time coupled with Bath's financial records filed during a divorce, that Bath had no substantial money of his own at the time the investment was made. In an interview with Beaty, White described a variety of backroom business deals with Bath, rich Arabs, Texas wheeler-dealers and the now defunct Bank of Credit & Commerce International (BCCI).

"You have to understand that they thought I was one of them," White explained. "Bath told me he was in the CIA. He told me he had been recruited by George Bush [Sr.] himself in 1976, when Bush was director of the agency. This made sense to me, especially in light of what I had seen once we went into business together. Bath and George, Jr., were pals and flew together in the same Air National Guard unit, and Bath lived just down the street from the Bush family when George, Sr., was living in Houston. He said Bush wanted him involved with the Arabs, and to get into the aviation business.

"That's how Bath, who didn't know anything about the aviation business, became one of the biggest jet aviation dealers in the country within a couple of years. Look, here's a Boeing he's leasing to the Abu Dhabi National Oil Company. That's a multimillion-dollar jet. That's how he became a representative for Sheikh Khalid bin Mahfouz, whose family controls the National Commerce Bank of Saudi Arabia."

White also said Bath was investigated by the DEA in the 1970s. He was suspected of flying currency to the Cayman Islands. Nothing came of the investigation when no evidence of drug involvement was found. It was at this same time that Main Bank, according to Beaty, "made the news when a bank examiner discovered that it was purchasing $100 million in hundred-dollar bills each month from the Federal Reserve, an amount that dwarfed its minuscule asset base."

While representing Mahfouz's business interests in Texas, Bath had racked up more than $12 million in contract overruns by overcharging for aviation fuel at his Southwest Aviation Services company at Houston's Ellington Field.

According to an October 28, 1991, report in *Time* magazine, Southwest in 1990 was charging government military aircraft - including then president Bush's Air Force One - anywhere from twenty-two to more than forty cents per gallon more than the Air National Guard base at Ellington was paying for jet fuel. The article pointed out that each time Bush's government-owned jet landed at Ellington, it was serviced by Bath's company rather than the lower-priced government facility. *Houston Post* reporter John Mecklin estimated that between 1985 and 1989, the Department of Defense paid Mahfouz's agent Bath more than

$16.2 million for fuel under government contracts that should have cost $3.6 million.

Also in 1990, when the elder Bush drew a "line in the sand" to block Iraqi intrusion into Saudi Arabia, it is interesting to note that this line was located between the Iraqi forces and the Harken oil interests owned by his son, then soon-to-be Texas Governor George W. Bush.

The president's eldest son was a $50,000-a-year "consultant" to and a board member of Harken Energy Corp. of Grand Prairie, Texas, near the home of the Texas Rangers baseball team of which Bush was a managing general partner.

It should be noted that while connected to Harken, the younger Bush received low-interest loans from the company while he served as a director and most certainly benefited from insider transactions, actions that Bush denounced in mid-2002 following the scandals of Enron and WorldCom. One Bush official explained, "Corporate officers should not be able to treat a public company like their own personal bank."

According to filings with the Securities and Exchange Commission, the low- interest Harken loans totaled more than $180,000 and allowed Bush to purchase 105,000 shares of stock through a stock option program for senior company officials.

In January 1991, just days before Desert Storm was launched, Harken shocked the business world by announcing an oil-production agreement with the small island nation of Bahrain, a former British protectorate and a haven for international bankers just off the coast of Saudi Arabia in the Persian Gulf. Bahrain was listed among the top forty countries of the world with the highest per capita Gross Domestic Product in 1996.

Harken Energy, of which President Bush was a director from 1986 to 1993, formed an offshore subsidiary in September 1989 in the Cayman Islands. The subsidiary, Harken Bahrain Energy Company, was set up in anticipation of the company's venture drilling for oil off the coast of Bahrain.

Veteran oilmen wondered aloud how unknown Harken, with no previous drilling experience, obtained such a potentially lucrative deal. Furthermore, it was reported that "Harken's investments in the area will be protected by a 1990 agreement Bahrain signed with the U.S. allowing American and 'multi-national' forces to set up permanent bases in that country."

The younger Bush in October 1990 told *Houston Post* reporter Peter Brewton accusations that his father ordered troops to the area to protect Harken drilling rights was "a little far-fetched." He further claimed he sold his Harken stock before the Iraqi invasion but Brewton could find no record of the sale in the files of the Securities and Exchange Commission (SEC).

Records of Bush's Harken stock sale finally turned up in March 1991, eight months after the July 10, 1990, SEC deadline for filing such disclosures. One week after Saddam's troops entered Kuwait, Harken stock had dropped to

$3.03 a share. The tardy SEC records revealed that by some good fortune, Bush had sold 66 percent of his Harken stock on June 22, 1990 - just weeks prior to Iraq's invasion - for the top-dollar price of $4 a share, netting him $848,560.

An *Austin American-Statesman* article detailed both the financial and social connections between the two families, stating "Binladens traveled in same financial circles as Bush." It was the Bush family, particularly Jeb and Neil, who were involved in the savings and loan debacle from 1989 to 1993 that cost taxpayers more than $500 billion.

Through a tangled web of Texas oilmen, wealthy Saudi sheihs and unscrupulous bankers connected to BCCI, the younger Bush eventually gained a sizable interest in a new oil company called Harken Energy. Two months before Saddam Hussein sent Iraqi troops into Kuwait, Bush sold two-thirds of his Harken stock, netting himself nearly a one-million-dollar profit. The stock dropped when the Iraqi invasion began.

It should be noted that during the Persian Gulf War, it was Binladen Brothers Construction (now the Binladen Group) that helped build airfields for U.S. aircraft. The bin Laden brothers were then described as "a good friend of the U.S. government."

Later the bin Laden firm continued to be hired to construct an American air base in Saudi Arabia despite the fact that Osama bin Laden had already been blamed for terrorist acts such as the truck bombing of the Khobar Towers at the Dhahran base that killed nineteen Americans. A WorldNetDaily writer commented, "So let's get this straight. Bin Laden blows up our facilities, and his family gets the contract for rebuilding them. Do you get the feeling there is more going on than meets the eye?"

The BCCI banking institution was closed by federal investigators in 1991 after suffering some $10 billion in losses. BCCI was a Pakistani-run institution with front companies in the Cayman Islands that used secret accounts for global money laundering and was used by U.S. intelligence to funnel money to bin Laden and the Mujahideen in Afghanistan fighting against the Soviet-backed government.

Another close connection between bin Laden and the Bush family is a $12 billion private international investment firm known as the Carlyle Group. Although it has removed its Web site since the September 11 attacks, it is known that Carlyle directors include former Reagan secretary of defense Frank Carlucci, former Bush secretary of state James Baker and former Reagan aide and GOP operative Richard Darman. The *New York Times* reported that former President Bush was allowed to buy into Carlyle's investments, which involve at least 164 companies around the world.

According to the *Wall Street Journal* (September 28, 2001), "George H. W. Bush, the father of President Bush, works for the bin Laden family business in Saudi Arabia through the Carlyle Group, an international consulting firm." It has been confirmed by the senior Bush's chief of staff that Bush sent a thank-you note to the bin Laden family after a social visit in early 2001.

With such connections and his son as a sitting president of the United States, the senior Bush's Carlyle involvement was questioned by Larry Klayman, chairman and general counsel of Judicial Watch, who said, "Any foreign government or foreign investor trying to curry favor with the current Bush administration is sure to throw business to the Carlyle Group. And with the former President Bush promoting the firm's investments abroad, foreign nationals could understandably confuse the Carlyle Group's interests with the interests of the United States government."

After detailing some of the Carlyle/bin Laden investments in several businesses, including aerospace industries as well as the tremendous defense buildup since 9/11, writer Michael C. Ruppert commented, "In other words, bin Laden's attacks on the WTC and Pentagon, with the resulting massive increase in the U.S. defense budget, have just made his family a great big pile of money."

Bin Laden even had followers within the U. S. military as evidenced by court records of a former Fort Bragg, North Carolina, sergeant who gathered "Top Secret" materials for more than two years.

Ali A. Mohamed, from 1987 until his arrest in 1989, served for a time at the John F. Kennedy Special Warfare Center and School. Mohamed, who once served as a major in the Egyptian army's special operations forces, was trained at the officer's course for Green Berets at Fort Bragg in 1981. At about that same time, he joined the terrorist group Islamic Jihad, responsible for the 1981 assassination of Egyptian president Anwar Sadat and later became a close adviser to bin Laden. He also tried unsuccessfully to join the CIA but did become a source of information for the FBI, according to Larry Johnson, a former CIA agent and director of counterterrorism at the State Department during the first Bush administration.

The FBI found documents, believed to have come from Mohamed, in the possession of one of the men convicted in the 1993 WTC bombing. Included were top secret papers belonging to the Joint Chiefs of Staff and the commander-in-chief of the army's Central Command.

One former Special Forces officer said, "There is no doubt that his proximity, in hindsight, was very harmful," adding, "Does this hurt our efforts now? Absolutely."

One of the biggest roadblocks in conducting the War on Terrorism seems to have been the close connections between President Bush, his family, the Republican Party and a wide variety of Arabic and Muslim groups and individuals.

There is evidence that President Bush and his father tried to block past efforts to find and prosecute Osama bin Laden. According to a special BBC investigation reported in the November 10, 2001, issue of the *Times of India*, a "secret FBI document, numbered 1991 WF213589" emanating from the FBI's Washington field office, blamed the recent terrorist attacks on "connections between the CIA and Saudi Arabia and the Bush men and bin Ladens."

The British newspaper the *Guardian* wrote apparently of another document, marked "Secret" and coded "199 (national security)," concerning two of bin Laden's relatives. These two documents allege that the FBI had been told to "back off" an investigation of his brother, Abdullah bin Laden, who along with another brother, Omar, lived in Falls Church, Virginia just outside Washington. Abdullah was the United States director of the World Assembly of Muslim Youth (WAMY) until 2000. Although listed in FBI files as a "suspected terrorist organization," WAMY was not placed on the Bush administration's terrorist list, which would have frozen its assets. Despite several grand jury probes, no charges have been brought against the organization, which claims to be dedicated to guarding Muslim youth against "destructive ideologies."

Yet according to journalist Gregory Palast, in mid-2002 Pakistan expelled several WAMY operatives, and officials in both India and the Philippines have accused WAMY of funding militant Muslim groups.

Documents disclosed that the FBI file on the two bin Laden brothers was closed in 1996. According to Palast, "High-placed intelligence sources in Washington told the *Guardian*: 'There were always constraints on investigating the Saudis.'" The source said restrictions became worse after Bush took office and added, "There were particular investigations that were effectively killed."

The Saudis' attempts to lobby in Washington brought several Muslim organizations into the far-flung web of post 9/11 investigations. In late March 2002, federal agents raided sixteen homes and offices in northern Virginia believed to be involved in a nexus of Saudi-backed organizations with connections to terrorist groups.

Office's of the now-defunct SAAR Foundation in Herndon, Virginia, along with affiliates the Safa Trust and the International Institute of Islamic Thought, were searched by agents who carted away files and computers. The sweeping raids infuriated many Muslim groups.

Grover Norquist, a Republican Party activist who shared offices with the Safa Trust and was a board member of the Islamic Institute, said the groups existed "to promote democracy and free markets. Any effort to imply guilt by association is incompetent McCarthysim." Norquist, along with Islamic Institute chairman Khaled Saffuri, helped arrange meetings between Islamic leaders and senior Bush administration officials.

According to the *Washington Post*, federal agents since the mid-1990s had sought to track an estimated $1.7 billion that moved between these organizations. Investigators said the groups were created in the 1970s by the al-Rajhi family, one of Saudi Arabia's primary banking dynasties. Collectively, the organizations own or control a number of businesses worldwide. A spokesman for the al-Rajhis denied any wrongdoing on their part.

One example of the intricate and complex transactions of these groups came in 2000 when the York Foundation, whose president was M. Yaqub Mirza, who also headed the SAAR-Safa network, received $400,000 from Safa. Later that year, York sent $400,000 to a related entity named the York International Trust located on the Isle of Man, a notorious tax haven where tax records are kept private.

Federal officials said the government raids were part of a broader effort to track funds through Saudi charities and firms that end up in the hands of al-Qaeda and Hamas.

Attorney John Loftus, who once tracked Nazis for the Justice Department and now represents intelligence community whistle-blowers, said he had notified the government on March 11 that he was preparing to file a lawsuit in Florida that would spell out the connections between some of the Muslim organizations and the Saudis. Speaking of the federal raids taking place as he prepared his lawsuit, Loftus said, "There was no coincidence."

Muslim leader Talat Othman is a longtime Bush family associate and offered a benediction during the 2000 Republican National Convention in Philadelphia. Othman served on the board of directors of Harken Energy Corp. along with George W. Bush in the 1980s and has been a significant campaign contributor to both son and father Bush.

Following the federal raids of Islamic groups in Virginia, Othman joined other Muslim activists in a meeting complaining to Treasury Secretary Paul O'Neill, whose agents had participated in the raids.

In a speech in fall 2001 to an Islamic conference in Qatar, Jamal Barzinji, president of Safa Trust, boasted of Muslim influence in the Bush White House, saying, "At this time, the President and his administration are continually seeking the counsel and input of American Muslim leaders. At no other time has the Muslim community in America been more effective in relation to the processes of American government."

Another example of Saudi aid to Osama bin Laden, though perhaps unintentionally, is the case of a former employee at the U.S. Consulate in Saudi Arabia who took bribes to provide fake visas. Abdullah Noman, fifty-four, a citizen of Yemen, worked at the consulate from September 1996 until November 2001. He admitted to taking bribes of both money and gifts worth thousands of dollars in exchange for visas for entry into the United States, making it appear that the bearers were members of legitimate trade delegations. "They would come in with everybody else and then disappear," noted Assistant U.S. Attorney Lee Vilker.

Vilker said there was no known connection between Noman and al-Qaeda terrorists but he admitted that authorities had not been able to locate all those who obtained visas from Noman, who was arrested in Las Vegas in late 2001 while accompanying a Middle Eastern trade delegation. He faced a prison term of fifteen years and a $250,000 fine plus deportation after serving time.

But even more ominous revelations came in 2002 from Michael Springman, a twenty-year veteran of the U.S. Foreign Service and former chief of the American visa bureau in Jeddah, Saudi Arabia, who told of suspicious behavior there years ago.

In a *BBC News* interview, Springman said, "In Saudi Arabia, I was repeatedly ordered by high level State Department officials to issue visas to unqualified applicants. These were, essentially, people who had no ties either to Saudi Arabia or to their own country. I complained bitterly at the time there. I returned to the U.S., I complained to the State Department here, to the General Accounting Office, the Bureau of Diplomatic Security and to the Inspector General's office. I was met with silence.

"What I was protesting was, in reality, an effort to bring recruits, rounded up by Osama bin Laden, to the U.S. for terrorist training for the CIA. They would then be returned to Afghanistan to fight against the then-Soviets."

The attack on the World Trade Center in 1993 did not shake the State Department's faith in the Saudis, nor did the attack on the American barracks at Khobar Towers in Saudi Arabia three years later, in which nineteen Americans died. FBI agents began to feel their investigation was being obstructed."

Part III – Reaction to September 11, 2001

"In order to make sure that we're able to conduct a winning victory, we've got to have the best intelligence we can possibly have. And my report to the nation is we've got the best intelligence we can possibly have."
-President George W. Bush in a September 26, 2001, speech to the CIA

Reaction to the attacks of 9/11 was so swift it lent support to the idea that planning for such reaction had been made months before. And the evidence indicates that planning for the War on Terrorism was indeed set into motion long before September 11.

On May 8, 2001, four months prior to the attacks and a week before convicted Oklahoma City bomber Timothy McVeigh was executed, the Bush administration was already addressing the problem of terrorism. On this day, Bush created a new office dedicated to national preparedness with the Federal Emergency Management Agency (FEMA) and named Vice President Dick Cheney to head a special task force to study terrorism and guide FEMA's antiterrorism efforts. Amazingly enough, such pre-9/11 contingency planning may have aided the success of the attacks.

The powerful but little publicized National Reconnaissance Office (NRO) had scheduled a test exercise for the morning of September 11, 2001, in which a corporate jet, crippled by mechanical failure, crashed into one of the four towers of the NRO headquarters building in Chantilly, Virginia, just about four miles from Washington's Dulles International Airport. No actual planes were to be used in the exercise but plans called for evacuating most of the three thousand NRO employees.

The exercise, later described as a "bizarre coincidence," was the brain-child of CIA officer John Fulton, who had been named chief of the NRO's strategic gaming division. A later announcement for a Homeland Security conference noted the exercise with the comment, "On the morning of September 11, 2001, Mr. Fulton and his team were running a pre-planned simulation to explore the emergency response issues that would be created if a plane were to strike a building. Little did they know that the scenario would come true in a dramatic way that day."

The exercise was canceled when the first plane struck the World Trade Center less than an hour before the test was to begin. All NRO employees, except for certain essential personnel, were sent home for the day.

Author Barbara Honegger pointed out the obvious lack of timely response to the 9/11 attacks, especially the one at the Pentagon, and suggested, "This is beyond comprehension over the nation's capital unless some previous piece of information or mental set led them to assume the Pentagon plane could not be a terrorist vehicle, or at least confuse them as to whether it was or not. If those looking on from inside the Pentagon as 9/11 unfolded believed Flight 77 was, or might be, part of a 'Red Team' counter-terror exercise set for that very morning, it would explain the otherwise incomprehensible delay, almost to the point of paralysis, in effectively scrambling interceptors."

Honegger, in her book *October Surprise*, revealed the elder Bush's role in dealing with Iranian terrorists to ensure the election of Ronald Reagan in 1980. She advanced the idea that the 9/11 attacks as a homegrown concept might explain why the leak of a September 10, 2001, NSA intercept message upset Vice President Cheney so much. That message reportedly was between hijacker leader Mohammed Atta and the purported attack mastermind, Khalid Shaikh Mohammed. It stated, "The Match is about to begin. Tomorrow is zero hour."

"'Match,' of course, is what you would expect if the speaker were referring to his discovery of the date that the US government had selected to conduct its counter-terror simulation/exercise on the scenario of plane(s) crashing into government buildings - one that was about to turn very real when the terrorists 'piggybacked' their long-planned plot onto it given the context in which all this finally begins to make sense, Atta was merely communicating to his boss, or visa versa, the date that the U.S. government exercise was to take place. Bin al-Shibh, Atta, and Mohammed didn't choose the date. The U.S. government did.

"That's why [Cheney] was in the White House Sit[uation] Room; and why President Bush kept reading to grammar school kids in Florida long after he should have instantly broken it off to perform his emergency duties as Commander-in-Chief. The reason was that Bush 'knew' - or thought he knew - that it was just a game," she added.

Could this NRO exercise explain the incredible lack of response on the part of the government to the hijackings on 9/11? If this could be a legitimate explanation for the lack of timely response, how come no one in government has offered it to the public?

A botched government exercise might also explain why so much of the material on still-missing Khalid Shaikh Mohammed remains classified. He might well be a U.S. intelligence "asset" that was actually working for someone else. And the 9/11 attacks may indeed have been a conspiracy wrapped inside another conspiracy, exactly as it appears to have been in the Murrah Federal Building bombing, both involving Middle Eastern terrorists.

Cheney's terrorism task force was scheduled to produce antiterrorism recommendations for Congress by October 1, 2001. Of course, by that time, the nation was well into the new War on Terrorism.

During that same time, Cheney also was in charge of another task force reviewing national energy policy. This panel later became the center of controversy when California's power woes indicated that corporate energy executives had unduly influenced national policies. Near the end of 2002, Cheney's task force was still refusing to hand over its internal papers and one GAO lawyer said suits concerning Cheney's energy group could continue through the 2004 election year. One setback came in early December 2002 when a Bush appointee, Federal District Judge John Bates, refused to support a Government Accounting Office (GAO) request for a court order demanding that Cheney's committee turn over its internal papers. Bates argued that since neither the House nor Senate had subpoenaed such documents and since the seven congressmen who supported the GAO request were all Democrats, he declined to set "such unprecedented judicial action." "What are they hiding?" asked Connecticut's Joseph Lieberman, one of the seven lawmakers supporting the GAO. Lieberman added that the public has a right to know who is influencing our national energy policy. It was known that Cheney met at least six times with officials of the failed energy company Enron.

In prophetic testimony before joint hearings of the Senate Armed Services Appropriations and Intelligence Committees in spring 2001, Secretary of State Colin Powell declared, "If we adopted this hunkered down attitude, behind our concrete and our barbed wire, the terrorists would have achieved a kind of victory."

After the 9/11 attacks, the rhetoric changed completely as new and constitutionally questionable laws and regulations were put into effect. Within days of the 9/11 attacks, President Bush declared a "War on Terrorism." Actually, he initially called it a crusade, but that term was quickly dropped when it was pointed out that Muslims, both within and without the Middle East, still remember the history of the word.

To initiate a war, there first must be a perceived enemy. That one grand enemy was Osama bin Laden and his al-Qaeda network. With almost unbelievable speed, the FBI announced a list of the suspected hijackers while at the same time acknowledging that the men used false identity papers. This list was questioned in many quarters, including government intelligence agents.

"There are people within the U.S. intelligence community who doubt that the hijacker list from 9/11 has much truth in it," one unnamed intelligence source was quoted by Internet writer Jon Rappoport. "They see it as a more or less invented list. They know that if you start with men showing false passports (or no passports) to get on four planes on 9/11, you can't assemble a correct list of nineteen suspects within a few days - especially since all those men are presumed dead and missing, untraceable.

"Al-Qaeda is being used as a term to convince people that these terrorists are all connected in a vast, very well organized network that is global in reach, that has a very sophisticated and far-flung communication set-up, that issues orders from the top down to cells all over the world," stated the intelligence source. "There are a number of people inside the U.S. intelligence agencies who know this is a false picture. They know that false intelligence is being assembled in order to paint this picture which is distorted, so that the American people will have a single focus on one grand evil enemy."

So began the War on Terrorism, yet few felt any more secure than before 9/11.

Creating Homeland Security

If the idea of strong federal protection during times of terrorist acts seems comforting, picture this: A pimple-faced eighteen-year-old dressed in camouflage and armed with a fully loaded M-16 arrives at your door and informs you that you must leave your home and come with him because the authorities fear a biological attack in your city. If you protest and say you'll stay and take your chances, you are in violation of the law and subject to arrest, fine and imprisonment. Then, after seeing the kid's armed companions, you decide to join your neighbors in a military truck destined for a "relocation camp" located more than fifty miles from your home. At the camp, you are instructed to stand in line for a vaccination against smallpox, anthrax or whatever the latest threat might be. If you refuse the inoculation, recalling that in past years so many such vaccines were proven to be tainted, you are again subject to fine and jail.

If this sounds like some paranoid's view of an Orwellian nightmare, you should know that laws authorizing such action had already been passed in sixteen states and the District of Columbia by the end of 2002. And don't take comfort if your state is not among these as most of this overreaching law was incorporated into the Homeland Security legislation.

Many states modified or outright rejected this legislation, which was drawn up as a model law for the federal Centers for Disease Control and Prevention following the anthrax attack that came on the heels of 9/11. The law was then sent to each state legislature with a federal endorsement for its passage. Federal officials claimed the laws were needed to provide local authorities the legal right to make quick decisions in an emergency involving contagious or deadly pathogens.

One advocate, Attorney Gene Matthews with the Department of Health and Human Services, argued, "We have not used emergency powers in probably fifty years. This is something we need to attend to."

Under this Model State Emergency Health Powers Act, authorities would be able to federalize all medical personnel, from EMTs to physicians, and enforce quarantines. They would have the right to vaccinate the public, with or without their consent, seize and destroy private property without compensation and ration medical supplies, food, fuel and water in a declared emergency.

By mid-2002, the District of Columbia as well as Maine, New Hampshire, Maryland, Virginia, South Carolina, Georgia, Tennessee, Florida, Missouri, Oklahoma, Minnesota, South Dakota, Utah, Arizona and New Mexico had passed all or parts of the model law. The other states had either rejected or stalled the legislation.

"[This act] goes far beyond bioterrorism," said Andrew Schlafly of the Association of American Physicians and Surgeons. "Unelected state officials can force treatment or vaccination of citizens against the advice of their doctors."

The Federal Emergency Management Agency (FEMA), designated as the lead agency under the new Department of Homeland Security, also has plans in its files for the evacuation of cities and sprawling temporary camps to house their residents.

Under planning for the War on Terrorism, FEMA has dusted off and augmented contingency plans to counter the effects of nuclear, biological and chemical attacks.

By mid-2002, FEMA was notifying its vendors, contractors and consultants to envision the logistics of millions of displaced Americans forced to leave cities that come under attack. The firms were given a deadline of January 2003 to be ready to establish such displaced person camps. FEMA made it known that it already has ordered significant numbers of tents and trailers to be used for housing. Well into the year

2002, incremental but significant changes were being made to the American system. This movement culminated in hurried passage of the Homeland Security bill in late November. This act, which authorized a whole new cabinet-level department, was the greatest restructuring of the federal government since the National Security Act of 1947 yet with none of its deliberation and review.

History has provided proof that traditional American openness and fairness will not necessarily be supported by the nation's highest authorities.

During the War Between the States, President Abraham Lincoln suspended the writ of habeas corpus, that mainstay of American justice that demands that the accused has the right to face his accusers. This action was later overturned by the U.S. Supreme Court but only because Lincoln had not sought approval from Congress.

During World War I, that same court upheld the right of the president to seize the property of enemy aliens without a hearing, stating, "National security might not be able to afford the luxuries of litigation and the long delays which preliminary hearings traditionally have entailed."

And, of course, the Supreme Court upheld the rounding up, incarceration and property seizure of Japanese Americans following the attack on Pearl Harbor.

Many Americans, from leading academics to Joe SixPack, wondered aloud what would become of traditional American liberties. Frank Serpico, the former New York policeman who turned in corrupt comrades in the 1960s and was the object of a popular film, spoke at a July 4, 2002, reading of the Declaration of Independence in Chatham, New York.

"It is my opinion that never before have we, as a nation, stood in greater danger of losing our individual liberties as we are today," he told the audience. "We, the people of this great nation, are being punished for the transgressions of our leaders and their consorts. When I still have the freedom to speak, I'll always use it." Ironically, several in the audience there to hear Serpico read the Declaration of Independence booed his remarks.

Even former attorney general Janet Reno, under whose leadership the tragedies at Ruby Ridge and Waco unfolded, expressed concern. "I have trouble with a war that has no endgame and I have trouble with a war that generates so many concerns about individual liberties," she told an audience at Old Dominion University in Norfolk, Virginia, in 2002.

Reno asked Americans to remember the lessons learned from the unjust imprisonment of Japanese Americans during World War II and added that she believed the government could be hard pressed to find a legal basis to prosecute many of the Taliban and al-Qaeda prisoners detained at Guantanamo Bay Naval Base in Cuba.

By November 3, 2001, more than 1,147 persons were being held without bail and without legal representation in connection with the 9/11 attacks by the U.S. government.

This action prompted cries of outrage from civil libertarians and even some congressmen. Senator Patrick J. Leahy of Vermont said the use of military tribunals could send "a message to the world that it is acceptable to hold secret trials and summary executions without the possibility of judicial review, at least when the defendant is a foreign national." In the days following the 9/11 attacks it was found that letters addressed to Osama bin Laden in Afghanistan were being held by the U.S. postal service. When Justice Department investigators wanted to open them, the Postal Service sought advice from the Customs Service. Customs rules prohibited the opening of private mail without a warrant based on probable cause, sound policy in a free society. "The mere fact that envelopes were addressed to Osama bin Laden without any other evidence was considered to be insufficient to establish probable cause to obtain a warrant authorizing the search of the envelopes," argued officials at the Custom's Service. The mail was allowed to proceed to Afghanistan. There was no word if anyone thought to stake out Osama's mailbox and perhaps catch the world's most wanted man. Editors at *U.S. News & World Report* seemed proud of the fact that "Congress has changed those silly rules and from now on Osama's mail and packages can be opened."

Presumably this could include anyone else's mail since in the pell-mell rush to wage war on terrorism, such niceties as legal warrants based on probable cause have fallen by the wayside.

Less than a month after the 9/11 attacks, Tom Ridge, a former governor of Pennsylvania, stepped into his new office only steps away from the Oval Office of President Bush, the man who created his job. Ridge's new job was chief of the Office of Homeland Security. Here was the man who was to coordinate forty-six different federal government agencies in an effort to protect the American people from terrorists, a position then scheduled to become a permanent government department.

It was announced that Ridge would work in conjunction with Bush's deputy national security advisor, Army General Wayne Downing, indicating that the military would play a prominent role in counterterrorism activities. No one thought to ask if this was a violation of the Posse Comitatus Act (PCA), the law that prohibits the U.S. military from conducting law enforcement duties against the American public.

It is a law that has never really been challenged in this nation's history because it addresses a concern dating back to the days of the American Revolution and has all but been forgotten today. The act embodies the traditional principle of separation of military and civilian authority, one of the fundamental precepts of our form of government.

The early colonists were distressed at being placed at the mercy of King George's troops and being forced to feed and quarter them. But the Posse Comitatus Act, Latin for a "companion group to law enforcement," a posse, was passed in 1878 as a direct result of the outrage over Reconstruction in the South following the War Between the States. Southern states were at the mercy of military authorities, many of whom proved inept or corrupt.

Yet, in recent years this act has been slowly shredded, beginning at least in 1981 when Congress allowed an exception to be made in the PCA for the War on Drugs. The military was allowed to be used for drug interdiction along the nation's borders. This small and what appeared to be sensible action at the time soon grew out of proportion. In 1989, Congress, still unable to come to grips with the true causes of drug abuse, designated the Department of Defense as the lead agency in drug interdiction.

In the tragedy at Waco on April 19, 1993, military snipers were on hand and tanks were used to bulldoze the burning Branch Davidian church. Use of the Fort Hood tanks came about because federal officials used the pretext that the Davidians were involved with drugs. No evidence of drugs was ever found. On April 19, 1995, when the Murrah Federal Building in Oklahoma City was bombed, President Clinton proposed yet another exception to the PCA to allow the military to aid civilian investigators looking into weapons of mass destruction. About this same time Congress considered but did not pass legislation to allow troops to enforce customs and immigration laws at the borders.

During the 1996 presidential campaign, Bob Dole promised to heighten the military's role in the War on Drugs, while another primary contender, Lamar Alexander, suggested that a new branch of the military be formed and substituted for the INS and Border Patrol.

"The need for reaffirmation of the PCA's principle is increasing," wrote Matthew Hammond in the *Washington University Law Quarterly* in 1997, "because in recent years, Congress and the public have seen the military as a panacea for domestic problems."

He added, "Major and minor exceptions to the PCA, which allow the use of the military in law enforcement roles, blur the line between military and civilian roles, undermine civilian control of the military, damage military readiness, and inefficiently solve the problems they supposedly address. Additionally, increasing the role of the military would strengthen the federal law enforcement apparatus that is currently [1997] under close scrutiny for overreaching its authority. Although it seems benign, such an increase in military authority revives fears of past overreaching during the late 1960s."

Yet in the wake of 9/11, military troops were seen patrolling airports and the streets of Washington and New York with no outcry from a citizenry appreciative of perceived new security. We have already had brief glimpses of how it will be to live under a martial law situation by observing recent airport security, as applied to the public, especially those old enough to remember what true freedom was like.

Eighty-year-old Fred Hubbell, a retired engineer from Texas visiting in Connecticut, was arrested and handcuffed at Bradley International Airport in August 2002 for mentioning one word. Cranky after enduring repeated searches at the airport, the World War II veteran observed a security guard poking through his wallet "What do you expect to find in there, a rifle?" Hubbell asked sarcastically. "Do you think that was an appropriate remark?" responded the guard. "I do," replied Hubbell, who was promptly arrested.

Judy Powell, a fifty-five-year-old tourist from Britain, bought a GI Joe toy soldier in Las Vegas and packed it in her bag for her return flight home. But she was refused boarding privileges when an airport security officer spotted GI Joe's tiny plastic rifle. "I was simply stunned when I realized they were serious," said Mrs. Powell. "I was really angry to start with because of the absurdity of the situation. But then I saw the funny side of it and thought this was simple lunacy." A spokesman for Los Angeles International Airport defended the action, saying, "We have instructions to confiscate anything that looks like a weapon or a replica. If GI Joe was carrying a replica then it had to be taken from him."

One can imagine Sergeant Schultz of *Hogan's Heroes* explaining, "I vas chust following orders." It is such unthinking responses to orders that so trouble civil libertarians.

And as always, planning for the eventuality of martial law did not start with the terrorist attacks on 9/11; just ask the residents of Kingsville, Texas.

Beginning on the night of February 8, 1999, a series of mock battles using live ammunition erupted around the twenty-five thousand inhabitants of the town, located near Corpus Christi. In a military operation named Operation Last Dance, eight black helicopters roared over the town. One nearly crashed when it hit the top of a telephone pole and started a fire near a home. Soldiers of the elite 160th Special Operations Aviation Regiment, known as the "Night Stalkers," ferried by the choppers, staged an attack on two empty buildings using real explosives and live ammunition. During the action, an abandoned police station was accidentally set on fire and a gas station was badly damaged when one or more helicopters landed on its roof.

Citizens of Kingsville were terrified during the drill as only Police Chief Felipe Garza and Mayor Phil Esquivel were notified of the attack in advance. Both men refused to give any details of the operation, insisting they had been sworn to secrecy by the military. Only Arthur Rogers, the assistant police chief, would admit to what happened. "The United States Army Special Operations Command was conducting a training exercise in our area," he said but refused to provide any details.

Local emergency management coordinator for FEMA, Tomas Sanchez, was not happy with the frightening attack and the lack of information and warning. Sanchez, a decorated Vietnam veteran with thirty years' service in naval intelligence, was asked what the attack was all about. He replied that based on his background and knowledge, the attack was an operational exercise based on a scenario where "Martial law has been declared through the Presidential Powers and War Powers Act, and some citizens have refused to give up their weapons. They have taken over two of the buildings in Kingsville. The police cannot handle it. So you call these guys in. They show up and they zap everybody, take all the weapons and let the local PD clean it up."

One resident told a reporter, "This is total BS. If we don't stop it now it's going to get worse."

Asked for comment, then Texas governor George W. Bush said it was not his job to get involved in the concerns over the Night Stalkers using live ammunition in a civilian area of his state.

Sanchez and other military experts told World Net Daily that the night attack indicated the use of Presidential Decision Directive (PDD) 25, a top-secret document that apparently authorizes military participation in domestic police situations. Some speculated that PDD 25 may have surreptitiously superceded the 1878 Posse Comitatus Act.

The events in Kingsville may date as far back as 1971, when plans were drawn up to merge the military with police and the National Guard (State Guards were gradually eliminated during the past two decades). In that year, Senator Sam Ervin's Subcommittee on Constitutional Rights discovered that military intelligence has established an intricate surveillance system to spy on hundreds of thousands of American citizen's, mostly

antiwar protesters. This plan was code-named "Garden Plot." Britt Snider, who worked for the subcommittee, said the plans seemed too vague to get excited about. "We could never find any kind of unifying purpose behind it all," he told a reporter. "It looked like an aimless kind of thing."

Four years later Garden Plot began to come into sharper focus. "[C]ode-named Cable Splicer [and] covering California, Oregon, Washington and Arizona, under the command of the Sixth Army, [it] is a plan that outlines extraordinary military procedures to stamp out unrest in this country," reported Ron Ridenhour and Arthur Lubow in *New Times.* "Developed in a series of California meetings from 1968 to 1972, Cable Splicer is a war plan that was adapted for domestic use procedures used by the U.S. Army in Vietnam. Although many facts still remain behind Pentagon smoke screens, Cable Splicer [documents] reveal the shape of the monster that the Ervin committee was tracking down."

During the time of Cable Splicer, several full-scale war games were conducted with local officials and police working side by side with military officers in civilian clothing. Many policemen were taught military urban pacification techniques. They returned to their departments and helped create the early SWAT (Special Weapons and Tactics) teams.

Representative Clair Burgener of California, a staunch Reagan Republican who had attended the Cable Splicer II kickoff conference, was flabbergasted when shown Cable Splicer documents. "I've read *Seven Days in May* and all those scary books and they're scary! This is what I call subversive."

Subcommittee chief counsel Doug Lee read through the documents and blurted, "Unbelievable. These guys are crazy! We're the enemy! This is civil war they're talking about here. Half the country has been designated as the enemy." Snider agreed, stating, "If there ever was a model for a takeover, this is it."

The War on Terrorism has provided the pretext for the activation of plans such as Cable Splicer, a clear violation of the Posse Comitatus Act. In June 2001, despite promises by the Bush administration that it would not initiate any new intelligence reforms until after the joint congressional committees had completed their inquiry into the 9/11 attacks, the Pentagon quietly requested to create a powerful new position - undersecretary of defense for intelligence. This request for yet another layer of authority was inserted into a Senate defense bill slated for Congress's approval.

"The Pentagon's gambit has been such a brilliant stealth attack that many members of Congress aren't even aware it is happening, let alone what it means," noted reporter Linda Robinson. "No hearings have been held, and Pentagon officials portray it as merely an internal managerial matter with few broader implications. But intelligence officials and experts say that could not be further from the truth. The new under secretary position is a bureaucratic coup that accomplishes many Pentagon goals in one fell swoop."

Insiders thought this slippery move served to garner even more power into the hands of top Bush administration officials Dick Cheney and Donald Rumsfeld. The man in line to become the new undersecretary for intelligence is Richard Haver. Haver was Rumsfeld's special assistant for intelligence and was Cheney's very first assistant secretary of defense for intelligence in the elder Bush's administration.

Even if the Posse Comitatus Act is rewritten or eliminated, the most recent exploits of the military do not inspire confidence. Following the 9/11 attacks, the Defense Department announced the creation of an Office of Strategic Information designed to present a more favorable view of the U.S. military to foreign news media. The new unit provoked an immediate controversy when it was learned that it planned to influence international opinion by planting false stories in the foreign media. Critics felt such phony stories might find their way back to the domestic media. This, of course, was nothing new. The CIA had done the same thing for years but this was too open and blatant. Even the major media, including the *New York Times*, was stirred to action.

In a rare step backward, the government announced that in early 2002 the office would be closed. Rumsfeld, while arguing that criticism of the office was "off the mark," nevertheless admitted that "the office has been so damaged that it is clear to me, it's pretty clear to me that it cannot function."

Later, in late summer 2002, the U.S. military engaged in "Millennium Challenge 2002," the largest military exercise conducted to that time, involving thirteen thousand troops. Additional foreign soldiers were called upon due to the fact that so many U.S. units were overseas. The scenario, largely conducted through computers, called for operations against a mythical rogue military commander operating in the Middle East.

The man in charge of the "enemy" forces was retired Marine Lieutenant General Paul Van Riper, and he played his part to the hilt. Instead of confronting the high-tech American military head-on, the general had his couriers send messages by hand to avoid electronic surveillance and his attack orders were shouted from mosques in the "enemy" nation. He also sent small boats and civilian planes filled with theoretical suicide-bent terrorists against the U.S. fleet.

Theoretically, Van Riper won. The friendly force commander was forced to reconstitute most of the U.S. fleet in order to continue.

Pentagon officials claimed Riper didn't play fair and reworked the exercise but denied that it was slanted toward an allied win. Riper, for his part, resigned in disgust, claiming the war game was fixed to avoid exposing flaws in the high-tech tactics favored by Rumsfeld. Some commentators even advanced the notion that the United States' slowness in attacking Iraq might have been due to the poor showing of the U.S. military in these war games.

Causing further anxiety among knowledgeable persons was a plan revealed in late 2002 for the U.S. Army to use computers to investigate hundreds of thousands of
law-abiding Americans on the chance one might be a terrorist. The plan called for the Army's Intelligence and Security Command (INSCOM), headquartered at Fort Belvoir, Virginia, to use high-powered computers to secretly search email messages, credit card purchases, telephone records and bank statements on the chance that one might be associated, or sympathetic to, terrorists. Known as the Pentagon's new Office of Information Awareness (OIA), this organization was to create a "vast centralized database" filled with information on the most minute details of citizens' private lives.

To add insult to injury in the minds of opponents of this plan was the appointment of former national security adviser Vice Admiral John Poindexter to head this new office. Poindexter lost his national security adviser job after being convicted of lying to Congress, defrauding the government and destroying evidence in the Iran-Contra scandal. That scandal involved the illegal sale of weapons to Iran and the profits being sent illegally to the CIA-backed "Contra" army fighting in Nicaragua, all done in defiance of Congress. But as vice president of Syntek Technologies, Poindexter worked with the Defense Advanced Research Projects Agency (DARPA) to develop Genoa, a powerful search engine and information harvesting program.

Critics, already suspicious over such an overreaching program so susceptible to abuse, were not assuaged by the DARPA logo, which depicts the occult "all-seeing eye" of knowledge perched on a pyramid looking over an image of the Earth.

Christopher H. Pyle, a teacher of constitutional law and civil liberties at Mount Holyoke College in Massachusetts, wrote, "That law enforcement agencies would search for terrorists makes sense. Terrorists are criminals. But why the Army? It is a criminal offense for Army personnel to become directly involved in civilian law enforcement [the Posse Comitatus law]. Are they seeking to identify anti-war demonstrators whom they harassed in the 1960s? Are they getting ready to round up more civilians for detention without trial, as they did to Japanese Americans during World War II? Is counterterrorism becoming the sort of investigative obsession that anti-Communism was in the 1950s and 1960s, with all the bureaucratic excesses and abuses that entailed? This isn't the first time that the military has slipped the bounds of law to spy on civilians. In the late 1960s, it secretly gathered personal information on more than a million law-abiding Americans in a misguided effort to quell anti-war demonstrations, predict riots and discredit protesters. I know because in 1970, as a former captain in Army intelligence, I disclosed the existence of that program."

Pyle, in writing two book-length reports on the army's spying for Senator Sam Ervin's Subcommittee on Constitutional Rights, was struck by the harm that could be done if the government ever gained untraceable access to the financial records and private communications of its critics. "Army intelligence was nowhere near as bad as the FBI [with its infamous COINTEL program], but it responded to my criticisms by putting me on Nixon's 'enemies list,' which meant a punitive tax audit. It also tried to monitor my mail and prevent me from testifying before Congress by spreading false stories that I had fathered illegitimate children. I often wondered what the intelligence community could do to people like me if it really became efficient." It is now becoming efficient, thanks to the computer, yet the public awareness of the danger is not near as great as it was in the pre-computer 1970s.

Many people fear any control over the civilian population by the military will lead to draconian measures such as the establishment of large concentration camps. FEMA's call for contractors to build such camps did little to assuage the anxiety of the more extreme conspiracy minded. The Internet is alive with sites detailing a string of concentration camps across America, just primed and waiting for the lines of detainees or dissidents to be marched through their gates.

Most people pay little attention to what they perceive as paranoid delusions, however the record clearly shows that such camps do exist. Many such camps are in actuality military bases, either reported closed or maintained by skeleton crews. Some were even World War II camps for Axis prisoners and others are operated by FEMA. For example, Fort Chaffee, Arizona, was used to house Cubans sent to the United States during Castro's Mariel Boatlift of 1980 and Elgin AFB was used to hold a group of Haitians who tried to enter the country in fall 2002.

"In actuality, there are two true sets of camps. First is the military, which can use any base at will to house detainees. Fort Chaffee, for instance, has in the past had warehouses full of mattresses, bunks, barbed-wire rolls, fence posts, etc. All of these were to be used around empty barracks to provide for a detention facility if needed. Some of the 'closed' military bases have been designated as 'emergency holding facilities' and already have barracks, mess halls, compounds and latrines in place. All they need are guards, administrators, logistics people and they're in business. All this can be accomplished in seventy-two hours. Operational plans are in existence for the 'handling of civilian prisoners and laborers on military installations, both male and female," said author and retired Lieutenant. Colonel Craig Roberts (USAR). "The second category is FEMA. We know they have let a contract for 1,000 'emergency relocation camps' in case of widespread terrorism, biological or chemical attacks on the cities. Again, this can be speedy. The president can declare a national emergency, evoke [Executive Order] 11490, and take over the country without deferring to Congress or the Constitution. Bingo! New World Order in a couple of days."

Roberts said the most ominous of these potential concentration camps is located at Elmendorf AFB in Alaska. "Millions of acres adjoining this base have been deeded to the federal government by the State of Alaska. Its designated use is for a 'mental health facility.' It is our version of Siberia and the gulag," he added.

The creation and maintenance - even the very existence - of such camps is lost in a maze of such Executive Orders (EO) dating back to World War II. Many EOs can be traced to the Kennedy presidency and were issued under the duress of the Cold War and the Cuban Missile Crisis. Many of the EOs detailed on the Internet are outdated, canceled, revoked or superceded by others. Even a careful search of the Federal Register Web site failed to clarify this issue.

It is clear from the FEMA Web site that that agency has many plans - including what to do in case of tornadoes, hurricanes, and flooding, in addition to a nuclear or biological strike - that include evacuation of major cities. Where are those people to go? Who will feed them? How will they live? The answers to these questions remain elusive. And in the meantime, dozens of large military installations sit, mutely awaiting future inhabitants.

As the Department of Homeland Security moved closer to reality in 2002, the U.S. military was also reshuffling its command structure to include a new United Command Plan, which would include a new combatant command responsible for homeland security called U.S. Northern Command (USNORTHCOM). Headed by at least a four-star general or Flag Officer, USNORTHCOM would control all military efforts in North America, to include Alaska, Canada, the United States and Mexico and out to five hundred nautical miles offshore. Conceived as part of the response to the War on Terrorism, an "appropriate" role also was under consideration for USNORTHCOM in the flagging War on Drugs.

Even though the Posse Comitatus Act seems to have been largely ignored in recent years, there were ongoing calls to alter or even abolish the law. In an October 2001 letter to Rumsfeld, Senator John Warner, a Republican from Virginia and a member of the Council on Foreign Relations, wrote, "Should this law [PCA] now be changed to enable our active-duty military to more fully join other domestic assets in this war against terrorism?"

This cry continued into late 2002 when Representative. Tom Trancredo, along with members of the Immigration Reform Caucus and families of victims slain in the course of immigration troubles, presented Congress with a petition demanding that military troops patrol the U.S. borders. Jumping on the antiterrorist bandwagon, Trancredo stated, "As long as our borders remain undefended, we cannot claim that we are doing everything possible to protect the nation from terrorism. It's time to authorize the deployment of military assets on our borders."

But "military assets" may lie at the heart of the problem as many police officials, military and paramilitary men from many nations, even including some al-Qaeda operatives, were trained by the U.S. military. One such training center was the infamous facility at Fort Benning, Georgia, until recently known as the School of the Americas, which even produced a handbook on torture and assassination.

In early June 2002, Bush began urging the creation of a permanent, cabinet level position for Ridge. And Ridge was calling for bringing myriad government agencies under one central control. And it all needed to be done rapidly, Bush argued, because "we face an urgent need, and we must move quickly, this year, before the end of the congressional session." Thus began the push to create the Department of Homeland Security, with Ridge holding a cabinet-level position controlling more than 170,000 federal employees and 22 federal agencies.

But Bush would not allow Ridge to confront Congress directly, claiming he was simply an adviser, not a policy maker. Congress fumed but, as usual, rolled over and played dead.

"The real losers are the American people." groused Senator Robert Byrd, a Democrat from West Virginia. "The Congress and the American people are forced to learn about the administration's homeland security efforts in piecemeal, patchwork fashion."

On July 15, 2002, Ridge finally submitted a written statement to the House Select Committee on Homeland Security. In it, Ridge stated, "We are today a Nation at risk to terrorist attacks and will remain so for the foreseeable future. The terrorist threat to America takes many forms, has many places to hide, and is often invisible. Yet the need for improved homeland security is not tied solely to today's terrorist threat. It is tied to our enduring vulnerability."

Ridge said in studying how best to implement homeland security, it became clear that the federal government would need reorganization, that "the structure of the federal government must be adapted to meet the challenges before us." He admitted that this new reorganization would result in the most significant transformation of the U.S. government in over a half century.

"It would transform and largely realign the government's confusing patchwork of homeland security activities into a single department whose primary mission is to protect our homeland," he wrote, adding the new department must have the "right set of tools to work with" and that undue oversight would be "damaging to the new Department's ability to carry out its mission successfully."

He stated that FEMA would be a leading component of the new Homeland Security Department. "The new Department would build on FEMA to consolidate the federal government's emergency response assets to better prepare all those pieces for all emergencies, both natural and man-made", stated Ridge. "Under the President's proposal, the Department of Homeland Security would consolidate existing federal government emergency response plans into one genuinely all-hazard plan, the Federal Incident Management Plan, and thereby eliminating the "crisis management" and "consequence management" distinction. This plan would cover all incidents of national significance, including acts of bioterrorism and agroterrorism, and would clarify roles and expected contributions of various emergency response bodies at different levels of government in the wake of a terrorist attack."

In addition to FEMA, the Office for Domestic Preparedness of the Office of Justice Programs, the National Domestic Preparedness Office of the FBI, the Domestic Emergency Support Teams of the Department of Justice, the Office of the Assistant Secretary for Public Health Emergency Preparedness (including the Office of Emergency Preparedness, the National Disaster Medical System, and the Metropolitan Medical Response System) of the Department of Health and Human Services (HHS), and the Strategic National Stockpile of HHS would be under the new chain of command.

He added that in a national emergency, Homeland Security would "provide a line of authority from the President through the Secretary of Homeland Security to one on-site federal coordinator. The single federal coordinator would be responsible to the President for coordinating the entire federal response to incidents of national significance." In vague generalities, Ridge indicated he sought changes deep within the American infrastructure. "We must therefore promote the efficient and reliable flow of people, goods, and services across borders, while preventing terrorists from using transportation conveyances or systems to deliver implements of destruction," he stated.

How to accomplish this? Ridge explained that "the principal border and transportation security agencies, the U.S. Customs Service, the U.S. Coast Guard, the Immigration and Naturalization Service (INS), the Animal and Plant Health Inspection Service, and the Transportation Security Administration, would be unified within a single, powerful division of the new Department of Homeland Security. The new Department also would control the issuance of visas to foreigners through the Department of State and would coordinate the border-control activities of all federal agencies that are not incorporated within the new Department. As a result, the Department would have sole responsibility for managing entry of people and goods into the United States and protecting our transportation infrastructure."

He added that the federal budget for 2003 provided $7.1 billion to the U.S. Coast Guard, "both the largest increase and the highest level of funding in Coast Guard history."

Ridge said his new department would also include "the U.S. Department of Agriculture's Animal and Plant Health Inspection Service, the agency that prevents and manages outbreaks of diseases and pests, and the Plum Island Disease Facility in the new Department to ensure integrated plans to address the threat of agroterrorism," and he mentioned control over the distribution of pharmaceuticals and medical supplies as well as a network of laboratories to "provide a multidisciplinary environment for developing and demonstrating new technologies for homeland security and would maintain a critical mass of scientific and engineering talent".

"The Department would establish a central management and research facility with satellite centers of excellence located at various national laboratories. A number of programs already exist at our National Laboratories that will benefit homeland security. These programs, most of which grew as part of various national security activities, would be transferred to the control and sponsorship of the new Department of Homeland Security."

Ridge argued that since a "core mission" of Homeland Security was detecting "weapons of mass destruction," the new department would engage in "the development of new technologies and systems for detecting fissile material at border crossings and technologies and systems that monitor the environment for the release of biological or chemical agents. The transfers to the new Department in this area would include $69 million in the Chemical and Biological National Security research and development program. In addition, the new Department would oversee $10 million in the Combating Nuclear Smuggling activity."

The new department also wanted transferred to its jurisdiction the new department the National Infrastructure Protection Center of the FBI, the National Communications System of the Department of Defense, the Critical Infrastructure Assurance Office of the Department of Commerce, the Computer Security Division of the National Institute of Standards and Technology, the National Infrastructure Simulation and Analysis Center of the Department of Energy, and the Federal Computer Incident Response Center of the General Services Administration.

Of course any effort to combat terrorism would require effective intelligence. So Ridge asked to incorporate the Department of Energy's National Laboratories in-house intelligence capabilities for assessing nuclear weapons and other WMD technologies throughout the world. This included analyses of Third World chemical, biological, and nuclear programs. He also asked that the Advanced Scientific Computing Research program, which supports researchers in applied mathematics and computer science, provide "a nucleus around which to grow Department of Homeland Security programs in, for example, advanced simulation, computer science, and scientific modeling to support such activities as complex nonlinear systems analysis, traffic flow modeling, and information extraction and analysis...

"To ensure that the new Department has access to all the intelligence and information it requires to assess terrorist threats, the draft legislation contains powerful assurances that the Secretary of Homeland Security will be provided such information by the intelligence community and federal law enforcement agencies," stated Ridge.

While Ridge paid some homage to the "longstanding principles" of the United States and said he believed that government intrusion into the daily lives of citizens should be strictly limited, he nevertheless noted that the president would serve as the ultimate authority over the control of sensitive intelligence information. "The President, as Commander-in-Chief, must have the ability to make decisions about how the Nation's most sensitive intelligence information is handled in order to carry out his sworn duties. The President will be able to exercise his authority in regard to intelligence distribution through such tools as Presidential Decision Directives and Executive Orders," Ridge explained.

"Therefore the new Homeland Security Department would incorporate the Secret Service and would have its director report directly to the Secretary of Homeland Security. It would also assume all authority for controlling the nation's borders."

"Terrorists are determined, opportunistic, and agile, and the Secretary [of Homeland Security] must build a department that can continually adapt to meet this rapidly changing threat," explained Ridge. "Moreover, even if our adversary were not so devious and nimble, the sheer organizational and management challenge confronting the new Secretary of Homeland Security is enormous. The creation of this new Department is larger and more complex than most corporate mega-mergers. History shows that a governmental reorganization of this magnitude is never easy. Providing the Secretary with the freedom to manage the Department is, therefore, profoundly important to achieving our goal of securing the homeland. Without this authority, an already challenging task will be far more difficult. If the new Department is to be greater than the sum of its parts, if it were not, it would obviously not be worth creating, its leadership must have the flexibility to organize it in the optimal way, create a new institutional culture, motivate and reward an outstanding workforce, and respond quickly to changing circumstances, emerging threats, and emergency situations."

In other words, give me the power and I will protect you.

None of this is really new. Plans to change America from a constitutional republic to an empirical state date back to 1984 when the Reagan National Security Council (NSC) drafted a plan to impose martial law in the United States through FEMA. Helping author this plan was marine Lieutenant Colonel Oliver North, who later admitted lying to Congress about a number of matters and has been rewarded by being hired as a highly paid talk show-host. But in 1987, when the plan leaked to the media, his work inspired a sharp protest from then attorney general William French Smith.

Arthur Liman, then chief counsel of the Senate Iran-Contra Committee, declared in a memo that North was at the center of what amounted to a "secret government-within-a-government,"a term similar to Bush's "shadow government." Officials at the time said North's involvement in the proposed plan to radically alter the American government by executive order was proof that he was involved in a wide range of secret activities, foreign and domestic, that went far beyond the Iran-Contra scandal.

North's shadow government plan called for suspension of the Constitution, turning control of the government over to the then largely unknown Federal Emergency Management Agency (FEMA), appointment of military commanders to run state and local governments and the declaration of martial law in the event of a crisis such as "nuclear war, violent and widespread internal dissent or national opposition to a U.S. military invasion abroad."

It's the last two scenarios that bother many people when they view the national events of today, especially since so many members of the Reagan administration are back in power. North, at the time he drafted these plans, was the NSC's liaison to FEMA.

Attorney General Smith was so alarmed at this plan to undercut the American constitutional republic that he fired off a letter to North's boss, Robert McFarlane, expressing the fear that FEMA was establishing itself as an "emergency czar."

This contingency plan was to be part of an executive order or legislative package that Reagan would sign but hold secretly within the NSC until such a time as a crisis arose. It was never announced whether Reagan signed the plan.

Could the consolidation of power within Homeland Security be a continuation of this plan? No one knows for certain as President Bush, shortly after the 9/11 attacks, ordered all records of former presidents, including Reagan, sealed from the public. To add to the concern was former Nixon counselor John Dean, who on June 7, 2002, warned that America was sliding into a "constitutional dictatorship" and martial law.

Further concerns were voiced by Timothy H. Edgar, legislative counsel for the American Civil Liberties Union, a nonpartisan, nonprofit organization dedicated to preserving civil liberties and the principles of constitutional democracy to include government openness and accountability.

In testimony to various congressional committees, Edgar noted that the Homeland Security Department would have substantial powers as well as more armed federal agents with arrest authority than any other government agency. He questioned whether the new department would have structural and legal safeguards to keep it open and accountable to the public.

"Unfortunately, the draft legislation not only fails to provide such safeguards, it eviscerates many of the safeguards that are available throughout the government and have worked well to safeguard the public interest," stated Edgar. He went on to enumerate the problem areas within the proposed Homeland Security Department, saying it:

- Hobbles the Freedom of Information Act (FOIA) by creating broad new exemptions to the act such as "any information voluntarily submitted to the department about threats to the nation's infrastructure." Edgar pointed out that exceptions to FOIA already include information concerning national security and sensitive law enforcement and confidential business information. "This is a deeply misguided proposal, and it should be rejected," he added.

- Limits citizen input by exempting advisory committees to Homeland Security from the Federal Advisory Act (FACA) passed in 1972 to ensure openness, accountability and the balance of viewpoints in government advisory groups. "By exempting from FACA requirements *any* [emphasis in original] advisory committees established by the Secretary of the Department of Homeland Security, [this act] severely undermines the openness and public-access goals of FACA," argued Edgar.

- Muzzles whistle-blowers protected under the federal Whistleblower Protection Act (WPA) by allowing the Homeland Security secretary to make his own personnel rules. "Title 5 [under the new department] does not guarantee employees of the Department of Homeland Security the protections of the WPA," stated Edgar. "Without such protection, employees who are in the best position to spot problems, violations of the law or dangers to the public are effectively silenced."

- Lacks strong oversight by allowing the Homeland Security secretary to override inspector general investigations in many areas including intelligence, criminal investigations, undercover operations, identity of confidential sources, protective matters of the Secret Service and any matter considered a threat to national security. "Given the mission of the Homeland Security Agency, it is conceivable that many of the functions performed by this new agency could be said to fall under one of these exempted categories," noted Edgar. "We are concerned that transferring these agencies [FEMA, INS, Animal and Plant Inspection Service of the Agriculture Department, Coast Guard] into a Department whose primary function is to protect the United States against terrorism could erroneously be perceived as elevating their regular duties to those of national security, thereby making such currently non-exempt activities exempt from Inspector General oversight."

- Threatens personal privacy and constitutional freedoms because the vagueness of the wording in the Homeland Security Act does not provide sufficient guarantees.

One huge concern voiced by the ACLU counsel concerned plans to combine the CIA and the FBI under Homeland Security.

"The CIA and other agencies that gather foreign intelligence abroad operate in the largely lawless environment," noted Edgar. "To bring these agencies into the same organization as the FBI risks further damage to Americans' civil liberties."

Edgar urged Congress to resist this move, instead placing clear limits on Homeland Security's ability to retain files on Americans that have no connection to criminal activity but relate to First Amendment freedoms.

He said combining domestic and foreign intelligence gathering under Homeland Security could have "a severe impact on civil liberties potentially leading to widespread spying on American's constitutionally protected political and religious activity."

"There is already a danger under the relaxed FBI guidelines for domestic investigations recently announced by Attorney General Ashcroft," Edgar added. "No one wants a repeat of the J. Edgar Hoover era, when the FBI [under the infamous Cointelpro program] was used to collect information about and disrupt the activities of civil rights leaders and others whose ideas Hoover disdained. Moreover, during the Clinton administration, the 'Filegate' matter involving the improper transfer of sensitive information from FBI background checks of prominent Republicans to the White House generated enormous public concern that private security-related information was being used for political purposes. Congress should not provide a future administration with the temptation to use information available in Homeland Security Department files to the detriment of its political enemies."

Interestingly enough, President Bush did have some conflict with Congress over the Homeland Security legislation, but it had nothing to do with the Constitution or common consideration. Congress wanted the department's employees covered by civil service protections and Bush did not.

Many observers believed this objection by Bush was a cover to exempt Homeland Security workers from the whistle-blower and Freedom of Information protections. If an employee did not go along with the Bush-Ridge program, they could be summarily fired and replaced with someone who would.

Some Democrats welcomed the new department, such as Senator Joseph Lieberman of Connecticut, an early advocate of the administration change, who said, "In fact, I think it will help us immediately." Others of his party objected to many provisions of the Homeland Security bill, charging that many had nothing to do with security, such as liability protection for vaccine manufacturers and exemptions to the Freedom of Information Act.

Despite misgivings, the Homeland Security Act passed speedily through Congress. In the U.S. Senate, the proposal passed on a 90/9 vote. Apparently senators were so confident that they were about to do a genuine service for America that on November 13 they voted themselves a pay raise for the fourth consecutive year. This vote was tighter, with 36 senators voting to reject a measure that would have denied them the raise.

The Homeland Security bill was signed into law by President Bush on November 25, 2002. Noting that the agencies responsible for border, coastline and transportation security were now under the same command structure, Bush said, "The continuing threat of terrorism, the threat of mass murder on our own soil, will be met with a unified, effective response."

To concentrate so much power in one government department head requires a thorough examination of the man who will wield such power. And in the case of Tom Ridge, there are worrisome aspects.

In the conventional biographies, Ridge is reported to have been a Catholic altar boy who won a scholarship to Harvard and went on to earn a B.A. in 1967. He was drafted into the army while attending Dickinson Law School in Carlisle, Pennsylvania. In Vietnam, he was awarded a Bronze Star for leading an action that cleared a small Vietcong force from an area. This war hero won six consecutive terms in the House before becoming the governor of Pennsylvania. Under that state's term limits, he was due to leave office in 2003.

But there is a disquieting side to this all-American-boy-makes-good story.

According to investigative reporters Jeffrey St. Clair and Alexander Cockburn, "He passed up officer training school because it would have meant an extra year of service. Ridge arrived in Vietnam [where he was given the nickname T-Bone] in November 1969, and joined Bravo Company, First Battalion, 20th Infantry Brigade, Americal Division."

One man who served with Ridge wrote to a veteran's Web page, stating, "The last several months I participated in the Pacification program along the Red Ball. My squad consisted of four other U.S. soldiers and up to ten ARVN [Army of the Republic of Viet Nam]. What a waste. I was not impressed with Ridge either. He was the squad leader of my squad before I became sergeant. The pathetic SOB would have caused all of us to get killed if we hadn't taken care of him. I was glad when he no longer led us."

But Ridge's leadership ability is not what concerned researchers the most. The "Pacification program" referred to by the Vietnam vet was the infamous Phoenix Program, in which more than 45,000 Vietnamese were assassinated and many thousands more tortured and abused.

Douglas Valentine, author of *The Phoenix Program*, explained, "During the Vietnam War, under the CIA's Phoenix Program - which is the model for the Homeland Security Office - a terrorist suspect was anyone accused by one anonymous source. Just one. The suspect was then arrested, indefinitely detained in a CIA interrogation center, tortured until he or she (in some cases children as young as twelve) confessed, informed on others, died, or was brought before a military tribunal (such as Bush is proposing) for disposition.

"In thousands of cases, innocent people were imprisoned and tortured based on the word of an anonymous informer who had a personal grudge or was actually a Viet Cong double agent feeding the names of loyal citizens into the Phoenix blacklist. At no point in the process did suspects have access to due process or lawyers, and thus, in 1971, four U.S. congresspersons stated their belief that the Phoenix Program violated that part of the Geneva Conventions guaranteeing protection to civilians in time of war."

Ridge received a medal for a small action during his stint in Vietnam. His Bronze Star citation states, "Sgt. Ridge moved forward and began placing accurate bursts of rifle fire on the insurgents, eliminating one and forcing the remainder of the hostile elements to take evasive action."

Vietnam veterans noticed that the citation did not mention enemy troops but instead "insurgents," a term given to any Vietnamese under suspicion by the U.S. authorities.

So, Tom Ridge, a man who participated in a CIA-sponsored terror program in Vietnam that included arrest without due process as well as torture and assassination, will now head our newest federal agency, one that is drawing power from more than two hundred existing agencies.

Another man who participated in the CIA Phoenix Program was Bruce Lawlor, who after serving in Vietnam went on to became a major general. Author Valentine said Lawlor admitted to his participation in Phoenix during an interview for Valentine's book. "What Lawlor told me basically confirmed everything. Except there were some additional, startling details. To begin with, Lawlor told me that he joined the CIA in 1967, while he was getting his B.A. at George Washington University. The CIA hired him to work the night shift, and after he graduated, he was given the chance to become a regular CIA staff officer. He took the paramilitary course, which included instruction in weapons and military tactics, but he was also trained as a foreign intelligence officer, the kind who manages secret agents. After that he was assigned to the Vietnam Desk at Langley headquarters, where he received specialized training in agent operations in Vietnam, and took a language course in Vietnamese. During this time, Lawlor formed a rapport with the Vietnam Desk officer, Al Seal, and when Seal was assigned as the base chief in Danang, he asked that Lawlor accompany him," stated Valentine.

In 1984, after leaving the military, Lawlor was the Democratic Party nomination for attorney general of Vermont. He listed the Phoenix Program on his political resume that was handed out to the press.

One journalist with a small weekly, *Vermont Vanguard*, published the first critical article about Lawlor and Phoenix. By the time of the state Democratic convention, activist groups in the state had organized and produced signs for convention delegates reading "No Assassins for Attorney General." Lawlor lost the fall primary despite a visit from former CIA director William Colby, the CIA official who headed the Phoenix Program.

"Imagine my surprise to learn that Bruce Lawlor is serving as the Office of Homeland Security's Senior Director for Protection and Prevention!" remarked Valentine. "To get right to the point, I have a sneaking suspicion that Lawlor…is still working for the CIA, and thus poses a major threat to democracy in America. He's someone who has access to Ashcroft's political blacklist, and he has control over the covert action teams that can be used to neutralize dissidents. One of the reasons I have this crazy feeling, is that nowhere in any of Lawlor's official-looking, online biographies is there any mention of his CIA service. It's like his biographers are deliberately trying to hide his CIA connection from us."

Yet another ranking Bush administration member with a checkered background is Richard Armitage, best friend of Colin Powell and unanimously endorsed by the Senate Foreign Relations Committee for his new position as Deputy Secretary of State. He too was a major Phoenix Program operative, according to Valentine and others.

Valentine noted, "HR 19, just introduced [in January 2001] by Georgia congressman Bob Barr, would repeal the Executive Orders of presidents Reagan and Carter prohibiting federal employees, including the military, from carrying out assassinations. This implies that the Bush administration plans to deal harshly with terrorists and other inconvenient persons. Richard Armitage, who was involved in the Iran-Contra deal as well as CIA covert operations in Vietnam, will reportedly head up what's called 'The Terrorist Elimination Act of 2001'. That's our new Deputy Secretary of State."

It should be noted that this was not the first time that Armitage's name has come up in connection with criminal behavior. Once again, the issue of illegal drugs cropped up.

Colonel James "Bo" Gritz, a much-decorated Vietnam veteran, in 1987 met with Burmese general Kuhn Sa, the head of the Golden Triangle drug trade, in an effort to locate American POWs. Gritz, in his 1988 book *A Nation Betrayed*, wrote that General Sa detailed for him the heroin trade and named then-assistant secretary of defense for international security affairs Armitage as the person who handled the financial end of the U.S. narcotics trade through banks in Australia. Armitage reportedly was involved in a shadowy group of U.S. government officials and mobsters to import heroin into the United States.

Shocked at this revelation, Gritz asked himself, "How could men sworn before God to defend the Constitution so befoul their office? What form of stand-up sewage would facilitate the movement of deadly addictive narcotics into their own homeland? It took several long moments for the full impact to be realized. Then it was as if someone had turned on a light in my mind. Until that moment my mental and emotional conditioning from a career of military service refused to allow such a contemplation. It was so un-American and alien as to be incomprehensible. But, if true, it explained a train of unexplained events. If Richard Armitage was, as Kuhn Sa avowed, a major participant in parallel government drug trafficking, then it explained why our efforts to rescue POWs had been inexplicably foiled."

But if illegal drugs continued to pour into the United States, more conventional products did not in mid-2002. A labor dispute between the International Longshore and Warehouse Union (ILWU) and the Pacific Maritime Association (PMA) caused a stack-up of cargo ships along the West Coast from San Diego to Seattle that threatened to cut deeply into the 2002/03 holiday season profits. The strike was broken in October when President Bush invoked the Taft-Hartley Act, a controversial 1947 union-busting law that was passed over President Truman's veto. Under this law, an eighty-day "cooling off" period can be ordered during a "national emergency."

Although Bush's action received scant attention in a media focused on the proposed invasion of Iraq, one official of ILWU, Jack Heyman, termed Bush's intervention "a historic juncture in the labor movement." Heyman added, "By invoking Taft-Hartley against the longshore workers, Bush is effectively declaring war on the working class here and the Iraqi people simultaneously."

It was not just labor unionists that were feeling the chill in the wake of the hot patriotism after 9/11. Two members of a Chicago group opposed to the sanctions against Iraq were confronted by police when they went to buy some postage stamps.

Daniel Muller, a coordinator for Voices in the Wilderness, along with Andrew Mandell, went to a Chicago post office to purchase a quantity of stamps. They were paying in cash. "We needed 4,000 stamps for a mailing we were doing," explained Muller, "and I asked for one not with the American flag on them." When the clerk asked if Statue of Liberty stamps were acceptable, Mandell replied, "Yes, we love liberty." "She asked us to step aside from the counter and she went to the back, out of view," recalled Muller. "I knew something was up because this was a bit out of the ordinary. And Andrew said, 'She's calling the cops,' but I didn't believe him."

However, about twenty minutes later two policemen entered and asked for the pair's identification. "They asked if we had any outstanding warrants. They ran a check on us. They asked why we had asked for stamps without American flags on them. I said we're very rooted in nonviolent activities and we would rather have the Statue of Liberty than the American flag."

The pair were finally released but had to return to the post office the next day to obtain their stamps, and then only after a further half-hour interview with a postal inspector.

"The fact that they did ask for anything but flag stamps did raise a question for the clerk," explained Silvia Carrier, a public relations officer for the Chicago Postal Inspector's office. "Right now, since September 11, clerks have been told to be cautious, to be looking out for anything suspicious."

The experience of Muller and Mandell shows that it matters little that the U.S. Postal Service in mid-July 2002 stated it would not participate in a snitch program called Operation TIPS.

TIPS, or Terrorism Information and Prevention System, was trotted out in midsummer 2002 and hailed on its Web site as "a national system for concerned workers to report suspicious activity." The program is part of the Citizen Corps, a program announced by President Bush in his State of the Union address and was originally scheduled to be launched by early fall 2002.

In a statement, the postal service stated it had "been approached by homeland security regarding Operation TIPS; however, it was decided that the postal service and its letter carriers would not be participating in the program at this time." Nothing was said about individual carriers deciding to join and the "at this time" left the final word unsaid.

And the experience of the men and the stamps indicated that some persons within the Postal Service still were reporting anything they viewed as suspicious behavior.

In published material, TIPS advocates said the program would be administered by the Justice Department coordinated with FEMA, which would bring it under the Homeland Security Department. It would involve "millions of American workers who, in the daily course of their work, are in a unique position to see potentially unusual or suspicious activity in public places." This, of course, referred to postmen, meter readers, repairmen or anyone who might have an axe to grind against their neighbors.

The TIPS plan was immediately compared to the Nazi Gestapo, the former East German secret police service, and Fidel Castro's Committees for the Defense of the Revolution (CDR) in which Cubans are encouraged to spy on and report any "counterrevolutionary" behavior by their neighbors. An estimated 8 million Cubans belong to more than 121,000 committees in the CDR, established by Castro on September 28, 1960.

In October 2000, the CDR held parties across the island nation to celebrate their forty years of existence. "If we see some sort of attack on society or the government, then that is counterrevolution and you have to root it out," voiced one jubilant CDR member while toasting with a glass of rum at a Havana street party.

The CDRs keep detailed records of all neighborhood inhabitants, not only listing each inhabitant but also keeping files on schooling and work history, spending habits, any potentially suspicious behavior, any contact with foreigners and attendance at pro-Castro meetings. The system has evolved into one that routinely provides an individual's information to prospective employers, medical authorities or any law enforcement official.

Needless to say, the American Civil Liberties Union (ACLU) and other public watchdog organizations reacted negatively to Operation TIPS, saying it would create an atmosphere in which Americans would be spying on each other. "The administration apparently wants to implement a program that will turn local cable or gas or electrical technicians into government-sanctioned Peeping Toms," declared ACLU legislative counsel Rachel King.

John Whitehead, executive director of the Rutherford Institute, said, "This is George Orwell's '1984.' It is an absolutely horrible and very dangerous idea. It's making Americans into government snoops. President Bush wants the average American to do what the FBI should be doing. In the end, though, nothing is going to prevent terrorists from crashing airplanes into buildings."

Even Homeland Security chief Ridge was forced to back pedal, saying, "The last thing we want is Americans spying on Americans. That's just not what the president is all about and not what the TIPS program is all about." However, he did not reject the program and most observers felt it would continue albeit with less publicity. "It is not a government intrusion," argued Ridge. "The president just wants people to be alert and aware. We're not asking people to spy on people."

Although Ridge still vouched for the TIPS program, a review of the Citizen Corps Web site showed a marked softening of both language and details after the program began to make a national stir.

In July 2002, the Web site stated Operation TIPS "will be a nationwide program giving millions of American truckers, letter carriers, train conductors, ship captains, utility employees and others a formal way to report suspicious terrorist activity. Operation TIPS, a project of the U.S. Department of Justice, will begin as a pilot program in 10 cities and that will be selected.

"Operation TIPS, involving 1 million workers in the pilot stage, will be a national reporting system that allows workers, whose routines make them well-positioned to recognize unusual events, to report suspicious activity. Everywhere in America, a concerned worker can call a toll-free number and be connected directly to a hotline routing calls to the proper law enforcement agency or other responder organizations when appropriate."

By early August, the list of occupations had been dropped and "suspicious terrorist activity" and "unusual events suspicious activity" had changed to "suspicious and potentially terrorist-related activity" and "Potentially unusual or suspicious activity in public places."

The TIPS program merely was an official extension of snooping in America, already so pervasive that author Jim Redden called modern life a "snitch culture." Neighborhood Watch groups already in existence were being brought into Homeland Security. In the spring of 2002, Ashcroft earmarked almost $2 million in an effort to double the number of Neighborhood Watch groups to about fifteen thousand. He claimed this would "weave a seamless web of prevention of terrorism" across the country.

TV personality Ed McMahon went from pitching for Publishers Clearing House Sweepstakes to pitching the War on Terrorism. The National Neighborhood Watch Institute already had been shipping out rectangular street signs reading "We Support Homeland Security."

From the school kid Drug Abuse Resistance Education (DARE) program to professional finger-pointers such as the Southern Poverty Law Center, more and more Americans are being encouraged to spy and report on one another.

In 1997, such activity was codified, at least for the federal government, when the Supreme Court in *U.S. vs. Singleton* exempted federal prosecutors from a statute prohibiting the bribery of witnesses to testify favorably for the government. There have been many cases, usually not played up in the media, in which innocent people have had their lives unsettled, ruined or even lost due to egregious snitching. Despite cases such as this, the purchase of information continues to be a mainstay of federal law enforcement. In 1994, the DEA spent $31.7 million while Customs spent $16.5 million on thousands of informants. Such practices have prompted protests from civil libertarians and attorneys but in today's fearful society, no one seems too concerned.

If opposition to the TIPS network and the growing "snitch culture" in America seems a bit paranoid, consider the plight of A. J. Brown, a freshman at Durham Tech in North Carolina who received some unwelcome visitors on October 26, 2001.

Answering a knock on her apartment door, Brown found herself face-to-face with two men in suits. "Hi, we're from the Raleigh branch of the Secret Service," said one of the men, flipping out an ID folder. "I was like, 'What?' recalled Brown. "And they say, 'We're here because we have a report that you have un-American material in your apartment.' And I was like, 'What? No, I don't have anything like that.' 'Are you sure? Because we got a report that you've got a poster that's anti-American.' And I said no." The agents wanted to enter Brown's apartment but she asked if they had a warrant. "And they said no, they didn't have a warrant but they wanted to just come in and look around. And I said, 'Sorry, you're not coming in.'"

Standing in her doorway, the agents said they knew she had a poster in her apartment of President Bush hanging himself. Brown denied this and after long minutes opened the door wide enough for the agents to see her poster. It was a picture of Bush holding a rope with the caption "We Hang on Your Every Word. George Bush Wanted: 152 Dead." The poster also contained drawings of people being hanged. It was a political poster referring to the number of persons subjected to the death penalty in Texas while Bush was governor.

The agents finally left after about forty minutes but called Brown back two days later to confirm her name, address, phone number and nicknames. "Obviously, I'm on some list somewhere," she commented.

And it's not all about college students. Katie Sierra, a fifteen-year-old sophomore at Sissonville High School in West Virginia, says that all she wanted to do was form an Anarchist Club at her school and she handed out fliers that stated, "Anarchism preaches to love all humans, not just of one country." She also wore a T-shirt that read "Racism, Sexism, Homophobia, I'm So Proud of People in the Land of the So-Called Free."

Sierra was suspended and her fellow students shoved her and posted pictures of the girl with bullet holes in her head. After losing a court battle for reinstatement in the state supreme court by a 3-to-2 vote, Sierra said, "I'm really disgusted with the courts right now and with the school. I'm being punished for being myself."

Children are especially susceptible to recruitment through the various programs being dreamed up today. And the U.S. military played it's own role. The principal of Mount Anthony Union High School in Bennington, Vermont, was shocked in the spring of 2002 to receive a letter from military recruiters demanding a list of all students, including names, addresses and telephone numbers. As the school's privacy policy prevented the disclosure of such individual information, the principal told the recruiters no. She was doubly shocked to learn that buried deep within President Bush's new education law passed earlier in 2002, the No Child Left Behind Act, public schools must provide such information to military recruiters or face a cutoff of federal funds.

Republican Representative David Vitter of Louisiana, who sponsored the recruitment requirement in the education bill, noted that in 1999, more than nineteen thousand U.S. schools denied military recruiters access to their records. Vitter said such schools "demonstrated an anti-military attitude that I thought was offensive."

"I think the privacy implications of this law are profound," commented Jill Wynns, president of the San Francisco Board of Education. "For the federal government to ignore or discount the concerns of the privacy rights of millions of high school students is not a good thing, and it's something we should be concerned about."

Even journalists and academics have come under fire for not acceding to the mob mentality. Robert Jensen is an associate professor of journalism at the University of Texas at Austin. He published a column in the *Houston Chronicle* on September 14, 2001, pointing out that while the 9/11 attacks were "reprehensible and indefensible," the acts were "no more despicable [than] the massive acts of terrorism, the deliberate killing of civilians for political purposes, that the U.S. government has committed during my lifetime."

Jensen's column was rebutted by the university president, Larry R. Faulkner, who labeled Jensen as "not only misguided but [he] has become a fountain of undiluted foolishness on issues of public policy." "I've been marginalized on this campus," said Jensen.

Newspaper writers Dan Guthrie of Oregon's *Grants Pass Daily Courier* and Tom Gutting of the *Texas City Sun* both wrote caustically of President Bush's irregular flight across America on 9/11. "What we are stuck with is a crippled President who continues to be controlled by his advisers. He's not a leader. He's a puppet," wrote Gutting, who said the day his piece ran his publisher assured him he would not be fired for expressing his opinion. But the publisher printed a front-page apology for Gutting's column and a few days later changed his mind about firing him.

Guthrie, who had won several awards, including best columnist in Oregon, wrote that Bush "skedaddled" on September 11. "The picture of Bush hiding in a Nebraska hole [was] an embarrassment," he wrote. Even though the paper's editor and his city editor had signed off on his piece, Guthrie soon joined Gutting in the ranks of the unemployed.

Still, the reporters got off lighter than Richard Allen Humphreys, who described himself as a religious prophet. He was found guilty in late October 2002 by a Sioux Falls jury of threatening President Bush and faced as much as five years in prison and a $250,000 fine. A bartender at a truck stop overheard Humphreys mention "burning bush" and called police. A search of Humphrey's hotel room yielded a card with President Bush's name on it and the words "Intimidation in the First Degree." In a transcript of a-Internet chat room conversation, Humphreys had written, "now going to ask Bush for justice, and if I don't get it don't be surprised to see a Burning Bush." Humphreys, who represented himself in court, said he was on a "discipleship journey" and was not threatening the president but merely exercising his right to religious expression.

Apparently not even traditional American activities such as taking pictures around town are exempt from the scrutiny of Homeland Security enforcers. Amateur photographer Mike Maginnis was intrigued by all the activity around Denver's Adams Mark Hotel in early December 2002, which included Denver police, army rangers and rooftop snipers. Maginnis, who works in information technology and frequently shoots photos of corporate buildings and communications equipment, took a few snapshots. He was then confronted by a Denver policeman who demanded his camera. When he refused to hand over his expensive Nikon F2, he was pushed to the ground and arrested.

After being held in a Denver police station, Maginnis was interrogated by a Secret Service agent. He learned that Vice President

Cheney was staying in the area and that he was to be charged as a terrorist under the USA PATRIOT Act. According to Maginnis, the agent tried to make him confess to being a terrorist and called him a "raghead collaborator" and "dirty pinko faggot."

After being held for several hours, Maginnis was released without explanation. When his attorney contacted the Denver police for an explanation, they denied ever arresting Maginnis.

Yet another case involved a kindergarten student who only wanted to play. Scot and Cassandra Garrick of New Jersey in May 2002 sued the Sayreville School District after their six-year-old and three kindergarten classmates were disciplined for playing cops and robbers. It seems other students saw the youngsters playing in the school yard, pretending their fingers were guns. They told a teacher and the kindergartners were suspended from school.

U.S. District Judge Katherine S. Hayden dismissed a civil suit filed by the parents, claiming school authorities have the right to restrict violent or disruptive games.

The parents' attorney, Steven H. Aden, commented, "They have the right to be children. The school and the courts shouldn't censor their play [even if] it's politically incorrect."

Such incidents are rarely covered in the corporate mass media and never distributed to a large audience, but they worry thoughtful people.

"I'm terrified," said Ellen Schrecker, author of *Many Are the Crimes: McCarthyism in America*. "What concerns me is we're not seeing an enormous outcry against this whole structure of repression that's being rushed into place by the Bush administration." ACLU president Nadine Strossen also voiced concern. "I've been talking a lot about the parallels between what we're going through now and McCarthyism. The term 'terrorism' is taking on the same kind of characteristics as the term 'communism' did in the 1950s. It stops people in their tracks and they're willing to give up their freedoms. People are too quickly panicked. They are too willing to give up their rights and to scapegoat people, especially immigrants and people who criticize the war."

Writing in *Executive Intelligence Review*, Edward Spannaus noted, "At this point, the new agency appears to be more of a coordination focal point, rather than a new command structure. But, potentially, such a structure could combine two of the worst features of the Reagan-Bush crisis-management structure, which ran what is known as 'Iran-Contra' and other covert operations."

"Besides being unconstitutional and un-American, snooping on innocent people in a free society is cowardly, divisive and just plan evil," argued Internet columnist Paul Proctor. "Regardless of whether or not President Bush's motives are honorable, the fact remains that in tattle tailing for the federal government, anyone with a personal grievance against another individual or group could literally wreck havoc on them with such powers. Needless to say, the potential for tragedy and abuse is huge.

"How secure do you think you are going to feel in this escalating 'War on Terrorism' burdened with the grim knowledge that you're always going to be watched by someone somewhere reporting your personal activities, conversations and correspondence to an unaccountable hierarchy that, in the interest of 'Homeland Security,' has the legal authority to take from you whatever they want, anytime they want, without so much as a warrant or a knock on the door."

Noting President Bush's claim that terrorism threatens our freedom, Proctor added, "But, you see - terrorists don't want your freedom - they want your life. It is tyrants and dictators that want your freedom."

The PATRIOT Act

The first advice any good lawyer gives his or her client is to not sign anything without first reading and understanding it.

Yet, a panicky House of Representatives, still in shock over 9/11 and the subsequent anthrax attacks, during Halloween week 2001 rushed the PATRIOT Act into law by a vote of 339/79 even though almost none of them had actually read the document. Many civil libertarians felt that fact alone should be cause for wholesale dismissals at the Capitol, even though House lawmakers tacked on a sunset provision that portions of the act must come under review in December 2004, unless President Bush decides to extend them in the "national interest." In 2003, several Republicans in Congress were already attempting to slip provisions into other legislation that would repeal the sunset provisions of the PATRIOT Act.

Judith Krug of the American Library Association and a leading expert on First Amendment rights was not optimistic about the sunset review process. "It's [the act] going to be used as long as they can get away with it," she said, adding that unless the act is challenged in court, "we'll be lucky if we can 'sunset' out any of it."

The official title of the bill is the Uniting and Strengthening America by Providing Appropriate Tools Required to Intercept and

Obstruct Terrorism Act - USA PATRIOT Act. The name was reminiscent of Hitler's 1933 legislation passed hurriedly following the burning of the Reichstag in 1933, which evolved into the Third Reich. It was called The Law To Remove the Distress of the People and State.

The Act is 342 pages long and makes changes, both great and small, to more than fifteen different U.S. statutes, most of them enacted after previous misuse of surveillance powers by the FBI and CIA. It was hurriedly and enthusiastically signed into law by President Bush on October 26, 2001.

Representative Dennis Kucinich, a Democrat from Ohio, described the atmosphere in which the PATRIOT Act was passed: "[T]here was great fear in our great Capitol. The great fear began when we had to evacuate the Capitol on September 11. It continued when we had to leave the Capitol again when a bomb scare occurred as members were pressing the CIA during a secret briefing. It continued when we abandoned Washington when anthrax, possibly from a government lab, arrived in the mail. It is present in the camouflaged armed national guardsmen who greet members of Congress each day we enter the Capitol campus. It is present in the labyrinth of concrete barriers through which we must pass each time we go to vote."

Representative Ron Paul, one of only three Republicans to vote against the House bill, said he objected to how opponents were stigmatized by the name alone. "The insult is to call this a 'patriot bill' and suggest I'm not patriotic because I insisted upon finding out what was in it and voting no. I thought it was undermining the Constitution, so I didn't vote for it - therefore I'm somehow not a patriot. That's insulting."

Paul confirmed rumors that the bill was not read by most members of the House prior to their vote. "It's my understanding the bill wasn't printed before the vote - at least I couldn't get it," he told *Insight* magazine. "They played all kinds of games, kept the House in session all night, and it was a very complicated bill. Maybe a handful of staffers actually read it, but the bill definitely was not available to members before the vote."

Paul's view of the PATRIOT Act was echoed by the only independent in the House, Representative Bernie Sanders of Vermont, who said, "I took an oath to support and defend the Constitution of the United States, and I'm concerned that voting for this legislation fundamentally violates that oath. And the contents of the legislation have not been subjected to serious hearings or searching examination."

The Electronic Frontier Foundation (EFF) of San Francisco, a donor-supported membership group dedicated to protecting freedom when "law and technology collide," published an overview of the PATRIOT Act. They concluded that "it seems clear that the vast majority of the sections included have not been carefully studied by Congress, nor was sufficient time taken to debate it or to hear testimony from experts outside of law enforcement in the fields where it makes major changes.

"This concern is amplified because several of the key procedural processes applicable to any other proposed laws, including inter-agency review, the normal committee and hearing processes and thorough voting, were suspended for this bill. The civil liberties of ordinary Americans have taken a tremendous blow with this law, especially the right to privacy in our online communications and activities. Yet there is no evidence that our precious civil liberties posed a barrier to effective tracking or prosecution of terrorists."

This act, which clearly abridges the rights of Americans, was built upon the little-known Foreign Intelligence Surveillance Act of 1978 (FISA), which cracked the door open to secret government searches. It was passed in the contingencies of the Cold War and in the wake of revelations of misused surveillance by the FBI and CIA.

Under FISA was created the secret federal Foreign Intelligence Surveillance Court (FISC), which meets in total secrecy to routinely approve covert surveillances on individuals by intelligence agencies. All applications to the court must be approved by the attorney general. Either the federal prosecutors are extremely efficient and effective in their work or the seven federal judges who make up this secret court are not picky about the Constitution because out of the some twelve thousand requests for secret surveillances and physical searches made during the twenty-year life of the FASC, not one application has been denied.

"Then came the USA PATRIOT Act," wrote journalist Walter Brasch, "drafted by the Bush administration and fine-tuned in secret by the House and Senate leadership following the September 11 terrorist attacks. The PATRIOT Act, which incorporates and significantly expands FISA to include American citizens, was overwhelmingly approved by the Congress, most of whom admit they read only a few paragraphs, if any at all."

"The intent behind the passage of the FISA legislation was to impose limits and a review process upon warrantless surveillance and searches conducted for 'national security' purposes in light of the numerous abuses by federal agencies against U.S. citizens," wrote Patrick S. Poole in a treatise on both the FISA and the FISC. "But the politicization and present use of the FISA process [now expanded through the PATRIOT Act] has resulted in the erosion of numerous constitutional rights and basic legal procedures that have their roots in free societies dating back to the Magna Carta."

The new act also greatly expands law enforcement power into areas that have little to do with terrorism. One provision provides for the collection of DNA from terrorists, then expands this to include anyone suspected of "any crime of violence." Both the scope and penalties under the Computer Fraud and Abuse Act were increased along with the use of wiretaps.

In fact, the act was so broad and subject to abuse that the Foreign Intelligence Surveillance Court took the unprecedented move of forcing Ashcroft to modify Justice Department guidelines concerning FBI terrorism searches and wiretaps. The FISC, for the first time in nearly two decades, rejected some of Ashcroft's guidelines as "not reasonably designed" to safeguard Americans' privacy.

Ashcroft's instructions came in March 2002 and were addressed to FBI Director Robert Mueller and senior Justice Department officials. They were intended to make it easier for investigators in espionage and terrorism cases to share information from searches or wiretaps. The FISC ruled that his guidelines could all the misuse of information in criminal cases that required higher legal standards to procure searches and wiretaps.

Ashcroft had cited the USA PATRIOT Act as the justification for expanded guidelines used in wiretaps and searches. "The attorney general seized authority that has not been granted to him by the Constitution or the Congress," noted Marc Rotenberg, head of the Washington-based Electronic Privacy Information Center.

The Electronic Frontier Foundation said Internet users particularly should be concerned about provisions of the act that expand government surveillance while reducing checks and balances, the forced handing over of records by Internet Service Providers (ISP), new and vague definitions of "terrorism," and surveillance without a court order.

Here are some of the provisions of the PATRIOT Act that concern civil libertarians:

- The federal government may now monitor religious and political institutions without suspecting criminal activity as an assist to terrorism investigations (a violation of the First Amendment right of association).

- The feds now can close to the public once-open immigration hearings and have detained secretly hundreds of people without charge while encouraging bureaucrats to resist Freedom of Information requests (a violation of Amendments 5 and 6 guaranteeing due process, speedy trials and freedom of information).

- The government may prosecute librarians or other keepers of records if they tell anyone that the government subpoenaed information related to a terrorism investigation (a violation of the First Amendment right of free speech).

- The government now may monitor conversations between federal prisoners and their attorneys and even deny lawyers to Americans accused of crimes (a violation of the 6th Amendment right to have legal representation).

- The government now may search and seize individual and business papers and effects without probable cause to assist an antiterrorism investigation (a violation of the 4th   Amendment right against unreasonable searches and seizures).

- The government now may jail Americans indefinitely without a trial or charges (a violation of the 6th Amendment right to a speedy trial and to be informed of the charges against them).

And lest anyone think that the government will hold in abeyance any power given to it, many incidents have already been reported.

John Ashcroft's Justice Department in March 2002 announced that it planned to use secret evidence to justify financial sanctions against a Chicago-area Muslim charity as part of its effort to stop the funding of terrorists.

Attorneys for Global Relief Foundation filed a lawsuit claiming the government violated the Constitution when it froze the charity's assets in December 2001. The government said it would share it's evidence with the judge but not with the charity or its attorneys. Legal experts said this may be the first time the government has tried to use secret evidence in a trial, citing the PATRIOT Act as its authority.

Global Relief, along with two other charities - Benevolence International and the Texas-based Holy Land Foundation for Relief and Development - had their assets frozen by the government pending an investigation of their links to terrorism

"It's completely contrary to anything that's ever happened in this country. This country was founded on the idea of confronting your accuser. If they submit secret evidence or present it to the judge in such a way that we can never see it, we can't cross examine and we can never rebut," said Global attorney Roger Simmons, adding such government action set "a very dangerous legal precedent."

Such concern takes on even more substance when viewed against the government's track record in such cases. Following the WTC bombing in 1993, a Palestinian named Hany Kiareldeen living in New Jersey was held after being secretly accused of meeting with one of the men convicted of the bombing. Kiareldeen suspected the information came from someone with an axe to grind.

A federal judge, after reviewing the case, questioned not only the evidence against Kiareldeen but the manner in which it was presented. He wrote, "The [Immigration and Naturalization Service's] reliance on secret evidence raised serious issues about the integrity of the adversarial process, the impossibility of self-defense against undisclosed charges, and the reliability of government processes initiated and prosecuted in darkness."

Niels Frenzen, a University of Southern California law professor, agreed with the judge, stating, "Without exception, when the government uses this one-sided evidence, it's gotten it wrong. Why should anyone think they are going to get it right now?"

Another example of what to expect under the new expanded powers of the federal government, already under fire for it's questionable actions at Ruby Ridge and Waco, came at 5 A.M. in San Antonio, Texas, the day after 9/11, when heavily armed federal agents raided the home of Dr. Al-Badr al-Hazmi. Al-Hazmi was a thirty-four-year-old radiology resident at the University of Texas Health Science Center who had been working in Lackland Air Force Base's military hospital in the days before September 11.

According to news reports, al-Hazmi's home was ransacked by agents without a search warrant, his wife and young children held at gunpoint, and later the doctor was thrown naked into a cold FBI holding cell without being charged with any crime. He was then flown to a New York prison, where al-Hazmi said he was beaten repeatedly during FBI interrogations. After a week, he finally was allowed to speak to his attorney and discovered the cause of his problems was that his name, a common name in the Middle East, was similar to that of two of the suspected 9/11 hijackers. Another week passed before al-Hazmi was released and allowed to return home, still without having been charged with any crime.

And don't think that something like this could only happen to someone with a Middle Eastern name and only in today's terrorist-sensitive environment. Robert Lee "Bob on the Job" Lewis is a fervent Christian who has spent decades researching government scandals. He worked with airline lawyers during the investigation of the bombing of Pan Am Flight 103 over Lockerbie, Scotland.

In April 1998, Lewis was in a restaurant in Houston, Texas, regaling waiters with his knowledge of government skullduggery, including little-reported information on former president George H. W.

Bush. Lewis admitted he made a remark about Bush along the lines of, "I'll have his ass."

Sitting in the restaurant was Secret Service agent Tim Reilly, who promptly placed Lewis under arrest for threatening the former president. The next day, in a short hearing, federal magistrate Marcia Crone avoided any First Amendment issue and instead accepted the hearsay testimony of Agent Reilly. The impecunious Lewis was held for nearly a year in federal custody. His ordeal included being sent to the Fort Worth Federal Correctional Institution, where he was placed in the same cell where Whitewater scandal figure James McDougal had been held. Lewis knew full well who McDougal had been and felt his placement was a form of intimidation. Some months later, Lewis was transferred to a federal hospital in Springfield, Missouri, where he was involuntarily drugged until letters from some journalists and academic contacts protesting his drugging gained him a release. There was never a court trial or even an adversarial hearing in the case.

Secret evidence, closed trials, false imprisonment, warrant-less searches, involuntary drugging, the seizing of private property all seem like something out of the Nazi era, but fear has pushed many Americans into a passive and accepting mode. Congressman Paul, when asked what was wrong with the PATRIOT Act, replied, "The worst part of this so-called antiterrorism bill is the increased ability of the federal government to commit surveillance on all of us without proper search warrants." Paul was referring to Section 213 of the act, entitled "Authority for Delaying Notice of the Execution of a Warrant," also called the "sneak-and-peek" provision, which allows authorities to search personal property without warning.

Insight magazine reporter Kelly Patricia O'Meara wrote that "With one vote by Congress and the sweep of the president's pen, say critics, the right of every American fully to be protected under the Fourth Amendment against unreasonable searches and seizures was abrogated".

Paul pointed out the obvious flaw in the idea that the government would act in a restrained and responsible manner when given this authority. "I don't like the sneak-and-peek provision because you have to ask yourself what happens if the person is home, doesn't know that law enforcement is coming to search his home, hasn't a clue as to who's coming in unannounced and he shoots them. This law clearly authorizes illegal search and seizure, and anyone who thinks of this as antiterrorism needs to consider its application to every American citizen."

One man who can testify in support of Paul's concern is San Diego computer executive Donald Carlson, who in 1994 was awarded a $2.75 million settlement following a 1992 raid on his home by federal agents. But money was a poor compensation for being shot three times, a six-week stay in intensive care, permanent lung damage and limited movement in one arm. Carlson was shot when he awoke in the night and tried to defend himself from strangers breaking down his door. The strangers were Customs and DEA agents acting on a tip from informant Ronnie Edmond, who told the feds Carlson's home contained more than five tons of cocaine. No drugs were found.

Another part of the PATRIOT Act (Section 215) prompted the concern of Representative C. L. "Butch" Otter of Idaho, another of the three Republicans who found the entire act potentially unconstitutional. "Section 215 authorizes the FBI to acquire any business records whatsoever by order of a secret U.S. Court. The recipient of such a search order is forbidden from telling any person that he has received such a request. This is a violation of the First Amendment right to free speech and the Fourth Amendment protection of private property," commented Otter, adding, "[S]ome of these provisions place more power in the hands of law enforcement than our Founding Fathers could have dreamt and severely compromises the civil liberties of law-abiding Americans. This bill, while crafted with good intentions, is rife with constitutional infringements I could not support."

In 1998, there was a brief furor over proposed new banking regulations that would require all banks to report to the government any large deposits or withdrawals or unusual activity on the part of the banking public. Euphemistically called the "Know Your Customer" program, it heralded a new era wherein law-abiding citizens might have to defend their financial matters before government agents. Under this program, banks would be required to create a profile of each customer and report any deviation from the profile to the feds. For example, consider a citizen who sold an unneeded car and deposited the cash in his bank account. Under this program, the bank computer would flag the transaction because this was an unusually large deposit based on the person's previous deposit record. Federal authorities would be notified and soon agents would be sent to interrogate the customer on the chance he or she might be a drug dealer or terrorist.

Representative Ralph Paul in 1998 planned to introduce legislation to stop this intrusive program but an irate citizenry saved him the trouble. The schemers behind the proposal, the Federal Deposit Insurance Corp, the IRS and other agencies, quickly backed off the proposal. Paul said quite prophetically, "Somehow, though, I imagine such action will not stop them, only slow them down."

Almost all of the provisions of the "Know Your Customer" program can be found in the PATRIOT Act.

Another of those who actually read the PATRIOT Act and were appalled at its unconstitutional provisions was Nadine Strossen, a professor of law at New York University and president of the American Civil Liberties Union. Her main complaint was that the sweeping changes codified by the act have little or nothing to do with fighting terrorism.

"There is no connection between the September 11 attacks and what is in this legislation," Strossen argued. "Most of the provisions related not just to terrorist crimes but to criminal activity generally. This happened too, with the 1996 antiterrorism legislation, where most of the surveillance laws have been used for drug enforcement, gambling and prostitution."

Reporter O'Meara noted that a similar antiterrorist act in England allows government investigators to obtain information from Internet Service Providers about their subscribers without a warrant. The British law is now being applied to minor crimes, tax collection and public health measures.

By mid-2002, the ACLU was already filing a number of lawsuits trying to make the government accountable in its actions under the PATRIOT Act. An ACLU press release stated the organization believed "it is critically important that the public learn how Attorney General Ashcroft is using the vast new surveillance powers granted the government." In their suit under the Freedom of Information Act, the ACLU wanted to know among other things:

- The number of times the FBI used pen registers [the numbers that a person has called is kept in a register] or trap and trace devices against U.S. citizens or permanent residents as provided in Section 214 of the PATRIOT Act.

- The number of times the FBI has ordered libraries, bookstores or newspapers to divulge records or other tangible things as provided in Section 215 of the act.

-The number of United States citizens or permanent residents who have been subjected to new surveillance orders since the enactment of the PATRIOT Act.

The ACLU stated that it did not believe that the release of such aggregate, statistical information would jeopardize national security or any other legitimate government interest. ACLU president Strossen said her overriding concern with the new act is the power that is being concentrated in the presidency. "The concern here is about the third branch of government," she explained. "One of the overreaching problems that pervades so many provisions is reduction of the role of judicial oversight. The executive branch is running roughshod over both of the other branches of government. I find it very bothersome that the government is going to have more widespread access to e-mail and Web sites and that information can be shared with other law enforcement and even intelligence agencies. So again, we're going to have the CIA in the business of spying on Americans."

Strossen, Paul, Otter and others were pointed but polite in their criticisms of the PATRIOT Act. Others were not so courteous. "In light of the egregious evisceration of the Bill of Rights that this law undertakes, those who blindly supported and signed this blatantly unconstitutional act into law should be collectively condemned and charged with high treason to the Constitution and the people of the United States," wrote columnist Doreen Miller for YellowTimes, an online publication of alternative news. "The USA PATRIOT Act creates and allows for a virtual police state with little to no judicial oversight. We, as a nation, are literally treading the razor's edge when it comes to flirting with the grave dangers inherent in giving up our rights for the empty promises of 'safety' and 'national security' masquerading under the guise of a 'patriotic' PATRIOT Act. Once we fall off that edge, reclaiming and reinstating our rights, authority and power as 'We The People' of this great nation might prove very difficult."

Karen G. Schneider, writing for the American Library Association Web site, wrote, "First of all, I'm a hawk. I believe we should be in Afghanistan, I'd like to see bin Laden oh, say, six feet under, and behind my bifocals, this middle-aged veteran cheers her colleagues in the armed forces defending our nation. However, the USA PATRIOT Act is treason pure and simple, and you need to know how and why, because it presents particularly pernicious issues for the users who rely on your Internet services. The PATRIOT Act is not antiterrorism legislation; it's anti-speech legislation, and is no more a direct response to the September 11 attacks than the Children's Internet Protection Act is a direct result of sincere concern by members of Congress about the safety of minors. The cold, cynical reality is that the PATRIOT Act is a bloated hodgepodge of speech-chilling law that lurked in congressional corridors not only before September 11 but in large part before the Bush administration. It was hustled into reality in the post 9/11 environment so quickly, secretively, and undemocratically that our Bill of Rights had been clocked with a one-two punch well before any of us realized it was under attack."

Schneider's concern was clearly illustrated in an incident in which FBI agents showed up some time back at a Bloomsburg, Pennsylvania, bookstore owned by Arline Johnson. The agents weren't tracking criminals, they were asking which customers bought copies of the Tom Clancy book *The Hunt for Red October.*

Johnson, who has been challenged for selling books on everything from Karl Marx to gay rights to dinosaurs, said she tells the "book police" that "it's important that people learn and read about everything, whether they believe it or not. It's not the government's job to tell me or anyone what they can read. I once lived and taught in Bulgaria and I don't like totalitarian regimes."

Book sellers do indeed seem most vulnerable to the PATRIOT Act. In November 2001, the American Booksellers Foundation for Free Expression (ABFFE) sent a letter to it members stating, "Dear Bookseller, Last week, President Bush signed into law an antiterrorism bill that gives the federal government expanded authority to search your business records, including the titles of the books purchased by your customers. There is no opportunity for you or your lawyer to object in court. You cannot object publicly either. The new law includes a gag order that prevents you from disclosing 'to any person' the fact that you have received an order to produce documents because of the gag order you should not tell ABFFE that you have received a court order you can simply tell us that you need to contact ABFFE's legal counsel."

Marsha Rummel of the Rainbow Bookstore Cooperative in Madison, Wisconsin, commented, "[T]he danger to booksellers is just one small part of this new landscape. We must collectively take a stand to defend our democratic rights, including the right to protest our government and oppose the war, and the right to read whatever we like."

According to *Newsweek,* the ACLU was searching for "Conan the Librarian," some librarian who would be willing to serve as a test case against the PATRIOT Act, with little success. The act was being used by the FBI as an excuse for broad new powers to check library records, Internet use and anything else that they claim might lead them to terrorists. "This statute trumps protections in place in 49 of 50 states," observed Gregory T. Nogeim of the ACLU.

"The effect of the USA PATRIOT Act upon businesses that loan, rent or sell books, videos, magazines and music CDs, is not to find and incarcerate terrorists - there are far more ways to investigate threats to the nation than to check on a terrorist's reading and listening habits - but to put a sweeping chilling effect upon constitutional freedoms," wrote Online Journal writer Walter Brasch.

James R. Elwood, executive vice president of the International Society for Individual Liberty, an umbrella organization representing individuals and groups in more than eighty countries, stated that the "rule of law - enshrined in the Bill of Rights - which protects the innocent - must be strictly upheld and that the new 'antiterrorist' laws be repealed."

According to Section 112 of the act, a "suspected terrorist" may be determined solely by certification by the attorney general on "reasonable ground" that he "believes" someone to be such.

"Section 236A gives the Attorney General unprecedented powers untouchable by any court, whereby he may detain a suspect in increments of up to six months at a time if he believes the suspect's release would threaten national security or the safety of the community or any person," wrote columnist Miller, noting that the act states, "At the Attorney General's discretion, no court shall have jurisdiction to review, by habeas corpus, petition, or otherwise, any such action or decision."

For such power to be concentrated in the hands of one man brings up the question of John Ashcroft's integrity, ambition and philosophical outlook. In 2000, the Democratic governor of Missouri, Mel Carnahan, was battling John Ashcroft for a U.S. Senate seat. Carnahan died in a small plane crash. His wife, Jean, was not with him. Jean agreed to fill the seat for her late husband should he win it, and Missouri voters delivered a blow to Ashcroft by casting their votes for a dead man, a clear indication of the respect held for Ashcroft in his home state.

A distinct warning about Ashcroft and what was to come came long before the 2001 terror attacks. In testimony opposing the nomination of John Ashcroft as attorney general given on January 16, 2001, Dr. Debra H. Freeman warned the Senate Judiciary Committee that Ashcroft would bring under the guise of "crisis management" a "form of brutal bureaucratic fascism on the United States that bears striking similarities to the conditions under which Adolf Hitler seized power in Germany in 1933."

Dr. Freeman, the national spokesperson for presidential candidate Lyndon H. LaRouche, said she wanted to present the "strongest possible opposition" to Ashcroft because "he would only augment the horrible abuses of power and criminal tyranny already rampant within the Justice Department and FBI bureaucracies."

Displaying remarkable foresight, Dr. Freeman said, "What you're going to get with a frustrated Bush administration, if it's determined to prevent itself from being opposed, you're going to get crisis management, where members of the special warfare types, of the secret government, the secret police teams, will set off provocations which will be used to bring about dictatorial powers and emotion, in the name of crisis management."

Until the 9/11 attacks, Ashcroft, who had been most noticeable to the American public when he ordered an exposed breast covered on the statue called The Spirit of Justice that stands in the Justice Departments's Hall of Justice, rapidly patched together a spate of antiterrorism laws, most of which would never have made it through Congress under normal circumstances. He already was warping U.S. laws beyond recognition by detaining as many as twelve hundred persons, most in violation of immigration laws.

But at least one vision of Ashcroft is absolutely outrageous. In a little-publicized announcement in August 2002, Ashcroft said he wanted the power to strip American citizens of their constitutional rights, including access to the court system, and indefinitely imprison them in interment camps on his word that they were "enemy combatants."

"The proposed camp plan should trigger immediate congressional hearings and reconsideration of Ashcroft's fitness for this important office," declared Jonathan Turley, a professor of constitutional law at George Washington University Law School who actively supported Ashcroft during his contentious nomination hearing. "Whereas al-Qaeda is a threat to the lives of our citizens, Ashcroft has become a clear and present threat to our liberties."

An example of the unevenness of Ashcroft justice was seen in the treatment of two Americans captured while fighting for the Taliban in Afghanistan - John Walker Lindh and Yasser Esam Hamdi. Lindh was given a lawyer and a trial where he plea bargained for a reduced prison sentence. Hamdi, a Louisiana-born prisoner captured in Afghanistan and held in the U.S. detention camp at the Guantanamo Bay naval base in Cuba, was transferred to a navy brig in Virginia, where he remained indefinitely floating off the Virginia coast.

When a federal judge ordered that the Justice Department present evidence justifying Hamdi's treatment, the government simply refused to comply, insisting that the judge could not interfere with the president's "absolute authority in a time of war."

Then there's the case of American citizen Jose Padilla, the "dirty" bomber. Padilla was arrested after federal authorities claimed they learned he was planning to construct a radioactive bomb. However, the Bush administration some time later quietly admitted they had no evidence that Padilla actually was planning anything like that. "What is clear [in this case] is that Padilla is an American citizen and was arrested in the United States - two facts that should trigger the full application of constitutional rights," said Turley.

"If you think this law applies only to foreign nationals, think again," admonished columnist Miller. "Jose Padilla, although by no means a model U.S.-born citizen, had his civil rights stripped from him [in May 2002] just by Ashcroft's uttering the magic words, 'enemy combatant' and 'suspected terrorist.' To this day, no solid evidence has been produced to substantiate Ashcroft's claims - neither bomb parts, nor bomb assembly instructions, nor any plans or maps of intended strike areas."

"Okay, now let's play a game," wrote columnist Carl Worden. "Replace the name Jose Padilla with Carl Worden. I get picked up and thrown into a military brig where I don't get my call or a visit with my attorney. I am being held without charges as an 'enemy combatant" and the government does not have to appear in open court to present evidence at my arraignment, and they don't have to release me until hostilities have ended - which in the case of the War on Terrorism, that would translate into a life sentence.

"In the meantime, they can say anything about me they want - but they don't have to prove it. They will probably allege a conspiracy of some sort, which means they don't have to produce hard evidence like illegal weapons or explosives. They will throw in a couple of verifiable facts for credibility purposes, such as my membership in the Southern Oregon Militia and my [proclaimed] outspoken 'anti-government,' 'Right Wing Extremist' rhetoric. They will display the weapons I own they will claim I had bomb-making supplies and equipment in my garage when they searched my premises [common household materials can be construed as bomb-making supplies]. That's right. They found my diabolical [ammunition] reloading bench. Now replace my name with yours and play the same game."

"We are only now getting a full vision of Ashcroft's America," mused Professor Turley. "Ashcroft is a catalyst for constitutional devolution, encouraging citizens to accept autocratic rule as their only way of avoiding massive terrorist attacks. His greatest problem has been preserving a level of panic and fear necessary to induce a free people to surrender rights so dearly won by their ancestors," he added. "Every generation has had Ashcrofts who view our laws and traditions as mere obstructions rather than protections in times of peril. But before we allow Ashcroft to denude our own constitutional landscape, we must take a stand and have the courage to say, 'Enough.' Every generation has its test of principle in which people of good faith can no longer remain silent in the face of authoritarian ambition. If we cannot join together to fight the abomination of American camps, we have already lost what we're defending."

Even the *New York Times* editorialized, "The Bush administration seems to believe, on no good legal authority, that if it calls citizens combatants in the war on terrorism, it can imprison them indefinitely and deprive them of lawyers. This defiance of the courts repudiates two centuries of constitutional law and undermines the very freedoms that President Bush says he is defending in the struggle against terrorism."

Writer Nat Hentoff grumbled, "It bothers me that the executive branch is taking the amazing position that just on the president's say-so, any American citizen can be picked up, not just in Afghanistan, but at O'Hare Airport or on the streets of any city in this country, and locked up without access to a lawyer or court just because the government says he's connected somehow with the Taliban or al-Qaeda. That's not the American way. It's not the constitutional way and no court can even figure out whether we've got the wrong guy."

When asked what the Founding Fathers might say about the Bush-Ashcroft vision for the PATRIOT Act, Congressman Paul laughed and said, "Our forefathers would think it's time for a revolution. This is why they revolted in the first place. They revolted against much more mild oppression."

Son of PATRIOT Act

In early 2003 there was an effort underway within the Justice Department to further expand the provisions and powers of the PATRIOT Act. And it was all done in such secrecy that even ranking members of congress did not know this act was in preparation.

Even Mark Corallo, deputy director of the Justice Department's Office of Public Affairs appeared unaware of the draft legislation. "This is all news to me. I have never heard of this," he told members of the Center for Public Integrity, a Washington-based group dedicated to "public service journalism." This center obtained a copy of the document and made it public in early 2003.

A spokesman for the House Judiciary Committee, Jeff Lungren, said, "We haven't heard anything from the Justice Department on updating the PATRIOT Act. They haven't shared their thoughts on that. Obviously, we'd be interested, but we haven't heard anything at this point."

After reviewing the draft legislation, Dr. David Cole of the Georgetown University Law School said raises a "lot of serious concerns." "It's troubling that they have gotten this far along and they've been telling people there is nothing in the works." He added the proposed changes "would radically expand law enforcement and intelligence gathering authorities, reduce or eliminate judicial oversight over surveillance, authorize secret arrests, create a DNA database based on unchecked executive 'suspicion,' create new death penalties, and even seek to take American citizenship away from persons who belong to or support disfavored political groups."

Innocently entitled the "Domestic Security Enhancement Act of 2003," this expansion of both police and government powers was kept deep within the confines of the Justice Department until leaked to the public. As usual, the corporate controlled mass media made little of the story but it sparked outrage on the Internet and from some columnists.

Editorial page writer Errol Louis of the *New York Sun* wrote, "[This] document is a catalog of authoritarianism that runs counter to the basic tenets of modern democracy." Columnist Jim Hightower termed it "Ashcroft's Latest Assault on Liberty."

A dissection of the PATRIOT Act expansion by Timothy H. Edgar, Legislative Counsel for the American Civil Liberties Union, revealed the legislation would diminish personal privacy by removing checks on government power by:

— Making it easier to initiate surveillance and wiretapping of U. S. Citizens under the authority of the little-known Foreign Intelligence Surveillance Court (FISC). (Sections 101, 102 and 107)

— Permitting the government, under certain circumstances, to bypass the FISC altogether and conduct warrantless wiretaps and searches. (Sections 103 and 104)

— Sheltering federal agents engaged in illegal surveillance without a court order from criminal prosecution if they are following the orders of Executive Branch officials. (Section 106)

— Creating a new category of "domestic security surveillance" that permits electronic eavesdropping of entirely domestic activity under looser standards than provided for ordinary criminal surveillance. (Section 122)

— Using an overly broad definition of terrorism that could cover some protest tactics such as those used by Operation Rescue or the protesters at Vieques Island, Puerto Rico, as a new predicate for criminal wiretapping and other electronic surveillance (Sections 120 and 121)

— Providing for general surveillance orders covering multiple functions for high-tech devices and by further expanding pen register and trap and trace authority for intelligence surveillance of U.S. citizens and lawful permanent foreign residents. (Sections 107-124)

— Creating a new and separate crime of using encryption technology that could add five years to any jail sentence for crimes committed with a computer. ((Section 144)

— Expanding the PATRIOT Act's definition of nationwide search warrants and giving the government secret access to credit reports with consent or judicial process (Sections 125 and 126)

— Enhancing the government's ability to obtain sensitive personal information without prior judicial approval and providing new penalties for failure to comply with written demands for such records. (Sections 128 and 129)

— Allowing for the sampling and cataloging of innocent Americans' genetic [DNA] information without a court order or the individual's consent. (Sections 301-306)

— Permitting sensitive personal information to be shared with state and local law enforcement agencies despite any connection to anti-terrorism measures, (Section 311)

— Terminating court-approved limits on police spying, put in place to prevent Mc-Carthy-era style police persecution based on political or religious affiliation. (Section 312)

— Permitting searches, wiretaps and surveillance of U.S. citizens on behalf of foreign governments - to include dictators and human rights abusers - in the absence of Senate-approved treaties. (Sections 321-322)

— Authorizing secret arrests in immigration, material witness and other cases where the detained person is not criminally charged. (Section 201)

— Threatening public health by severely restricting access to crucial information concerning health risks by facilities that use dangerous chemicals. (Section 202)

— Diminishing corporate responsibility by grant immunity to businesses that provide information to government terrorism investigations even if such actions are taken with disregard for the customer's privacy and show reckless disregard for the truth. (Section 313)

— Undermines basic constitutional rights by overly broad definitions of "terrorism" and "terrorist organization" which could result in stripping a native-born American of citizenship if they wittingly or unwittingly support any organization deemed terrorist by government officials. (Section 501)

— Creating 15 new categories of the death penalty, including one should a death result from otherwise peaceful protests such as Operation Rescue. (Section 411)

— Permitting arrests and extradition of American citizens to any foreign country including ones with bad human rights records, in the absence of a Senate-approved treaty and unfairly targeting immigrants by opening sensitive personal visa files to local law enforcement agencies and extended jail terms for common immigration offenses. (Sections 322, 311 and 502)

— Permitting summary deportations of American citizens deemed a threat to national security by Attorney General Ashcroft, even with no evidence of criminal activity, intent or terrorism. (Section 503)

—Completely abolishing fair hearings for American citizens convicted of minor criminal offenses through a retroactive "expedited removal" procedure and preventing any court from questioning the government's unlawful actions by explicitly exempting these cases from habeas corpus review. (Section 504)

ACLU counsel Edgar noted that the constitutional protection of habeas corpus (the right to a hearing to determine if any criminal offense has been committed) has not been exempted since the War Between the States.

Edgar added that despite the Justice Department's efforts to characterize both the PATRIOT Act and its proposed expansion as minor tinkering with statutory language, "the DOJ's modest descriptions of the powers it is seeking, and the actual scope of the authorities it seeks, are miles apart." "The USA PATRIOT Act undercut many of the traditional checks and balances on government power, " he explained. "The new draft legislation threatens to fundamentally alter the constitutional protections that allow us as Americans to be both safe and free. If adopted, the bill would diminish personal privacy by removing important checks on government surveillance authority, reduce the accountability of government to be public by increasing government secrecy, further undermine fundamental constitutional rights of Americans under an already over broad definition of 'terrorism,' and seriously erode the right of all persons to due process of law."

Many of the provision of the expansion of the PATRIOT Act seem to be so draconian and reprehensible that many people felt it could never be passed in the light of day. But, as noted by Professor Cole, author of *Terrorism and the Constitution*, this legislation may lay awaiting yet another pretext to make it law.

He said PATRIOT Act II "is troubling as a generic matter that they have gotten this far along and tell people that there is nothing in the works. What that suggests is that they're waiting for a propitious time to introduce it, which might well be when a war is begun. At that time there would be less opportunity for discussion and they'll have a much stronger hand in saying that they need these things right away."

Author and Internet commentator Whitley Strieber expressed similar sentiments by writing, "If there is a horrendous terrorist attack on our country in the next few weeks or months, and there emerges a similar lack of official will to prevent it, and then the Domestic Security Enhancement Act is placed before a terrified and compliant congress, then, in my opinion, the conclusion will be inescapable: the United States of America will have ceased to be a free nation and the first American dictatorship will be under way."

Big Brother's Technology

The only thing that is really required today to turn the United States into a *1984*-type controlled society is the technology to do so. Such technology was not available in 1984 but it is today. A national identification card has been talked about for years but civil libertarians have consistently cooled the public's receptivity to such a concept - until now.

In mid-2002, even as the initial fear over 9/11 began to subside, Representative Jim Moran of Virginia, citing increased concerns over terrorism, introduced legislation in Congress called the Driver's License Modernization Act of 2002 (H.R. 4633). This bill was styled as a law that would set uniform standards for driver's license's in all fifty states and the District of Columbia.

But it also included provisions to establish a national database and identification system. This bill codified a plan previously sent by Congress to the Department of Transportation urging the development of electronic "smart" drivers' licenses that contain imbedded programmable computer chips that could be checked by law enforcement authorities across the nation.

"So it's more of a national ID *system* [emphasis in the original], a linking of Department of Motor Vehicles - and the records they keep on you - across state lines, with some extra on-card security measures thrown in," wrote Frank Pellegrini of Time.com. "The plan, Congress hopes, will be cheaper and easier to implement, and less likely to incur the talk-show ire of civil libertarians and states' rights purists (the same type who squawked in 1908 when the FBI was born). But the approach is mere stealth - 50 different state ID cards all linked together is pretty much the same as one national ID card, just as all those new quarters are still worth 25 cents each, no matter which state is on the back."

The House bill also states the new ID card must "conform to any other standards issued by the Secretary [of Transportation]," an open invitation for bureaucrat tinkering.

New York City will be one of the first major cities to try out microchipped identification cards for the city's 250,000 employees. Some 50,000 officers and workers for the NYPD were scheduled to begin receiving their new ID cards before the end of 2002. The state-of-the-art plastic cards contain microchips, holograms and other security devices to prevent theft and to track employee work hours. On the front of this picture ID is the Statue of Liberty and two chips, one containing fingerprints and handprints and the other filled with personal information, including blood type and emergency telephone numbers. Police officials said eventually the ID cards will be used in conjunction with "biometric" hand scanners to ensure the person bearing the card is the correct one. They also hoped to save money in computing paychecks by using the cards to keep track of employee hours.

Pellegrini and others have warned that the real fight will come over when and where citizens will have to show such IDs. "The average American's driver's license gets a pretty good workout these days," he said, "certainly far more than traffic laws themselves would seem to warrant - but you can only get arrested for *driving* without one. If the U.S. domestic response starts to resemble Zimbabwe's, which passed a law in November [2001] making it compulsory to carry ID on pain of fine or imprisonment, well, that's something to worry about."

Quietly, the U.S. government has already been turning previous forms of recognition into full-fledged identity cards. According to the *El Paso Times*, Mexican immigrants are now using Mexican consular cards, known as *matriculas*, as identification.

In October 2002, the Mexican consul's office in El Paso announced a new "high security" consular card that carried a digital photo, holographic letters and a magnetic band for storing readable data. This program of consular cards began growing in 2000, after several large U.S. banks, including Wells Fargo, Bank of America and JP Morgan Chase agreed to accept the card from immigrants wanting to open a bank account. Today at least thirteen states accept the *matriculas* card as identification for persons applying for a driver's license and some cities and police departments recognize the card as legal identification.

The Mexican Consul in El Paso, Juan Carlos Cue Vega, said Mexico's Foreign Ministry was working to persuade the State of Texas to accept the card for driver's license applications. In 2002 alone, Mexico has issued 740,000 *matriculas*. Many saw this plan as nothing more than an under-the-table attempt to build a national computer database on every American. Tom Ridge of Homeland Security is all for it and President Bush, while claiming he opposed a national ID card, nevertheless supported the bill to standardize driver's licenses.

According to author Steven Yates, a teaching fellow at the Ludwig von Mises Institute "The long and the short of it is, the Driver's License Modernization Act of 2002 would bring us closer than ever before to establishing a comprehensive national ID system. The present excuse is that extreme measures are necessary to 'protect us against terrorism.' Such [previous] efforts existed as stealth measures little-noticed provisions buried in large, omnibus bills like the Welfare Reform Act, the Illegal Immigration Reform and Immigration Responsibility Act and the Kennedy-Kassenbaum Health Care Reform Acts, all in 1996. The provisions were to go into effect in October of 2000. The feds didn't think anyone would notice until it was too late, since no one had noticed the stealth measures that gave us civil forfeiture - those nasty provisions that allow the feds to take your car without compensation if they find, say, a certain amount of marijuana or some other illegal substance in it."

Yates also took note of the fact that in today's fearful climate, no one seems too concerned about the traditional wariness of such schemes. "It is a testimony to how much this country has changed since 9/11 that no one has visibly challenged H.R. 4633 as unconstitutional and incompatible with the principles of a free society. The 1990s gave us the obviously corrupt Clinton Regime and a significant opposition to federal power grabs. Now it's Bush the Younger, beloved of neocons [neo-conservatives] who see him as one of their own and believe he can do no wrong. Clearly, the slow encirclement of law-abiding U.S. citizens with national ID technology would advance such a cause [globalism or The New World Order] while doing little if anything to safeguard us against terrorism."

Yates also offered up a vision of the near future that disturbs many thinking people. He noted that if the feds really wanted to stifle dissent, they could 'freeze' the dissident's assets by reprogramming his database information. Scanners would not recognize him and he would become officially invisible, unable to drive or work legally, have a bank account, buy anything on credit, or even see a doctor. "Do we want to trust *anyone* [emphasis in the original] with that kind of power?" he asked.

It is just such a prospect that concerns many Christians, who see government control through computers and identification computer chips as the fulfillment of biblical prophecy warning that no one will be able to conduct business without the "mark of the Beast." This theme also was the premise of the popular Sandra Bullock film *The Net*.

Lest anyone think this is naïve or even paranoid nonsense, consider that in late October 2002, Applied Digital Solutions, Inc., a high-tech development company headquartered in Palm Beach, Florida, announced the launching of a national promotion for its new subdermal personal verification microchip. Entitled "Get Chipped," the promotion is hyping a device that can be implanted under a person's skin to transmit data to various locations. Describing the "VeriChip," company literature states it is "an implantable, 12mm by 2.1mm radio frequency device about the size of the point of a typical ballpoint pen. It contains a unique verification number. Utilizing an external scanner, radio frequency energy passes through the skin energizing the dormant VeriChip, which then emits a radio frequency signal containing the verification number. The number is displayed by the scanner and transmitted to a secure data storage site by authorized personnel via telephone or Internet."

In addition to "VeriChip Centers" in Arizona, Texas and Florida, the firm also fields the "ChipMobile," a motorized marketing and "chipping" vehicle. The new "Get Chipped" campaign was launched just days after the Food and Drug Administration ruled that the chip is not a regulated medical device.

Uses for the chip include controlling access to nonpublic facilities such as government buildings and installations, nuclear power plants, national research laboratories, correctional institutions and transportation hubs, either by itself or in conjunction with existing security technologies such as retina scanners, thumbprint scanners or face recognition devices. Company officials envision the chip will come to be used in a wide range of consumer products including PC and laptop computers, personal vehicles, cell phones, homes and apartments. They said the implanted chip will help stop identity theft and aid in the war against terrorists.

Several members of Congress seem quite at home with the idea of a national ID card or chip. Representative Jane Harman of California said, "I think this issue must be looked at. We don't automatically have to call it a national ID card, that's a radioactive term, but we can certainly think about smart cards for essential functions, but we need the database to support that."

This need for a national database was addressed in the USA PATRIOT Act, which authorized $150 million in tax money for the "expansion of the Regional Information Sharing System [to] facilitate federal-state-local law enforcement response related to terrorist acts."

Harman was one of many members of Congress who expressed a desire to speed up the process of identifying, categorizing and perhaps even chipping the population. In a statement prior to passage of the Patriot Act, she contended, "Never has someone been given such an immensely difficult job and so little authority to do it. Tom Ridge needs to be a Cabinet level official subject to Senate confirmation, with budgetary authority and accountability to Congress for a homeland security strategy and budget. Rather than give him a letter grade for his first six months on the job, I would use the administration's own color-coding system and assign the overall Homeland Security effort a red for severely behind schedule."

Asked if she thought the public was ready for such measures, Harman replied, "I think most people are really there. Keep in mind that if we have a second wave of attacks, the folks who are raising objections will probably lose totally."

Others agree, such as District of Columbia mayor Anthony A. Williams, who only added to the fear factor when he warned, "We are in a new really dangerous world now, and we have to maintain a higher level of security."

Williams's plan for increased security was to emulate such cities as London and Sydney by installing hundreds of video cameras throughout the city of Washington, all linked to a central command office. Williams predicted that Washington eventually will have such a surveillance system as England, which boasts more than two million cameras in airports, train stations, streets and neighborhoods.

Asked if such a scheme would seriously impact individual civil rights, Williams replied, "There will be trade-offs."

The Nevada Supreme Court in spring 2002 ruled it was okay for police to hide electronic monitoring devices on people's vehicles without a warrant for as long as they want. The court ruled that there is "no reasonable expectation of privacy" on the outside of one's vehicle and that attaching an electronic device to a man's car bumper did not constitute unreasonable search or seizure.

Then there must be consideration of satellite technology, which includes the two greatest electronic threats to privacy and individual freedom - Echelon and Tempest.

"The secret is out," wrote Jim Wilson in *Popular Mechanics* in early 2002. "Two powerful intelligence gathering tools that the United States created to eavesdrop on Soviet leaders and to track KGB spies are now being used to monitor Americans."

Echelon, the previously discussed global eavesdropping satellite and mainframe computer system, is operated from the Maryland headquarters of the National Security Agency. It intercepts and analyzes phone calls, faxes and e-mail sent to and from the United States, both with or without encryption. Encrypted messages are first decrypted and then joined with clear messages. The total is then checked by software known as "Dictionary" for "trigger words." Such terms as "nuclear bomb", "al-Qaeda", "Hamas", "anthrax", and others are then shuttled to appropriate agencies for analysis.

Although speculation and warnings about Echelon were circulating on the Internet for a number of years, it was not until 2001 that the U.S. government finally admitted to its existence. This came about because of high-profile investigations in Europe, where it was discovered that Echelon had been used to spy on Airbus Industrie and Thomson-CSF, two European companies. In actuality, the government had been using Echelon even as it was evolving into the multinational tool of today. In the late 1960s and 1970s, Presidents Lyndon Johnson and Richard Nixon used NSA technology to gather files on more than seven thousand American citizens and one thousand organizations, mostly those opposed to the Vietnam War.

Although paid for primarily by U.S. taxpayers, Echelon is multinational, involving the United Kingdom, Canada, Australia, New Zealand and even Italy and Turkey. Information gleaned from Echelon flows mostly to the CIA. According to investigator Wilson, "Based on what is known about the location of Echelon bases and satellites, it is estimated that there is a ninety percent chance that NSA is listening when you pick up the phone to place or answer an overseas call. In theory, but obviously not in practice, Echelon's supercomputers are so fast, they can identify Saddam Hussein by the sound of his voice the moment he begins speaking on the phone."

Amazing as all this may sound to those unfamiliar with Echelon, the sheer fact that the government now acknowledges it tells many that it already has become obsolete, largely due to burgeoning Internet traffic. Researchers now believe that Echelon may be phased out in favor of a ground-based technology known as "Tempest," which secretly read the displays on personal computers, cash registers, television sets and automatic teller machines (ATM).

Wilson said documents now available from foreign governments and older sources clearly show how these systems are used to invade our right to privacy. "We think you will agree it also creates a real and present threat to our freedom," he added.

In September 2002, the Associated Press obtained U.S. government documents showing that the Bush administration was considering the creation of a fund that would combine tax dollars with funds from the technology industry to pay for "Internet security enhancements." The documents, one under the title "executive summary for the National Strategy to Secure Cyberspace," discussed "sweeping new obligations on companies, universities, federal agencies and home users" to make the Net more secure, presumably from terrorists.

The new Net strategy was being headed up by Richard Clarke, top counterterrorism expert in both the Bush and Clinton administrations, and Howard Schmidt, a former senior executive at Microsoft Corp. The plan was expected to offer up more than eighty recommendations to tighten Internet security.

The Associated Press also wrote about a "key-logger" device which, during the new "sneak and peek" incursions by federal agents, can be secreted inside a computer using a viruslike program. The device, code named "Magic Lantern," records every key stroke on the computer, allowing authorities to capture passwords, which then allows them to enter encrypted data files. The FBI has acknowledged using such a device in a recent gambling investigation.

William Newman, director of the ACLU in Western Massachusetts, said the use of such technology could easily spread to all Americans. He pointed out that federal law enforcement agencies now are permitted "the same access to your Internet use and to your e-mail use that they had to your telephone records." He said this could lead to agencies overstepping their authority. "The history of the FBI is that they will do exactly that."

Other high-tech items to be employed in the War on Terrorism include a program being developed by the CIA called Fluent, which searches foreign Web sites and displays an English translation back to Langley. This may be used in conjunction with Oasis, a technology that transcribes worldwide radio and TV broadcasts.

The FBI and some police departments are now using a software program called dTective to trace financial transactions by dramatically improving the grainy video of surveillance cameras at banks of ATMs.

The feds are even working on techniques for restoring videotapes and computer disks that have been destroyed, cut up or tossed in water. One software program called Encase can recover deleted computer files and search for incriminating documents on any computer. This is being used by the FBI to examine computers seized in the wake of the 9/11 attacks.

Consider the gradual encroachment made by the government in assigning each and every member of the United States a computer or identity number:

· Social Security started in 1935.

· The current numbering system started in 1936.

· The IRS started requiring Social Security numbers on tax returns in 1962. Social Security cards plainly stated the number was "Not For Identification."

· In 1970, all banks were required to have your Social Security number.

· Military ID numbers were changed to Social Security numbers in 1971.

· By 1982, everyone receiving any sort of government largesse was required to obtain
   a Social Security number.

· By 1984, any person being declared a dependent for IRS tax purposes required a Social Security number. Within two years, even newborn babies were required to have a Social Security number under penalty of fine.

Numbering individual humans is already in place.

A tracking system will be next. And don't count on government watchdog organizations to maintain your privacy rights. In late 2002, the American Civil Liberties Union gave its stamp of approval to an electronic tracking system utilizing Global Positioning System (GPS) satellites to track suspects and criminals. This "VeriTracks" system is offered by the Veridan company of Arlington, Virginia Such GPS tracking not only keeps tabs on convicted criminals but also suspects and can even correlate their position with high-crime areas or crime scenes. Law enforcement agencies can create "electronic fences" around areas they deem off-limits to wearers of cell-phone-size GPS receivers. The module that records its exact position is carried on the waist while an electronic bracelet worn on the ankle acts as an electronic tether to the GPS receiver.

The module is placed in a docking system at night to recharge batteries and upload its data to a central headquarters, which checks to see if the wearer has been at any crime scenes.

How do you get someone to agree to this monitoring system? Sheriff Don Eslinger of Seminole County, Florida, answered, "It's either wear the GPS device or go to jail. Most of them find this much more advantageous than sitting in a cold jail cell, and it also saves us between $45 and $55 a day." Eslinger said his county had equipped ten pretrial suspects with the GPS device as a condition of making bond and that county officials hoped to expand the program to include nonviolent probationers and parolees.

And such surveillance technology is not being limited to felons and probationers. In Texas, some one thousand drivers allowed an insurance company to place a transponder in their vehicles to keep track of teenaged drivers and their speed.

The firm Digital Angel was developing a wristband that allows parents to log on to the Internet and instantly locate their children while another company, eWorldtrack, is working on a child-tracking device that will fit inside athletic shoes. The German firm Siemens has tested a seven-ounce tracking device that allows constant communication between parents and their children. Author Joe Queenan quipped, "Fusing digital mobile phone technology, a satellite-based global positioning system and good old-fashion insanity, the device can pinpoint a child within several yards in a matter of seconds."

Such GPS devices reminded civil libertarians of the 1987 film *The Running Man*, in which Arnold Schwarzenegger is equipped with a collar that will blow his head off if he leaves a prescribed area. They also note that the difference between a suspect and an innocent man is often unclear.

All this technology leads to scary scenarios, such as this one envisioned by *Village Voice* writer and editor Russ Kick: "You just got a call that your sister is in critical condition in the hospital. So you jump in your car and hit the gas. Trouble is, the speed limit is thirty miles per hour and your car won't let you drive any faster. Or maybe you're lucky enough to have a vehicle that still lets you drive at the speed you choose. A cop pulls you over and demands a saliva sample, so he can instantly match your DNA to a data bank of criminals' genes. You refuse and are arrested. After booking you, the authorities force you to submit to 'brain fingerprinting,' a technology that can tell if memories of illegal events are in your mind.

"By this point, you're thinking this is a worst-case scenario, a science-fiction dysphoria. Well, wake up and smell the police state, because all this technology - and more - is already being implemented."

Governing By Secrecy And Decree

While waging its War on Terrorism, the Bush administration has expanded government secrecy in ways hardly imaginable just a few years ago. Information has been sequestered away from the public and the Congress while law enforcement agencies have been allowed to operate in the shadows.

And this was not all in response to the 9/11 attacks. Well before September 11, Bush kept secret some four thousand pages related to presidential pardons granted by President Clinton as he was leaving office. The administration shielded Vice President Cheney by keeping secret the members and minutes of an energy policy task force headed by Cheney.

Shortly after 9/11, Bush held up the release of presidential papers from the Reagan administration in which his father played such a big role.

Among President Bush's many secrets was the fact that he has gathered around him one of the most wealthy circle of government officials in the history of the United States, earning mention in the *Guinness World Records 2000.*

According to *Guinness,* "George W. Bush (inaugurated as the 43rd U.S. president on January 20, 2001) has assembled the wealthiest cabinet in American history by appointing more multimillionaires to the top rank of his government than any of his predecessors. Of the 16 full government members at the heart of the Bush administration, 13 are multimillionaires, seven of them own assets more than $10 million. His cabinet has acquired the nickname 'tycoon's club.' Defense Secretary Donald Rumsfeld and Treasury Secretary Paul O' Neill each have declared assets of at least $61 million, while Secretary of State Colin Powell has at least $18 million."

Information such as this seeped into the public's consciousness during 2001 despite the distraction of the terrorist attacks and the subsequent bombing of Afghanistan and the war talk against Iraq. A mid-2002 telephone poll by the *New York Times* and *CBS News* found that out of one thousand adults polled, 58 percent - a clear majority - thought that big business had too much influence on government and Bush himself. The poll also showed that a majority of respondents felt Bush was hiding some things about his own corporate past and that the national economy was in its worst shape since 1994. By more than two to one, respondents said the Bush administration was more interested in protecting the interests of large companies than those of ordinary Americans.

And Bush was only slightly ahead of Cheney when it came to belief in their word that they had not done anything wrong while in the business sector. Of those surveyed, only 17 percent thought Bush was telling the truth about his dealings at Harken Energy, while only 11 percent thought Cheney was truthful about the accounting practices of Halliburton while under his control.

Of course, this means that the majority in both cases thought the two top national leaders were hiding something or outright lying about their business dealings. And no one was asked about Halliburton's under-the-table dealings with Iraq despite U.S. sanctions.

Amazingly, 80 percent of those polled said they thought that Bush shared the moral values that most Americans try to live by, which may explain Bush's continued high approval ratings - almost 70 percent in mid-2002. This was a significant drop from the peak of 89 percent in the days just after 9/11 but still impressive.

The poll respondents concern over big business exerting undue influence over the government is fully supported by a brief survey of top Bush administration leaders and their connection to multinational corporations, especially oil companies. This survey was conducted by the Center for Responsive Politics, a Washington-based nonprofit research group.

Defense Secretary Donald Rumsfeld has close ties to both multinational drug companies such as G. D. Searle, now a subsidiary of Pharmacia, as well as defense giants like General Dynamics and Motorola. He served on the boards of Gilead Sciences, Amylin Pharmaceutical, Kellogg, Sears and Allstate and the Tribune Company, which owns the *Los Angeles Times* and the *Chicago Tribune*.

Secretary of State Colin Powell has tight connections to Gulfstream Aerospace and General Dynamics as well as the media giant AOL Time Warner. His son Michael was the only commissioner on the Federal Communications Commission that advocated allowing the AOL Time Warner merger to go through without scrutiny. It was estimated that Powell's stock in the company increased in value by $4 million.

National Security Adviser Condoleezza Rice so impressed her fellow board members at Chevron they named a 130,000-ton oil tanker after her. She also served on the board of the multinational brokerage firm of Charles Schwab and the insurance giant Transamerica Corp.

Attorney General John Ashcroft has connections, through campaign contributions during his time as a Missouri senator, to AT&T, Microsoft, Schering-Plough, Enterprise Rent-A-Car and Monsanto. Microsoft was hoping Ashcroft would dismiss the anti-trust suit against the computer giant.

Director of the Office of Management and Budget Mitch Daniels Jr. was a former senior vice president of the pharmaceutical giant Eli Lilly. Daniels also had stock holdings of up to $100,000 in Citigroup, General Electric and another drug company, Merck.

Chief of Staff Andrew Card had been chief lobbyist for General Motors for more than a year before joining the Bush White House.

Secretary of Veterans Affairs Anthony Principi, formerly with the Federal Network and president of QTC Medical, also had significant holdings in Lockheed Martin, Microsoft, Schering-Plough, Ford Motor Co. and Qualcomm Inc.

Treasury Secretary Paul O'Neill was the former CEO and chairman of Alcoa, the world's largest manufacturer of aluminum, which was represented by the Texas law firm of Vinson & Elkins. This firm managed to find a loophole in Texas's environmental regulations that brought Alcoa to the top of the list of lead Texas polluters. Vinson & Elkins also happened to be George Bush's third largest campaign contributor. O'Neill was also a past president of International Paper and served on the boards of Lucent Technologies and Eastman Kodak.

Transportation secretary Norman Y. Mineta, the only Democrat in the Bush cabinet, nevertheless has a solid background in aerospace and aviation. He resigned his twenty-one-year seat in the House to take a job with Lockheed Martin. He also has corporate connections to Northwest Airlines, Greyhound, United Airlines, Union Pacific and Boeing.

Labor secretary Elaine Chao served as CEO of United Way and worked for the Peace Corps. But she also sat on corporate boards, including Dole Food, Clorox, and the health care companies C. R. Bard and HCA. She also was an executive at Bank of America.

Interior secretary Gale Norton's selection by Bush was a disappointment to environmentalists as she had represented several corporations in suits charging environmental and health hazards. Her corporate connections include Brownstein, Hyatt & Faber, Delta Petroleum, NL Industries, BP Amoco and Ford Motor Co.

Health and Human Services secretary Tommy G. Thompson, a former Wisconsin governor, reportedly sold his stock in pharmaceutical giants Merck and Abbott Laboratories when he signed on with the Bush administration but he retained his holdings in AOL Time Warner and General Electric. While serving as governor, Thompson received privileges, trips and contributions from the Philip Morris tobacco company.

Energy secretary Spencer Abraham, a one-term senator from Michigan, was the primary recipient of automotive industry campaign contributions, having received more than $700,000 from General Motors, Ford Motor Company, Lear Corp. and DaimlerChrysler.

Agriculture secretary Ann M. Veneman worked in the U.S. Deptartment of Agriculture under the former President Bush and was head of California's Department of Food and Agriculture in 1995. In 1994, she was on the board of directors of Calgene, Inc., the first company to bring genetically engineered food - the Flavr Savr tomato - to the public. Calgene was bought out by Monsanto, the nation's leading biotech company, which in turn was bought by Pharmacia in 2000. She also served on the International Policy Council on Agriculture, Food and Trade, a group funded by Cargill, Nestle, Kraft and Archer Daniels Midland.

Commerce secretary Donald L. Evans, an old buddy from Bush's early days in the oil business, was chairman and CEO of the Denver-based oil and gas company Tom Brown, Inc. He also sat on the board of another oil and gas firm, TMBR/Sharp Drilling. Evans broke all previous contribution records when he garnered more than $100 million for Bush's presidential campaign. As chief of the National Oceanic and

Atmospheric Administration, Evans will have control over the nation's coastline, the source of about 25 percent of U.S. gas and oil.

Rice, O'Neill, Powell and Chao are members of either the Council on Foreign Relations or the Trilateral Commission, both groups avowed proponents of globalism or one-world government.

The evidence is clear. The idea that America today is run by corporate executives for corporate executives is no conspiracy theory, it is a fact. And they are doing their best to see that it all operates in secrecy.

And while Bush has had meager experience in the corporate world, his 2000 campaign contributions tell a different story. According to *Sierra* magazine, the president received almost $1.9 million from the gas and oil industry, $203,000 from the mining industry and $300,000 from the timber and forest-products industry. The Republican Party got more than $20 million from the gas and oil industry, $4.7 million from the mining industry and $5.4 million from the timber and forest-products industry.

Enron's CEO, Kenneth Lay, as a "Bush Pioneer," personally raised more than $550,000 for the Bush campaign. More than thirty former energy executives, lobbyists and lawyers now serve in high-level jobs for the Bush administration. "The people running the United States government are from the energy industry," acknowledged Peabody Energy executive Fredrick Palmer. If the close corporate connections aren't enough to raise questions about government integrity, some have even raised the specter of nepotism.

In late February 2002, Elizabeth Cheney, the vice president's daughter, was named as a deputy secretary of state. Within about a week, her husband, Philip Perry, became chief counsel for the Office of Management and Budget, where he joined Director Mitchel Daniels, whose sister is an assistant attorney general.

"That's just the beginning," noted *Washington Post* reporter Dana Milbank. "Among Deborah Daniels's colleagues at Justice is young Chuck James, whose mother, Kay Coles James, is the director of the Office of Personnel Management, and whose father, Charles Sr., is a top Labor Department official. Charles James Sr.'s boss, Labor Secretary Elaine L. Chao, knows about having family members in government: Her husband is [Kentucky] Sen. Mitch McConnell and her department's top lawyer, Labor Solicitor Eugene Scalia, is the son of Supreme Court Justice Antonin Scalia.

"Everybody knows the Bush administration is famously loyal. One reason Bush aides are like family is because some of them *are* family. Ken Mehlman, the White House political director, regularly calls his younger brother Bruce, an assistant commerce secretary, to get his input. 'He's a great adviser -- I trust him like a brother,' quips Ken.

"Secretary of State Colin L. Powell is the father of Michael Powell, chairman of the Federal Communications Commission," added Milbank. "The director of the Federal Trade Commissions office of policy planning, Ted Cruz, is married to a senior official in the U.S. Trade Representatives office, Heidi Cruz. 'It's a little bit like having adjoining booths at the county fair,' she says."

The *Post* article goes on to name numerous familial connections between members of the Bush administration, which argues that there is no nepotism involved and that all office holders are qualified in their own right.

Another secret of the Bush presidency is that his contention that he must defend his office from the loss of power is blatantly untrue. The American president today carries far more power than ever imagined by our Founding Fathers or even more modern chief executives like Franklin D. Roosevelt.

Yet, Bush argues that his actions to ride roughshod over both the Congress and the Constitution are somehow necessary to preserve the presidency.

"I have an obligation to make sure that the presidency remains robust and that the legislative branch doesn't end up running the executive branch," Bush argued in mid-2002. He either ignored or didn't realize that by preparing an attack on Iraq, he was preempting the power of Congress. When he and his appointees rammed the USA PATRIOT Act through a Congress that had little or no input, he likewise took powers from the representatives of the people.

Bush's press secretary, Ari Fleischer, also failed to study recent history when he stated that presidential powers have been diminished "in multiple ways" as part of a "long-standing, gradual process."

Perhaps this effort to take power away from legislators was the reason that Bush announced his legal advisers had told him he did not need to consult Congress before ordering a strike on Iraq, despite the fact that war-making powers are explicitly granted the Congress by the U.S. Constitution.

"What the president is claiming is legally and historically absurd and politically stupid," stated Bruce Fein, a former Justice Department official who worked for several past Republican administrations. "[The United States] has never had a more imperial presidency, at least since Roosevelt during his conduct of World War II."

Bush argued that he must work in secrecy to regain open dialog with his advisers and various experts. Bush-appointed chairman of the

Republican National Committee, Mark Racicot, explained that "the ability of the president to carry on communications and get unvarnished advice has eroded over a period of time."

Many Washington insiders, including Fein, scoffed at this argument. "I've been around this town a long time, almost 30 years, and I've never encountered one individual who told me he's not going to the Oval Office unless he's promised confidentiality. It's the biggest hoax in the world. Why he's making up all this stuff is utterly and completely baffling."

Since taking office in January 2001, President Bush has wrapped the Oval Office in more secrecy than any previous president. President Bill Clinton's White House looked absolutely transparent compared to Bush's. One of Bush's first efforts as president was to freeze the release of papers from the Reagan administration, which had been scheduled to be released in 2001.

But in the matter of executive privilege, Bush was two-faced - documents that placed President Clinton in a bad light were released with impunity while documents that might have put Clinton in a more favorable light were withheld as executive privilege. For example, in summer 2001, when congressional investigators requested transcripts of three discussions between Clinton and Israeli Prime Minister Ehud Barak concerning a Clinton pardon for Marc Rich, the financial wizard who stiffed the IRS for $48 million and claimed citizenship in the United States, Israeli and Spain, the Bush White House promptly turned them over with the explanation that they were not classified.

"Given the secrecy that the Bush-Cheney administration has pursued, it's inconceivable that they would turn this information over if it affected President Bush," commented Democratic staff director for the House Government Reform Committee Phil Schiliro.

On November 1, 2001, with the nation in turmoil following the 9/11 attacks, Bush signed an executive order "reinterpreting" the 1978 Presidential Records Act, which provided for the public release of former presidents' documents after they left office. Bush claimed the executive privilege to veto the release of any such documents and thereby establish a "process that I think will enable historians to do their job and at the same time protect state secrets."

Historians were so unimpressed with Bush's logic that before the month was out a group had filed a lawsuit to stop his executive order. Parties to the suit included the American Historical Association, the National Security Archive at George Washington University, the Organization of American Historians, Public Citizen, the Reporter's

Committee for Freedom of the Press and history professors Hugh Graham and Stanley Kutler.

"The Presidential Records Act of 1978, which specified that after January 20, 1981, all official presidential and vice presidential records became the property of the federal government, was meant to shift power over White House documents from former presidents to professional government archivists, and ultimately, to the public," said Thomas Blanton, director of the National Security Archives. "But the Bush order attempts to overturn the law, take power back, and let presidents past and present delay public access indefinitely."

Joan Claybrook, president of Public Citizen, charged that Bush's decree "violates not only the spirit but the letter of the law." "We will not stand by while the administration tramples on the people's right to find out about their own government," she added.

The group's attorney, Scott Nelson, summed up the feeling of many people when he said, "It's interesting that the first beneficiary of this new doctrine would be the father of the man who announced it." He referred, of course, to Bush's father, who served as vice president and virtually ran the government for some time after Ronald Reagan was seriously wounded in March 1981.

"This administration is the most secretive of our lifetime, even more secretive than the Nixon administration," said Larry Klayman, chairman of Judicial Watch, the conservative group that sued the government for release of the names of Cheney's energy task force. "They don't believe the American people or Congress have any right to information."

Just after the 9/11 attacks, Attorney General Ashcroft sent a memo to all government agencies urging them to turn down more Freedom of Information requests in favor of "institutional, commercial and personal privacy interests."

This represented a dramatic reversal of decades of open government. "We are moving from a right to know to a need to know society," observed Gary Bass of OMB Watch, a private group that monitors government spending and legislation.

Since 9/11, thousands of pages of documents have vanished from the Internet. Some that might have a direct impact on security measures are understandable, others less so. But the new heightened security has proven a boon to corporate despoilers who would like their sordid track records on safety and environmental pollution kept from the public. Activists and newsmen can no longer gain information on polluting chemical plants or locate hazardous waste dumps.

"There is a pattern of secrecy that is a defining characteristic of the Bush administration," noted Steven Aftergood, who heads government secrecy research for the Federation of American Scientists. "It resists even the most mundane requests for information."

Taking a cue from President Clinton, Bush turned to executive order, many activated without fanfare or publicity, to effect his rule.

Then there is the issue of the "shadow government." On March 1, 2002, well after the 9/11 attacks, President Bush announced that the American public needn't worry about the survival of vital federal government functions because a "shadow government" made up of unelected bureaucrats were working in underground bunkers stocked with supplies of food, water and electric generators to preserve the government. Many people found little consolation in the idea that while their cities might be devastated by biological, chemical or nuclear terrorism, the Agriculture Department and the IRS would still be there for them. Plans for COG, or Continuity of Government, have been in place since the beginning of the Cold War but only revved up by the Bush administration in the wake of the 9/11 attacks.

Actually, authors and commentators have spoken out about a shadow government that runs the country in secret for many years. Colonel Fletcher Prouty called it the "Secret Team," while Bill Moyers called it the "Secret Government."

The shadow government made public by President Bush in 2002 was only about the bureaucrats that would try to continue government services in the event of a massive attack or emergency. There was no mention of the shadow or parallel government that has operated since the signing of the National Security Act of 1947 and the coup that took place in Dallas in 1963.

The federal shadow government could well have been named the "Secret Government." The Republican Speaker of the House Dennis Hastert said he only had a vague idea of this sub-rosa government and he is third in line to assume the presidency.

Although some one hundred senior government managers go to one of two secret East Coast underground destinations on a rotating basis to work within the "Shadow Government," according to the *Washinton Post*, "Only the executive branch is represented in the full-time shadow government."

Following a catastrophic attack, these shadow bureaucrats would try to contain national disruption of food, water, transportation, energy and telecommunications, then move on to reconstitute the federal government. But this is all hush-hush. Participants cannot reveal the whereabouts of these underground retreats even to their own families, who are not allowed to join them.

And the shadow government has now been tied to Tom Ridge and his Homeland Security apparatus. And Ridge won't reveal any details on its cost or budget.

This prompted a threat from Senate Majority Leader Tom Daschle that he might issue a subpoena to Ridge in order to find out what all these secret preparations are costing the American taxpayer. Bush had even refused to allow Ridge to testify to Congress about his plans and their costs. Ridge finally sent a written statement to a joint meeting of several committees.

Daschle said secrecy about the shadow government was so tight he had not learned about it until he read about it in the *Washington Post*. "We have not been informed at all about the role of the shadow government or its whereabouts or what particular responsibilities they have or when they would kick in," groused Daschle.

Klayman, executive director of Judicial Watch, the group that criticized President Clinton so doggedly, stated, "This is a case of where left and right agree. True conservatives don't act this way. We see an unprecedented secrecy in this White House that we find very disturbing."

Michael Ventura of the *Austin Chronicle* wrote, "Without an active free press (especially the *New York Times*, the *Washington Post* and the *Los Angeles Times*) our elected representatives in Congress would know virtually nothing of most of the major steps the Bush administration has taken not only since September 11, but since last spring [2001]. If America means to you a republic governed according to a Constitution that carefully stipulates checks and balances among the White House, Congress, and the judiciary - a system in which none can overwhelm the others, and in which each is responsible to the others - then you no longer live in America.

"This is not some dire warning about the future. This has happened and is happening. A free press is noting the process step by step: braver members of Congress, Republican and Democrat, have voiced alarm and are attempting legal measures to exercise their constitutional duties (so far to no avail); watchdogs on the right and left agree on the urgency of the situation while most citizens say and do nothing, giving tacit approval to a new (yes, new!) de facto system of government that recognizes no obligation to obey or enforce the letter or spirit of the Constitution."

The Bush administration is packed with men and women who claim to be conservatives. But what is it they wish to conserve? It would appear not to be the conservation of a constitutional republic.

"[Conservative] does not describe the Bush administration at all," added Ventura. "They ignore Congress almost completely on crucial issues; they feel no obligation to inform American citizens of the White House's deliberations or even its policies, whether or not national security is at stake; they concentrate tremendous power among the very few. That is not conservatism. There is only one word that adequately describes the bent and preference of George W. Bush's White House: Totalitarianism."

The Crimes Of Henry Kissinger

If conspiracy theorists wanted proof of a plot by the globalists to manipulate any investigation into 9/11, it came in late November 2002 when President Bush named former secretary of state Henry Kissinger to head a ten-person commission to probe the events of 9/11. This appointment created a firestorm in some quarters.

After all, most thoughtful people realized that any terrorism problems the USA is experiencing are the result of many years of neocolonial foreign policy. Much of that policy came under the direction of Kissinger. Many people asked if anyone truly believed the public would get an honest and in-depth investigation by Kissinger concerning the context of the September 11 attacks. Critics of this appointment compared it to that old bromide of "putting the fox in charge of the hen house." Even the *New York Times* in a November 29, 2002, editorial suggested that the White House selected Kissinger "to contain an investigation it has long opposed."

Therefore, it came as no great surprise to those who have tracked Kissinger's exploits through the years when he abruptly resigned on Friday, December 13, 2002, ostensibly to prevent any questions of conflict of interest. His company, Kissinger Associates, a privately held international consulting company, represents worldwide clients as well as some nations. Questions arose when Kissinger learned that as chairman of the 9/11 commission (the Kissinger Commission?) he would have to submit a list of his firm's clients. In a letter to President Bush, he wrote "It has become clear the controversy would quickly move to the consulting firm I have built and own. To liquidate Kissinger Associates cannot be accomplished without significantly delaying the beginning of the joint commission's work. I have, therefore, concluded that I cannot accept the responsibility you have proposed."

Even before the 9/11 commission was fully constituted, conspiracy researchers were urging the public to keep a watchful eye on both members and their business and societal connections. Based on

Internet chatter, they obviously were concerned that the new commission might become a clone of the Warren Commission, which conducted a largely discredited investigation of the JFK assassination in 1964.

The selection of Kissinger did however open a window on the inner connections between the U.S. government and secret societies. Most Americans, those who get their news and information exclusively from the six o'clock news and the local newspaper, knew little of Kissinger except he was 56th secretary of state and winner of the 1973 Nobel Peace Prize. He also served as assistant to the president for national security affairs to both Nixon and Gerald Ford.

Kissinger was born in Fuerth, Germany, on May 27, 1923. He came to the United States in 1938 when his parents immigrated from Nazi Germany and gained U.S. citizenship on June 19, 1943. He gained entrée to American military and intelligence circles when he served in the U.S. Army Counter-Intelligence Corps and was a captain in the Military Intelligence Reserve from 1943 to 1949. He received his B.A. degree graduating summa cum laude, at Harvard College in 1950 and his M.A. and Ph.D. degrees at Harvard University in 1952 and 1954 respectively. From 1954 until 1971 he was a member of the Faculty of Harvard University, both in the Department of Government and at the Center for International Affairs. He was associate director of the Center from 1957 to 1960. He served as Study Director, Nuclear Weapons and Foreign Policy, for the Council on Foreign Relations from 1955 to 1956; director of the Special Studies Project for the Rockefeller Brothers Fund from 1956 to 1958; director of the Harvard International Seminar from 1951 to 1971, and director of the Harvard Defense Studies Program from 1958 to 1971 while on leave of absence.

He has written many books and articles on U.S. foreign policy, international affairs, and diplomatic history and has received numerous prestigious awards, chiefly from globalist organizations. He also served as a consultant to the Department of State (1965~68), United States Arms Control and Disarmament Agency (1961~68), Rand Corporation (1961~68), National Security Council (1961~62), Weapons Systems Evaluation Group of the Joint Chiefs of Staff (1959~60), Operations Coordinating Board (1955), Director of the Psychological Strategy Board (1952), Operations Research Office (1951), and Chairman of the National Bipartisan Commission on Central America (1983~84).

But there is a darker side to Kissinger. He must be careful in his travels because in certain countries there are warrants outstanding on Kissinger, who has been charged with war crimes and complicity in murder. Christopher Hitchens, author if several books and the *Harper's* magazine article "The Case Against Henry Kissinger," presents a wealth of documentation showing that Kissinger was the responsible party behind a number of acts that can be considered war crimes and that, in 1970, Kissinger ordered the removal of Chilean army Commander-in-Chief Rene Schneider. Schneider, a supporter of Chile's constitution and opposed to a right-wing coup against Socialist president Salvadore Allende, was murdered in 1970 by right-wing plotters within the Chilean military. In early September 2001, *60 Minutes* aired interviews with former U.S. ambassador to Chile Edward Korry and Peter Kornbluh of the National Security Archives, both of whom confirmed Kissinger's responsibility in Schneider's death. On September 10, Schneider's family filed suit against Kissinger as well as former CIA director Richard Helms in the U.S. District Court for the District of Columbia, accusing them of responsibility for the murder. The case still was undecided in late 2002 but many observers felt the suit may have played a role in President Bush's opposition to joining a World Criminal Court. He reportedly feared that Kissinger and other Americans might be hauled before the judges.

Author Hitchens pointed to the basis for this fear, writing that the murder of General Schneider was "a lay-down case from soup to nuts: we know who commissioned it, who paid for it, who organized it, who shipped the illegal money, who shipped the dirty weapons to Chile to have it done, and who paid the murderers after the crime had been committed. And the same name and the same face recurs throughout. We charge Henry Kissinger with murder for that and we say that the society that tolerates it is tolerating murder, too. And that's, therefore, a big reproach to a society that claims to be bound by law and responsive to justice."

The controversial death of the leftist Allende - he reportedly committed suicide following a right-wing coup backed by Chilean military leaders in 1972 - already has received voluminous publicity. Most researchers believe his death and the coup were orchestrated by Kissinger and the CIA. It was during this time that Kissinger stated, "I don't see why we need to stand by and watch a country go communist due to the irresponsibility of its own people."

Hitchens further accused Kissinger of helping sabotage the 1968 presidential election by undermining the Paris peace talks regarding Vietnam, which assured the election of Richard Nixon. "The combination of the subversion of that election and the extension of that war qualifies, I think, to be termed the single wickedest act in the history of this republic," commented Hitchens. Of the four people who concerted that policy - Richard Nixon, Attorney General John Mitchell, Vice President Spiro Agnew and Henry Kissinger - only one has escaped any kind of indictment so far." Many commentators have written about the deceptions of Congress and the unconstitutional measures against antiwar protesters by Nixon and Kissinger.

Yet another individual and controversial death has been attributed to Kissinger. In the early 1980s, Italian authorities discovered a conspiracy to overthrow their government centered around a Masonic Lodge known as Propaganda Masonica Due or P2. The P2 Lodge plot involved three cabinet ministers, forty members of Parliament, forty-three military generals, eight admirals, security service chiefs, the police chiefs of four major cities, industrialists, financiers, entertainment celebrities, twenty-four journalists and hundreds of diplomats and civil servants.

The lodge was founded by a leader of a secret society called the Knights of Malta. Modern American Knights included CIA directors John McCone and William Casey. Casey, along with Reagan's first secretary of state, Alexander Haig, has been connected to fellow Knight Licio Gelli, who during the 1980s turned this little-used Italian Masonic Lodge into what was termed a "worldwide fascist conspiracy" with the help of the Mafia, the Vatican Bank and the CIA. Gelli was a "business partner of [Nazi war criminal] Klaus Barbie, a financial backer of [fascist South American dictator] Juan Peron, a paid CIA contact and an honored guest at Ronald Reagan's 1980 inauguration," according to authors Jonathan Vankin and John Whalen. He created what an Italian court indictment called a "secret structure [that] had the incredible capacity to control a state's institutions to the point of virtually becoming a state-within-a-state." Gelli also claimed to be on friendly terms with former president George Bush, who some claimed was an "honorary" P2 Lodge member.

During subsequent trials in Italy involving P2 members, one prominent American name kept cropping up - a name with close connections to secret societies in the United States. Italian prime minister Giulio Andreotti, a close friend of Gelli on trial for his Mafia involvement, named Henry Kissinger as a character witness. In addition, both a close associate and the widow of former Italian prime minister Aldo Moro - kidnapped and murdered reportedly by the leftist Red Brigade in 1978 - testified that Moro had been threatened by Kissinger to stop his stabilizing financial polices or "you will pay dearly for it."

Then there are the many questions concerning Kissinger's role in the estimated 700,000 deaths of Cambodian peasants. Edward S. Herman, professor emeritus of the Wharton School at the University of Pennsylvania, wrote extensively on Kissinger's involvement in these deaths during the Vietnam War and pointed to his dubious achievement as the person responsible for more deaths in Southeast Asia than the infamous Pol Pot. Likewise, it was Kissinger as secretary of state under Ford who approved Indonesian president Suharto's invasion of East Timor, which resulted in yet another bloodbath.

Upon departing as U.S. secretary of state, Kissinger trucked State Department records to the Rockefeller estate at Pocantico Hilla near Tarrytown, New York. These documents were subsequently recovered for their rightful owners, the American public, but not before Kissinger made a substantial amount of money publishing three volumes of memoirs. These writings left out significant issues of his years of service - including deals with China, the loss of Angola in Africa and the East Timor affair - and even proved to be untrue in some incidences after official documents were later declassified.

After leaving government, Kissinger set himself up as a national security adviser to many nations by forming and serving as chairman of Kissinger Associates. According to author Walter Isaacson, Kissinger started his consulting firm with $350,000 loaned to him by Goldman Sachs and three banks. Early on, he hired Brent Scowcroft and Lawrence Eagleburger, both of whom later left to join the first Bush administration. It should be noted that Eagleburger has been a member of both the Council on Foreign Relations and the Trilateral Commission.

It is such secret societies as these that form a hidden backdrop to the events most Americans only know about from superficial reporting in the corporate mass media. An excellent example of the influence of such globalist organizations can be found in Kissinger's own meteoric rise to power. In 1955, Kissinger was merely another unknown ex-military academic until he attended a meeting at the Marine Corps School at Quantico, VA, hosted by then presidential foreign affairs assistant Nelson Rockefeller. This meeting was the start of a lengthy friendship between the two, culminating in a $50,000 outright gift to Kissinger from Rockefeller. Kissinger soon was introduced to David Rockefeller and other prominent members of the Council on Foreign Relations (CFR). Through the CFR, Kissinger obtained funding and entree to ranking officials of the Atomic Energy Commission, the three branches of the military, the CIA and the State Department, which he used to produce a best-selling book entitled *Nuclear Weapons and Foreign Policy,* in which he argued that a nuclear war might be "winnable."

Even today Kissinger remains a formidable force in world affairs. He is the consummate secret-society insider and his career has been surrounded by persons connected to these globalist groups. For example, according to several researchers large amounts of funding for organizations of both the left and right comes from CFR connected groups, including the Rubin Foundation, represented by the New York law firm of Lord, Day and Lord. The Lord family has counted members on the rolls of Skull and Bones since 1898. Winston Lord [The Order, 1959], a former aide to Henry Kissinger, in 1983 was chairman of the Council on Foreign Relations and later President Reagan's ambassador to China.

In late 2002, President Bush, after naming secret-society insider Kissinger to head the 9/11 investigation, turned to other leading members. Following the resignation of Securities and Exchange chairman Harvey Pitt, Bush chose as a replacement William Donaldson, head of an investment research firm and first dean of the Yale School of Management. Donaldson also had been undersecretary of state for Henry Kissinger and a member of the CFR. Bush's replacement for outgoing chief economic assistant to the president Lawrence Lindsey was former Goldman Sachs chairman Steven Friedman, who has held membership in the Trilateral Commission, Council on Foreign Relations and the secretive and powerful Bilderbergers.

Secret Societies

Do such groups actually exist and do they truly exert power beyond their numbers? Secret societies not only exist, they have played an important role in national and international events right up to this day.

The Trilateral Commission publishes its membership as well as position papers but its inner workings are secret. The CFR also publishes a membership roll but members are pledged to secrecy regarding its goals and operations. The Bilderberg group keeps both its agenda and membership a secret. These are not secret societies so much in the sense that no one knows about them, but rather that one cannot freely join any of them. One must be invited and then adhere to stringent membership criteria, one such being the support of globalism often referred to as the New World Order after several comments by former president Bush. A pledge never to make public what is discussed in their sessions qualifies these groups as secret societies.

It is obvious why these people want their discussions kept from the public. The July 20, 1992, issue of *Time* magazine quoted CFR member Strobe Talbot as saying, "In the next century [today], nations as we know it will be obsolete; all states will recognize a single, global authority." This was an extremely explicit articulation of the goals of the New World Order. Talbot, who as President Clinton's deputy secretary of state presumably swore an oath to protect and defend the U.S.

Constitution, then added, "National sovereignty wasn't such a great idea after all."

Publisher John F. McManus noted that in the fall of 1998 as impeachment loomed over Clinton, he hurried to New York to seek support from his CFR friends. "Bill Clinton knows well that he serves as President because the members of the 'secret society' to which he belongs chose him and expect him to carry out its plans," wrote McManus.

Clinton was not the only recent president with connections to these groups. President George H. W. Bush was a Trilateralist, a CFR member and a brother in the mysterious Order of Skull and Bones. George W. Bush, however, was also a member of the secretive and exclusive Order of Skull and Bones while at Yale.

While the younger Bush has remained off the published membership lists of these societies, it has been charged from several quarters that he takes his orders from his father and others well connected to these groups, such as Vice President Dick Cheney, undoubtedly the most powerful vice president in history. He has carried membership in both the Trilateral Commission and the Council on Foreign Relations. And amazingly enough, the Bush family are direct blood relatives to the royal family of England going all the way back to King Charles II. And there's more.

"[President George W. Bush] is closely related to every European Monarch both on and off the throne," stated Harold Brooks-Baker, publishing director for *Burke's Peerage*, a prestigious genealogical publication that has researched royal bloodlines in Britain since 1826. Commenting on his genealogical search of the Bush family history dating back one thousand years, Brooks-Baker added, "Not one member of his family was working class, middle class, or even middle, middle class." They were all aristocrats, those same people that most early settlers in America came here to escape.

President Ronald Reagan did not officially belong to these groups but his administration was packed with both current and former members. After being shot less than two months after taking office, much of the early Reagan administration was run by his vice president, George Herbert Walker Bush.

President Jimmy Carter's administration was so filled with members of the Trilateral Commission that conspiracy researchers had a field day. The issue even prompted much commentary in the corporate mass media but soon dropped from sight.

By the early 1970s, thanks to burgeoning communications technology, many Americans were becoming more aware of secretive organizations such as the Council on Foreign Relations. Former CFR chairman David Rockefeller, apparently in an effort to deflect public attention from CFR activities, instigated the creation of a more public offshoot organization - the Trilateral Commission.

Both the commission and its predecessor, the CFR, are held out by conspiracy researchers as the epitome of covert organizations that may be guiding public policy in directions opposite to those either in the best interest of or desired by the public.

The concept of the Trilateral Commission was originally brought to Rockefeller by Zbigniew Brzezinski, then head of the Russian Studies Department at Columbia University. While at the Brookings Institution, Brzezinski had been researching the need for closer cooperation between the trilateral nations of Europe, North America and Asia.

In 1970, Brzezinski wrote in *Foreign Affairs*, a CFR publication, "A new and broader approach is needed - creation of a community of the developed nations which can effectively address itself to the larger concerns confronting mankind. A council representing the United States, Western Europe and Japan, with regular meetings of the heads of governments as well as some small standing machinery, would be a good start."

Brzezinski's vision raised the suspicions of those opposed to the consolidation of world political and economic power. Declaring "National sovereignty is no longer a viable concept," he predicted "movement toward a larger community by the developing nations through a variety of indirect ties and already developing limitations on national sovereignty." He foresaw this larger community being funded by "a global taxation system." In explaining that a cooperative hub, such as the Trilateral Commission, might set the stage for future consolidation, he reasoned, "Though the objective of shaping a community of developed nations is less ambitious than the goal of world government, it is more attainable."

Brzezinski's hope for a global society did not exclude nations then under the rule of Marxism, which he described as "a further vital and creative stage in the maturing of man's universal vision" and "a victory of the external man over the inner, passive man, and a victory of reason over belief."

Brzezinski's plan for a commission of trilateral nations was first presented during a meeting of the ultra-secret Bilderberg group in April 1972 in the small Belgian town of Knokke. Reception to Brzezinski's proposal reportedly was enthusiastic. With the blessing of the Bilderbergers and the CFR, the Trilateral Commission began organizing on July 23~24, 1972, at the 3,500-acre Rockefeller estate at Pocantico

Hills, a subdivision of Tarrytown, New York. Participants in this private meeting included Rockefeller, Brzezinski, Brookings Institution director of Foreign Policy Studies Henry Owen, McGeorge Bundy, Robert Bowie, C. Fred Bergsten, Bayless Manning, Karl Carstens, Guido Colonna di Paliano, Francois Duchene, Rene Foch, Max Kohnstamm, Kiichi Miyazawa, Saburo Ikita and Tadashi Yamamoto. Apparently these founders were selected by Rockefeller and Brzezinski.

The Trilateral Commission officially was founded on July 1 1973, with David Rockefeller as chairman. Brzezinski was named founding North American director. North American members included Georgia governor Jimmy Carter, U.S. Representative John B. Anderson [another presidential candidate] and Time, Inc., editor-in-chief Hedley Donovan. Foreign founding members included the late Reginald Maudling, Lord Eric Roll, *Economist* editor Alistair Burnet, FIAT president Giovanni Agnelli and French vice president of the Commission of European Communities Raymond Barre. The total exclusive membership remains about three hundred persons.

Although the commission's official yearly publication, *Trialogue*, stated, "The Trilateral Commission was formed in 1973 by private citizens of Western Europe, Japan and North America to foster closer cooperation among these three regions on common problems," skeptical conspiracy authors saw "closer cooperation" as more like "collusion" of the multinational bankers and corporate elite with an eye toward one-world government.

The Trilateral Commission has headquarters in New York, Paris and Tokyo. An executive committee of thirty-five members administers the commission, which meets roughly every nine months, rotating between the three regions.

It is not surprising that the question of who funds this group has arisen. Commission spokesmen stress that the group does not receive any government funding. A report in 1978 showed that commission funding from mid-1976 to mid-1979 was $1,180,000, much of which came from tax-exempt foundations such as the Rockefeller Brothers Fund, which in 1977 alone put up $120,000. Donations also came from the Ford Foundation, the Lilly Endowment, the German Marshall Fund and corporations such as Time, Bechtel, Exxon, General Motors, Wells Fargo and Texas Instruments.

In addition to *Trialogue*, the commission has regularly issued a number of "Task Force Reports" or "Triangle Papers," which are publicly available. "For years, conspiracy-oriented newsletters of the Right and Left have been peddling Trilateral 'secrets' which were obtained directly from the Commission!" snickered journalist and

Trilateral Commission researcher Robert Eringer. It is obvious to most researchers that, as these papers are available to the public, they don't contain any true inner "secrets."

One such paper, entitled "The Crisis of Democracy", was published by the commission in 1975. One of its authors, Harvard political scientist Samuel P. Huntington, avowed that America needed "a greater degree of moderation in democracy." He argued that democratic institutions were incapable of responding to crises such as the Three Mile Island nuclear accident or the Cuban refugee boat lift operation. The paper suggested that leaders with "expertise, seniority, experiences and special talents" were needed to "override the claims of democracy."

Just a few examples indicate that those espousing Trilateralist policies often end up implementing those same policies in the government. Three years after his paper was published, Huntington was named coordinator of security planning for Carter's National Security Council. In this capacity, Huntington in 1979 prepared Presidential Review Memorandum 32, which led to the 1979 Presidential Order creating the Federal Emergency Management Agency, a civilian organization with the power to take totalitarian control of government functions in the event of a national "emergency."

Yale University economist Richard Cooper headed the commission's task force on monetary policy, which recommended selling "official" gold reserves to private markets. Cooper became under secretary of state for economic affairs, presiding as the International Monetary Fund sold a portion of its gold.

Trilateralist John Sawhill authored an early commission report entitled "Energy: Managing the Transition," which made recommendations on how to manage a movement to higher-costing energy. Carter appointed Sawhill deputy secretary of the Department of Energy. C. Fred Bergsten aided in the preparation of a commission report called "The Reform of International Institutions," then went on to become assistant secretary of the U.S. treasury for international affairs. "Many of the original members of the Trilateral Commission are now in positions of power where they are able to implement policy recommendations of the Commission; recommendations that they, themselves, prepared on behalf of the Commission," noted journalist Eringer. "It is for this reason that the Commission has acquired a reputation for being the Shadow Government of the West."

"The Trilateral Commission's tentacles have reached so far afield in the political and economic sphere that it has been described by some as a cabal of powerful men out to control the world by creating a supernational community dominated by the multinational corporations," wrote researcher Laurie K. Strand in a piece entitled "Who's in charge - Six Possible Contenders" for the *People's Almanac #3*.

Even *U.S. News & World Report* took note of the commission's globalist agenda, reporting, "The Trilateralists make no bones about this: They recruit only people interested in promoting closer international cooperation."

Researchers Anthony C. Sutton and Patrick M. Wood in their book *Trilaterals Over Washington* voiced suspicions of the group and offered this view of its inception. "The Trilateral Commission was founded by the persistent maneuvering of David Rockefeller and Zbigniew Brzezinski. Rockefeller, [then] chairman of the ultra powerful Chase Manhattan Bank, a director of many major multinational corporations and 'endowment funds' has long been a central figure in the mysterious Council on Foreign Relations. Brzezinski, a brilliant prognosticator of one-world idealism, has been a professor at Columbia University and the author of several books that have served as 'policy guidelines' for the CFR. Brzezinski served as the [Trilateral] commission's executive director from its inception in 1973 until late 1976 when he was appointed by President Carter as assistant to the president for national security affairs."

It was Brzezinski who recruited Carter for the Trilateral Commission in 1973. In fact, during President Jimmy Carter's administration, so much Trilateral material was made public that considerable debate ensued within the news media.

Even the Establishment-oriented *Washington Post* pondered in early 1977, "But here is the unsettling thing about the Trilateral Commission. The President-elect [Carter] is a member. So is Vice-President-elect Walter F. Mondale. So are the new secretaries of State, Defense and Treasury, Cyrus R. Vance, Harold Brown and W. Michael Blumenthal. So is Zbigniew Brzezinski, who is a former Trilateral director and Carter's national security advisor, also a bunch of others who will make foreign policy for America in the next four years."

Sutton and Wood commented, "If you are trying to calculate the odds of three virtually unknown men [Carter, Mondale and Brzezinski], out of over 60 [Trilateral] commissioners from the U.S., capturing the three most powerful positions in the land, don't bother. Your calculations will be meaningless."

Carter administration Trilaterals also included ambassadors Andrew Young, Gerard Smith, Richard Gardner and Elliot Richardson, White House economic aide Henry Owen, Deputy Secretary of State Warren Christopher, Director Paul Warnke of the Arms Control and Disarmament Agency, Under-secretaries of State Richard Cooper for economic affairs and Lucy Benson for security assistance, Under-secretary of the Treasury Anthony Solomon, Robert Bowie of the CIA and Assistant Secretary of State Richard Holbrooke.

Lest anyone think that The Trilateral Commission was simply some organ of the Democratic Party, *U.S. News & World Report* in 1978 listed prominent Republicans who were members. These included former secretaries Henry Kissinger (State), William Coleman (Transportation), Carla Hills (Housing and Urban Development), Peter Peterson (Commerce) and Casper Weinberger (Health, Education and Welfare).

Also listed were ex~Energy administrator Sawhill, ex~CIA director and future President George Bush, ex~deputy secretaries of state Robert Ingersoll and Charles Robinson, ex~deputy defense secretary David Packard, former Environmental Protection Agency administrator Russell E. Train, ambassadors William Scanton to the United Nations and Anne Armstrong to Britain and members of Congress John Anderson, William Brock, William Cohen, Barber Conable, John Danforth, Robert Taft Jr. and Marina Whitman, former member of the Council of Economic Advisers.

Provoking additional concern among conspiracy researchers was President Carter's selection of banker Paul Volcker to head America's powerful central bank - the Federal Reserve. Appointed reportedly on instructions from David Rockefeller, Volcker had been the North American chairman of The Trilateral Commission as well as a member of those other secret groups, the Council on Foreign Relations and the Bilderbergers. He was replaced as chairman of the Federal Reserve during the Reagan administration by current chairman Alan Greenspan, also a member of the Trilateral Commission, the CFR and the Bilderbergers.

It is easy to see why so many people believed that U.S. government policy was being directed from these Rockefeller-dominated organizations.

Despite having been written nearly twenty years ago, the words of Sutton and Woods ring true today for many average Americans concerned over the state of the nation and suspicious of a super elite trying to gain world control. They wrote, "By Biblical standards, the United States most certainly deserves judgment - perversion runs amok, child abuse is common, greed and avarice are the passwords to success and morals have rotted. If we are about to be thrown into the pits of the dark ages, the most logical catalyst, or motivator on the horizon is the Trilateral Commission." Former senator and presidential candidate Barry Goldwater echoed the fears of many when he wrote, "What the Trilaterals truly intend is the creation of a worldwide economic power superior to the political government of the nation-states involved. As managers and creators of the system they will rule the world."

Such criticism prompted David Rockefeller to defend the commission in a 1980 edition of the *Wall Street Journal*. "[F]ar from being a coterie of international conspirators with designs on covertly ruling the world, the Trilateral Commission is, in reality, a group of concerned citizens interested in fostering greater understanding and cooperation among international allies."

But some criticism came from within the Carter administration itself. Secretary of State Edmund Muskie charged that Brzezinski was making foreign policy rather than coordinating it. William Sullivan, who had been U.S. ambassador to Iran, accused Brzezinski of sabotaging U.S. efforts to ease relations with Iran following the departure of the Shah. "By November 1978, Brzezinski began to make his own policy and establish his own embassy in Iran," complained Sullivan.

It was accusations such as these that prompted sudden concern in Washington over secret and semi-secret organizations. Columnist Nicholas von Hoffman noted, "Brzezinski has long spooked those who worry about the Trilateral Commission, that Rockefeller-inspired group of globally minded big shots from the major industrial powers. For countless Americans of both a rightward and a leftward persuasion, the commission, which tried to influence governments' trade and diplomatic policies, is a worrisome conspiracy."

Concern spilled over into veterans organizations. In 1980, the American Legion National Convention passed Resolution 773, which called for a congressional investigation of the Trilateral Commission and its predecessor, the Council on Foreign Relations. The following year a similar resolution was approved by the Veterans of Foreign Wars (VFW).

Representative Larry McDonald introduced these resolutions in the House of Representatives but nothing came of it. McDonald, who as national chairman of the John Birch Society was a vocal critic of these secret societies, died in the still-controversial downing of Korean Airlines 007 on September 1, 1983.

During the 1980 presidential campaign, Republican candidate Ronald Reagan went on the record blasting the nineteen Trilaterals in the Carter administration - including Carter himself, who wrote that his association with the commission was "a splendid learning opportunity" - and vowed to investigate the group if elected. While competing with George Bush for the nomination, Reagan lambasted Bush's membership in both the Trilateral Commission and the CFR and pledged not to allow Bush a position in a Reagan government.

Yet during the Republican National Convention a strange series of events took place. While Reagan was a shoe-in as the presidential candidate, the vice presidency was the object of a contentious fight. In midweek, national media commentators suddenly began talking about a "dream ticket" to be composed of Reagan and former president Gerald Ford. Pressure began building for this concept, which would have created a shared presidency and, hence, divided power. It was even suggested that since Ford had been president he should choose half of the Reagan cabinet. Faced with the prospect of presiding over half a government, Reagan rushed to the convention floor late at night and announced, "I know that I am breaking with precedent to come here tonight and I assure you at this late hour I'm not going to give you my acceptance address tonight. But in watching at the hotel the television, and seeing the rumors that were going around and the gossip that was taking place here. Let me as simply as I can straighten out and bring this to a conclusion. It is true that a number of Republican leaders felt that a proper ticket would have included the former president of the United States, Gerald Ford, as second place on the ticket. I then believed that because of all the talk and how something might be growing through the night that it was time for me to advance the schedule a little bit. I have asked and I am recommending to this convention that tomorrow when the session reconvenes that George Bush be nominated for vice president."

Reagan never again uttered a word against the commission or the CFR. Following his election, Reagan's fifty-nine-member transition team was composed of twenty-eight CFR members, ten members of the elite Bilderberg group and at least ten Trilaterals. He even appointed prominent CFR members to three of the nation's most sensitive offices - Secretary of State Alexander Haig, Secretary of Defense Casper Weinberger and Secretary of the Treasury Donald Regan. Additionally, he named Bush's campaign manager, James A. Baker III, who then served as chairman of the Reagan-Bush campaign committee, as his chief of staff. Baker is a fourth-generation member of a family long connected to Rockefeller oil interests.

Then little more than two months after taking office, President Reagan was struck by an assassin's bullet which, but for a quarter of an inch, would have propelled Bush into the Oval Office eight years before his time. Oddly enough, the brother of the would be assassin, John W. Hinckley, had scheduled dinner with Bush's son Neil the very night Reagan was shot. Hinckley's Texas oilman father and George Bush were longtime friends. It should also be noted that Bush's name - including his then little-publicized nickname "Poppy" - address and phone number were found in the personal notebook of oil geologist George DeMohrenschildt, the last known close friend of Lee Harvey Oswald. The existence of a 1963 FBI report mentioning a "George Bush of the CIA" in connection with reactions of the U.S. Cuban community to the JFK assassination drew media attention during the 1992 election. Many researchers view these seemingly small unconnected and little-reported details as collectively pushing the notion of coincidence to the breaking point.

The undeniable ties connecting America's leadership to the CFR and The Trilateral Commission - along with the fact that globalist banker David Rockefeller was a leading luminary in both groups - has prompted much anxiety among conspiracy writers on both the left and right.

"If the Council on Foreign Relations can be said to be a spawning ground for the concepts of one-world idealism, the Trilateral Commission is the 'task force' assembled to assault the beachheads," wrote authors Sutton and Wood in 1979. "Already the commission has placed its members in the top posts the U.S. has to offer." In his 1979 book, *With No Apologies*, Goldwater warned, "David Rockefeller's newest international cabal [the Trilateral Commission] is intended to be the vehicle for multinational consolidation of the commercial and banking interests by seizing control of the political government of the United States."

Such allegations resulted in a 1981 commentary by *Washington Post* writers normally disinterested in any conspiracy theory. They at last acknowledged the Trilateral presence by sarcastically writing, "Remember those dreaded three-sided Trilateralists, the international conspirators headed by David Rockefeller who were going to take over the world? Jimmy Carter was one. George Bush used to be one too and it cost him dearly in his campaign last year against Ronald Reagan.

"Well, guess who's coming to the White House. Guess who invited them. Guess who will lead the delegation. Right. The Trilateralists are coming. President Reagan has asked them to come. They will be led by David Rockefeller. The Trilateralists have landed and the conspiracy theorists no doubt will be close behind," they sneered.

The Trilateral Commission most certainly represents an extension of the activities of the even more secretive Council on Foreign Relations, as all eight North American representatives to the founding meeting of the Trilateral Commission were CFR members.

Globalism, the concept of one-world government, stretches back far beyond the twentieth   century, but became concentrated in the granddaddy of the modern American secret societies - the Council on Foreign Relations (CFR).

The council began as an outgrowth of a series of meetings conducted during World War I. In 1917 New York, Colonel Edward Mandell House, President Woodrow Wilson's confidential advisor, had gathered about 100 prominent men to discuss the post-war world. Dubbing themselves "the Inquiry," they made plans for a peace settlement which eventually evolved into Wilson's famous "fourteen points" which he first presented to Congress on January 8, 1918. They were globalist in nature, calling for the removal of "all economic barriers" between nations, "equality of trade conditions" and the formation of "a general association of nations..."

Col. House, who once described himself as a Marxist socialist but whose actions more reflected Fabian socialism, was the author of a 1912 book entitled *Philip Dru: Administrator.* In this work, House described a "conspiracy" within the United States with the goals of establishing a central bank, a graduated income tax and the control of both political parties. Two years after the publication of his book, two, if not all three, of his literature's goals had been met in reality.

By late 1918, stalemate on the Western Front and the entry of America into the war forced Germany and the Central Powers to accept Wilson's terms for peace. The subsequent Paris Peace Conference of 1919 resulted in the harsh Treaty of Versailles which forced Germany to pay heavy reparations to the Allies. This ruined the German economy, leading to depression and the eventual rise of Adolf Hitler and his Nazis.

Attending the Paris Peace Conference were President Woodrow Wilson and his closest advisers, Colonel House, bankers Paul Warburg and Barnard Baruch and almost two dozen members of "the Inquiry." The conference attendees embraced Wilson's plan for peace, including the formation of a League of Nations. However, under American law, the covenant had to be ratified by the U.S. Senate, which failed to do so, apparently distrusting any supranational organization.

Undaunted, Colonel House, along with both British and American peace conference delegates, met in Paris's Majestic Hotel on May 30, 1919, and resolved to form an "Institute of International Affairs," with one branch in the United States and one in England. The English branch became the Royal Institute of International Affairs. This institute was to guide public opinion toward acceptance of one-world government. The U.S. branch was incorporated on July 21, 1921, as the Council on Foreign Relations. Article II of the new CFR's bylaws stated that all meetings were secret and anyone revealing details of CFR discussions in contravention of CFR rules and regulations could be dropped from membership, thus qualifying the CFR as a secret society.

This secrecy has been assiduously protected by America's corporate mass media. "Analysts of the Soviet press say the Council crops up more regularly in *Pravda* and *Izvestia* than it does in the *New York Times*," noted journalist J. Anthony Lucas in 1971.

Since 1945, the CFR has been headquartered in the elegant Harold Pratt in New York City. The building was donated by the Pratt family of Rockefeller's Standard Oil. The mansion, with its painted French doors, elegant tapestries and fireplaces, presents a clublike atmosphere. Characterization of the CFR as an "Old Boy's" club is enhanced by the fact that many members belong to other upper-crust Social Register groups, such as the Century Association, the Links Club, the University Club and Washington's Metropolitan Club. In the CFR's 1997 annual report, board chairman Peter G. Peterson acknowledged that there was a "kernel of truth" to the charge that the council was an organization of "New York liberal elite," but stated the CFR today is "reaching further into America" with an increasing number of members now living outside New York and Washington.

The CFR's invitation-only membership, originally limited to sixteen hundred participants, today numbers more than thirty-three hundred, representing the most influential leaders in finance, commerce, communications and academia. Admission was a very discriminating and painful process - candidates had to be proposed by a member, seconded by another member, approved by a membership committee, screened by the professional staff and finally approved by the board of directors. In an effort to adjust to the modern world, the council had extended its membership by the early 1970s to include a few blacks and more than a dozen women. To broaden its influence beyond the eastern seaboard, the CFR created Committees on Foreign Relations composed of local leaders in cities across the nation. More than thrity-seven such committees comprising about four thousand members existed by the early 1980s.

Original CFR members included Colonel House, former New York senator and secretary of state Elihu Root, nationally syndicated columnist Walter Lippmann, John Foster Dulles and Christian Herter, who both later served as secretaries of state, and Dulles's brother Allen, who later served as director of the CIA.

Founding CFR president millionaire John W. Davis was financier J. P. Morgan's personal attorney, while Vice President Paul Cravath also represented Morgan properties. The council's first chairman was Russell Leffingwell, one of Morgan's partners. Since most of the earliest CFR members had connections to Morgan in one way or another, it could be said that the council was heavily influenced by Morgan interests.

Funding for the CFR came from bankers and financiers such as Morgan, John D. Rockefeller, Bernard Baruch, Jacob Schiff, Otto Kahn and Paul Warburg. Today, funding for the CFR comes from major corporations such as Xerox, General Motors, Bristol-Myer's Squibb, Texaco and others, as well as the German Marshall Fund, McKnight Foundation, Dillion Fund, Ford Foundation, Andrew W. Mellon Foundation, Rockefellers Brothers Fund, Starr Foundation and the Pew Charitable Trusts.

According to the Capital Research Center's *Guide to Nonprofit Advocacy and Policy Groups*, CFR board members are associated with such influential organizations as the Committee for Economic Development, Institute for International Economics, Committee for a Responsible Federal Budget, the Business Enterprise Trust, the Urban Institute, the Business Roundtable, Council on Competitiveness, U.S. Chamber of Commerce, National Alliance for Business, Brookings Institution, Business~Higher Education Forum, Washington Institute for Near East Policy, Ethics and Public Policy Center, Hoover Institution, Center for Strategic and International Studies, Wilderness Society and the American Council for Capital Formation.

The CFR played a key role in American policy during World War II and journalist J. Anthony Lucas noted, "From 1945 well into the sixties, Council members were in the forefront of America's globalist activism."

In a 1997 "Mission Statement," CFR officials, whose "ranks include nearly all past and present senior U.S. government officials who deal with international matters," stated the council is merely "a unique membership organization and think tank that educates members and staff to serve the nation with ideas for a better and safer world."

Critics dispute this, noting that the CFR has had its hand in every major twentieth century conflict. Many writers view the CFR as a group of men set on world domination through multinational business, international treaties and world government.

Even insiders seem to have a hard time convincing their fellows that there is no attempt at conspiratorial control. Admiral Chester Ward, retired judge advocate general of the U.S. Navy and a longtime CFR member, was quoted as saying, "CFR, as such, does not write the platforms of both political parties or select their respective presidential candidates, or control U.S. defense and foreign policies. But CFR members, as individuals, acting in concert with other individual CFR members, do." Journalist Lucas agreed, commenting that even if one rejects a "simple-minded" dictatorial view of the CFR, "one must also recognize that influence flows as well through more intricate channels:

the personal ties forged among men whose paths have crossed time and again in locker rooms, officers' messes, faculty clubs, embassy conference rooms, garden parties, squash courts and board rooms. If the Council has influence - and the evidence suggests that it does - then it is the influence its members bring to bear through such channels."

Admiral Ward went on to explain that the one common objective of CFR members is "to bring about the surrender of the sovereignty and the national independence of the United States. Primarily, they want the world banking monopoly from whatever power ends up in the control of global government," Ward added.

He detailed CFR methods in a 1975 book coauthored with Phyllis Schlafly entitled *Kissinger on the Couch.* "Once the ruling members of the CFR have decided that the U.S. government should adopt a particular policy, the very substantial research facilities of CFR are put to work to develop arguments, intellectual and emotional, to support the new policy, and to confound and discredit, intellectually and politically, any opposition," he explained.

The public manifestation of the CFR is its publication *Foreign Affairs*, termed informally "the voice of the U.S. foreign-policy establishment." Although council supporters claim "articles in *Foreign Affairs* do not reflect any consensus of beliefs", critics counter that the CFR signals members to its desired policies through such articles.

Even the stodgy *Encyclopedia Britannica* noted, "Ideas put forward tentatively in this journal often, if well received by the *Foreign Affairs* community, appear later as U.S. government policy or legislation; prospective policies that fail this test usually disappear."

Alvin Moscow, a sympathetic biographer of the Rockefeller family, wrote more to the point-stating, "So august has been the membership of the Council that it has been seen in some quarters as the heart of the eastern Establishment. When it comes to foreign affairs, it *is* [emphasis in the original] the eastern Establishment. In fact, it is difficult to point to a single major policy in U.S. foreign affairs that has been established since [President] Wilson which was diametrically opposed to then current thinking in the Council on Foreign Relations."

The council has two methods of communicating the thoughts and desires of its inner circle of leadership - regular luncheon or dinner meetings where prominent thinkers and leaders from around the world address council members, and council study groups that periodically present position papers on subjects of interest.

The Council also offers a Corporation Service, through which subscribing companies were provided twice-a-year dinner briefings by government officials such as the Treasury secretary or CIA director.

Noted author John Kenneth Galbraith, who resigned from the CFR in 1970 "out of boredom," called such off-the-record talks a "scandal." "Why should businessmen be briefed by government officials on information not available to the public, especially since it can be financially advantageous?" he reasoned.

G. Edward Griffin, author of *The Creature from Jekyll Island* which chronicled the creation of the Federal Reserve System, noted that initially the CFR was a front for the British Round Table Group and was dominated by the J. P. Morgan family. "The Morgan group gradually has been replaced by the Rockefeller consortium, and the roll call of participating businesses now reads like the Fortune 500," he wrote in 1994.

One example of Rockefeller domination of the CFR came in the early 1970s when David Rockefeller went over the heads of a nominating committee and offered the editorship of *Foreign Affairs* to William Bundy, a former CIA official instrumental in prosecuting the Vietnam War.

Demonstrating how every U.S. government administration since the council's inception has been packed with CFR members, conservative journalist and CFR researcher James Perloff noted, "The historical record speaks even more loudly. Through 1988, 14 secretaries of state, 14 treasury secretaries, 11 defense secretaries and scores of other federal department heads have been CFR members." Nearly every CIA director since Allen Dulles has been a CFR member, including Richard Helms, William Colby, George Bush, William Webster, James Woolsey, John Deutch and William Casey. "Many of the council's members have a personal financial interest in foreign relations," noted researcher Laurie Strand, "because it is their property and investments that are guarded by the State Department and the military (and the CIA)."

Many researchers have alleged that the CIA, in fact, serves as a security force not only for corporate America but for friends, relatives and fraternity brothers on the CFR. This may be a two-way street. According to former executive assistant to the deputy director of the CIA Victor Marchetti, along with former State Department analyst John D. Marks, "[T]he influential but private Council, composed of several hundred of the country's top political, military, business, and academic leaders, has long been the CIA's principal 'constituency' in the American public. When the agency has needed prominent citizens to front for its proprietary companies or for other special assistance, it has often turned to Council members."

CFR members who take government positions tend to bring in fellow members. When CFR member Henry Stimson came to

Washington as secretary of war in 1940, he brought with him fellow member John J. McCloy as assistant secretary for personnel. McCloy, in turn, did his part over the years to bring more CFR members to government. "Whenever we needed a new man [for a government position], we just thumbed through the roll of council members and put through a call to New York," once commented McCloy, a former CFR chairman, chairman of Chase Manhattan Bank, mentor to David Rockefeller and himself foreign policy adviser to six U.S. presidents and a member of the discredited Warren Commission.

According to published reports, the Clinton administration was top-heavy with more than one hundred CFR members helping to begin the Clinton years. CFR members were named ambassadors to Spain, Great Britain, Australia, Chile, Syria, South Africa, Russia, Romania, Japan, Korea, Mexico, Italy, India, France, the Czech Republic, Poland, Nigeria and the Philippines. Currently, more than a dozen members of both the House and Senate are CFR members. Author Robert Anton Wilson commented, "If the CFR had millions of members like, say, the Presbyterian Church, this list might not mean much. But the CFR only has 3,200 members."

Because of its Wall Street/banking origins and its inherent secrecy, the Council on Foreign Relations came under strident attack by conservative writers. This public attention led to the creation of the less-secretive Trilateral Commission. Public awareness of the pervasive CFR presence in government became so widespread that the late Gary Allen, whose book on globalist organizations, *None Dare Call It Conspiracy*, sold more than five million copies despite being ignored by the Establishment media, commented just before the 1972 national elections, "There really was not a dime's worth of difference [between presidential candidates]. Voters were given the choice between CFR world government advocate Nixon and CFR world government advocate [Hubert] Humphrey. Only the rhetoric was changed to fool the public."

In a call to action, Allen echoed the admonition of many researchers who are suspicious of the CFR's motives when he wrote, "Democrats and Republicans must break the Insider control of their respective parties. The CFR types and their flunkies and social climbing opportunist supporters must be invited to leave or else the Patriots must leave." Many conspiracy researchers today see a parallel situation in the 2000 election between Democrat Al Gore and Republican George W. Bush, both of whom have long-standing business and family ties to oil companies, Wall Street and CFR members.

Author Perloff warned from a Christian perspective that a monumental battle is shaping up between the Kingdom of Christ and "an evil, one-world government: the kingdom of the Antichrist. Many notables of the American Establishment have given themselves over to one side in this conflict, and it is not the side the ancient scriptures recommend. Whether or not they are conspirators, whether they are conscious or not of the ultimate consequences of their actions, their powerful influence has helped move the world toward apocalyptic events."

Clearly the CFR has exerted a powerful influence, if not outright control, over U.S. policies for nearly the past century. But for almost fifty years, this influence has been shared with another closely connected secretive group.

The Bilderbergers are a group of powerful men and women - many of them European royalty - who meet in secret each year to discuss the issues of the day. Many suspicious researchers claim they conspire to manufacture and manage world events.

Despite the fact that many highly regarded American media members meet with the Bilderbergers, little or nothing gets reported on the group or its activities, leading writers to claim censorship and news management.

As with The Trilateral Commission and the Council on Foreign Relations, Bilderbergers often carry cross-membership in one or more of these three groups.

The Bilderbergers have no official name but were identified with the Bilderberg Hotel in Oosterbeek, Holland, where they were first discovered by the public in 1954. Its meeting in February 1957 on St. Simon Island near Jekyll Island, Georgia, was the first on U.S. soil.

National leaders often have been first prepped by the Bilderbergers. In 1991, then Arkansas Governor Bill Clinton was honored as a Bilderberg guest and the next year he ran for and won the presidency of the United States. After his election, Clinton made no mention of the Bilderberg meetings but, according to the *Spotlight*, a Washington tabloid that has covered Bilderberg conferences for years, Hillary Clinton attended in 1997, becoming the first American first lady to do so. Thereafter, talk steadily grew concerning her future role in politics.

Beginning as unofficial meetings between members of Europe's elite in the 1940s, the official creation of this highly secret organization came about in the early 1950s following discussions regarding regular meetings of Europe's foreign ministers between Holland's Prince Bernhard and Polish socialist Dr. Joseph Hieronim Retinger, a founder of the European movement after World War II. Retinger became known as the "father of the Bilderbergers."

Retinger was brought to America by Averell Harriman (CFR), then U.S. ambassador to England, where he visited prominent citizens such as David and Nelson Rockefeller, John Foster Dulles and then~CIA director Walter Bedell Smith. Previously, Retinger had formed the American Committee on a United Europe along with future CIA director and CFR member Allen Dulles, then~CFR director George Franklin, CIA officials Thomas Braden and William Donovan, former chief of the Office of Strategic Services (OSS), forerunner of the CIA. Donovan began his intelligence career as an operative of J. P. Morgan Jr. and was known as an "Anglophile," a supporter of close British-American relations. Retinger continued his participation in Bilderberg meetings until his death in 1960. Another CIA-connected person who helped create the Bilderbergers was *Life* magazine publisher C. D. Jackson, who served under President Eisenhower as "special consultant for psychological warfare."

From these associations came the idea of holding regular meetings of prominent businessmen, politicians, bankers, educators, media owners and managers and military leaders from around the world. The Bilderbergers also are closely tied to Europe's nobility, including the British Royal Family. According to several sources, meetings are often attended by royalty from Sweden, Holland and Spain.

The primary impetus for the Bilderberger meetings came from Dutch Prince Bernhard, whose full name is Bernhard Leopold Frederick Eberhart Julius Coert Karel Godfried Pieter, Prince of the Netherlands and Prince of Lippe-Biesterfeld. Bernhard was a former member of the Nazi *Schutzstaffel* (SS) and an employee of Germany's I.G. Farben in Paris. In 1937, he married Princess Juliana of the Netherlands and became a major shareholder and officer in Dutch Shell Oil, along with Britain's Lord Victor Rothschild. After the Germans invaded Holland, the royal couple moved to London. It was there, after the war, that Rothschild and Retinger encouraged Prince Bernhard to create the Bilderberger group. The prince personally chaired the group until 1976, when he resigned following revelations that he had accepted large payoffs from Lockheed to promote the sale of its aircraft in Holland.

Since 1991 the Bilderberg chairmanship has been held by Britain's Lord Peter Carrington, former cabinet minister, secretary-general of NATO and president of the Royal Institute of International Affairs, a sister organization to the CFR. Carrington has been linked to the Rothschild banking empire by both business connections and marriage.

Americans with famous names who have attended Bilderberger meetings include CFR members George Ball, Dean Acheson, Dean

Rusk, McGeorge Bundy, Christian Herter, Zbigniew Brzezinski, Douglas Dillon, J. Robert Oppenheimer, Walter Reuther, Jacob Javits, Robert McNamara, Walter Bedell Smith and General Lyman Leminitzer. Other noteworthy attendees have included J. William Fulbright, Henry Ford II, George Pompidou, Giscard d'Estaing, Helmut Schmidt and France's Baron Edmond de Rothschild. "in fact, the Bilderbergers are a sort of unofficial CFR, expanded to an international scale," stated author Neal Wilgus.

Author and former intelligence officer Dr. John Coleman claimed, "the Bilderberger Conference is a creation of [Britain's] MI6 under the direction of the Royal Institute of International Affairs." Considering the U.S. intelligence connections, it also can be legitimately argued that the Bilderberg conferences have been at least partially organized and sponsored by the CIA.

According to "Strictly Confidential" minutes of the first Bilderberg conference later leaked to the public, "Insufficient attention has so far been paid to long-term planning, and to evolving an international order which would look beyond the present-day crisis [the Cold War]. When the time is ripe our present concepts of world affairs should be extended to the whole world."

Investigative reporter James P. Tucker, who has doggedly tracked the Bilderbergers for years, wrote, "The Bilderberg agenda is much the same as that of its brother group, the Trilateral Commission the two groups have an interlocking leadership and a common vision of the world. David Rockefeller founded the Trilaterals but shares power in the older Bilderberg group with the Rothschilds of Britain and Europe."

The Bilderbergers usually meet once a year at plush resorts around the globe and their activities are cloaked in total secrecy despite the attendance of top-level American media members. Although the group claims to merely hold informal discussions on world affairs, there is evidence that often its recommendations become official policy. The concept of a unified Europe under centralized control, a goal of the medieval Knights Templar, appears well along the way to becoming a reality thanks to the Bilderbergers. George McGhee, a Bilderberger and former U.S. ambassador to West Germany, acknowledged that "the Treaty of Rome, which brought the [European] Common Market into being, was nurtured at Bilderberg meetings." The Common Market evolved into the present European Union. Jack Sheinkman, chairman of Amalgamated Bank and a Bilderberger member, stated in 1996, "In some cases discussions do have an impact and become policy. The idea of a common European currency was discussed several years back before it became policy. We had a discussion about the U.S. establishing formal relations with China before Nixon actually did it."

Sheinkman may be one of those Bilderberger members who do not understand the true goals of the group's elite leadership. According to several researchers, the Bilderberg inner core elite coordinate the meetings. They know the real game plan, while those invited on a rare or one time basis may not know the true agenda of the organization and can be fed the party line that Bilderberg goals lead to peace and prosperity." And what is this "true agenda"? It may have been revealed when Prince Bernhard stated, "It is difficult to reeducate the people who have been brought up on nationalism to the idea of relinquishing part of their sovereignty to a supernational body."

So a global, centrally run government is the plan. But how could they get American citizens to willingly part with the Constitution and Bill of Rights? Kissinger may have given the game away back in 1992. According to several separate sources, a Swiss delegate to that year's Bilderberg conference in Evian, France, secretly taped this quote; "Today Americans would be outraged if UN troops entered Los Angeles to restore order [the LA riots were in progress]; tomorrow they will be grateful! This is especially true if they were told there was an outside threat from beyond, whether real or promulgated, that threatened our very existence. It is then that all people of the world will plead with world leaders to deliver them from this evil. The one thing every man fears is the unknown. When presented with this scenario, individual rights will be willingly relinquished for the guarantee of their well-being granted to them by their world government." Was Kissinger merely speculating or was this a plan that was postponed in favor of the War on Terrorism? Could this scenario be the next plan if the terrorism war fails to achieve the objective of world governmen?. Answers to these questions are hard to come by because the American corporate mass media, owned by many of these same secret-society members, has declined to discuss the matter, just as they fought against addressing the Kennedy assassination for nearly thirty years.

Unlike their American brethren, the Canadian media actually reported news of the 1996 Bilderberg meeting near Toronto with such headlines as "[Canadian prime minister Jean] Chretien To Speak at Secret World Meeting," "[Canadian publisher Conrad] Black Plays Host to World Leaders" and "World Domination or a Round of Golf?"

When asked to comment about the lack of reporting by journalist William F. Buckley, who attended the Bilderberg meeting in Canada, a secretary commented, "I don't think that is the nature of the meeting, is it?" Paul Gigot of the *Wall Street Journal*, another attendee, explained,

"The rules of the conference, which we all adhere to, are that we don't talk about what is said. It is all off the record. The fact that I attended is no secret."

Perhaps these reporters don't talk about what they learn at these secret meetings, but it is clear that their association shapes their editorial positions. Media critics have long charged that the differences in editorial positions of America's major news outlets are negligible. "If the Bilderberg Group is not a conspiracy of some sort, it is conducted in such a way as to give a remarkably good imitation of one," wrote journalist C. Gordon Tether of London's *Financial Times* in 1975. About a year later, following ongoing arguments over censorship, Tether was fired by *Financial Times* editor Max Henry "Fredy" Fisher, a member of the Trilateral Commission.

The Bilderbergs met in late spring 2002 at the Westfields Marriott in Chantilly, Virginia. Outside was a sign advising that the "Westfields Marriott will not be accessible to the general public from May 30th to June 2nd." Reports leaked from this meeting indicated concern on the part of many European members over a precipitous invasion of Iraq. "[Defense Secretary] Rumsfield is known to have been summoned to reassure the Europeans there would be 'no immediate' U.S. invasion of Iraq as had been planned by the White House," wrote journalist Tucker. He reported that European members chastised the United States for its one-sided policies in the Middle East and voiced some dissension over a possible war with Iraq. As Christmas 2002 neared, there was still no war. That came in March 2003.

Part IV – Historical Precedents

"Redefining the role of the United States from enablers to keep the peace to enablers to keep the peace from peacekeepers is going to be an assignment."
-President George W. Bush, *New York Times,*
January 14, 2001

The historical precedents that may provide insight into the events of 9/11 are so numerous that there is not enough space to present them all.

But consider what happened just last century.

The Gulf War

The Gulf War was all about oil, from the accusation that Kuwait was slant-drilling into Iraq's southern Rumaila reserves to the destruction of the oilfields at its finish. Here we found a new enemy in Saddam Hussein, an enemy armed and financed by the CIA, an agency whose top officials have long been connected to oilmen and Council on Foreign Relations globalists.

The Allied victory in the Persian Gulf War of 1991 was loudly trumpeted by the American mass media, but the actions leading to this conflict were sparsely reported throughout the coverage. These machinations involved people in secret societies and indicated a very different rationale for the war than the one presented to the public.

No one can argue that the U.S. military, with some assistance from British, French and Arab forces, did not perform magnificently during this brief conflict. It only took between January 17 and February 28, 1991, for the coalition of Operation Desert Storm to soundly defeat the Iraqi forces of Saddam Hussein, then representing the fifth largest army in the world. This astounding military success was due primarily to the Allied forces' superiority in both weaponry and training, as opposed to Saddam's conscripts who, though veterans of combat against Iran, had limited training and low morale.

This created a lopsided war that resulted in more than 300,000 Iraqi casualties, both military and civilian, and 65,000 prisoners, compared to the extraordinarily low Allied losses of 234 killed, 470 wounded and 57 missing.

The primary leader of the war was U.S. President George Herbert Walker Bush, a former CFR member, Trilateralist and Skull and Bonesman.

Both Bush and then~secretary of state James Baker were deeply involved in the oil business. Any Bush policy that increased the price of oil meant more profit to his companies, those of his oilmen supporters and, of course, to the Rockefeller-dominated oil cartel.

An added bonus was that any conflict that divided the Arab world would only strengthen the power of the United States, Britain and Israel in the region, and a coalition of countries fighting for the United Nations could only advance the globalists' plan for a one-world military force. This "battle of the New World Order was some kind of manufactured crisis with a hidden agenda," concluded researchers Jonathan Vankin and John Whalen after careful study of the events leading to this conflict.

Bush and Saddam Hussein had had a close relationship for many years. In his role as CIA director, then vice president, George Bush along with the Agency had supported Hussein through his eight-year war against Iran, following the surprise ouster of the Shah in 1979.

By 1990, Hussein's Iraq was a primary threat to the balance of power between Israel and its Arab neighbors, but Hussein was strapped for cash due to the Iraq-Iran War and couldn't pay his bills. Under pressure from the international bankers for slow repayment of loans and from the Organization of Petroleum Producing Countries (OPEC), which refused to allow him to raise oil prices, Saddam turned his eyes to Kuwait as a source of income, since it was the third largest producer of oil next to Iraq and Saudi Arabia.

Kuwait had been carved out of Iraq by Britain, who in 1899 took control of Kuwait's foreign policy under an agreement with the dictatorial Sabah family. The Sabahs had produced a series of ruling sheikhs since assuming control of the area's nomad tribes in 1756. Kuwait became a British Protectorate in 1914 when German interest suddenly gave the area strategic importance. British dominance was solidified by sending British troops to the area in 1961 after Iraq sought to reclaim it.

The Pentagon had known that Iraqi troops were massing along the Kuwait border since mid-July 1990. On July 25, Saddam sought advice from the United States on his intentions to reclaim Kuwait. He met with U.S. ambassador April Glaspie, who told him, "I have direct instructions from President Bush to improve our relations with Iraq. We have considerable sympathy for your quest for higher oil prices, the immediate cause of your confrontation with Kuwait.

"I have received an instruction to ask you, in the spirit of friendship not confrontation, regarding your intentions: Why are your troops massed so very close to Kuwait's borders?"

According to transcripts released long after the war, Hussein explained that, while he was ready to negotiate his border dispute with Kuwait, his design was to "keep the whole of Iraq in the shape we wish it to be." This shape, of course, included Kuwait, which Hussein considered still a part of Iraq. "What is the United States' opinion on this," he asked.

"We have no opinion on your Arab-Arab conflicts, like your dispute with Kuwait," replied Glaspie. "Secretary Baker has directed me to emphasize the instruction, first given to Iraq in the 1960s, that the Kuwaiti issue is not associated with America."

"Shortly after this, April Glaspie left Kuwait to take her summer vacation, another signal of elaborate American disinterest in the Kuwait-Iraq crisis," noted authors Webster Griffin Tarpley and Anton Chaitkin in *George Bush: The Unauthorized Biography* . On July 31, Bush met with GOP congressional leaders but said nothing about the Gulf situation.

The crisis escalated on August 2, when Iraqi troops moved into Kuwait. Bush froze all Iraqi assets in the United States, adding to Saddam's money woes, which had worsened in 1990 after international bankers refused him further loans. Glaspie was prohibited from speaking out by the State Department, so the American public could not learn of Bush's duplicity.

In later testimony before the Senate Foreign Relations Committee, Glaspie pointed out that the July 25 conference was her first and only meeting with Hussein, who had not met with any foreign ambassador since 1984, the midpoint of his war with Iran.

But if Hussein had not met with U.S. diplomats, the same could not be said of American businessmen. Economist Paul Adler noted, "it was known that David Rockefeller met with the Iraqi leader on at least three known occasions after the Chase Manhattan consortium became the lead banker in a number of major Iraqi credit syndications." It was also reported that Alan Stoga, a vice president of [Henry] Kissinger Associates met with Iraqi leaders during a two-year period preceding the Gulf conflict.

"Saddam began to realize that he could not get what he wanted from the striped pants set. He began doing business with the people who mattered to him - foreign businessmen, defense contractors, technologists and scientists, occasionally even visiting newsmen," reported the Washington newspaper, the *Spotlight*.

Following the money trail of such non-diplomatic contacts that led to the Gulf War, Representative Henry Gonzalez, chairman of the House Committee on Banking, Finance and Urban Affairs, discovered that almost $5 billion in loans had been passed to Saddam Hussein in the 1980s through the Atlanta, Georgia, branch of Italy's government-owned bank, Banca Nazional del Lavoro (BNL). The branch manager, Christopher Drogoul, was finally brought into federal court, where he pled guilty to approving this huge cash transfer without the approval of BNL's head office in Italy. However, the whole investigation was put on hold during the Gulf War.

Most observers disbelieved that Drogoul could have conducted such a massive transaction without the knowledge of his superiors. Bobby Lee Cook, one of Drogoul's several defense attorneys, argued that his client had been made the patsy in "a scheme orchestrated at the highest levels of the U.S. government."

In court, BNL official Franz Von Wedel testified that his boss, Drogoul, had acted on the advice of the bank's consultants, Kissinger Associates. In both 1989 and 1990, the Bush Justice Department had quashed indictments against the BNL by the Atlanta attorney general's office following an FBI raid on the bank on August 4, 1989. Action against the bank managers was held up for more than a year. Indictments were finally handed down one day after Bush declared a cease-fire in the Gulf War. This scandal - dubbed "Iraqgate" - prompted Gonzalez to prepare a House resolution calling for the impeachment of Bush attorney general William Barr for "obstruction of justice in the BNL scanda.." House Judiciary Committee chairman Representative Jack Brooks called on Barr to appoint a special prosecutor in the case.

In a classic case of who-will-watch-the-watchers, Barr said he could find no evidence of wrongdoing on his part and refused to appoint a special prosecutor. It was one of the only times that an attorney general had failed to appoint a special prosecutor when asked to do so by Congress.

The clincher of this sordid story of financial scheming and official malfeasance was that not only had most of the $5 billion been used by Hussein to buy weaponry to be used against American servicemen but the U.S. taxpayers picked up the tab!

Gonzalez said $500 million of the loans to Hussein came through the government-backed Commodity Credit Corporation (CCC) and had been intended to purchase grain from U.S. farmers. However, grain shipped through the port of Houston had gone to then~Soviet bloc nations in exchange for weapons, while the remainder of the grain purchase had freed Hussein's limited cash reserves to buy more military materials. The Bush administration had pledged taxpayer guarantees should Hussein default on the loans, which he did after sending troops to Kuwait. According to at least one public source, more than $360 million in American tax money was paid to the Gulf International Bank in Bahrain, which was owned by seven Gulf nations, including Iraq. This amount was only the first of an estimated $1 billion to be paid to ten banks by the CCC to cover the $5 billion of Hussein's defaulted loans.

"The $1 billion commitment, in the form of loan guarantees for the purchase of U.S. farm commodities, enabled Saddam to buy needed food on credit and to spend his scarce hard currency on the arms buildup that brought war to the Persian Gulf," wrote Russell S. Bowen, author of *The Immaculate Deception.*

Even after the Iraqi invasion began on August 2, Bush publicly appeared strangely noncommittal. Asked by reporters if he intended any intervention in the Gulf crisis, Bush said, "I'm not contemplating such action."

His attitude apparently changed drastically that same day after meeting with British prime minister Margaret Thatcher, a regular attendee of Bilderberg meetings who had been implicated with Bush in both the Iran-Contra and October Surprise scandals.

After meeting with Thatcher, Bush began to describe Hussein as a "new Hitler" and said "the status quo is unacceptable and further expansion [by Iraq] would be even more unacceptable." Despite assurances from Hussein that Kuwait was his only objective and with no concrete evidence to the contrary, Bush nevertheless personally telephoned the leaders of Saudi Arabia and warned that they would be the next target of this "new Hitler."

Panicked, the Saudis handed over as much as $4 billion to Bush and other world leaders as secret payoffs to protect their kingdom, according to Sabah family member Sheikh Fahd al-Sabah, chairman of the Kuwait Investment Office.

Long after the Persian Gulf War, when audits found this money had been diverted into a London slush fund, anti-Sabah elements in Saudi Arabia criticized the payoff. They were told by al-Sabah, "That money was used to buy Kuwait's liberation. It paid for political support in the West and among Arab leaders - support for Desert Storm, the international force we urgently needed."

Whether this money played any role or not, Bush soon drew a "line in the sand" to block further Iraqi intrusion, then launched Desert Storm, an offensive that drove Iraqi troops from Kuwait.

Yet, even as America's patriotic soldiers closed in on Hussein, the whole war stopped and George H. W. Bush's old business partner remained in power and the "Great Game" continued.

Even through the Clinton administration periodic air forays into Iraq continued, ostensibly to punish Hussein for preventing UN inspection of his development centers for biological and nuclear weaponry. However, this time there was a big difference - probing questions were raised by both a suspicious public and a few less-timid members of the news media.

Following missile and bombing strikes in late 1998, a letter writer to a national news magazine asked, "By using weapons of mass destruction to deter Iraq from manufacturing weapons of mass destruction, would America not be doing the very thing we're warning Iraq not to do?" Others raised the question of why we attacked Iraq for refusing UN inspection of its sensitive military installations when President Clinton also had refused to allow such inspections in the United States - a refusal greeted with general approval by the American public.

Scott Ritter, a member of the United Nations Special Commission (UNSCOM), created to locate and eliminate Saddam Hussein's secret weapons caches, resigned in August of 1998 and accused the U.S. government of using the commission to justify an attack on Iraq. Ritter said before his resignation he disbelieved Baghdad's minister of defense, who told him the UNSCOM team was being used to "provoke a crisis," but slowly came to agree with the charge. Ritter's superiors scoffed at the allegation, claiming Ritter's knowledge of the situation was "limited."

However, in early 1999 it was reported that Washington had used UNSCOM to plant electronic bugs in the Ministry of Defense (Iraq's Pentagon) and other U.S. officials confirmed much of Ritter's accusations.

"The relationship between the United States and the inspection commission has long been a subject of debate," wrote   *U.S. News & World Report* reporter Bruce B. Auster. "The issue is sensitive because UNSCOM is an arm of the UN Security Council, not an agency of the United States, although it does rely on the United States for intelligence and personnel."

Again, the hidden hand of the secret-society members who both created and in many ways control the UN could be briefly seen manipulating events.

On December 15, 1998, after stockpiling cruise missiles in the Persian Gulf during the fall, the U.S. launched a much-delayed air strike against Baghdad.

But with Christmas nearing, most Americans couldn't get too worked up over civilian casualties halfway around the world. And any doubts about United States involvement in the Persian Gulf - except among those unfortunates having to deal with Gulf War Syndrome caused by a lethal combination of oil fires, biological agents and radioactive uranium-tipped artillery and tank shells - had been thrown away, along with the yellow ribbons that had proudly displayed the total support of the uninformed.

The Reichstag Fire

In January 1933, Germany, with one of the most educated and cultured populations in the world at that time, was at peace and enjoying a blossoming of democratic freedom under the coalition government of the Weimar Republic. But on February 27, 1933, the German *Reichstag*, or Parliament building, was destroyed by fire. In those slower, gentler times, this act was as great a shock to the German people as the destruction of the World Trade Center was to Americans.

German Chancellor Adolf Hitler and his Nazis blamed the destruction on communist terrorists. They even caught one, a retarded Dutch youth named Marinus van der Lubbe, who carried a Communist Party card. After some time in custody, the youth confessed to being the arsonist. However, later investigation found that one person could not have started the mammoth blaze and that incendiaries had been carried into the building through a tunnel that led to the offices of Hitler's closest partner, Hermann Goering, head of the German air force, the *Luftwaffe*.

Despite misgivings in many quarters about the official explanation of the fire, it was announced, "the government is of the opinion that the situation is such that a danger to the state and nation existed and still exists." Law enforcement agencies quickly moved against not only the communists, but also pacifists, liberals and democrats.

Less than a month later, on March 24, 1933, at Hitler's urging, a panicky German Parliament voted 441 to 94 to pass an "Enabling Act," which was the starting point for Hitler's dictatorship.

As a result of this act, Germans soon saw national identity cards, racial profiling, a national homeland security chief (SS Commander Heinrich Himmler), gun confiscation, and later mass murders and incarcerations in concentration camps. In fact, according to Jews for the Preservation of Firearms Ownership (JPFO), a close examination of the U.S. Gun Control Act of 1968 (Public Law 90-618) revealed it to be nearly word for word the gun legislation passed in Germany under Hitler.

"When Germany awoke," wrote British reporter Douglas Reed, "a man's home was no longer his castle. He could be seized by private individuals, could claim no protection from the police, could be indefinitely detained without preferment of charge; his property could be seized, his verbal and written communications overheard and perused; he no longer had the right to foregather with his fellow countrymen, and his newspapers might no longer freely express their opinions."

When the war in Europe ended, the immense amount of loot accumulated by the Nazis was missing.   It seems that by late August 1944, many top Nazi officials saw the handwriting on the wall. When the French town of St. Lo, center of the German defense line facing the Normandy beachhead, had fallen on July 18, opening all of southern France to Allied armor and infantry, Nazi leaders knew the end of the war was only a matter of time.

Adolf Hitler, who according to captured medical records was on a roller-coaster ride of euphoria and depression due to large daily doses of amphetamines, increasingly lost contact with reality. However, the second most powerful man in the Reich, Hitler's deputy Martin Bormann, was not so incapacitated. On August 10, 1944, Bormann called together German business leaders and Nazi Party officials. They met in the Hotel Maison Rouge at Strasbourg. Bormann explained the purpose of the meeting to one attendee: "German industry must realize that the war cannot now be won, and must take steps to prepare for a postwar commercial campaign which will in time insure the economic resurgence of Germany."

These "steps" came to be known as *Aktion Adlerflug*, or Operation Eagle Flight. It was nothing less than the perpetuation of Nazism through the massive flight of money, gold, stocks, bonds, patents, copyrights and even technical specialists from Germany. As part of this plan, Bormann, aided by the black-clad SS, the central Deutsche Bank, the steel empire of Fritz Thyssen and the powerful I.G. Farben combine, created 750 foreign front corporations - 58 in Portugal,

112 in Spain, 233 in Sweden, 214 in Switzerland, 35 in Turkey and 98 in Argentina.

Bormann's efforts were substantially helped by close connections with foreign banks and businesses begun long before the war. According to former U.S. Department of Justice Nazi War Crimes prosecutor John Loftus, much of the wealth was passed out of Germany by German banker Thyssen through his Rotterdam Bank in Holland, which, in turn, owned the Union Banking Corporation (UBC) in New York City. On the board of directors of Union was shareholder Prescott Bush. Attorneys for these dealings were John Foster and Allen Dulles. John was secretary of state under Eisenhower while Allen became one of the longest serving CIA directors. Both were deeply involved with the Council on Foreign Relations.

Two ranking U.S. business leaders who supported Hitler and his policies were George Herbert Walker and his son-in-law Prescott Bush, father of George Herbert Walker Bush and grandfather of President George Walker Bush.

On October 20, 1942, the U.S. Alien Property Custodian, operating under the Trading With the Enemy Act, seized the shares of UBC and said the bank was financing Hitler. Also seized were Bush's holdings in the Hamburg-America ship line that had been used to ferry Nazi propagandists and arms. Another firm essential to the passing of Nazi money was another Holland American Trading Company, a subsidiary of UBC. It was through this Dutch bank, originally founded by Thyssen's father in 1916, that Nazi money was passed. This Dutch connection tied the Bush and Nazi money directly to former SS officer and founder of the Bilderbergers Prince Bernhard of the Netherlands

The leading shareholder in UBC was E. Roland Harriman, son of Edward Harriman, the person who had been a mentor to Bush. All had been members of the Yale secret society Skull and Bones and all were closely connected to the globalists at the Council on Foreign Relations.

On November 17, 1942, U.S. authorities also seized the Silesian-American Corporation, managed by Bush and his father-in-law, George Herbert Walker, and charged the firm with being a Nazi front company supplying vital coal to Germany.

Illustrating the interconnecting business associations of this time was ITT's German chairman Gerhardt Westrick, a close associate of John Foster Dulles, who was a partner to Dr. Heinrich Albert, head of Ford Motor Co. in Germany until 1945. Two ITT directors were German banker Baron Kurt von Schroeder and Walter Schellenberg, head of counterintelligence for the Nazi Gestapo. Rockefeller-owned

Standard Oil also came under investigation during World War II for a series of complex business deals that resulted in desperately needed gasoline reaching Nazi Germany.

Nazi-American business connections were further buttressed by the 1936 partnership between the J. Henry Schroeder Bank of New York and Rockefeller family members. According to author Charles Higham, "Schroeder , Rockefeller and Company, Investment Bankers, was formed as part of an overall company that *Time* magazine disclosed as being 'the economic booster of the Rome-Berlin Axis.' The partners in Schroeder, Rockefeller and Company included Avery Rockefeller, nephew of John D., Baron Bruno von Schroeder in London, and Kurt von Schroeder of the Bank of International Settlements and the Gestapo in Cologne. Their lawyers were John Foster Dulles and Allen Dulles of Sullivan and Cromwell. Allen Dulles (later CIA director and Warren Commission member) was on the board of Schroeder. Further connections linked the Paris branch of (the Rockefeller) Chase National Bank to Schroeder as well as the proNazi Worms Bank and Standard Oil of New Jersey in France. Standard Oil's Paris representatives were directors of the Banque de Paris et des Pays-Bas, which had intricate connections to the Nazis and to Chase."

It is interesting to note that throughout the war, Chase maintained its financial connections with the Nazis through its Paris bank and that I.G. Farben chief Hermann Schmitz served as Chase president for seven years prior to the war and eventually held as much stock in Standard Oil of New Jersey as the Rockefellers. "Schmitz's wealth - largely I.G. Farben bearer bonds converted to the Big Three successor firms, shares in Standard Oil of New Jersey. General Motors, and other U.S. blue chip industrial stocks, and the 700 secret companies controlled in his time by I.G., as well as shares in the 750 corporations he helped Bormann establish during the last years of World War II - has increased in all segments of the modern industrial world. The Bormann organization in South America utilizes the voting power of the Schmitz trust along with their own assets to guide the multinationals they control, as they keep steady the economic course of the Fatherland," wrote journalist Paul Manning, who added, "The Bormann organization is not merely a group of ex-Nazis. It is a great economic power whose interests today supersede their ideology."

These long-standing banking and business connections coupled with the Schmitz business network allowed *Reichsleiter* Bormann to forge a formidable Nazi-controlled organization for postwar activities.

Jim Keith, author of numerous conspiracy books, wrote, "in researching the shape of totalitarian control during this century, I saw that the plans of the Nazis manifestly did not die with the German loss of World War II. The ideology and many of the principal players survived and flourished after the war, and have had a profound impact on postwar history, and on events taking place today."

"It is bad enough that the Bush family helped raise the money for Thyssen to give Hitler his start in the 1920s, but giving aid and comfort to the enemy in time of war is treason," declared Nazi prosecutor Loftus. "The Bush's bank helped the Thyssens make the Nazi steel that killed allied soldiers. As bad as financing the Nazi war machine may seem, aiding and abetting the Holocaust was worse. Thyssen's coal mines used Jewish slaves as if they were disposable chemicals. There are six million skeletons in the Thyssen family closet, and a myriad of criminal and historical questions to be answered about the Bush family complicity."

Being so closely connected to the Nazis, patriarch Bush must have taken notice of Hitler's method for gaining unwarranted power - fabricate a crisis, call for sweeping powers to protect the population and slowly take totalitarian control.

Luftwaffe chief Goering verbalized this method clearly when he spoke at the Nuremberg War Crimes Trials following the war: "Naturally, the common people don't want war; neither in Russia, nor in England, nor for that matter in Germany. That is understood. But, after all, it is the leaders of the country who determine the policy and it is always a simple matter to drag the people along, whether it is a democracy, or a fascist dictatorship, or a parliament, or a communist dictatorship. Voice or no voice, the people can always be brought to the bidding of the leaders. That is easy. All you have to do is tell them they are being attacked, and denounce the peacemakers for lack of patriotism and exposing the country to danger. It works the same in any country."

Since the Reichstag fire, the Bush family and their associates in the Council on Foreign Relations, Trilateral Commission and Bilderbergers have often mimicked Hitler's tactics of creating a problem, offering a draconian solution and advancing their agenda through any resulting compromise. Such comparison is now widespread, even in Germany.

In mid-2002, when German Justice Minister Herta Daubler-Gmelin commented on President Bush's threats against Iraq, she noted, "Bush wants to distract attention from his domestic problems. That's a popular method. Even Hitler did that." She was quickly forced to resign for calling attention to this aging but effective ploy.

Pearl Harbor

Controversy has raged for years over the question of Roosevelt's foreknowledge of the December 7, 1941, attack on Pearl Harbor.

The situation following the World Trade Center attack is comparable to the aftermath of Pearl Harbor. While some few journalists and Republicans accused the Roosevelt administration of foreknowledge, government spokesmen and Establishment historians blamed the attack on the failure of U.S. intelligence and incompetence within the naval high command.

Today, the accumulation of available information has now caused wide acceptance of the idea that the devastating attack was tolerated, even encouraged, in an effort to galvanize public support for America's participation in the war.

It cannot be denied that Roosevelt's Depression-era social and economic policies greatly centralized the federal government and initiated social engineering that continues to this day, and he was quite open in his allegiance to England. While proclaiming neutrality, Roosevelt had sent warships and ammunition to Britain, just as proposed by the Century Group composed of CFR members. He ordered the occupation of Iceland, closing it off to the Germans, and authorized attacks on U-boats. He openly approved loans to Japan's enemy, nationalist China, and quietly approved the recruitment of well-paid American "volunteers" for Chiang Kai-shek's famous "Flying Tigers." Much of this was in violation of international war rules and was guaranteed to provoke the Axis powers.

"Roosevelt was himself a prototypic Wall Streeter," wrote CFR researcher James Perloff. "His family had been involved in New York banking since the eighteenth century. His uncle, Frederic Delano, was on the original Federal Reserve Board." Roosevelt's son-in-law, Curtis B. Dall, wrote, "Most of his (Roosevelt's) thoughts, his political 'ammunition,' as it were, were carefully manufactured for him in advance by the CFR~One World Money group."

Those who accept the idea that Roosevelt and a few other insiders knew that Pearl Harbor was to be attacked point to these facts:

- During Pacific naval exercises in 1932 and 1938, and with Japanese military attaches closely observing, U. S. Navy officers theoretically destroyed the Pacific Fleet at Pearl Harbor both times.

- Roosevelt ordered the Pacific fleet moved to the exposed position at Pearl Harbor over the vigorous objections of

Admiral James O. Richardson, who was replaced for refusing to issue the order.

    - Roosevelt, Secretary of State Cordell Hull and other high-level officials knew that war was inevitable and that negotiations with Japan's Kichisaburo Nomura were hopeless because the broken Japanese code revealed Nomura was instructed not to yield to Hull's harsh demands.

    - They also knew that a large Japanese task force, including six aircraft carriers, had dropped from sight after moving toward America.

    - This prompted U.S. Army Chief of Staff George C. Marshall, a close associate to many CFR members, to send an oddly worded message to Pearl Harbor commanders on November 27, 1941: "Hostile action possible at any moment. If hostilities cannot, repeat CANNOT, be avoided, the United States desires that Japan commit the first overt act. This policy should not, repeat NOT, be construed as restricting you to a course of action that might jeopardize your defense." Despite this clear warning, with its accompanying suggestion not to attack any attackers, Pacific Fleet ships remained at anchor and aircraft were bunched into clusters of "sitting ducks" as "security" against saboteurs.

    - During the first week of December, Americans intercepted the Japanese diplomatic "Purple" code ordering the Washington embassy to destroy all secret papers and prepare to evacuate.

    - On December 4, Australian intelligence reported sighting the missing Japanese task force moving toward Pearl Harbor but Roosevelt dismissed it as a rumor begun by pro-war Republicans.

    - A British agent named Dusko Popov learned of Japan's plans from German sources but his warnings to Washington were ignored.

    - According to John Toland, author of *Adolf Hitler*, separate warnings regarding a pending attack on Pearl Harbor, though varying as to a specific time, came from U.S. ambassador to Japan Joseph Grew, FBI Director J. Edgar Hoover, Senator Guy Gillette, Representative Martin Dies, Brigadier General Elliot Thorpe in Java and Colonel F. G. L. Weijerman, the Dutch military attaché in Washington. Later, Dutch naval officer Captain Johan Ranneft said sources in U.S.

intelligence told him on December 6 that the Japanese carriers were only four hundred miles northwest of Hawaii.

- During investigations after the attack, Marshall and navy secretary Frank Knox both testified they could not recall their whereabouts the night of December 6. It was later revealed that they were both in the White House with Roosevelt.

Then there is the issue of the aircraft carriers. In 1941, the American public, as well as a few hidebound military officers, still believed that the battleship was the ultimate weapon. But anyone who had been paying attention knew that General Billy Mitchell had proven in the mid-1920s that a single bomb-loaded airplane could destroy a battleship. Battleships were obsolete. Victory in any Pacific war would go to the side with the strongest air power and that meant aircraft carriers.

Not one aircraft carrier was present when Pearl Harbor was attacked.

On November 25, 1941, Secretary of War Henry Stimson had a conversation with Roosevelt, after which he wrote in his diary, "The question was how we should maneuver them into the position of firing the first shot without too much danger to ourselves. It was desirable to make sure the Japanese be the ones to do this so that there should remain no doubt in anyone's mind as to who were the aggressors."

The answer to this dilemma came within twenty-four hours. The most damning evidence yet of Roosevelt's foreknowledge of an attack came from the 1948 interrogation of Germany's Gestapo chief Heinrich Mueller. In a 1995 book by Gregory Douglas, based on previously secret files, Mueller stated that on November 26, 1941, the Germans in Holland had intercepted a private transatlantic telephone conversation between Roosevelt and British prime minister Churchill.

Churchill informed Roosevelt of the movements of the missing Japanese fleet and stated, "I can assure you that their goal is the (conversation broken) fleet in Hawaii, at Pearl Harbor." "This is monstrous," exclaimed Roosevelt, "Can you tell me indicate the nature of your intelligence?..." "Reliable," answered Churchill, who mentioned agents within the Japanese military and foreign service as well as their broken code.

"The obvious implication is that the Japs are going to do a Port Arthur on us at Pearl Harbor. Do you concur?" asked Roosevelt. Churchill replied, "I do indeed unless they add an attack on the Panama Canal to this vile business." Port Arthur, today called Pinyun Lu-shun, was a strategic Russian port on China's Liaotung Peninsula. The

Japanese launched a surprise torpedo attack against the port, which began the 1904~05 Russo-Japanese War.

Roosevelt then said, "I will have to consider the entire problem. A Japanese attack on us, which would result in war between - and certainly you as well - would certainly fulfill two of the most important requirements of our policy." Roosevelt speaks about absenting himself from the White House on some pretext, adding, "What I don't know, can't hurt me and I cannot understand messages at a distance."

Addressing the unlikely proposition that U.S. military officers would have knowingly allowed American units to be attacked, author Douglas explained, "(T)he warning did not come to Roosevelt from below but on a parallel level and from a foreign intelligence source which was far better equipped to decode and translate the Japanese transmissions."

Would Americans Allow Attacks On Americans?

The WTC and Pentagon attacks certainly provided a convenient excuse to launch the prelaid plans for military action against Afghanistan. But were they simply allowed to happen or were they contrived? Again the question arises: Would any American allow an attack on fellow Americans just to further his own business or political agenda? Unfortunately, the answer is yes.

Incredibly, forty-year-old government documents thought to have been destroyed long ago recently were made public. They show the U.S. military in the early 1960s proposed making terrorist attacks in the United States and blaming them on Fidel Castro. Between the failure of the Bay of Pigs invasion of Cuba in April 1961 and the Cuban Missile Crisis of 1962, there was a time when the Pentagon was given authority over the ongoing, and mostly secret, war against Fidel Castro's Cuba.

The entire project was known as Operation Mongoose and was headed by General Edward Lansdale, then~deputy director of the Pentagon's Office of Special Operations. Mongoose was a gathering point for CIA agents, virulent anti-Castro Cubans, gung-ho military operatives and even organized crime figures, all of whom detested President Kennedy and thought him "soft" on communism and a threat to their own preserves.

From this volatile fusion of violent elements came Operation Northwoods, which was to end up with then, Defense secretary Robert McNamara. Today McNamara says, "I never heard of it." However, then~chairman of the Joint Chiefs had heard of it, for it was General

Lyman Lemnitzer who recommended that the Joint Chiefs oversee this plan to generate world opinion against Castro.

These Operation Northwoods documents were discussed in a recent book on the National Security Agency (NSA) entitled *Body of Secrets: Anatomy of the Ultra-Secret National Security Agency* by James Bamford. After a careful study of the documents, Bamford concluded that the Joint Chiefs "proposed launching a secret and bloody war of terrorism against their own country in order to trick the American public into supporting an ill-conceived war they intended to launch against Cuba."

Following the ill-fated Bay of Pigs invasion of Cuba, President Kennedy, angered by the inept actions of the CIA, had shifted responsibility for Cuba from that agency to the Department of Defense. Here, military strategists considered plans to create terrorist actions that would alarm the American population and stampede them into supporting a military attack on Cuba.

Under consideration in Operation Northwoods were plans to create "a series of well-coordinated incidents" in or around the U.S. naval base at Guantanamo Bay, Cuba, to include inciting riots, blowing up ammunition stores, aircraft and ships.

They also planned to "develop a Communist Cuba terror campaign in the Miami area, in other Florida cities and even in Washington" or to "sink a boatload of Cubans en route to Florida (real or simulated) foster attempts on the lives of Cuban refugees in the United States."

Other highlights of Operation Northwoods included the tactics of exploding bombs in carefully chosen locations along with the release of "prepared documents" pointing to Cuban complicity, the use of fake Russian aircraft to harass civilian airliners and "Hijacking attempts against civil air and surface craft," even to simulating the shooting down of a civilian airliner.

The Joint Chiefs of Staff were going along with this pernicious program but President Kennedy rejected Operation Northwoods. Senior military officers ordered the documents destroyed. But someone slipped up and the papers were discovered by the Assassination Records Review Board and recently released by the National Archives.

In late 2002, it appeared that Operation Northwoods was not forgotten. In fact, it seemed like covert and "Black Operation" programs might be making a comeback.

In addition to the tremendous military buildup following the 9/11 attacks, the military affairs analyst for the *Los Angeles Times* reported "what may well be the largest expansion of covert action by the armed forces since the Vietnam Era."

"The Defense Department is building up an elite secret army with resources stretching across the full spectrum of covert capabilities," wrote William M. Arkin. "New organizations are being created. The missions of existing units are being revised. Spy planes and ships are being assigned new missions in anti-terror and monitoring the 'axis of evil.'"

In summer 2002, Defense Secretary Rumsfeld's Defense Science Board (DSB) conducted a "Summer Study on Special Operations and Joint Forces in Support of Countering Terrorism." The panel recommended "new strategies, postures and organization."

One such new organization would be a super Intelligence Support Activity called the Proactive, Preemptive Operations Group (P2OG), a unit combining the CIA, military covert action, information warfare, intelligence, and cover and deception. One line of the classified study, which was leaked to the public by Federation of American Scientists, called for "preemption/proaction/interdiction/disruption/quick-response capabilities"; in other words, dirty fighting.

According to Arkin, the group would, among other things, "launch secret operations aimed at 'stimulating reactions' among terrorists and states possessing weapons of mass destruction ~ that is, for instance, prodding terrorist cells into action and exposing themselves to 'quick-response' attacks by U.S. forces. Such tactics would hold 'states/sub-state actors accountable' and 'signal to harboring states that their sovereignty will be at risk.'"

Under the reorganized military, responsibility and accountability for the P2OG group would be held by a "Special Operations Executive" within the National Security Council (NSC). According to *Asia Times* writer David Isenberg, "The NSC would plan operations but not oversee their execution in order to avoid comparisons to past abuses, such as Iran-Contra operations run out of the NSC by Oliver North during the Reagan administration. Under the board's proposal, NSC plans would be executed by the Pentagon or the CIA."

Several commentators could not help but recall the CIA's Phoenix Program in Vietnam and the Operation Northwoods plan of the Pentagon that followed the disastrous Bay of Pigs invasion of Cuba, a joint military-CIA activity.

The thought of such past abuses prompted one writer, Chris Floyd, to rail against "Bush and his cohorts [who] are plunging the world into an abyss, an endless night of black ops, retribution, blowback, deceit, or murder and terror,"

Now consider that such dirty tricks may already be afoot.

Late on Saturday, May 11, 2002, an astute deputy sheriff in Jacksonville, Florida, stopped a speeding late-model pickup truck. The deputy was amazed to find the truck's driver dressed all in black, wearing a pistol in a shoulder holster and plastic pads on his elbows and knees. In the truck also were large knives, a 12-gauge shotgun, shotgun and pistol ammunition, four ammo magazines, a six-volt battery, duct tape, speaker wire and place from an explosive device. He was further amazed to find the suspect was a soldier from Fort Stewart, Georgia.

Arrested was army specialist Derek Lawrence Peterson. The arresting officer recognized Peterson's truck as one seen earlier parked near the main gate of a nearby Florida Power and Light station. Tracking footprints from where the truck had been parked, investigating officers discovered an explosive device beneath power lines.

The twenty-seven-year-old soldier explained he was practicing night reconnaissance tactics.

A spokesman for Fort Stewart confirmed that Peterson had been stationed there for about a month with B Company, 1st Battalion, 64th Armored Division. If Peterson was simply an idiot who somehow made it into the army, one would expect widespread news coverage to demonstrate how seriously authorities were taking attempted bombing attempts. On the other hand, if Peterson was carrying out some undisclosed covert military orders, one would expect the incident to be hushed up. The soldier was held in a Jacksonville jail without visitors in lieu of $5 million bail. Somebody was taking this case quite seriously, yet there was no national news coverage of this incident at a time of heightened fear and excitement over terrorist incidents, and the initial court hearing for Peterson was postponed.

Next consider the case of the man who tried to stop the first World Trade Center bombing.

According to the *New York Times*, an FBI informant named Emad Salem early in 1993 was involved with Middle Eastern terrorists connected to Osama bin Laden. They were developing a bomb for use against New York's World Trade Center. Salem, a forty-three-year-old former Egyptian army officer, wanted to substitute a harmless powder for the explosive but his plan to thwart the attack was blocked by an FBI official who apparently did not want to expose the inside informant. The attack was allowed to proceed. The February 26 explosion in the WTC resulted in six deaths, more than one thousand casualties and damage in excess of a half billion dollars.

Salem said he wanted to complain to FBI Headquarters in Washington but was dissuaded from doing so by another FBI agent. Salem said the agent told him, "I don't think that the New York [FBI] people would like the things out of the New York Office to go to Washington, D.C."

We now see that creating crises to further political goals is a methodology well understood and utilized in the twentieth century. Is this the game afoot today?

War As An Economic Boost

Even the most cursory examination of past military actions shows a distinct correlation between such warfare and the national economy. Marine Major General Smedley D. Butler, writing in the 1930s, stated, "War is a racket. War is largely a matter of money. Bankers lend money to foreign countries and when they cannot pay, the President sends Marines to get it."

The controversial *Report From Iron Mountain* makes clear that war is not only necessary to maintain societal control but to prop up a sagging financial system. The study that led to the "Report from Iron Mountain" reportedly began in 1961 with Kennedy administration officials such as McGeorge Bundy (CFR, Bilderberger and Skull and Bones), Robert McNamara (Trilateralist, CFR and Bilderberger) and Dean Rusk (CFR and Bilderberger). Knowing of Kennedy's goal of ending the Cold War, these men were concerned that there had been no serious planning for long-term peace.

The genesis of this report came, according to Leonard C. Lewin, in early 1963, when a Special Study Group was selected to study the hypothetical problems of peace just as government think tanks such as Rand Corporation and Hudson Institute studied war. Its principal meetings were at Iron Mountain, a huge underground corporate "nuclear hideout" near Hudson, New York, site of the Hudson Institution, widely regarded as a CFR think tank. Here, in case of nuclear attack, were housed redundant corporate offices of Rockefeller-controlled Standard Oil of New Jersey, the Morgan bank, Manufacturers Hanover Trust, and Dutch Shell Oil, then headed by Bilderberger founder Prince Bernhard. According to Lewin, a copy of the "Report from Iron Mountain" was leaked by a man identified only as "John Doe," a Midwest university professor who claimed to have been a participant. It was published by the Dial Press in 1967 with a foreword by Lewin.

Lewin warned that the report would be "unsettling" to the general reader. "He may not be prepared for some of its assumptions -

for instance, that most medical advances are viewed more as problems than as progress; or that poverty is necessary and desirable, public postures by politicians to the contrary notwithstanding; or that standing armies are, among other things, social-welfare institutions in exactly the same sense as are old-people's homes and mental hospitals."

"John Doe" told the publisher that, while he agreed with the findings of the study, he disagreed with the group's decision to conceal their work from a public "unexposed to the exigencies of higher political or military responsibility." He said he believed the American public, whose tax money paid for the report, had a right to know its disturbing conclusions, while his fellow authors feared "the clear and predictable danger of a crisis in public confidence which untimely publication of the Report might be expected to provoke." He said the report was submitted in March 1966.

Over the years, the *Report from Iron Mountain* has received little or no publicity and certain members of the government and media have attempted to brush it off as a joke or satire. In 1972, Lewin confessed to writing the book himself and the whole thing has been dismissed as a hoax. Yet, questions remain.

But Dial Press published this work with no disclaimers and the serious and erudite tone of this footnoted study along with its global and macroanalytical approach belies the charge of fiction. It is an amazing document, written at the onset of our national experience in Vietnam, and most certainly reflects the elitist views of those who are said to have solicited the study.

According to the report, "War itself is the basic social system, within which other secondary modes of social organization conflict or conspire. It is the system which has governed most human societies of record, as it is today." The report's authors saw war as both necessary and desirable as "the principal organizing force" as well as "the essential economic stabilizer of modern societies."

They expressed concern that through "ambiguous leadership" the "ruling administrative class" might lose its ability to "rationalize a desired war," leading to the "actual disestablishment of military institutions," an eventuality they viewed as "catastrophic."

Therefore, the report writers concluded, "we must first reply, as strongly as we can, that the war system cannot responsibly be allowed to disappear until (1.) we know exactly what (forms of social control) we plan to put in its place and (2.) we are certain, beyond reasonable doubt, that these substitute institutions will serve their purposes."

Most significantly, the report states, "The elimination of war implies the inevitable elimination of national sovereignty and the traditional nation-state," and added, "The possibility of war provides the sense of external necessity without which no government can long remain in power; The basic authority of a modern state over its people resides in its war powers."

The report goes on to say that war "has served as the last great safeguard against the elimination of necessary social classes hewers of wood and drawers of water" and that war functions serve to control "essential class relationships."

Its authors credited military institutions with providing "antisocial elements with an acceptable role in the social structure (I)t is not hard to visualize, for example, the degree of social disruption that might have taken place in the United States during the last two decades if the problem of the socially disaffected of the post~World War II period had not been foreseen and effectively met" noted the report. "The younger, and more dangerous, of these hostile social groupings have been kept under control by the Selective Service System." In the past, juvenile delinquents often were given the choice of going to jail or into the army.

The report suggests what should be done with the "economically or culturally deprived" among us. "A possible surrogate for the control of potential enemies of society is the reintroduction, in some form consistent with modern technology and political process, of slavery the development of a sophisticated form of slavery may be an absolute prerequisite for social control in a world at peace." Perhaps this refers to the current growing practice of private businesses utilizing prison labor or to "wage slaves," those so mired in credit that they have lost any option but to continue working for wages in an unfulfilling job.

It is highly intriguing to compare the recommendations of this report with life in the United States today. The Iron Mountain "boys" listed these possible substitutes for the "functions of war":
  - A comprehensive social-welfare program.
  - a giant open-end space research program aimed at unreachable targets (missions to Jupiter, etc.).
  - A permanent, ritualized, ultra-elaborate disarmament inspection system [as in Iraq and Bosnia].
  - An omnipresent, virtually omnipotent international police force [a UN peacekeeping force as in the Persian Gulf War or the Balkans].
  - An established and recognized extraterrestrial menace [UFOs and alien abductions].
  - Massive global environmental pollution.

- Fictitious alternate enemies [Saddam Hussein, Muammar Qaddafi, Slobodan Milosevic, Osama bin Laden and whoever follows them].

- Programs generally derived from the Peace Corps model [the Job Corps, Volunteers In Service To America].

- A modern, sophisticated form of slavery [addressed above].

- New religions or other mythologies [New Age theologies, cults, etc.].

- Socially oriented blood games [the National Football League, World Wrestling Federation].

- A comprehensive program of applied eugenics (abortion and birth control).

The authors admitted that "alternative enemies" might prove unlikely, but stressed that "one   *must* be found" (emphasis in the original) or, more probably, that "such a threat will have to be invented."

Why was there no legal action taken against an admitted hoaxer who used the good names of several prominent government officials? Why has the corporate mass media attempted to stifle any discussion of the report rather than sensationalize the hoax? Could it be that there is more than a little truth behind this little-known, but controversial, document?

In 2001, a document examiner with deep connections into the military and defense communities made a study of the *Report From Iron Mountain*. The man, who asked not to be identified, reported, "[His company] finds it to be neither a hoax and likely, in its original conception and production, not intended by its author as a satire. [We] are aware of no internal nor external evidence that RFIM nor its production was funded by the U.S. government, neither from vouchered nor from unvouchered funds of the public trust."

This document analyst stated that it was his opinion that the report was written by John Kenneth Galbraith as it closely mimicked Galbraith's 1967 book, *The New Industrial State*. The analyst went on to say, "[T]he usual idiosyncrasies and stylistic comparisons are highly persuasive and replete. The motifs, topics, logic, mode of presentation, vocabulary and arguments of [the two books] are so closely congruent that the two works almost certainly could not have been authored by two different educated and highly perceptive writers."

Galbraith, one of the most influential sociopolitical philosophers of the last century, was an adviser to President Kennedy and later his ambassador to India. As a teacher at Princeton, Harvard and other institutions, as well as a Paul Warburg [one of the creators of the

Federal Reserve System] professor of economics, Galbraith was certainly in a position to know what he was writing about.

And what is to be said for former high-ranking Pentagon Colonel Donn de Grand Pre who worked for Robert McNamara in the early 1960's? In a 2001 interview, Grand Pre, said, "One of the policy makers that I was associated with at the time - for good or for ill - was Henry Kissinger. At that time Henry was an untenured professor at Harvard University and he was also working for the Operations Research Office at the Pentagon, which was paying him a stipend for that work. Simultaneously, Henry was also working for the Council on Foreign Relations under Nelson Rockefeller; Henry would come to the Pentagon and since my boss, General [Robert] York was his contact there, I became Henry's contact [while General York was off on a lengthy study in Vietnam]. It evolved into informal luncheons where Henry would come down from the Hudson Institute, which is close to Iron Mountain, where he and fourteen others were working on this study. Henry was a little bit reluctant to talk about this study, but he gave us enough information to enable us to realize that there was such a study going on. It lasted anywhere from eight to ten months. The Iron Mountain study was not fiction by any means.

"Here was the overall purpose of the study: to analyze different ways a government can perpetuate itself in power, control its citizens and prevent them from rebelling. Their major conclusion was that, in the past, war was the only reliable means to achieve that goal. Remember, this study was in the process of being formulated in early 1963. Kissinger's intellectual buddies from Harvard and also from Yale were already formulating this no-win war in Vietnam."

Regardless of its origin, the tone of the report is certainly conspiratorial and it most certainly reflects the mindset and class-conscious views of men connected to the secret societies. These same men were responsible for the involvement of America in Vietnam in the 1960s and 1970s, and their mindset was behind the attempt to foment war in Nicaragua in the 1980s as well as the conflicts of the 1990s in the Middle East and Balkans. Is what we are seeing today merely a continuation of the policies of such men?

One indication of the behind-the-scenes manipulation that takes place to support the ever-growing world economy was revealed by the London *Observer* shortly after the 9/11 attacks. According to this newspaper, a "secretive committee," called the Working Group on Financial Markets, was prepared to coordinate intervention by the Federal Reserve on "an unprecedented scale" when the markets opened a week after the events of 9/11.

Unofficially called "the plunge protection team," this group, made up of bankers and representatives of the New York Stock Exchange, Nasdaq and the U.S. Treasury, was prepared to spend billions of dollars to purchase equities from mutual funds and other institutional sellers if panic selling had taken place. This was a plan in readiness to prevent a replay of the stock market crashes of 1929 and 1987.

The "plunge protection team" was created by a special executive order of President Ronald Reagan in 1989. "It is known to include senior bankers at leading Wall Street institutions such as Merrill Lynch and Goldman Sachs. It has acted before, in the early 1990s and during the 1998 hedge fund crisis," noted *Observer* reporter Richard Wachman.

Georgia Democratic representative Cynthia McKinney was verbally eviscerated in the mass media for charging that friends of George W. Bush and other corporate bigwigs were profiting from the War on Terror. Yet, on December 20, 2001, war hero and senator John McCain chided his fellow senators about pork and profits accumulated since 9/11 with no appreciable media reaction. McCain was particularly miffed at a proposal to lease one hundred Boeing 767s as refueling tankers for ten years and then spend $30 million to reconfigure the planes as commercial airliners and return them to Boeing. "This is the wrong thing to do," groused McCain. "We're going to spend $20 billion plus over a 10-year period and 10 years from now are going to have nothing to show for it."

"This kind of behavior cannot go on," he later told the Senate. "You will lose the confidence of the American people. This is called war profiteering."

There was no hand-wringing by the mass media about his comments. Only on several Internet sites and in some alternative media were there snickers of understanding. For some time, rumors had flown that Boeing was being offered a sweetheart money package as a bribe to keep quiet about the fatal crash of TWA 800.

Controversy has continued to swirl around the crash, which involved a Boeing 747 passenger jetliner that crashed off Long Island on July 17, 1996. Although hundreds of witnesses reported seeing a streak in the sky prior to the plane exploding and the fact that military exercises were being conducted in the area at the time, the government concluded that a spark had somehow gotten into a central fuel tank and caused the explosion, which killed 230 passengers and crew.

Books, magazine articles and the Internet have been filled with speculation that TWA 800 was accidentally shot down when its late departure took it into a weapons testing zone. Boeing officials initially objected to the conclusion that somehow their craft were defective, yet later became strangely silent, giving birth to the rumors that the aircraft company was being paid off for its silence.

The last-minute and little-publicized add-on to a defense spending bill that caused McCain such concern only added to such speculation. Apparently McCain and other senators had not heard this speculation. Junior Senator Rick Santorum of Pennsylvania naively asked a colleague why the air force could not simply keep the Boeing 767s after they were paid for. He was told, "We can't do that. It will queer the deal."

In the wake of the 9/11 attacks, Americans were asked to give up many things including some constitutional rights in the War on Terrorism. However, government contractors, especially those delivering military goods, gave up nothing. In fact, they gained, and plenty, even companies that had been caught in past scandals.

Take Lockheed Aircraft Inc., for example. In the mid-1970s, Prince Bernhard of the Netherlands was forced to resign the secretive and exclusive Bilderbergers, which represented the inner core elite of more than one secret society. In London, just after World War II, Lord Rothschild and Dr. Joseph Hieronim Retinger had encouraged Prince Bernhard to create the Bilderberger group. The prince personally chaired the group until 1976, when he resigned following revelations that he had accepted large payoffs from Lockheed to promote the sale of its aircraft in Holland. Today, Texaco Inc. has sold its U.S. gas stations to Dutch Shell, drawing yet another American firm into even closer ties with the global economy.

Despite the bribery scandal involving the Dutch prince and other public officials worldwide, Lockheed continued to enjoy the largesse of the U.S. government. Despite pledges to institute ethical reforms, Lockheed officials again came under fire in the mid-1990s. The company pled guilty to making payoffs to an Egyptian official to win approval for a deal involving C-130 cargo planes.

Since 1995, Lockheed, which has since changed its name to Lockheed Martin, has been named in thirty-three more court cases involving charges of overcharging on government contracts, improper technology transfers to China, falsifying the results of nuclear safety tests, job discrimination, environmental pollution and more.

This dismal public record did not deter the U.S. government in October 2001 from awarding Lockheed Martin a contract to build the nation's newest military jet, the F-35 Joint Strike Fighter. The contract was expected to exceed $200 billion during its decades-long life. It was called "the richest military contract in history."

Lockheed Martin is not alone in repeatedly violating both laws and regulations while continuing to collect vast amounts of public money. According to *U.S. News & World Report*, "In the past dozen years, 30 of the 43 largest federal contractors have racked up more than 400 enforcement cases, resulting in at least 28 criminal convictions, 286 civil settlements, mostly involving their government contracts. Allegations included price fixing, bogus testing, polluting, overcharging, hiding product defects, violating export laws and withholding financial data from the government. They also represent more than accounting quibbles: Company workers have been killed and seriously injured and national security potentially put at risk."

Yet four out of every ten federal procurement dollars go to these same companies. "If it was a food-stamp recipient, they'd go to jail," complained Oregon Democrat Representative Peter DeFazio. "It's an extraordinary double standard."

In research conducted by *U.S. News & World Report*, it was determined that only one of the government's thirty largest contractors - General Electric Co. - has ever been denied new contracts and that punishment only lasted a few days.

Due to the cost, bureaucratic paperwork and apparent indifference - not to mention undiscovered bribes - no government agency keeps tabs on which company has broken the law. So the fat contracts just keep coming.

Following the trend of the big corporations getting bigger, many defense contractors have merged into huge multinational entities, making it even more difficult for government watchdogs to detect unlawful activities and make cases. No one - either in the major news media or the government - seems capable of determining exactly which individuals are in control of these corporate behemoths.

With the sudden and burgeoning national defense buildup following the 9/11 attacks, no one expects these corporate zebras to change their stripes any time soon.

Meanwhile, the grand plan to level out the economies of the trilateral nations of Asia, North America and Europe continued. The infrastructure of the United States continued to crumble, jobs continued to disappear as the NAFTA and WTO agreements encouraged companies to move out of the country and social services continued to lag behind demand.

Part V – *Qui Bono?* Who Benefits?

"But as the result of evil, there's some amazing things that are taking place in America."
- President George W. Bush, Daytona   Beach, Florida, January 30, 2002

Detectives long have used the question of   *qui bono*, who benefits, as the beginning of their investigation's. Journalists also use this method, couching it in the old adage "Follow the money."

The Mass Media

But don't look to the corporate mass media to seek truth in this new war as they have all agreed not to broadcast anything that might detract from the official government story, even though it is acknowledged that Bush's media denunciations of bin Laden have been more filled with adjectives like "evil" and "evildoer" than specific evidence.

Fairness & Accuracy in Reporting (FAIR) noted that on October 10, network executives representing ABC, NBC, CBS, Fox and CNN were involved in a conference call with National Security Adviser and Council on Foreign Relations heavyweight Condoleezza Rice. The executives apparently agreed to limit how and what they would broadcast regarding bin Laden or his al-Qaeda group. Bush people even tried unsuccessfully to have Al-Jazeera, described as the "CNN of the Mideast," tone down its coverage of bin Laden. When this effort failed, Al-Jazeera was "accidentally" bombed off the air by U.S. military war planes.

The Bush administration's effort to block any far-reaching inquiry was even more successful with members of our Congress. Free speech was curtailed when they threatened to cut off intelligence reports to legislators who spoke offhandedly to the media. White House spokesman Ari Fleischer, already on the record saying Americans "need to watch what they say," extended this constraint by contacting major newspapers asking that they not print full transcripts of bin Laden's interviews.

According to a FAIR news release, "The point is not that bin Laden or al-Qaeda deserve 'equal time' on U.S. news broadcasts, but that it is troubling for the government to shape or influence news content. Withholding information from the public is hardly patriotic. When the White House insists that it's dangerous to report a news event 'in its entirety,' alarm bells should go off for journalists and the American public alike."

Another small but telling example of the media glossing over 9/11 issues and questions came on April 18, 2002, when Associated Press writer Sheila Hotchkin talked with relatives of the victims of Flight 93 after the government allowed them to listen to cockpit audiotapes from the doomed plane. No reporters were allowed in and the relatives were encouraged not to speak to the media.

But a few did, such as Hamilton Peterson, whose father, Donald A. Peterson, had perished in the crash. In an initial version of the story, Hotchkin quoted Peterson as saying "he learned things from the tape he did not know before, but declined to elaborate." By the next day, Peterson's observation regarding things he had not known was deleted. What did Peterson learn that the rest of us are forbidden to know? Who is behind this mass media control? Particular attention should be paid to the four major corporations that dominate the American mass media - GE, the Walt Disney Co., Viacom and AOL Time Warner. This represents a concentration of media power unthinkable prior to the Clinton years.

One of the few members of Congress to address this monopoly of the news media by an increasingly small number of giant corporations was Representative Bernie Sanders, an independent from Vermont.

"[O]ne of the best-kept secrets is the degree to which a handful of huge corporations control the flow of information in the United States. Whether it is television, radio, newspapers, magazines, books or the Internet, a few giant conglomerates are determining what we see, hear and read," he said.

During the 1990s, "Telecommunication firms were engaged in the most visible and dramatic drive for corporate alliance and consolidation," wrote author William Greider in *One World, Ready or Not.* "AT&T, Time Warner, TCI, MCI, Ameritech and Nynex, CBS, ABC, Disney and many others - the overlapping deals were stunning as U.S. firms rushed to unite market power and technological assets in cable and telephone systems, broadcasting, film-making, publishing and other media, while simultaneously forging telecom partnerships abroad. U.S. consumers would provide the capital for these huge new conglomerates through the deregulated rates they paid to cable and telephone companies. The winners, it was clear, would be a handful of broad and powerful media combines, as dominant as the railroad and oil trusts were in the 1890s."

Apart from the concentration of media ownership is a corporate system that rewards mediocrity and conformity while stifling initiative and hard-hitting investigative journalism. Reporters may go after the occasional crooked siding salesman or auto mechanic but they know well enough to leave the big guys alone.

"Much of what is reported as 'news' is little more than the uncritical transmission of official opinions to an unsuspecting public," wrote media critic Michael Parenti. "What [reporters] pass off as objectivity, is just a mindless kind of neutrality," said journalist Britt Hume, who added reporters "shouldn't try to be objective, they should try to be honest."

The power of this combined media behemoth is overwhelming. A 1994 study by the research firm of Veronis, Suhler & Associates revealed that the typical American spends more than four hours a day watching TV, three hours listening to radio, forty-eight minutes listening to recorded music, twenty-eight minutes reading newspapers, seventeen minutes reading books and fourteen minutes reading magazines.

Over and above ownership consolidation, there is a corresponding decrease in the number of distribution companies, critical to the widespread dissemination of information. Standard & Poor's editors noted that in 1996, distribution problems caused by the consolidation of formerly independent distributors "disrupted deliveries and relationships with retail clients canceled, missed and late deliveries were common occurrences." Authors have complained for years that books on controversial subjects always seem to encounter distribution or publicity problems. With an estimated eight hundred new magazines added each year to the existing eighteen thousand or so (most fail within the first year), it is easy to understand the importance of distribution.

Major banks, most controlled by secret-society members, own significant amounts of stock in the ever-decreasing number of media corporations. "Through elite policy shaping groups like the Council on Foreign Relations and the Business Roundtable, they steer the ship of state in what they deem to be a financially advantageous direction," noted authors Martin A. Lee and Norman Solomon in 1990. "GE, CapCities, CBS, the *New York Times* and the *Washington Post* all have board members who sit on the Council on Foreign Relations."

Little has changed today. A cursory glance at the 1998 edition of *Standard & Poor's Corporation Records* showed several CFR and Trilateral members sit on the boards of the major media corporations.

Corporate ownership intermingled with secret-society members, many of whom are employed in the media, may explain why Bilderberg, Trilateral and CFR meetings are not reported by America's "watchdog" media. In fact, the membership lists of these societies read like a "Who's Who" of the mass media.

These members include many past and present media corporate leaders such as Laurence A. Tisch and William Paley of CBS; John F. Welch Jr. of NBC; Thomas S. Murphy of ABC; Robert McNeil, Jim Lehrer, Hodding Carter III and Daniel Schorr of Public Broadcast Service; Katherine Graham, Harold Anderson and Stanley Swinton of Associated Press; Michael Posner of Reuters; Joan Ganz Cooney of Children's TV Workshop (Sesame Street); W. Thomas Johnson of CNN; David Gergen of *U.S. News & World Report* ; Richard Gelb, William Scranton, Cyrus Vance, A. M. Rosenthal and Harrison Salisbury of the *New York Times* ; Ralph Davidson, Henry Grunwald, Sol Linowitz and Strobe Talbbott of *Time*; Robert Christopher and Phillip Geyelin of *Newsweek*; Katherine Graham, Leonard Downie Jr. and Stephen S. Rosenfeld of the *Washington Post* ; Arnaud de Borchgrave of the *Washington Times*; Richard Wood, Robert Bartley and Karen House of the *Wall Street Journal*; William F. Buckley Jr. of *National Review*, and George V. Grune and William G. Bowen of *Reader's Digest*. Furthermore, sitting on the boards of directors of the corporations that own the media are secret-society members.

Some of the well-known reporters, anchors and columnists who are members of the CFR and/or the Trilateral Commission include Dan Rather, Bill Moyers, C. C. Collinwood, Diane Sawyer, David Brinkley, Ted Koppel, Barbara Walters, John Chancellor, Marvin Kalb, Daniel Schorr, Joseph Kraft, James Reston, Max Frankel, David Halberstram, Harrison Salisbury, A. Ochs Sulzberger, Sol Linowitz, Nicholas Katzenbach, George Will, Tom Brokaw, Robert McNeil, David Gergen, Mortimer Zuckerman, Georgie Ann Geyer and many others. Small wonder so many researchers see a conspiracy of silence among these media peers.

Then there are "media watchdog" organizations such as Accuracy in Media (AIM). Many persons assume such groups are watching out for the public's interests. Not according to writer Michael Collins Piper, who in 1990 made public that AIM founder Reed Irvine was paid $37,000 a year as an "adviser for the division of international finance" of the Federal Reserve System. Noting that many Fed members also belong to the secret societies, Piper wrote, "To this day, Irvine and AIM never touch on any subject which is sensitive to the interests of the international Establishment: whether it be the Bilderberger group, the Trilateral Commission, the Council on Foreign Relations or the truth about the privately owned Federal Reserve."

There are also choke points within the flow of information, such as the international desk at Associated Press headquarters in New York, where one person decides what news from outside the United States makes it onto the wire service. It is important to understand that the real control over the mass media is not direct control over the thousands of hardworking editors, reporters and news directors throughout the nation, but rather the control over the distribution of the information. If one doesn't see or hear about a story, to them it didn't happen.

Then there is the tremendous pressure created by fear of job loss and loss of sources. Many national columnists must rely on insider sources to provide juicy information. Much of this information comes from government sources that would dry up if they published the wrong story. Even the more hard-hitting national reporters still must pull their punches if they want to maintain their insider sources.

The ever-concentrated corporate ownership of the media has meant objective news, long viewed as a public service, flies out the window in favor of bottom-line profits based on ratings. At the time of the JFK assassination, the three major TV networks - ABC, CBS and NBC - supported their news departments with public service funds. Today, these same news departments are funded as programming with a resultant concern over ratings. News today is "a kind of commodity in the marketplace, no longer a holy profession," commented former CBS correspondent Daniel Schorr, "Today, it doesn't matter anymore. You just make your money and to hell with public service."

Veteran newsman Walter Cronkite agreed. Quoted in a professional journal, he said the current state of television journalism is "disastrous and dangerous" and decried "unreasonable profits to satisfy shareholders." "(I)n demanding a profit similar to that of the entertainment area, they're dragging us all down."

"I challenge any viewer to make the distinction between [TV talk show host] Jerry Springer and the three evening newses and CNN," commented *60 Minutes* correspondent Morley Safer.

The watchdog media in America, as they like to portray themselves, appear to be more like lap dogs to their corporate owners. This can be seen in a quick glance at Project Censored, a yearly posting of stories judged to be of importance to the public but which are downplayed or spiked by the major mass media corporations. The censored list clearly showed that the bulk of such stories concern U.S. foreign policy, misdeeds by American businesses or the steady globalism of both governments and multinational firms. Project Censored was conducted through a media research group at Sonoma State University. Nearly two hundred members of the faculty and student body reviewed more than nine hundred nominations from national journalists and academics.

According to this study, the top censored stories of 2001~2002 in order of perceived importance were:

- The attempt by the Federal Communications Commission to privatize the public airwaves, thus enabling tighter corporate control. This plan was conceived during the Clinton administration but never pushed because it was considered too ambitious even for Clinton.

- A new treaty proposed by the World Trade Organization to privatize almost all government public services, which would then be run by multinational corporations.

- How United States policies supported mass murder in Colombia through drug spraying and the use of unrestrained paramilitary groups.

- How the Bush administration hampered FBI investigations into the bin Laden family before the 9/11 attacks.

- A description of how the United States intentionally destroyed Iraq's water supply.

- How the U.S. government is pushing for a revival of the accumulation of nuclear weapons despite several nonproliferation conventions.

- How large corporations are pressing for an HMO model for the administration of school districts.

- How the North American Free Trade Agreement (NAFTA) destroys farming communities both in the United States and abroad.

- The facts behind a national housing crisis in the United States.

- How the CIA destabilized the political balance in Macedonia to allow easier access for an American-British oil pipeline.

Other stories largely missed by the American corporate mass media included how President Bush has appointed former criminals who lied to Congress about their roles in the Iran-Contra Scandal; how President Gerald Ford and his secretary of state Henry Kissinger, lied to the American public about their approval of Indonesia's 1975 invasion of East Timor; how NAFTA's Chapter 11 overrides national public protection laws; how the CIA kidnaps and tortures suspects overseas and how the corporate mass media ignores the key issues behind anti-globalization protests.

"The first step in liquidating a people is to erase its memory. Destroy its books, its culture, its history. Then have somebody write new books, manufacture a new culture, invent a new history. Before long the nation will begin to forget what it is and what it was," wrote author Milan Kundera in *The Book of Laughter and Forgetting.*

A Dismal Foreign Policy Record

Osama bin Laden's allegation that U.S. foreign policy attempts to enslave other nations gains weight when viewed in the context of the past fifty years. The record of United States foreign policy since World War II has indeed been contrary to the peace and prosperity envisioned by the American public.

"I don't think we, the American people, deserved what happened [on 9/11]. Nor do we deserve the sort of governments we have had over the last forty years," said Gore Vidal in a mid-2002 interview. "Our governments have brought this upon us by their actions all over the world. Unfortunately, we only get disinformation from the *New York Times* and other official places. Americans have no idea of the extent of their government's mischief. The number of military strikes we have made unprovoked, against other countries, since 1947~48 is more than 250. These are major strikes everywhere from Panama to Iran. And it isn't even a complete list. It doesn't include places like Chile, as that was a CIA operation. I was only listing military attacks."

As confirmed by the *New York Times* years ago, U.S. foreign policy has been in the hands of the Council on Foreign Relations elite since at least 1939. This elite and its associates include former presidents Bush and Bill Clinton, Gerald Ford, Jimmy Carter and Richard Nixon, virtually every CIA director as well as a considerable number of familiar past and present government officials such as Dick Cheney, Henry Kissinger, Wesley Clark, Strobe Talbot, Alexander Haig, Alan Greenspan, Bruce Babbitt, James A. Baker III, Sandy Berger, Colin Powell, Harold Brown, Zbigniew Brzezinski, Frank C. Carlucci, Richard Darman, John Deutch, Lawrence Eagleburger, Robert McFarlane, Brent Scowcroft, Condoleezza Rice and Casper Weinberger.

Within three hours of the attacks of 9/11, Kissinger, Talbot, Clark and Haig were all prominently seen on both CNN and the broadcast networks. Their message was so similar that one would have thought they were reading from the same CFR script: The attacks were terrible, something must be done, terrorism transcends national boundaries and therefore, all the nations must come together under the United Nations to successfully combat this new type of warfare.

This clarion call was seen by some as nothing more than support for America's ongoing policy of neocolonialism, the subjugation and control of other nations through military dictators or wealthy families supported by, and often placed in power by, the U.S. military or intelligence services.

The result of this neocolonial policy has been dismal at best and catastrophic at worst. Never mind the historical aggression displayed by American foreign policy in the Mexican War of 1848 and the Spanish-American War of 1898. Consider this policy just since World War II:

In 1951, when Iran's prime minister Mohammed Mossadegh nationalized the oil industry in that Mideast nation, he was deposed by a coup instigated by the CIA and the Shah came to power, assuming complete control in 1963. Thousands of Iranians, perhaps millions died during the repressive rule of the Shah and his SAVAK secret police. The Shah was finally forced out in 1979 by the Ayatollah Khomeini, who quickly became the United States' latest foreign enemy despite the fact that he had been on the CIA payroll while living in Paris. The Shah was granted asylum in the United States.

In Guatemala in 1954, the CIA toppled the popularly elected government of Jacobo Arbenz, which had nationalized United Fruit property. Prominent American government officials such as former CIA director Walter Bedell Smith, then~CIA director Allen Dulles, Secretary of State for Inter-American Affairs John Moors Cabot and Secretary of State John Foster Dulles were all closely connected to United Fruit. An estimated 120,000 Guatemalan peasants died in the resulting military dictatorships.

Fidel Castro, with covert aid from the CIA, overthrew the military dictatorship of Fulgencio Batista and instituted sweeping land, industrial and educational reforms as well as nationalizing American businesses. Castro was swiftly labeled a communist and the CIA then organized anti-Castro Cubans, resulting in numerous attacks on Cuba and the failed Bay of Pigs invasion in 1961. The island nation has been the object of U.S. economic sanctions since that time.

More than three thousand persons died in the wake of an invasion of the Dominican Republic by U.S. Marines in 1965. The troops ostensibly were sent to prevent a communist takeover, although later it was admitted that there had been no proof of such a takeover.

Also in 1965, the United States began the bombing of North Vietnam after President Lyndon Johnson proclaimed the civil war there an "aggression" by the north. Two years later, American troop strength in Vietnam had grown to 380,000. U.S. dead by the end of that Asian war totaled some 58,000, with casualties to the Vietnamese, both north and south, running into the millions.

In 1973, the elected government of Salvador Allende in Chile was overthrown by a military coup aided by the CIA. Allende was killed and some thirty thousand persons died in subsequent violence and repression, including some Americans.

In 1968, General Sukarno, the unifier of Indonesia, was overthrown by General Suharto, again with aid from the CIA. Suharto proved more dictatorial and corrupt than his predecessor. A reported 800,000 people died during his regime. Another 250,000 persons died in 1975 during the brutal invasion of East Timor by the Suharto regime aided by the U.S. government and Henry Kissinger.

In 1979, the powerful Somoza family, which had ruled Nicaragua since 1937, was finally overthrown and Daniel Ortega was elected president. CIA-backed Contra insurgents operating from Honduras fought a protracted war to oust the Ortega government in which an estimated thirty thousand people died. The ensuing struggle came to include such shady dealing in arms and drugs that it created a scandal in the United States called Iran-Contra, which involved persons connected to the National Security Council selling arms to Iran, then using the profits to buy drugs in support of the Contras. All of those indicted or convicted of crimes in this scandal were pardoned by then~president George H. W. Bush.

U.S. Marines landed in Lebanon in 1982 in an attempt to prevent further bloodshed between occupying Israeli troops and the Palestine Liberation Organization. Thousands died in the resulting civil war, including several hundred Palestinians massacred in refugee camps by Christian forces. Despite the battleship shelling of Beirut, American forces were withdrawn in 1984 after a series of bloody attacks on them.

In 1983, U.S. troops invaded the tiny Caribbean island nation of Grenada after a leftist government was installed. The official explanation was to rescue a handful of American students who initially said they didn't need rescuing. The only real damage in this tiny war was to a mental health hospital partly owned by a White House physician and widely reported to be a CIA facility.

During the 1970s and 1980s, the U.S. government gave aid and arms to the right-wing government of the Republic of El Salvador for use against it's leftist enemies. By 1988, some seventy thousand Salvadorans had died.

More than one million persons died in the fifteen-year battle in Angola between the Marxist government aided by Cuban troops and the

National Union for the Total Independence of Angola, supported by South Africa and the U.S. government.

When Muammur al-Qaddafi tried to socialize the oil-rich North African nation of Libya beginning with his takeover in 1969, he drew the wrath of the U.S. government. In 1981, it was claimed that Qaddafi had sent hit teams to the United States to assassinate President Reagan and in 1986, following the withdrawal of U.S. oil companies from Libya, an air attack was launched that missed Qaddafi but killed several people including his infant daughter.

In 1987, an Iraqi missile attack on the U.S. frigate *Stark* resulted in thirty-seven deaths. Shortly afterward, the Iraqi president apologized for the incident. In 1988, a U.S. Navy ship shot down an Iranian airliner over the Persian Gulf, resulting in 290 deaths. The Reagan administration simply called it a mistake.

Thousands of freedom-seeking Chinese were killed in Beijing's Tiananmen Square in 1989 after government hard-liners there conferred with former president Richard Nixon on how to deal with the dissidents. Nixon, of course, was the only U.S. president to resign under threat of criminal indictment and was in power during the shooting of students at Kent State University on May 4, 1970.

As many as eight thousand Panamanians died over Christmas 1989 when President George H. W. Bush sent U.S. troops to invade that Central American nation to arrest his former business partner Manuel Noriega. The excuse was that Noriega was involved in the importation of drugs to the United States. *U.S. News & World Report* noted that in 1990, the amount of drugs moving through Panama had doubled.

Iraqi casualties, both military and civilian, totaled more than 300,000 during the short Persian Gulf War of 1991. It has been estimated that more than one million Iraqis, including women and children, have died as a result of the continued missile and air attacks over the past decade as well as economic sanctions against that nation.

Also in 1991, the United States suspended assistance to Haiti after the election of a liberal priest sparked military action and disorder. Eventually, U.S. troops were deployed.

Other nations that have felt the brunt of U.S. CIA and/or military activity as a result of foreign policy include Somalia, Afghanistan, Serbia, Kosovo, Bosnia, Brazil, Chad, Sudan and many others. As Dr. Martin Luther King Jr. stated during the Vietnam War, "My government is the world's leading purveyor of violence."

He did not say "my country" or "my people," it is the government, or rather those who control it, who are responsible. Although we, the distracted and unaware citizens who claim to live in a democracy must take our fair share of the blame as accessories after the fact.

Robert Bowman flew 101 combat missions in Vietnam and so he knows the results of U.S. foreign policy firsthand. He later became bishop of the United Catholic Church in Melbourne Beach, Florida Bowman noted, "President Clinton [and later President Bush] did not tell the American people the truth about why we are the targets of terrorism when he explained why we bombed Afghanistan and Sudan. [They both] said that we are a target because we stand for democracy, freedom, and human rights in the world. Nonsense!

"We are the target of terrorists because, in much of the world, our government stands for dictatorship, bondage and human exploitation. We are the target of terrorists because we are hated. And we are hated because our government has done hateful things."

The solution, Bowman said, is to change our ways. "Getting rid of our nuclear weapons, unilaterally if necessary, will enhance our security. Drastically altering our foreign policy will ensure it. In short, we should do good instead of evil. Who would try to stop us? Who would hate us? Who would want to bomb us? That is the truth the American people need to hear."

If such a dismal and counterproductive foreign policy was simply the result of incautious and insipid blundering, one might expect that occasionally mistakes would be made in favor of the American people. But a careful study of the United States' errant policies during the past century clearly indicate a persistent pattern of policies that only enrich the wealthy and further the goals of the globalist elite.

Manufactured Enemies

Many of our worst enemies of the past were created by the U.S. government. Again, the primary question is whether America simply has a penchant for creating Frankenstein monsters or are such creations part of a conscious agenda?

The history of the Vietnam War can be personified in Nguyen Tat Thanh, the son of a lowly Vietnamese rural educator. This man later changed his name to Ho Chi Minh {He Who Enlightens} and became the driving force behind Indochinese nationalism for three decades. As a young man during World War I, Ho Chi Minh lived in France, where he came into contact with French socialists and their Illuminati and Masonic philosophies. In 1919, he spoke before the attendees of the Versailles Peace Conference, calling for expanded rights in Indochina.

In 1930, Ho founded the Vietnamese Communist Party, which later was changed at the urging of Soviet leaders to the Indochinese Communist Party to avoid being perceived as simply a national movement. However, the nationalism of Ho's party was reaffirmed in 1941 when he and others entered Vietnam and created the League for the Independence of Vietnam, or the Viet Minh. When the Japanese overran Indochina in 1945, Ho and General Vo Nguyen Giap began working with the American Office of Strategic Services to oust the occupation forces.

Ho continued to receive American aid after the Japanese withdrew from Vietnam following their surrender on August 14, 1945. "We had a trusted agent whom we regularly supplied with weapons, radio equipment, operators and medicine. All of it served to reinforce his position and status," wrote journalist Lloyd Shearer.

There exists a wealth of documentation indicating that the Russian Revolution - indeed the very creation of communism - sprang from Western conspiracies beginning even before World War I. "One of the greatest myths of contemporary history is that the Bolshevik Revolution in Russia was a popular uprising of the downtrodden masses against the hated ruling class of the Czars," wrote author G. Edward Griffin, who said both planning and funding for the revolution came from financiers in Germany, Britain and the United States.

In January 1917, Leon Trotsky was living in New York City working as a reporter for the *New World*, a communist newspaper. Trotsky had escaped an earlier failed attempt at revolution in Russia and fled to France, where he was expelled for his revolutionary behavior. "He soon discovered that there were wealthy Wall Street bankers who were willing to finance a revolution in Russia," wrote journalist William Still.

One of these bankers was Jacob Schiff, whose family had lived with the Rothschilds in Frankfurt. Another was Elihu Root, attorney for Paul Warburg's Kuhn, Loeb & Company. According to the *New York Journal-American*, "(I)t is estimated by Jacob's grandson, John Schiff, that the old man sank about $20 million for the final triumph of Bolshevism in Russia." Root, a CFR member, contributed yet another $20 million, according to the Congressional Record of September 2, 1919.

To illustrate the interconnectedness of America's wealthy elite, another grandson, Andrew Schiff, is married to the daughter of Democratic presidential contender Al Gore.

Author Gary Allen noted, "In the Bolshevik Revolution we have some of the world's richest and most powerful men financing a movement which claims its very existence is based on the concept of stripping of their wealth men like the Rothschilds, Rockefellers, Schiffs, Warburgs, Morgans, Harrimans and Milners. But obviously these men have no fear of international communism. It is only logical to assume that if they financed it and do not fear it, it must be because they control it. Can there be any other explanation that makes sense?"

This conspiratorial view was echoed by none other than Winston Churchill, who in 1920 wrote, "From the days of Spartacus-Weishaupt {head of the mysterious Illuminati}) to those of Karl Marx, to those of {Socialists Leon} Trotsky, Bela Kun, Rosa Luxembourg, and Emma Goldman, this worldwide conspiracy for the overthrow of civilization has been steadily growing.

"It played a definitely recognizable role in the tragedy of the French Revolution. It has been the mainspring of every subversive movement during the nineteenth century, and now at last this band of extraordinary personalities from the underworld of the great cities of Europe and America have gripped the Russian people by the hair of their heads, and have become practically the undisputed masters of that enormous empire."

If there can be identified one single motivating factor behind the horror and tragedy experienced in the twentieth century, it is surely anti-communism. The animosity between the so-called democracies of the West and the communism of the East produced continuous turmoil from 1918 through the end of the century.

As mentioned previously, more recent manufactured enemies include Saddam Hussein, the Shah of Iran, Manuel Noriega, Ferdinand Marcos and many others.

But then such enemies are necessary to convince an otherwise peaceful population on the need for wars and foreign expeditions. It's all part of a formula that has proved quite successful down through the centuries. Create a boogeyman enemy to keep the public distracted but focused, then play both ends against the middle to maintain profits and control.

The Hegelian Dialectic

Conspiracy researchers were mystified for years how such high-level capitalists as the Morgans, Warburgs, Schiffs and Rockefellers could condone, much less support, the Communists who espoused an ideology that overtly threatened their position and wealth.

To understand this seeming dichotomy, indeed to understand how the secret-society members operate, one must study the philosopher who most greatly influenced these men - the founder of idealism, Georg Wilhelm Friedrich Hegel.

Coming on the heels of the Age of Reason - the intellectual revolt against the authority of the church - German philosophers Hegel, Johann Gottlieb Fichte and Immanuel Kant inspired future generations with the idea that modern man, need not be chained by religious dogma and tradition. These iconoclasts differed only in that Kant believed that things which cannot be experienced in the material world cannot be known to man while the metaphysical Fichte and Hegel believed that man's reason is "the candle of the Lord," that intuition and love create a unity of man with the Divine that brings understanding and equality.

Hegel's claim to the rational interpretation of the human essence, termed the "Hegelian System," was an attempt to reconcile opposites, to comprehend the entire universe as a systematic whole. It was a mind-boggling effort and has not yet been fully completed. Adherents and opponents of Hegel may well continue to philosophize into the next millennium. It is easy to understand why such abstract thinking has been interpreted in so many ways by Hegel's followers, who included Karl Marx and Adolf Hitler

Hegel's fellow idealist and the man who most influenced his work, Fichte, was a member of secret societies. Both he and Hegel espoused the Freemason theology of rationalism.

Marx turned Hegel's theoretical philosophy to the material and developed an exceptional tool for manipulating people and events. This has become known as the Hegelian Dialectic, the process in which opposites - thesis and antithesis - are reconciled in compromise or synthesis.

Hegel simply reduced human interaction to a simple formula: One person or group desires one thing, another desires something else, and whatever comes from their interaction - whether this be compromise, arbitration or a fight - is the end result or synthesis.

The application relevant here is the idea that Western capitalists created communism on one side (thesis) as a perceived enemy of the democratic nations on the other side (antithesis). The ensuing conflict produced huge markets for finance and armaments and eventually a general leveling of both sides (synthesis). Often during the past fifty years it was said that the USA was becoming more like Russia, while Russia was becoming more like the USA.

The members of secret societies traceable to Cecil Rhodes's Round Tables and the Illuminati understood the Hegelian Dialectic quite well. Their predecessors had successfully used it for centuries. These early-day Machiavellis found it was but a small step to the realization that one needn't wait for crisis and turmoil. It could be created and controlled to their benefit. Hence came the cycles of financial booms and busts, crises and revolutions, wars and threats of war, all of which maintained a "Balance of Power."

Social activists and bureaucrats alike have learned this both-ends-against-the-middle stratagem well, whether by experience, intuition or study. Demand more than you really need (thesis) from your opposition or employer (antithesis) and, even after compromises, you'll usually end up with what you wanted in the first place (synthesis).

"This revolutionary method - the systematic working of thesis vs. antithesis = synthesis - is the key to understanding world history," declared conspiracy author Texe Marrs.

Russian revolutionaries such as Lenin and Trotsky were being used to get Russia out of World War I, to the benefit of Germany. But at the elite level, communism was being created to stimulate the division of fear and mistrust presented as communism verses capitalism verses fascism.

Even Lenin apparently came to understand that he was being manipulated by more powerful forces. "The state does not function as we desired," he once wrote. "A man is at the wheel and seems to lead it, but the car does not drive in the desired direction. It moves as another force wishes."

This other "force" were the members of the secret societies that were behind the birth of communism itself, "monopoly finance capitalists" as Lenin described them.

What Do We Know Now?

The question then becomes, was 9/11 truly an unprovoked and surprise attack by a handful of Muslim zealots or was it yet another case of the Hegelian method being used to promote an existing agenda?

The record is clear that since the National Security Act of 1947 the United States has slowly been turned into a national security state with more and more power being concentrated in the federal government, particularly the executive branch. Law's are being enacted by presidential orders rather than through reasoned debate and careful study by our elected representatives. And no one seems to notice, especially since the news media have now come under the total control of a mere handful of international corporations. Trained and dedicated newsmen, in the mold of a Walter Cronkite, have been replaced by air personalities who are more conscious of ratings than world and national events. Citizens are compelled to study and learn for themselves, drawing from a variety of nontraditional news sources.

What have we learned from the 9/11 attacks and their aftermath?

We know that mere incompetence cannot explain the systematic failure of the normal security protections codified in both the civilian aviation and military sectors and we know that not one single person has yet been reprimanded for this failure. Why did it take a year to learn that Cheney's antiterrorism task force was alerted to the problem and that an NRO exercise involving the idea of planes crashing into buildings was scheduled for 9/11?

The evidence of foreknowledge of the attacks, particularly within the FBI and CIA, is overwhelming. This raises the question of who precisely blocked this information and why. Why was there no warning to the public or beefed up security? Who had the power to misdirect and block official investigations?

We also know that action against the Taliban in general and Osama bin Laden in particular were well under way long before the attacks. How is it that bin Laden remains at large as of this writing despite what we are told are the best efforts of the world's foremost superpower? Does anyone truly believe that the Mossad, and hence the CIA, has no clue as to bin Laden's whereabouts, especially at a time when every American can be tagged by computer?

It is now clear that the bombing of Afghanistan had more to do with oil and gas pipelines and restoring the poppy fields than with catching bin Laden. And the War on Terrorism shifted from finding those responsible for the attacks to enforcing a "Pax Americana" on the world, exactly as articulated by Cheney, Rumsfeld, Perle and Wolfowitz even before Bill Clinton was elected. If they are unable to generate a war in Iraq, there surely will be new provocations and excuses for foreign adventurism. Unlike every past American administration, this group has actually proposed a first-strike use of nuclear weapons in this new war.

We know now that Bush spurned more international treaties than any other world leader and released funds for North Korea's nuclear program at a time when he was preparing to seek war with Iraq, claiming Saddam Hussein *might* be capable of building a weapon of mass destruction. If the United States is not at war with Iraq soon after the holiday season of 2002~03, it will not be due to lack of interest on the part of the Bush administration. This issue seemed to indicate a schism within the ranks of the New World Order. The Bush forces pushed hard for an attack while the United Nations worked hard behind the scenes to ensure compliance by Saddam Hussein to UN demands.

We now know that plans to circumvent the Constitution were laid as far back as the Nixon years and that the new Department of Homeland Security carries within it concepts and programs that would have been greeted with howls of protests just a few short years ago. And the new technology to identify and classify each individual citizen is now in place. Administration critics cannot be summarily dismissed for using terms like "dictatorship," "1984" and "totalitarianism." Considering the close ties between Prescott Bush, his father-in-law, George Herbert Walker, and Hitler's Nazis, it is no stretch of the language to call the grandson's programs "fascist."

Bush and Cheney consistently fought any truthful investigation into the tragedies of 9/11, and when popular opinion in this matter turned against them, they turned to one of the leading lights of the secret societies - Henry Kissinger. Again, a groundswell of public opinion as well as the possibility of dredging up old war crimes prompted Kissinger's resignation even before he began work. It can also be seen that President Bush is trying to place persons sympathetic to his worldview on the Supreme Court, the place where his father's friends handed him his office. And shifting to a Democrat won't make things better as most of the groundwork for the current War on Freedom was laid during the CFR-dominated Clinton administration.

We now know that both Bush and most other members of his cabinet are too locked into the monopolies of energy, pharmaceuticals, telecommunications and military/aerospace to allow alternative views to be heard. Bush, Cheney and many others are guilty of the same corporate shenanigans they were forced to criticize in the summer of 2002 following the collapse of Enron, WorldCom and others.

We now clearly see that the privatization of both U.S. industry, energy and institutions to include health care and education does not fulfill the promise of better service at less cost. If the game plan of the masterminds behind the 9/11 attacks was to curtail American freedom, centralize more power in the federal government and set back the social agenda of the United States in favor of an open-ended military and intelligence buildup, then they succeeded admirably. To many longtime researchers, it all has a familiar ring to it.

In many ways, the aftermath of the 9/11 attacks fits the same template as the assassination of President Kennedy in 1963:

- Within hours, despite a lack of real evidence, one man was blamed for the event along with hints that he was connected to foreign enemies.

- Official pronouncements were widely publicized only to be quietly admitted as errors later on.

- Although within the jurisdiction of the local authorities, the entire case was usurped by the FBI and CIA, both agencies under the control of a president who benefited from the tragedy.

- A group of specialists (medical in JFK's case and engineers in the WTC) was convened but limited in what they could view and study, blocked from conducting an objective probe by federal officials.

- Evidence in the case was hastily removed and destroyed, forever lost to an impartial and meaningful investigation.

- More evidence was locked away in government files under the excuse of "national security."

- Federal malfeasance was excused by claiming lack of manpower and resources and no one was disciplined or fired. Federal agency budgets were increased.

- Any alternative to the official version of events was decried as "conspiracy theory" and "unpatriotic."

- The federal government used the event to increase its own centralized power.

- A foreign war (Vietnam in JFK's case and Afghanistan today), which would have been otherwise opposed, was supported by a grieving population.

- Top government leaders (then LBJ and now Bush), formerly under suspicion for election fraud and corrupt business dealings, was suddenly propelled to new heights of popularity.

- Many citizens knew or suspected that the official version of events was incorrect but were afraid to speak out.

- A compliant and sycophantic mass media was content to merely parrot the official version of events and studiously avoided asking the hard questions that might have revealed the truth.

One major difference in the two cases is that following JFK's death, less than ten days went by before President Lyndon Johnson appointed a special commission to investigate the crime. Well more than a year after the events of 9/11, there was still only talk of creating some sort of investigative body, the time lag due primarily to pressure from President Bush and Vice President Cheney not to convene such an inquiry.

In the case of the Pearl Harbor attack, the JFK assassination and 9/11, a common denominator was the failure of normal security precautions. This is the tip-off.

As Colonel L. Fletcher Prouty, former Pentagon-CIA liaison officer, stated in regards to the Kennedy assassination, "The active role is played secretly by permitting it to happen. That was why President Kennedy was killed. He was not murdered by some lone gunman or by some limited conspiracy, but by the breakdown of the protective system that should have made assassination impossible. This is the greatest single clue to the assassination - Who had the power to call off or reduce the usual security precautions that are always in effect whenever a president travels? Castro did not kill Kennedy, nor did the CIA. The power source that arranged that murder was on the inside. It had the means to reduce normal security and permit the choice of a hazardous route. It also had the continuing power to cover that crime for years."

The same question could be asked regarding the tragedies of September 11, 2001:

Who had the power to call off or reduce normal airline and NORAD security procedures and who had the power to deflect any meaningful investigation into the events? This kind of power can only be found at the highest levels of government and corporate control. Today's big-time criminals no longer worry about what the government might do to them because they *are* the government. It therefore becomes essential to identify and connect the inner core elite of the world's secret societies, to demonstrate their ownership and interlocking control over the multinational corporations that dominate our national life.

"Most people prefer to believe their leaders are just and fair even in the face of evidence to the contrary, because once a citizen acknowledges that the government under which they live is lying and corrupt, the citizen has to choose what he or she will do about it. To take action in the face of a corrupt government entails risks of harm to life and loved ones. To choose to do nothing is to surrender one's self-image of standing for principles. Most people do not have the courage to face that choice. Hence, most propaganda is not designed to fool the critical thinker but only to give moral cowards an excuse not to think at all," noted Internet commentator Michael Rivero.

But the time has come for persons of good heart and conscience to stand up and regain the country handed down to them by men and women who not only were discomforted by fighting for a free and democratic republic but risked their very lives and fortunes.

Look to local leaders as they are the ones most likely to look out for the public welfare. Our democratic republic, with its Constitution and Bill of Rights, is without a doubt the greatest form of government ever initiated in the written history of this planet. Let's make it work as it was intended.

By the time you read this, there is every likelihood that another major terrorist attack will have taken place and that some form of warfare will have broken out in some far corner of the world. There will be more "experts" brought forward to generate fear and instruct us on the need to curtail freedom to save democracy.

Do Not be stampeded. We all agree that the true culprits, of this or any future tragedy, must be identified and punished. But we must make certain through an objective investigation and cool reasoning that we indeed have the true culprits. We must not be played for suckers as so many times in the past.

The corporate mass media has bombarded the public with facts, statistics, personal opinion and commentary to the point of distraction and confusion.

Viewed in its broadest perspective, however, the picture is both clear and appalling:

The United States today is under the control of a dynastic family, blood relatives to virtually all European monarchs, whose patriarch can be shown to have been both in sympathy and in business with Hitler and his Nazis.

Through this man's son, the family has been involved with the CIA since at least the time of the 1961 Bay of Pigs invasion, with all that implies regarding covert wars, drug smuggling and assassinations, not to mention the creation of Saddam Hussein as well as Osama bin Laden and his al-Qaeda network. One would imagine that the public would finally catch on after realizing that three major world evildoers were financed by the same family.

And each generation has belonged to a secret college society linked to the German Illuminati as well as prominent members of other such societies, whose avowed purpose is to end United States sovereignty in favor of globalism. The family has even been linked to accused assassin, John Hinckley and Lee Harvey Oswald. What are the odds?

At least two sons were at the heart of the savings and loan debacle that cost every man, woman and child in the United States thousands of dollars. The eldest son, not elected but selected by a Supreme Court packed by previous Republican presidents, including his father, has been linked to Enron and other shady oil company dealings and has surrounded himself with men of questionable ethics and truthfulness.

Collectively, this family and their corporate cronies are today seeking what amounts to dictatorial powers to combat the proclaimed War on Terrorism, despite the growing evidence that the attacks that launched this war were known in advance and were allowed to happen to bring about the erosion of individual rights and the centralization of even more power unto themselves. And that view is putting the very best possible light on the affair.

Considering the long-standing connections between this family, the secret societies, the CIA, the bin Laden family, Saddam Hussein and the al-Qaeda network as well as Global Hawk technology, a case can be made that the 9/11 attacks were instigated by persons other than Osama bin Laden.

The nature of public life in the United States today has begun to resemble the very despotic societies - Hitler's Third Reich, Stalinist Russia, Communist Eastern Europe and China - that America contested during the last century. Such totalitarian regimes stemmed from centralized governments that served themselves rather than the people, that responded more swiftly to policies of the central government than evidence of criminal activities or public need and used every means at their disposal to spy on and intimidate their citizens. Thoughtful observers see much of that same trend in the United States today.

These are not conjectures or conspiracy theories. These are the facts. The questions raised regarding the 9/11 attacks and their aftermath bring only further questions. These questions concern what the American people intend to do about all this.

Will they continue to be led by the corporate mass media that deceives by omission more than commission and distracts them from the real issues? Will they continue to reelect politicians who have been in office while all the causes of current problems were put into place? Will they continue to blindly follow the standards of the two major political parties that have demonstrated that precious little difference exists in their major policies? Will they continue to support a foreign policy that angers and alienates peoples all across the globe with its thinly disguised neocolonialism? Will they allow the U.S. military to continue enforcing this foreign policy while gaining unwarranted control over their own nation and lives? Will they continue to permit their nation to be the primary seller of arms to the world and then bemoan the fact that those same arms are used against them? Will they finally take a look behind the green curtain of media spin to identify the globalists who own and control that media as well as the government and, hence, the military? Will they stand up and exercise their own individual power or stand idly by, frozen by fear, intimidation or confusion, while their remaining liberties are lost?

Only you, the reader, can answer these questions.

The War on Freedom

SOURCES:

PAGE   INTRODUCTION

5   State of Emergency: www.whitehouse.gov/news/releases/2001/09/20010914-4.html .

6   "We haven't heard from him…": Editors, "Bush: Nuclear Weapons Are Still an Option," *People's Daily* (March 14, 2002); http://english.peopledaily.com.cn/200203/14/eng20020314_92081.shtml

Definitions

Democracy or Republic?

8   One tenth of one percent: Editors, "Big-Time Donors Small in Number: Less Than One-Tenth of 1 percent of Population," Center for Responsive Politics Media Advisory (Dec. 11, 2002); www.opensecrets.org

PART I – THE EVENTS OF 9-11

A Summery of Events

9   Various mainstream publications.

Unresolved Issues and Questions

12   Rumsfeld's missile quote: http://www.defenselink.mil/news/Nov2001/t11182001_t1012pm.html

12   Steganography: Editors, "Digital moles in the White House?" *WorldNetDaily.com* (2001); www.worldnetdaily.com/news/article.asp?ARTICLE_ID=24594

12   Flying bin Ladens: Jane Mayer, "The House Of Bin Laden," *The New Yorker* (Nov. 12, 2001)

13   No stone unturned: Editors, "They Saw It Happen," *America at War,* (New York: Personality Profiles Presents, 2001)

14   Some identified hijackers still alive: Editors, "Hijack `suspects' alive and well," *BBC News* (Sept. 23, 2001)

14   Arab names similar: Hanna Rosin, "Some Cry Foul As Authorities Cast a Wide Net," *Washington Post* (Sept. 28, 2001)

14   Kristin Breitweiser: Jim Miklaszewski, "U.S. had 12 warnings of jet attacks," NBC, MSNBC, *The Associated Press* and *Reuters* (Sept. 18, 2002).

14   Passport found: http://www.cnn.com/2001/US/09/16/gen.america.under.attack/

14   Terrorists looked for hookers: Editors, "Reports: Hijack Suspects Looked for Hookers in Boston," *Reuters* (Oct. 10, 2001)

15   Controlled implosions: Olivier Uyttebrouck, "Explosives Planted In Towers, N.M. Tech Expert Says," *Albuquerque Journal* (Sept. 11, 2001)

16   Bombs set in building: Editors, "New York City," *People.com* (Sept. 12, 2001); http://people.aol.com/people/special/0,11859,174592-3,00.html

17   Teresa Veliz and bombs: Dean E. Murphy, "Teresa Veliz: A Prayer to Die Quickly and Painlessly," *September 11: An Oral History* (New York: Doubleday, 2002)

18   Ross Milanytch: *America at War,* op. cit.

18   Steve Evans of BBC: Christopher Bollyn, "New York Firefighters' Final Words Fuel Burning Questions about 9-11," *American Free Press* (Aug. 19, 2002)

19   Explosion at base of building: Col. Donn de Grand Pre, "Many Questions Still Remain About Trade Center Attack," *American Free Press* (Feb. 11, 2002)

19   Tom Elliott: Peter Grier, "A Changed World – Part 1: The Attack," *The Christian Science Monitor* (Sept. 17, 2001)

19   CNN videotapes smoke from WTC 6: Christopher Bollyn, "Unexplained 9-11 Explosion at WTC Complex," *American Free Press* (July 22, 2002)

19   Firefighters Palmer and Bucca: Bollyn (Aug. 19, 2002), op. cit.

19   Seismic evidence of two shocks: Christopher Bollyn, "Seismic Data Refutes Official Explanation," *American Free Press* (Sept. 9, 2002)

19   Loizeaux's speculation: Ibid.

19   Arthur Lerner-Lan: Ibid.

19   Eric Hufschmid: Ibid.

20   WTC steel sold for scrap: Bill Manning, "Selling Out the Investigation," *Fire Engineering* (January, 2002)

20   Evidence treated like garbage: Francis Brannigan, "WTC 'Investigation'?: A Call To Action," *Fire Engineering* (January, 2002)

21   W. Gene Corley and team complaints: Avery Comarow, "After the fall," *U.S. News & World Report* (May 13, 2002)

The Tracks of Foreknowledge

22     $30 billion: Editors, "The Road to Sept. 11," *Newsweek* (Oct. 1, 2001).

22   Kenneth Katzman: www.washingtonpost.com/wo-dyn/articles/A14120-2001Sep11.html

23   Snider resigns from joint committee: Tabassum Zakaria, "Head of Congressional Probe Into Sept. 11 Quits," *Reuters* (April 29, 2002)

23   Small teams of investigators: Greg Miller, "Tactics Impede Investigation," *Los Angeles Times* (May 4, 2002)

23   FBI investigates leaks: Christopher Newton, "FBI Asks Lawmakers to Take Lie Detector Test in Sept. 11 Leak Investigation," *Associated Press* (Aug. 2, 2002)

23   Congressmen warned: Jeff Johnson, "Congress Was Warned Two Months Before 9/11 Attacks," *NewsMax.Com* (Sept. 19, 2002)

24   Sen. Richard Shelby: Miklaszewski, op. cit.

24   Sen. Bob Graham: Ibid.

24   McCain co-sponsors inquiry: Lisa Stein, "Private Eye," Top of the Week, *U.S. News & World Report* (Oct. 7, 2002)

24   Rep. Ray Lahood: Miklaszewski, op. cit.

24   Eleanor Hill noted consistent theme: Editors, "US 'failed to heed' terror warnings," *BBC News* (Sept. 18, 2002)

25   Terrorist trained to crash airliners: Yossef Bodansky, *Target America: Terrorism in the US Today* (New York: Shapolsky Publishers, 1993)

25   Italian wiretaps: Sebastian Rotella and Josh Meyer, "Wiretaps May Have Foretold Terror Attacks," *Los Angeles Times* (May 29, 2002)

25   Spanish wiretaps: Ibid.

25   Cayman Islands warning: Chris Hansen, "Warning Signs," *MSNBC* (Sept. 23, 2001)

26   Taliban warning: Kate Clark, "Revealed: The Taliban minister, the US envoy and the warning of September 11 that was ignored," *The Independent* (September 7, 2002). http://news.independent.co.uk./world/politics/story.jsp?story=331115

26	Manila warning: Editors, "Flashback: Airliner terror plan was code-named `Project Bojinka'," *World Tribune.com* (Sept. 25, 2001)
26	Air France Flight 8969: Matthew L. Wald, "Earlier Hijackings Offered Signals That Were Missed," *New York Times* (Oct. 3, 2001)
26	Philippine warnings: Dorian Zumel Sicat, "Abu's long-standing ties to global terrorism bared," *The Manila Times* (Feb. 15, 2002)
27	Terry Nichols and terrorists: Dorian Zumel-Sicat, "RP cops aware of long-term rightwing, Muslim connection," *The Manila Times* (April 26, 2002); www.manilatimes.net/national/2002/apr/26/top_stories/20020426top6.html
27	Chinese manual: www.newsmaxstore.com/nms/showdetl.cfm?&DID=6&Product_ID=886&CATID=9&GroupID=1 2...
27	China enters WTO: http://www.cnn.com/2001/WORLD/asiapcf/central/11/10/china.WTO/
28	Dr. Koryagina: www.newsmax.com/archives/articles/201/10/3/212706.shtml
28	Egyptian warning: Patrick E. Tyler and Neil MacFarquhar, "Egypt Warned U.S. of a Qaeda Plot, Mubarak Asserts," *The New York Times* (June 4, 2002).
29	Atwan warning: Editors, "Expert: Bin Laden Warned of 'Unprecedented' US Attack," *Reuters New Service*, Sept. 11, 2001.
29	Arab MBC channel: Editors, "US Airlines May Be a Terror Risk Over Next Three Days," *Airjet Airline World News* (June 23, 2001).
30	Letter to NY Times: http://judiciary.senate.gov/oldsite/childers.htm

The FBI Couldn't or Wouldn't Connect the Clues

30	Carnivore and FBI memos: Editors, "FBI `Carnivore' glitch hurt al Qaeda probe," *Reuters* (May 29, 2002). www.cnn.com/2002/US/05/28/attack.carnivore.reut
31	Promis software: Carl Cameron, Fox News (Oct. 16, 2001)
31	"most committed tracker": Lawrence Wright, "The Counter Terrorist," *The New Yorker*, January 14, 2002.
31	"dealt with dolts": Ibid.
31	Jamal Ahmed al-Fadl: Ibid.
31	"it *is* the eastern Establishment": Alvin Moscow, *The Rockefeller Inheritance* (Garden City, New York: Doubleday & Company, Inc., 1977), p. 225.
32	Groups ability to strike: Wright, op. cit.
32	No government support: Wright, op. cit.
32	Valarie James: Wright, op. cit.
32	Something big to happen: Wright, op. cit.
33	FBI not protecting: Wes Vernon, "Agent: FBI Could Have Prevented 9-11," *NewsMax.com* May 31, 2002.
33	Phoenix suspicions: Editors, "FBI Agent Warned of Suspicious Flight Students Last Summer," *Fox News* May 3, 2002.
33	Agent Williams' memo: Richard Behar, "FBI's `Phoenix' Memo Unmasked," *Fortune.com* (May 22, 2002)
33	FBI agents indicted: Alex Berenson, "Five, Including F.B.I. Agents, Are Named in a Conspiracy," *New York Times* (May 23, 2002)
33	Asst. US Atty. Kenneth Breen: Whitley Strieber, "Is the FBI Penetrated?" *Unknown Country.com* (May 25, 2002); www.unknowncountry.com/journal/print.phtml?id=95
34	Mission jeopardized: Vernon, op. cit.

36   Gary Aldrich: www.newsmaxstore.com

36   FBI Agent Ivan C. Smith: Paul Sperry, "Why FBI missed Islamic threat Agents: Clinton shifted counterterror efforts to fighting 'right-wing' groups," *WorldNetDaily* (July 25, 2002)

37   40 boxes of evidence: Ibid.

37   Commerce Dept. report sanitized: Ibid.

37   FBI Director Robert Mueller: Eric Lichtblau and Josh Meyer, "Terrorist Signs Were Missed, FBI Chief Says," *The Los Angeles Times* (May 30, 2002)

37   Randy Glass: John Mintz, "U.S. Reopens Arms Case In Probe of Taliban Role," *The Washington Post* (Aug. 2, 2002); Wanda J. DeMaarzo, "Feds reopen probe of Florida arms deal," *The Miami Herald* (Aug. 2, 2002)

37   David Schippers: http://www.infowars.com/transcript_schippers.html

37   A general disbelief: Wright, op. cit.

37   FBI and Clinton White House: James Risen, "C.I.A.'s Inquiry on al-Qaeda Aide Seen as Flawed," *The New York Times* (Sept. 22, 2002).

37   Atta's email with Moussaoui: Spotlight, "The strange case of Mr. M." *U.S. News & World Report* (Sept. 232, 2002)

37   FBI docs in Moussaoui's cell: Lisa Stein, op. cit.
Ramzi al-Shibd in custody: Lisa Stein, "Man of the hour," *U.S. News & World Report* (Sept. 23, 2002)

38   Colleen Rowley: http://www.counterpunch.org/sperry0613.html
http://www.apfn.org/apfn/WTC_whistleblower1.htm;

39   Rowley testimony defused: Steve P---- "-----

---   Ashcroft rejects FBI request for $50 million: Julian Borger, "Bush held up plan to hit Bin Laden," *The Guardian* (Aug. 5, 2002)

----

39   NIC report: John Solomon, "1999 Report Warned of Suicide Hijack," The Associated Press, May 17, 2002.

39   Echelon like vacuum cleaner: Ned Stafford: "Newspaper: Echelon Gave Authorities Warning of Attacks," *Newsbytes.com* (Sept. 13, 2001)

39   French probe Echelon: Warren P. Strobel, "A fine whine from France," *U.S. News & World Report* (July 17, 2000)

40   Osama as Tim Osman: Mike Blair, "Public Enemy No. 1 Was Guest of Central Intelligence Agency," *American Free Press* (Jan. 7 & 14, 2002)

40   "Olberg" in Durenberger's office: Ibid.

40   Unnamed agent's warning: Brian Blomquist, "FBI Man's Chilling 9-11 'Prediction,'" *New York Post*, May 9, 2002.

40   Ben Fenton and John Steele, "Bin Laden Told Mother to Expect 'Big News', *Daily Telegraph* (Oct. 2, 2001)

40   Rumsfeld grounds Predator: Michael Hirsh and Michael Isikoff, "What Went Wrong," *Newsweek* (May 27, 2002)

40   "it's unconscionable": Interview, "Has someone been sitting on the FBI?" *News Night*, BBC Television (June 11, 2002)

41   Kahlid al-Midhar and Nawaq Alhazni: Risen, op. cit.

41   Khalid Shaikh Mohammed: Ibid.

42   Mohammed identified before 9-11: Ibid.

42   FBI tracked Mohammed Atta in Germany: Audrey Gillan, Giles Tremlett, John Hooper, Kate Connolly and Jon Henley, "Dozens detained as net spreads from US to Europe," *The Guardian* (Sept. 27, 2001); http://www.guardian.co.uk/waronterror/story/0,1361,558871,00.html

43   Osama bin Laden in Dubai: Alexandra Richard, "The CIA met Bin Laden While undergoing treatment at an American Hospital last July in Dubai," *Le Figaro* (Oct. 11, 2001), translation by Tiphaine Dickson; www.globalresearch.ca/articles/RIC111B.html

43   CIA team in Afghanistan: Editors, "Newspaper: Afghans tracked bin Laden," In brief, *USA Today* (Dec. 24, 2001)

43   CIA's James Pavitt: www.cia.gov/cia/public_affairs/speeches/pavitt_04262002.html

44   Delmart "Mike" Vreeland: http://www.fromthewilderness.com/free/ww3/index.html#vree

45   LAPD cocaine bust: Ibid.

45   Attorney Galati: Nick Pron, "Did this man predict 9-11? Strange story of a jailed spy unfolds in Toronto court," *Toronto Star* (Feb. 5, 2002)

46   Internet domain names: Jeff Johnson, "Internet Domain Names May Have Warned of Attacks," *Cybercast News Service* (Sept. 19, 2001); http://www.middleeastwire.com/atlarge/stories/20010919_3_meno.shtml

46   Editor Russ Kick: Russ Kick, "September 11, 2001: No Surprise," *Everything You Know Is Wrong* (New York: The Disinformation Company, 2002).

46   Willie Brown's warning: Phillip Matier and Andrew Ross, "Willie Brown got low-key early warning about air travel," *San Francisco Chronicle* (September 12, 2001).

47   Pentagon officials won't fly: Evan Thomas and Mark Hosenball, "Bush: 'We're At War'," *Newsweek* (Sept. 24, 2001).

47   Ashcroft uses charter jets: Jim Stewart, "Ashcroft Flying High," *CBS News*, July 26, 2001.

47   David Welna report: www.thememoryhole.org/tenet-9-11.htm

47   Rumsfeld lays off blame: http://www.defenselink.mil/news/Nov2001/t11182001_t1012pm.html

48   Senior officials warned: Risen, op. cit.

48   Bush warned at Crawford: Hirsh and Isikoff, op. cit.

Selling Stocks Short Indicates Foreknowledge

48   James Doran, "Millions of shares sold before disaster," *The Times* (Sept. 18, 2001). http://www.thetimes.co.uk/article/0,,2001320007-20011323297,00.html

49      $15 billion worldwide: Christopher Bollyn, "Revealing 9-11 Stock Trades Could Expose The Terrorist Masterminds," *American Free Press* (May 13, 2002).

49   U.S. Treasury notes: Ibid.

50   Dylan Ratigan: Ibid.

50   Alex Popovic: Marcy Gordon, "SEC Investigating Trading in Shares of 38 Companies; Asks Brokerages to Review Records," *The Associated Press* (Oct. 2, 2001).

50   Harvey Pitt: Ibid.

50   Other suspicious trading: Michael C. Ruppert, "Suppressed Details of Criminal Insider Trading lead directly into the CIA's Highest Ranks," *From The Wilderness Publications* (October 9, 2001).

50   Tracks lead to Deutsche Bank: Ibid.

51   A. B. "Buzzy" Krongard: http://www.cia.gov/cia/information/krongard.htm

52   Michael Ruppert: Kellia Ramares and Bonnie Faulkner, "The CIA's Wall Street connections," *Online Journal* (Oct. 12, 2001).

52   Don Radlauer: Bollyn, op. cit.

52	Chicago affidavit: Alex Jones, op. cit.
52	Jerry Bremer: Elizabeth Neuffer, "Officials Aware in 1998 of Training," *Boston Globe* (Sept. 15, 2001)
53	Credibility gap: Hirsh and Isikoff, op. cit.

Israeli Foreknowledge?

53	Germans say U.S. and Israelis warned: Ned Stafford, "Newspaper: Echelon Gave Authorities Warning of Attacks," *The Washington Post,* Newsbytes (Sept. 13, 2001)
53	Odigo message warnings: Editors, "Instant Messages To Israel Warned of WTC Attack," *The Washington Post* (Sept. 28, 2001)
53	CEO Micha Macover: Yuval Dror, "Odigo says workers were warned of attack," *Ha'aretz Daily* (Nov. 3, 2001)
54	ZIM American Shipping Co.: Christopher Bollyn, "Who Knew? Israeli Company Mum About WTC Pullout," *American Free Press* (Dec. 10, 2001)
54	4,000 Israelis reported missing: Editors, "Thousands of Israelis missing near WTC, Pentagon," *Jerusalem Post* (Sept. 12, 2001
54	Israelis film WTC: Editors, "The White Van: Were Israelis Detained on Sept. 11 Spies?" *ABC News* (June 21, 2002); http://abcnews.go.com/sections/2020/DailyNews/2020_whitevan_020621.html
55	Maps in car: Paulo Lima, "Five Men Detained As Suspected Conspirators," *The Bergen* [New Jersey] *Record* (Sept. 12, 2001)
55	Foreign Counterintelligence Investigation: Marc Perelman, "Spy Rumors Fly on Gusts of Truth," *Forward* (March 15, 2002)
55	Stoffer and Berlet: Ibid.
55	DEA report leaked: Ben Fenton, "US arrests 200 young Israelis in spying investigation," *Telegraph* (July 3, 2002); www.telegraph.co.uk/news/main.jhtml?xml=/news/2002/03/07/wspy07.xml&sSheet
55	Guillaume Dasquie: Christopher Bollyn, "120 Spies Deported," *American Free Press* (March 25, 2002)
56	Carl Cameron quotes investigators: Michael Collins Piper, "Israel Knew: Israel Conducts Massive Spying Operation in U.S.," *American Free Press* (Dec. 24, 2001)
56	Served in intel or signal intercepts: Ibid.
56	National Counterintelligence Center warning: Ibid.
57	*Le Monde* on cell phones from vice consul: John F. Sugg, "Israeli Spies Exposed," [Tampa] *Weekly Planet* (April 2, 2002)
57	Military bases and petroleum facilities: Justin Raimondo, "The 'Urban Myth' Gambit," *Antiwar.com* (March 13, 2002)
57	German paper *Die Zeit*: Rob Broomby, "Report details US 'intelligence failures'," *BBC News* (Oct. 2, 2002)
57	Insulated from foreign influence: Charles R. Smith, "FBI Investigates Foreign Spy Ring - U.S. Companies Deny Involvement," *NewsMax.com* (Jan. 16, 2002); www.newsmax.com/archives/articles/2002/1/16/110443.shtml
57	Reversed wiretaps: Charles R. Smith, "U.S. Police and Intelligence Hit by Spy Network," *NewsMax.com* (Dec. 19, 2001); www.newsmax.com/archives/articles/2001/12/18/224826.shtml
58	Pipes and conspiracy theories: Daniel Pipes, "An Israeli spy network in the United States?" *Jewish World Review* (March 11, 2002)
58	Hands off Israel: Raimondo, op. cit.; Smith (Jan. 16, 2002)
58	Lisa Dean and Brad Jansen: Smith (Sec. 19, 2001)

58	Israeli policy foisted on Bush: Lyndon LaRouche, "The Pollard Affair Never Ended!" www.larouchein2003.com
59	IASPS "Clean Break" paper: www.israeleconomy.org/strat1.htm
60	Rothschilds and Israel: Jim Marrs, *Rule by Secrecy*(New York: HarperCollins Publishers, 2000)
60	Mossad prime suspect: Dick Eastman, "Here is how the WTC/Pentagon crash bombing operation came...," http://disc.server.com/discussion.cgi?9d=149495&article=10401
61	Jack Anderson: Michael Collins Piper, "Were the 9-11 Hijackers Really Arabs? Maybe not," *American Free Press* (Dec. 24, 2001)
62	Gen. Hameed Gul: Michael Collins Piper, "Former Pakistani Intelligence Chief Alleges Rogue Spook Agencies Behind Terror Attacks," *American Free Press* (Dec. 5, 2001)
62	Werthebach and von Bulow: Christopher Bollyn, "European Spooks Say Mideast Terrorists Needed State Support," *American Free Press* (Dec. 24, 2001)
63	Mossad has capability: "US troops would enforce peace under Army study," *The Washington Times* (Sept. 10, 2001).

Remote Controlled Aircraft A Reality

63	Global Hawk in Afghanistan: Editors, "Operational debut for Global Hawk," *Jane's Aerospace* (Oct. 8, 2001); www.janes.com/serospace/military/news/misc/globalhawk_ppv.shtml
63	Global Hawk made history: www.dsto.defence.gov.au/globalhawk/releases/parlsec18801.html
63	First flight: News Release, "Global Hawk Completes First Flight," United States Department of Defense (March 2, 1998); www.defenselink.mil/news/Mar1998/b03021998_bt091-98.html
64	Andreas Von Buelow: Joe Vialls, "'Home Run' Electronically Hijacking the World Trade Center Attack Aircraft," http://geocities.com/mknemesis/printer.html
64	Joe Vialls: Ibid.
66	Flight 77 and skilled pilot: "On Flight 77: 'Our Plane Is Being Hijacked'," *The Washington Post* (Sept. 12, 2001), p. 1.
66	Hani Hanjour: Justin Paprocki, "Airport Owners Panic Over Plummeting Profits," *MarylandNewsline* and *Capital News Service* (Sept. 19, 2001).
66	Bush in *Times*: Editors, "Bush to Increase Federal Role in Security at Airports," *The New York Times* (Sept. 28, 2001).
66	NFERS white paper: www.kinetx.com
66	Hijackers flying skills: "Hijackers Suspects Tried Many Flight Schools," *The Washington Post* (Sept. 19, 2001).
67	Al-Hazmi and al-Mahar: "San Diegans See Area as Likely Target," *The Washington Post* (Sept. 24, 2001).
67	Transponder explanation: Vialls, op. cit.
68	Objective is loss of national sovereignty: Col. Donn de Grand Pre, "The Enemy Is Inside The Gates," *American Free Press* (Feb. 11, 2002)
69	Glen Cramer: John Carlin, "Unanswered Questions - The Mystery of Flight 93," *The Independent* (Aug. 13, 2002)
69	Seismic boom recorded: Robb Magley, "Seismic Event: The Final Moments of Flight 93," http://members.fortunecity.com/seismicevent/ author's email correspondence, Feb. 15, 2003.
69	Cheney acknowledges shoot-down order: Editors, "Cheney Says Military Was Ordered To Shoot Down Planes," *Online NewsHour*, Public Broadcasting Service (Sept. 16, 2001)
70	Paul Wolfowitz: Ibid.
70	Bill Wright: Carlin, op. cit.
70	Wally Miller: Ibid.

73   Biblical prophets: Trent C. Butler, gen. ed., *Holman Bible Dictionary* (Nashville, TN: Holman Bible Publishers, 1991) p. 1142.

73   Deborah: The Holy Bible, Judges 4: 4-16.

73   St. Paul: The Holy Bible, 1 Thessalonians 5:20-21 (Living Bible edition).

73   Severely monitored scientific experiment: Ronald M. McRae, *Mind Wars: The True Story of Government Research into the Military Potential of Psychic Weapons*, (New York: St. Martin's Press, 1984)

PART II – WAR FOR OIL AND DRUGS

77   Weekly report: James P. Tucker Jr., "White House Whitewash: No Justice for Pearl Brass," *American Free Press*, July 8, 2002.

77   Tuckers statement: Ibid.

78   Loans to Russia: G. Edward Griffin, *The Creature from Jekyll Island* (Westlake Village, CA: American Media, 1994)

78   Real reason for Gulf War never known: Jonathan Vankin and John Whalen, *Fifty Greatest Conspiracies of All Time* (New York: Citadel Press, 1995)

The Central Asian Gas Pipeline

79   CENTGAS: Editors, *BBC NEWS*, (May 13, 2002); http://news.bbc.co.uk/1/hi/business/1984459.stm

79   Pipeline timeline: http://www.worldpress.org/specials/pp/pipeline_timeline.htm

79   Khalilzad played important part: Mike Fox, "Bush Appoints Afghan Envoy", *BBC News*, (Jan. 1, 2002)

80   Khalilzad supports Taliban: Joe Stephens and David B. Ottaway, "Afghan Roots Keep Adviser Firmly in the Inner Circle," *Washington Post* (Nov. 23, 2001)

80   French authors quote O'Neill: http://www.rense.com/general17/deal.htm.

80   Former Saudi oil minister: Editors, "Yamani: importance of Gulf oil collapses in the interests of the Caspian Sea," *Arabic News.com* (Feb. 1, 2002) www.arabicnews.com/ansub/Daily/Day/020201/2002020118.html

81   Hydrogen can replace petroleum: Harry Braun, "A Legislative Plan for Sustainable Economic Prosperity Without Pollution," *Hydrogen Political Action Committee Newletter* (Nov. 12, 2002)

Afghan Action Planned Long Ago

81   US aligns with Russians: S. Frederick Starr, "Afghanistan Land Mine," *Washington Post* (Dec. 19, 2000)

81   Anti-Taliban military plan: Correspondent, "India in anti-Taliban military plan," News Insight.net (June 26, 2001).

82   Pakistani Naik warned: http://news.bbc.co.uk/1/hi/business/1984459.stm (May 13, 2002).

83   Brzezinski's admission: Bill Blum, translator; Zbigniew Brzezinski interview, *Le Nouvel Observateur* (France), January 15-21, 1998, p. 76.

83   Break up of the Soviet empire: Ibid.

83   What is most important?: Ibid.

83   External threat needed for consensus: Zbigniew Brzezinski, *The Grand Chessboard: American Primacy and its Geostatic Imperatives* (New York: Basic Books, 1997); http://www.foreignaffairs.org/19971101fabook3692/zbigniew-brzezinski/the-grand-chessboard-american-primacy-and-its-geostrategic-imperatives.html.

84   Niaz Naik: Jonathan Steele, Ewen MacAskill, Richard Norton-Taylor and Ed Harriman, "Threats of US strikes passed to Taliban weeks before NY attack," *The Guardian*, September 22, 2001.

86   Pre-emptive strike: Ibid.

86   Regime change in Iraq: http://www.sundayherald.com/27735

86   Pre-attack plans against Iraq: http://www.newamericancentury.org/RebuildingAmericasDefenses.pdf

87   Bombing a PR fiasco: http://www.zmag.org/flandersarabcnn.htm

87   Bombs destroy music cache: Laure Flanders, "'Arab CNN' First Berated, then Bombed by U.S.," *WorkingForChange.com* (Nov. 14, 2001); www.alternet.org/print.html?StoryID=11921

87   Blueprint for US global hegemony: Jay Tolson, "World Disorder?" *U.S. News & World Report* (Oct. 21, 2002)

87   Col. Brian Hoey: Ibid.

87   Gore Vidal's statement on Bush's plea for no investigation: Marc Cooper, "The Last Defender of the American Republic?" *LA Weekly* (July 5-11, 2002)

Wag the Dog in Iraq?

88   North Korean nuke news withheld: Paul Bedard, "Going Nuclear," Washington Whispers, *U.S. News & World Report* (Oct. 28, 2002)

88   Bush give okay for nukes: Editors, "US grants N Korea nuclear funds," *BBC News* (April 3, 2002)

88   Letter to Bush: Editors, "Top Officials Reject Iraq War," *American Free Press* (Feb, 11, 2002)

89   Sen. Robert Byrd: Paul J. Nyden, "Bush's War Plans are a Cover-Up, Byrd Says," *West Virginia Gazette* (Sept. 21, 2002)

89   Rumsfeld notes: Editors, "Rumsfeld Wanted to Hit Iraq Hours After 9-11!" *Newsmax* (Sept. 8, 2002); www.newsmax.com/archive/

89   Bush on IAEA report: Joseph Curl, "Agency disavows report on Iraq arms," *Washington Times* (Oct. 1, 2002)

89   IAEA denies reports: Ibid.

90   1998 report: Ibid.

90   Ron Kuby: Fox TV News, Oct. 30, 2001.

90   Powell's UN report: Williams Rivers Pitt, "Blair-Powell UN Report Written by Student," *Truthout* (Feb. 7, 2003); http://truthout.org/docs_02/020803A.htm

91   Two Democrats argue against war: Editors, "Democrat Congressman Accuses Bush of Lying to Provoke War!" *Newsmax.com* and UPI (Sept. 30, 2002)

91   Lott remark: http://www.cnn.com/2002/ALLPOLITICS/09/29/iraq.debate/

91   Clinton's remarks: Editors, "Clinton: Get Bin Laden Before Pursuing Saddam," *The Associated Press* (Sept. 5, 2002)

92   Constitution no longer relevant: http://www.rense.com/general32/longer.htm

92   McKinney's remarks: Rep. Cynthia McKinny, "We Come For Peace," *Truthout* (April 20, 2002); www.truthout.org/docs_02/04.24A.McKinney.Peace.htm

92   Grassy knoll in Roswell: Editors, "McKinney implied Bush knew of Sept. 11 plot," *Atlanta Journal-Constitution* (April 12, 2002)

92   Irate columnist: Kathleen Parker, "McKinney's minions march to a different drummer indeed," *Orlando Sentinel* (April 21, 2002)

92   Bush and the Saudi prince: Patricia Wilson, "Bush Celebrates Saudi Ties Before Meeting Envoy," *Reuters* (August 27, 2002)

92   Rand analyst: Ibid.

93	David Hernandez: Kristen Wyatt, "G. Rep. McKinney Draws Support," *The Associated Press* (May 11, 2002)

93   David Hernandez: Kristen Wyatt, "G. Rep. McKinney Draws Support," *The Associated Press* (May 11, 2002)

93   Favored to win: Ibid.

93   McKinney's defeat: Stephen Zunes, "Don't Blame the Jews for Cynthia McKinney's Defeat," *CommonDreams.org* (Aug. 25, 2001)

94   Bush tore up international treaties: George Monbiot, "The logic of empire," *The Guardian* (Aug. 6, 2002)

95   Newspaper poll showed 47 percent believed officials knew of attacks: Michael Davidson, "Kill the Messenger," *From The Wilderness* (May 6, 2002)

96    $3.8 billion welfare hog: Knut Royce and Nathanial Heller, "Cheney Led Halliburton To Feast at Federal Trough," Investigative Report, *The Center for Public Integrity* (August 2, 2000)

97   Cheney making policy: Kenneth T. Walsh, "Cheney: Out of the bunker," *U.S. News & World Report* (March 25, 2002)

97   Kellogg Brown & Root: Jeff Gerth and Don Van Natta Jr., "In Tough Times, a Company Finds Profits in Terror War," *New York Times* (July 13, 2002)

97   Halliburton misdeeds: Editors, "Cheney accused of corporate fraud," *BBC News* (July 10, 2002); http://news.bbc.co.uk/1/hi/world/americas/2119981.stm

98   Judicial Watch suit against Cheney, Halliburton: Editors, "Cheney, Halliburton face suit," *CNNMoney* (July 10, 2002); http://money.cnn.com/2002/07/10/news/cheney_lawsuit/

98   GAO pressured: Peter brand and Alexander Bolton, "GOP threats halted GAO Cheney suit," *The Hill* (Feb. 19, 2003)

97   SEC probes Halliburton: Editors, "Suit accuses Cheney, firm of fraudulent accounting," *CNN.com* (July 11, 2002); http://www.cnn.com/2002/LAW/07/10/cheney.suit/

98   Cayman Island subsidiaries: Arianna Huffington, "Huffington: Holding Dick Cheney 'Accountable'," *AlterNet* (Aug. 5, 2002); www.alternet.org/story.html?StoryID=13757

98   Firm sidesteps US orders: Carola Hoyos, "A discreet way of doing business with Iraq," *Financial Times* (Nov. 3, 2000); www.truthout.org/docs_01/02.23D.Cheney.Circumvented.htm

98   Raad Alkadiri: Ibid.

100   Hoyos quote: Ibid.

100   Iraqi column showed foreknowledge: Larry Neumeister, "Lawsuit: Iraq Knew of 9/11 Attacks," *Associated Press* (Sept. 4, 2002)

100   Iraqis brought to US: Craig Roberts, *The Medusa File,* (Tulsa, OK: Consolidated Press International, 1997)

101   Four reasons for foreknowledge: Rep. Charles Key, "Rep. Charles Key on the Facts of the Oklahoma Bombing," mailed letter, March 12, 1997.

102   Carol Howe, Dennis Mahon and Andreas Strassmier: Editors, "Informant's Story Due Movie Treatment," *Associated Press* (Feb. 13, 2000).

102   Reporter had evidence rejected: Editors, "Oklahoma City blast linked to bin Laden," *WorldNetDaily.com* (March 21, 2001)

103   Motel witnesses: Jim Crogan, "The Terrorist Motel: The I-40 connection between Zacaria Moussaoui and Mohamed Atta," *LA Weekly* (July 29, 2002)

104   McVeigh had Iraqi phone numbers: Paul Bedard, Washington Whispers, *U. S. News & World Report* (Oct. 29, 2001)

104   Artifacts in Iraq: Editors, "Artifacts Uncovered in Iraq," *ABC News.com* (Dec. 28, 1999)

104   Loss of antiquities: McGuire Gibson, : "The loss of archeological context and the illegal trade in Mesopotamian antiquities," *Culture without Context* (Issue 1, Autumn, 1997)

105	Pentagon alerted to museum importance: Andrew Curry, "History's loss," *U.S. News & World Report* (April 28, 2003)
105	Looters had keys to vaults: Jocelyn Gecker, "Experts: Looters Had Keys to Iraq Museum," *Associated Press* (April 17, 2003)
105	Robert Fisk: Christopher Bollyn, "Iraqis Robbed," *American Free Press* (April 21, 2003)
106	Martin E. Sullivan: Gecker, op. cit.
106	Protest marches: Editors, "US Peace Marches Draw Large Crowds," *BBC News* (Oct. 27, 2002)

Destroyed Crops Impact World Drug Trade

108	Afghan drug trade: www.bbc.co.uk/radio4/today/reports/ international/afghanistan_drugs.shtml
108	Citibank and M.A. Bank: Tim Reason, "Shell Banks: Filthy Lucre," *CFO Magazine*(May 7, 2001). http://www.cfo.com/printarticle/0,5317,3034IA,00.html
108	Sen. Carl Levin: http://levin.senate.gov/releases/020501pr1.htm
108	CIA in Afghanistan: Alfred McCoy, "Drug fallout: the CIA's Forty Year Complicity in the Narcotics Trade," *The Progressive*(August 1, 1997)
109	Taliban ban effective: Richard Wolffe, "US prepares for long battle against heroin trade", *Financial Times,* February 5, 2002.
109	Opium production rises in 2002: Pam O'Toole, "Afghanistan opium production leaps," *BBC News* (Oct. 25, 2002) http://specials.ft.com/afghanfuture/FT394ET19WC.html
109	Story of opium and Empire: Webster Griffin Tarpley and Anton Chaitkin, *George Bush: The Unauthorized Biography* (Washington, D.C.: Executive Intelligence Review, 1992), p, 119. Families named: Ibid.
109	Tom Carew: www.sabawoon.com/articles.asp?id=132&view=detail
110	DEA "sting": Daniel Hopsicker, *Barry & 'the boys': The CIA, The Mob and America's Secret History,* (Noti, OR: Mad Cow Press, 2001), p. 311-312.
111	George Bush's kids: Terry Reed and John Cummings, *Compromised: Clinton, Bush and the CIA* (New York: S.P.I. Books, 1994), pp. 212-213.
112	George Bush and airplane: Hopsicker, p. 312.
112	Tyumen Oil and Langdon: Royce and Heller, op. cit.

WHO AND WHERE IS OSAMA BIN LADEN?

116	Osama bin Laden background: Anonymous source, translated document provided to *Frontline* Public Broadcasting System; www.angelfire.com/home/pearly/hjtmis1/osama-bio.html
116	President Clinton's address: Transcript of President Clinton's Oval Office remarks on anti-terrorist attacks, United States Information Agency, (Aug. 20, 1998)

OSAMA BIN LADEN REPLIES

117	*Ummat* interview with bin Laden: http://www.americanfreepress.net/10_22_01/Al-Qaeda_Not_Involved__Says_bi/al-qaeda_not_involved__says_bi.html.
117	Mother claims tape doctored: Editors, "Bin Laden's mother says video 'doctored'," In Brief, *USA Today* (Dec. 24, 2001)
118	German experts rip videotape: Christopher Bollyn, "Bin Laden Tape Dupes Public, Say Experts," *American Free Press* (Jan. 4-14, 2001)

THE BIN LADENS AND FRIENDS

118	Republicans suppress Saudi information: http://pub12.ezboard.com/fnuclearweaponsnuclearweaponsforum.showMessage?topicID=282.topic

119   Saudi oil production tripled: Michael Field, "Good for business," *Financial Times* (Feb. 21, 1991)

119   CFR report on Saudis: George Gedda, "Report: Saudi Charities Back al-Qaida," *Associated Press* (Oct. 17, 2002); http://story.news.yahoo.com/news?tmpl=story2&cid=513&u=/ap/20021017/ap_on_go_ot/us_saudi_terror_.

119     $1 trillion suit against Saudis and quotes: Philip Shenon, "U.S. May Ask Court to Dismiss a $1 Trillion Suit Linking Saudis to Al Qaeda," *The New York Times* (Oct. 25, 2002)

120   Wahabbis as functionally illiterate: http://www.john-loftus.com/press_release.asp

121   FBI Agent Steven Butler and the Saudis: Gloria Borger, Edward T. Pound and Linda Robinson, "The Road to Riyadh," *U.S. News & World Report* (Dec. 9, 2002)

121   Saudi bank connected to JPMorgan and Bank of America: Martin Mbugua, "Saudi Bank Tied To Terror Has U.S. Banks," *The Daily News* (Nov. 10, 2001)

122   Salem bin Laden in Texas: Mike Ward, "Bin Laden relatives have ties to Texas," *Austin American-Statesman* (Nov. 9, 2001)

122   Close ties between bin Ladens and Bushes: Ibid.

122   James Bath: Ibid; Jonathan Beaty and S. C. Gwynne, *The Outlaw Bank: A Wild Ride into the Secret Heart of the BCCI* (New York: Random House, 1993); *American Free Press* (October 15, 2001)

122   Bath's connection to Saudi bank: Pete Brewton, "The Mafia, CIA and George Bush," (New York: S.P.I.Books/Shapolsky Publishers, Inc. 1992)

123   Mahfouz and BCCI: J. H. Hatfield, *Fortunate Son: George W. Bush and the Making of an American President* (New York: St. Martin's Press, 1999)

124   Bill White: Beaty and Gwynne, op. cit.

124   Main Bank: Ibid.

124   John Mecklin's estimates: http://newsandviews9.tripod.com/news/timeline.html

125   1990 Bahrain agreement for bases: Russell S. Bowen, *The Immaculate Deception* (Carson City, NV: America West Publishers, 1991)

125   Harken low-interest loans to Bush: Editors, "Bush Received Company Loans He Now Wants Banned," *Reuters* (July 11, 2002)

125   Harken stock sale: Bowen, op. cit.
155   Cloaked in third parties: Ward, op. cit.

126   *WorldNetDaily* commentator: http://alexconstantine.50megs.com/the_cia_osama.html

126   George H. W. Bush and Carlyle Group: Michael Ruppert, "Must Read: The Best Enemies Money Can Buy," *Guerilla News Network* (Oct. 11, 2001) http://www.guerrillanews.com/newswire/164.html

127   Larry Klayman of Judicial Watch: http://www.judicialwatch.org/archive/2001/863.shtml

127   Attacks make big money: Ruppert, (Oct. 11, 2001), op. cit.

127   Sgt. Ali A. Mohamed: John Sullivan and Joseph Neff, "An Al Qaeda operative at Fort Bragg," *Raleigh News & Observer* (Nov. 13, 2001)

127   Pakistan, India and Philippines: Interviews, "Has someone been sitting on the FBI?" *News Night*, BBC News (June 11, 2002)

128   Constraints on investigating Saudis: Gregory Palast, "FBI and US Spy Agents Say Bush Spiked Bin Laden Probes Before 11 September," *The Guardian* (Nov. 7, 2001)

128   Grover Norquist: Duncan Campbell, "FBI Raids pro-Republicans," *The Guardian* (March 25, 2002)

| 128 | Al-Rajhi banking family: John Mintz and Tom Jackman, "Finances Prompted Raids on Muslims; U.S. Suspected Terrorism Ties to N. Va. For Years," *The Washington Post* (March 24, 2002) |

129   John Loftus: Ibid.

129   Jamal Barzinji: Chuck Baldwin, "War on Terrorism Abroad – Support for Islam at Home," *Chuck Baldwin Live* (June 14, 2002); www.chuckbladwinlive.com/bush14jun02.html

129   Abdullah Noman: Associated Press, "Official Took Bribes for U.S. Visas," *The New York Times* (May 21, 2002)

130   Michael Springman: http://news.bbc.co.uk/1/hi/events/newsnight/1645527.stm

PART III – REACTIONS

131   Cheney heads task force and Powell's comments: Frank Bruni, "Bush Taps Cheney to Study Antiterrorism Steps," *The New York Times* (May 8, 2001)

131   NRO 9-11 exercise: Editors, "Agency was to simulate plane crash on September 11," *Associated Press* (Aug. 22, 2002)

132   Govt. set 9-11 date: Barbara Honegger, "Feature: The U.S. Government, Not the Hijackers, 'Chose' the Date of the 9-11 Attacks;" www.911pi.com/honegger.htm

133   Federal Judge John Bates: Pete Yost, "Bush appointee dismisses GAO suit against Cheney's energy task force," *Associated Press* (December 9, 2002)

134   Unnamed intelligence source: Jon Rappoport, "Briefing on Al Quaeda,"*StratiaWire* (Sept. 5, 2002)

Creating Homeland Security

135   Model State Emergency Health Powers Act: Mimi Hall, "Many states reject bioterrorism law," *USA Today* (July 23, 2002)

135   FEMA plans tent cities: John O. Edwards, "FEMA Preparing for Mass Destruction Attacks on Cities," *NewsMax* (July 15, 2002)

136   History of repression in emergencies: Pamela Sebastian Ridge and Milo Geyelin, "Civil Liberties of Ordinary Americans May Erode --- Legally --- Because of Attacks," *The New York Times* (Sept. 17, 2001)

136   Frank Serpico booed: Editors, "Serpico decries anti-terrorism measures," *Associated Press* (July 6, 2002)

136   Janet Reno's remarks: Jim Burns, "William Bennett Hopes to Shape Public Opinion of War on Terrorism," *Cybercast News Service* (March 12, 2002); www.snsnews.com/ViewPolitics.asp?Page=\Politics\archive\200203\POL20020312

137   Sen. Patrick Leahy: Matthew Purdy, "Bush's New Rules to Fight Terror Transform the Legal Landscape," *The New York Times* (Nov. 25, 2001)

137   Osama's mail: Paul Bedard, "Neither Sleet nor G-men stopped bin Laden's mail," Washington Whispers, *U.S. News & World Report* (Oct. 7, 2002)

138   Military as panacea for domestic problems: Matthew Carlton Hammond, "The Posse Comitatus Act: A Principle in Need of Renewal," *Washington University Law Quarterly*(summer, 1997)

139   WWII vet Fred Hubbell arrested: Paul Marks, "Texan Learns to Rue Remark," *The Hartford Courant* (Aug. 3, 2002)

139   GI Joe disarmed: Editors, "Soldier toy disarmed at airport," *BBC News* (August 5, 2002)

139   Attack on Kingsville: David M. Bresnahan, "What happened in Kingsville, Texas, Monday night?" *World Net Daily* (Feb. 10, 1999)

141   Britt Snider and Garden Plot: Ron Ridenhour with Arthur Lubow, "Bringing the War Home," *New Times* (Nov. 28, 1975)

141   Cable Splicer: Ibid.

142   New under secretary of defense for intelligence: Linda Robinson, "Moves that matter," *U.S. News & World Report* (Aug. 12, 2002)

142   Office of Strategic Information closed: Editors, "US closes `disinformation' unit," *BBC News* (Feb. 26, 2002)

142   Millennium Challenge 2002: Pauline Jelinek, "Pentagon holds largest-ever exercise to prepare for future warfighting," *Associated Press* (July 29, 2002)

142   Lt. Gen. Paul Van Riper: Richard Sisk, "All's not fair in love – and war game," *New York Daily News* (August 20, 2002)

143   Army plan to spy on Americans: Christopher H. Pyle, "Be afraid, be very afraid, of spying by the U.S. Army," *The Hartford Courant* (Dec. 5, 2002)

145   Detention camps: Author's interview with retired Lt. Col. Craig Roberts, Nov. 4, 2002.

146   Sen. John Warner: http://www.freedomcommittee.com/freedom/fpc-news-archive/2001-Oct/msg00012.html.

146   Petition to put military on borders: James P. Tucker Jr., "Defend US Borders With US Army Troops," *American Free Press* (Oct. 21, 2002)

146   Bush's urgent need: news.bbc.co.uk/2/hi/americas/2031255.stm.

146   Real losers are American people: Editors, "Sen. Lashes Out Over Ridge No-Show," *Associated Press* (April 30, 2002)

149   Statements in support of Homeland Security: Tom Ridge, written statement to the House Select Committee on Homeland Security (July 15, 2002)

151   Oliver North's martial law plan: Alfonso Chardy, "Plan called for martial law in U.S." *Knight-Ridder News Service* (July 5, 1987)

151   John Dean's concern: Ritt Goldstein, "Foundations Are In Place For Martial Law In The US," *The Sydney Morning Herald* (July 27, 2002)

152   ACLU objections to Homeland Security: Timothy H. Edgar, Testimony before the House Select Committee on Homeland Security and others (June 25-28, 2002)

153   Sen. Joseph Lieberman: http://www.cnn.com/2002/ALLPOLITICS/11/25/homeland.security/

154   Bush quote on Homeland Security: Editors, "Bush signs Homeland Security bill, *CNN News* (Nov. 25, 2002); www.cnn.com/2002/ALLPOLITICS/11/25/homelandsecurity.

154   Vietnam veteran writes: Jeffrey St. Clair and Alexander Cockburn, "Tom Ridge in Vietnam: Tarnished Star," *Counterpunch* (Oct. 1, 2001)

155   Lawlor as Phoenix operative: Douglas Valentine, "Flight Of The Phoenix - From Vietnam To Homeland Security," *Counterpunch* (Aug. 25, 2002); www.rense.com/general28/dsdu.htm

156   Richard Armitage: Ibid.

157   Armitage major participant in narcotics: James "Bo" Gritz, *A Nation Betrayed* (Sandy Valley, NV: Bo Gritz, 1988)

157   A historic juncture in labor movement: Lee Sustar, "Taft-Hartley, Bush and the Dockworkers," *Counterpunch* (Oct. 11, 2002)

158   Post office incident: Matthew Rothschild, "The New McCarthysim," *The Progressive* (January, 2002)

159   Operation TIPS: Citizen Corps website; www.citizencorps.gov/tips.html

159   Cuba's Committees for the Defense of the Revolution: Isabel Garcia-Zarza, "Big Brother at 40: Cuba's revolutionary neighborhood watch system," *Reuters* (Oct. 120, 2000)

159   ACLU opposition to TIPS: Randolph E. Schmidt, "Postal Service Won't Join TIPS Program," *Associated Press* (July 17, 2002)

160   John Whitehead: Ellen Sorokin, "Bush Wants Letter Carriers, Meter Readers As Informants," *The Washington Times* (July 16, 2002)

160   TIPS website changes: Editors, "Website for Operation TIPS Quietly Changes," The Memory Hole; www.thememoryhole.org/policestate/tips-changes.htm

161   Neighborhood Watch: Darragh Johnson and David A. Fahrenthold, "Watching the Homeland," *Washington Post* (March 8, 2002)

161   A.J. Brown and the Secret Service: Rothschild, op. cit.

162   Katie Sierra, Robert Jensen, Dan Guthrie and Tom Gutting: Ibid.

162   Military recruiters denied, Rep. Vitter and Jill Wynns: David Goodman, "No Child Unrecruited," *Mother Jones* (November-December, 2002)

163   Richard Allen Humphreys: Robert Wilson, "Man Convicted of Threatening President Bush in Sioux Falls," *KSFY, Dakota First News* (Oct. 22, 2002)

163   Denver photographer Mike Maginnis: Editors, "Photographer Arrested For Taking Pictures Near Cheney Hotel," *2600 News* (Dec. 5, 2002); www.2600.com/news/display/display.shtml?id=1441

164   Kindergartners disciplined: Editors, "'Gun-toting' tot loses suspension suit," *Associated Press* (May 1, 2002)

164   Ellen Strecker and Nadine Strossen: Ibid.

164   New command structure: Edward Spannaus, "Ashcroft Seeks Hitler-Style Dictatorship Measures," *Executiove Intelligence Review* (Oct. 5, 2001)

164   Snooping is Un-American: Paul Proctor, "The War on Freedom," *News With Views* (July 17, 2002); www.newswithviews.com/war_on_terror/war_on_terrorism1.htm

The PATRIOT Act

164   Judith Krug: Walter Brasch, "The fiction behind national security," *Online Journal* (July 25, 2002)

165   Rep. Dennis Kucinich: Eli Pariser, editor, "Can Democracy Survive An Endless 'War'?" *MoveOn Bulletin* (July 18, 2002); www.moveon.org/moveonbulletin

165   Rep. Ron Paul: Kelly Patricia O'Meara, "Police State," *Insight Magazine* Nov. 9, 2001)

165   Rep. Bernie Sanders: Ibid.

166   PATRIOT Act expands FISA: Brasch, op. cit.

166   Erosion of Constitutional rights: Patrick S. Poole, "Inside America's Secret Court: The Foreign Intelligence Surveillance Court – FISA," *American Patriots Friends Network* (Aug. 2, 2002); http://disc.server.com/discussion.cgi?id=149495&article=31500

166   FISC rejects Ashcroft's guidelines: Ted Bridis, "Special Court Rejects Ashcroft's Rules," *Associated Press* (Aug. 22, 2002)

167   Normal processes suspended for this bill: Editors, "EFF Analysis of The Provisions of the USA Patriot Act," *Electronic Frontier Foundation* (Oct. 31, 2001); www.eff.org/Privacy/Surveillance/Terrorism_militias/20011031_eff_usa_patriot_analysis.html

167   Patriot Act provisions that cause concern: Editors, "Overview of Changes to Legal Rights," *Associated Press* (Sept. 5, 2002); www.newsday.com/news/nationworld/wire/sns-ap-sept-11-legal-rights-glance0905sep05.story

168   Global Relief Foundation faces secret evidence: Geoff Dougherty and Laurie Cohen, "U.S. Using New Law on Secret Evidence: Patriot Act invoked to fight lawsuit by Muslim group," *Chicago Tribune* (March 15, 2002)

168   Global attorney Roger Simmons: Ibid.

168   Hany Kiareldeen: Stephen Franklin and Ken Armstrong, "Secret evidence bill raises concerns," *Chicago Tribune* (Sep. 30, 2001)

169   Niels Frenzen: Ibid.

169   Dr. Al-Badr Al-Hazmi: Editors, "Saudi doctor returns to San Antonio, denounces terrorist attacks as having 'nothing to do with Islam'" *Associated Press* (Sept. 25, 2001); James R. Elwood and Jarret B. Wollstein, "Dictatorship At Your Door," *International Society for Individual Liberty* (May, 2002); www.isil.org/resources/lit/dictatorship-at-doorstep.html

169   Robert Lee Lewis: Author's interviews, summer, 1999.

170   Ron Paul on sneak-and-peek: O'Meara, op. cit.

170   Donald Carlson compensated for raid: Peter Katel, "The Trouble With Informants," *Newsweek* (Jan. 30, 1995)

171   Rep. Butch Otter: O'Meara, op. cit.

171   Rep. Paul on "Know Your Customer": Ron Paul, "Privacy Busters: Big Bank is watching," *Ron Paul Newsletter* (December, 1998)

172   ACLU's Nadine Strossen and O'Meara's comment on British law: Ibid.

173   Law signer should be held for high treason: Doreen Miller, "High Treason in the U.S. Government," *YellowTimes.org* (July 4, 2002); www.yellowtimes.org/article.php?sid=444

173   Patriot Act is treason: Karen G. Schneider, "Patriot Act: Last Refuge of a Scoundrel," *American Libraries* (March, 2002); http://www.ala.org/alonline/netlib/il302.html

174   Act trumps protections in 49 of 50 states: Adam Piore, "USA Patriot Act: Librarians Keep Quiet," *Newsweek* (Oct. 28, 2002)

174   A chilling effect on constitutional freedoms: Brasch, op. cit.

174   James R. Elwood: Elwood and Wollstein, op. cit.

176   The Padilla Game: Carl Worden, "The Padilla Test Run," *Free American* (August, 2002)

173   Arline Johnson: Brasch, op. cit.

174   ABFFE's letter to members: Rothschild, op. cit.

175   Crisis management: Dr. Debra H. Freeman, Testimony delivered to the Senate Judiciary Committee, Jan. 16, 2001; http://larouchein2004.net/pages/other/2001/0101116ashcrofttest.htm

177   Ashcroft's camps: Jonathan Turley, "Camps for Citizens: Ashcroft's Vision," *Los Angeles Times* (August 14, 2002)

178   Defiance repudiates two centuries of constitutional law: Nat Hentoff, "General Ashcroft's Detention Camps Time to Call for His Resignation," *VillageVoice.com* (Sept. 4-10, 2002)

178   Not the American way: Ibid.

178   Forefathers revolted against more mild oppression: O'Meara, op. cit.

Son of PATRIOT Act

178   Mark Corallo: Charles Lewis and Adam Mayle, "Justice Dept. Drafts Sweeping Expansion of Anti-Terrorism Act," New Release from The Center for Public Integrity; www.public-i.org/dtaweb/report.asp?ReportID=502&L1=10&L3=10=L3=o&L4=0...
178   Dr. David Cole: Ibid.

179   ACLU's Edgar: Timothy H. Edgar, "Interested Persons Memo: Section-by-Section Analysis of Justice Department draft 'Domestic Security Enhancement Act of 2003,' also known as 'PATRIOT Act II,'"; www. clu.org/SafeandFree/SafeandFree.cfm?ID=11835&c=206.

224   New law threatens Constitution: Ibid.

182   Troubling as generic matter: Lewis and Mayle, op. Cit.

Big Brother's Technology

182   National ID system: Frank Pellegrini, "The National ID Card That Isn't, Yet," *Time.com* (Jan. 8, 2002)

182   NYPD to issue microchip ID cards: Murray Weiss, "City Adds High-Tech I.D. Cards," *New York Post* (Nov. 1, 2002)

183   Mexican *matriculas*: Diana Washington Vakdez, "Mexican IDs prove versatile, popular," *El Paso Times* (Oct. 17, 2002)

184   The long and short of it: Steven Yates, "'Your Papers, Please': National ID, 2002," *LewRockwell.com* (Oct. 12, 2002); http://www.lewrockwell.com/yates/yates64.html

185   VeriChip: Press releases and website, Applied Digital Solutions, Inc. http://www.adsx.com/prodservpart/verichip.html

185   Rep. Jane Harman and "smart card": Dee Ann Davis and Nicholas M. Horrock, "Ridge eyes new driver's licenses," *The Washington Times* (May 2, 2002); www.newdem.org/press/newsreleases/2002-04-08.304.phtml

186   A second wave of attacks: Press Release, *dojgov.net*; www.dojgov.net/national_license-01.htm

186   Anthony Williams on trade-offs: Brian DeBose, "Increase Government Surveillance," *Washington Times* (March 7, 2002)

186   Nevada Court rules for electronic devices: Brendan Riley, "Nevada High Court Says Police Can Hide Monitoring Devices on Cars Without Warrant," *Associated Press* (April 25, 2002)

187   Echelon and Tempest: Jim Wilson, "Spying on Us," *Popular Mechanics* (January, 2001)

187   New Cyberspace security plan: Ted Bridis, "U.S. Considers Cybersecurity Plan," *Associated Press* (Sept. 7, 2002)

188   Key logger used by FBI: Ted Bridis, "Anti-Terror Tools Include High-Tech, " *Associated Press* (Oct. 28, 2001)

188   William Newman: Nat Hentoff, "The Sons and Daughters of Liberty," *Village Voice* (June 21, 2002)

188   Oasis, Fluent, dTective, Encase: Ibid.

189   GPS tracking: Julia Scheeres, "GPS: Keeping Cons Out of Jail," *Wired News* (Oct. 15, 2002); http://www.wired.com/news/privacy/0,1848,55740,00.html

189   Siemens tracking device: Joe Queenan, "Electronic Leashes for Teenagers," *The New York Times* (May 24, 2001)

189   Child tracking devices: Ibid.

190   Worst-case scenario: Russ Kick, "Machine Age --- Gotcha!" *Village Voice* (Feb. 27, 2001)

Governing by Secrecy and Decree

193   Corporate connections: The Center for Responsive Politics; http://www.opensecrets.org/bush/cabinet.asp

194   Campaign contributions: Editors, "Did You Know?" *Sierra Magazine* (September-October, 2002)

194   Fredrick Palmer: Ibid.

195   Bush Administration nepotism: Dana Milbank, "In Appointments, Administration Leaves No Family Behind," *The Washington Post* (March 12, 2002)

195   Bush and Fleischer's arguments: Bill Straub, "Bush Seeks to Redefine Entirely, The Power of the Presidency," *Scripps Howard News Service* (May 20, 2002)

196   Bruce Fein: Ibid.

196   Sealed records: Joshua Micah Marshall, "Bush's executive-privilege two-step," *Salon.com* (Feb. 7, 2002); http://www.salon.com/politics/feature/2002/02/07/bush_records/?x

196   Protect state secrets: Editors, "Historians File Suit to Quash White House Decree on Presidential Records," *Agence France Presse* (Nov. 29, 2001)

196   Historians file suit: Ibid.

197   Thomas Blanton: Ibid.

197   More secretive administration than Nixon: Alan Elsner, "Bush Expands Government Secrecy, Arouses Critics," *Reuters* (Sept. 3, 2002)

197   Gary Bass and Steven Aftergood: Ibid.

199   Only executive branch represented: Barton Gellman and Susan Schmidt, "Shadow Government Is at Work in Secret," *Washington Post* (March 1, 2002)

| 199 | True conservatives don't act this way: Michael Ventura, "The Shadow of Totalitarianism," *The Austin Chronicle* (March 22, 2002) |

The Crimes of Henry Kissinger

| 201 | Kissinger resigns: Editors, "Kissinger resigns as head of 9/11 commission," *CNN.com* (Dec. 15, 2002); http://www.cnn.com/2002/ALLPOLITICS/12/13/kissinger.resigns/ |

| 201 | Kissinger's quote and involvement in Chile: Christopher Hitchens, "Regarding Henry Kissinger: A panel discussion on the making of a war criminal," National Press Club (February 22, 2001) |

| 202 | A reproach to society: Ibid. |

| 203 | Licio Gelli and the P-2 Lodge: Jonathan Vankin and John Whalen, *Fifty Greatest Conspiracies of All Time* (New York: Citadel Press, 1995); Jim Marrs, *Rule by Secrecy* (New York: HarperCollins Publishers, 2000) |

| 204 | Kissinger's associates Snowcroft and Eagleburger: Walter Isaacson, *Kissinger: A Biography* (New York: Simon & Schuster, 1992) |

Secret Societies

| 206 | Clinton hurried to CFR: John F. McManus, "Insiders Call the Shots", *The New American* (October 12, 1998) |

| 206 | Bushes relatives to Royals: Tony Eufinger, "Political Blue Blood," *ABC News* (Oct. 25, 2000); http://abcnews.go.com/sections/world/DailyNews/london001025.html |

| 207 | A council…would be a good start: Zbigniew Brzezinski, "America and Europe," *Foreign Affairs* (October, 1970) |

| 207 | National sovereignty no longer a viable concept: Zbigniew Brzezinski, *Between Two Ages: America's Role in The Technetronic Era* (New York: Viking Press, 1970) |

| 207 | "More attainable": Ibid. |

| 207 | Victory of reason over belief: Ibid. |

| 207 | Bilderbergers at Knokke: Robert Eringer, *The Global Manipulators* (Bristol, England: Pentacle Books, 1980) |

| 208 | Founding members: Ibid. |

| 208 | "foster closer cooperation": *Trialogue: A Bulletin of North American, European, Japanese Affairs*, No. 16 (Winter, 1977-78), p. 12. |

| 208 | $120,000: Annual Report of Rockefeller Brothers Fund, Inc., 1977. |

| 209 | Leaders needed: David Wallechinsky and Irving Wallace, editors, *The People's Almanac #3* (New York: Bantam Books, 1981) |

| 209 | Huntington and FEMA: A. Ralph Epperson, *The Unseen Hand: An Introduction to the Conspiratorial View of History* (Tucson, AZ: Publius Press, 1985) |

| 209 | Cooper, Sawhill and Bergsten: Eringer, op cit. |

| 209 | Shadow Government: Ibid. |

| 209 | Tentacles have reached: Wallechinsky and Wallace, op cit. |

| 210 | Trilateralists make no bones: Editors, "We've Been Asked, Trilateral Commission: How Influential?" *U./S. News & World Report* (May 22, 1978) |

| 210 | Persistent maneuvering: Anthony C. Sutton and Patrick M. Wood, *Trilaterals Over Washington* (Scottsdale, AZ: The August Corp., 1979) |

| 210 | The unsettling thing: William Greider, "The Trilateralists are coming! The Trilateralists are coming!" *Dallas Times Herald* (February 3, 1977) |

| 210 | Calculations meaningless: Sutton and Wood, op. cit. |

| 211 | Most logical catalyst: Ibid. |

211   World economic power: Barry M. Goldwater, *With No Apologies* (New York: William Morrow, 1979)

212   "Concerned citizens": David Rockefeller, "Foolish Attacks on False Issues," *Wall Street Journal* (April 30, 1980)

212   Brzezinski makes his own policy and "a worrisome conspiracy": Nicholas von Hoffman, "Who's running foreign policy, anyhow?" *Fort Worth Star-Telegram* (October 21, 1980)

213   Reagan accepts George Bush: Ronald Reagan's remarks to the Republican National Convention, *Congressional Quarterly Weekly Reports, July-September, 1980,* Vol. 38, No. 29 (July 19, 1980)

213   Reagan's transition team: Epperson , op cit.

214   Trilateral "task force": Sutton and Wood, op cit.

214   Rockefeller's newest cabal: Goldwater, op cit.

214   "Guess who's coming to the White House": Washington Post Wire, "Trilateralists get invited to White House," *Dallas Times Herald* (March 18, 1981)

215   "The Inquiry": James Perloff, *The Shadows of Power: The Council on Foreign Relations And The American Decline* (Appleton, WS: Western Islands, 1988)

215   Article II: Epperson, op cit.

216   Council in Soviet press: J. Anthony Lucas, "The Council on Foreign Relations --- Is It a Club? Seminar? Presidium? `Invisible Government'? *The New York Times Magazine*(November 21, 1971)

216   "New York liberal elite": Peter G. Peterson, "Letter from the Chairman", *Council on Foreign Relations 1997 Annual Report*

216   Early CFR officers: Perloff, op cit.

217   Funding for CFR: Epperson, op cit.

217   Globalist activism: Lucas, op cit.

217   "Mission Statement": *Council on Foreign Relations 1997 Annual Report*

218   Admiral Chester Ward's comments: Barry Goldwater, op cit.

218   "intricate channels": Lucas, op cit.

218   World banking monopoly: Epperson, op cit.

270   CFR...put to work: Phyllis Schlafly and Chester Ward, *Kissinger on the Couch* (New Rochelle, NY: Arlington House, 1975)

218   *Foreign Affairs'* voice becomes policy: *The New Encyclopeadia Britannica*, Vol. 4

218   "It *is* the eastern Establishment": Alvin Moscow, *The Rockefeller Inheritance* (Garden City, New York: Doubleday & Company, Inc., 1977)

219   John Kenneth Galbraith: Lucas, op cit.

219   Morgan control moves to Rockefellers: Griffin, op cit.

219   "Historical records speaks...loudly": Perloff, op cit.

219   "It is their property": Wallechinsky and Wallace, op cit..

219   CIA's principal constituency: Victor Marchetti and John D. Marks, *The CIA and the Cult of Intelligence* (New York: Dell Publishing Co., 1974)

220   "Put through a call to New York": Ibid.

220   "CFR only has 3,200 members": Robert Anton Wilson, *Everything Is Under Control: Conspiracies, Cults and Cover-ups* (New York: HarperPerennial, 1998)

220	"Not a dime's worth of difference": Gary Allen, *None Dare Call It Conspiracy* (Seal Beach, CA: Concord Press, 1971)

220   Break the insider control: Ibid.

221   Move toward "apocalyptic events": Perloff, op cit.

221   First American meeting: Neal Wilgus, *The Illuminoids* (New York: Pocket Books, 1978)

221   Clinton at Bilderberg: "Clinton To Attend Meeting in Germany," *Arkansas Democrat Gazette* (June 4, 1991)

221   Hillary Clinton at Bilderberg: James P. Tucker Jr., "Bilderberg Tracked to Scotland," *The Spotlight* (May 18, 1998)

221   Retinger and friends: Eringer, op cit.

222   Donovan as "Anglophile": John Ranelagh, *The Agency: The Rise and Decline of the CIA* (New York: Simon & Schuster, 1987)

222   C. D. Jackson as Bilderberger: Vankin and Whalen, op cit.

222   "unofficial CFR": Wilgus, op cit.

222   MI6 creation: Dr. John Coleman, *Conspirators' Hierarchy: The Story of the Committee of 300* (Carson City, NV: America West Publishers, 1992)

223   "evolving an international order": Ibid.

223   "The Bilderberg agenda…": James P. Tucker Jr., "TC, Bilderberg Set to Meet," *The Spotlight*, (April 30, 1990)

223   Common Market nurtured at Bilderberg: Eringer, op cit.

224   Jack Sheinkman: Trisha Katson, "Some U.S. Bilderbergers Break Silence," *The Spotlight*, (June 24, 1996)

224   Prince Bernhard: Epperson, op cit.

224   William F. Buckley and Paul Gigot: Katson, op cit.

225   C. Gordon Tether: Eringer, op cit.

225   Rumsfield summoned: James P. Tucker Jr., "Bilderberg Batters Bush; But Unity Remains on NOW," *American Free Press* (June 17, 2002)

PART IV – HISTORICAL PRECEDENTS

The Gulf War

227   "Battle of the New World Order": Jonathan Vankin and John Whalen, *Fifty Greatest Conspiracies of All Time* (New York: Citadel Press, 1995)

228   Glaspie and Saddam's conversation: Russell S. Bowen, *The Immaculate Deception* (Carson City, NV: America West Publishers, 1991); Tarpley and Chaitkin, op. cit.;

228   Glaspie's summer vacation: Webster Griffin Tarpley and Anton Chaitkin, *George Bush: The Unauthorized Biography* (Washington, D.C.: Executive Intelligence Review, 1992)

229   Paul Adler: Warren Hough and Lawrence Wilmot, "Saddam: Bush-Whacked?" *The Spotlight* (April 8, 1991)

229   Bobby Lee Cook: Warren Hough, "Iraq Policy No Accident," *The Spotlight* (October 5, 1992)

229   Kissinger Associates: Ibid.

229   Barr's impeachment: Mike Blair, "Gonzalez: Impeach Top Cop," *The Spotlight* (September 28, 1992).

230   Bush administration repayments: Mike Blair, "You Pay for Bad Loans to Iraq," *The Spotlight* (April 27, 1992)

230   Loan guarantees enabled arms buildup: Bowen, op. cit.

230   Bush quote: Tarpley and Chaitkin, op. cit.

230    $4 billion secret payoff: Warren Hough, "Did George Bush Get a Big Payoff?" *The Spotlight* (August 30, 1993)

231   "Weapons of mass destruction": Jay Higgnbotham, "Letters," *U.S. News & World Report* (January 18, 1999)

231   Scott Ritter and Auster quote: Bruce B, Auster, "Inspecting the Inspectors," *U.S. News & World Report* (January 18, 1999)

231   Inspection account: Ibid.

The Reichstag Fire

233   Nazi gun laws lifted almost verbatim: www.jpfo.org/GCA_68.htm

233   Douglas Reed's comments: Louis L. Snyder, *Encyclopedia of The Third Reich* (New York: McGraw-Hill Book Company, 1976)

233   Operation Eagle Flight: Paul Manning, *Martin Bormann: Nazi in Exile* (Secaucus, NJ: Lyle Stuart, Inc., 1981)

233   750 front corporations: Manning, op. cit.
234   Prescott Bush's Nazi connections: http://www.wikipedia.org/wiki/Prescott_Bush

234   ITT: Charles Higham, *Trading With The Enemy: An Expose' of the Nazi-American Money Plot 1933-1949*, (New York: Delacorte Press, 1983)

234   Gerhardt Westrick: Ibid.
234   Schroder and Schellenberg: Ibid.
235   oil to Spain: Ibid.
235   Banking connections: Ibid.
235   Chase and Schmitz: Manning, op. cit.
235   Schmitz's wealth": Ibid.
235   Nazis did not die: Jim Keith, *Casebook on Alternative 3: UFOs, Secret Societies and World Control*, (Lilburn, GA: IllumiNet Press, 1994)

236   Bush family complicity: John Loftus, "The Dutch Connection," *Robert Lederman* (Feb. 9, 2002); http://baltech.org/lederman/bush-nazi-fortune-2-09-02.html.

236   Goering's quote: G. M. Gilbert, *Nuremberg Diary* (New York: Signet Books, 1947)

236   Bush like Hitler: John F. Dickerson, "Bush's Furor Over Der Fuhrer," *Time* (Sept. 30, 2002)

Pearl Harbor

236   CFR and State Department: J. Anthony Lucas, "The Council on Foreign Relations --- Is It a Club? Seminar? Presidium? 'Invisible Government'? *The New York Times Magazine* (November 21, 1971)

237   Ads calling for war: James Perloff, *The Shadows of Power: The Council on Foreign Relations And The American Decline* (Appleton, WS: Western Islands, 1988)

237   Justification for world government: Ibid.

237   Roosevelt "prototypic Wall Streeter": Ibid.

237   CFR-One World Money group: Curtis B. Dall, *FDR: My Exploited Father-in-Law* (Washington, D. C.: Action Associates, 1970)

237   Admiral James O. Richardson: Robert Anton Wilson, *Everything Is Under Control: Conspiracies, Cults and Cover-ups* (New York: HarperPerennial, 1998)

237   Japanese war preparations known: Carroll Quigley, *Tragedy and Hope: A History of the World in Our Time* (New York: MacMillan, 1966)

238   Marshall's message: Litchfield, op. cit.
238   Australian intelligence and Popov reports: Vankin and Whaley, op. cit.

238   Toland's names: Perloff, op. cit.

239   Marshall and Knox in White House: Ibid.

239   Stimson's diary entry: Wilson, op. cit.

239   Germans intercept Roosevelt-Churchill conversation: Gregory Douglas, *Gestapo Chief: The 1948 Interrogation of Heinrich Muller* (San Jose, CA: R. James Bender Publishing, 1995)

240   Warning came on parallel level: Douglas, op. cit.

Would Americans Allow Attacks on Americans?

240   A secret and bloody war of terrorism: Edward Spannaus, "When U.S. Joint Chiefs Planned Terror Attacks on America," *Executive Intelligence Review* (Oct. 12, 2001)

241   Largest expansion of covert action: William M. Arkin, "The Secret War: Frustrated by intelligence failures, the Defense Department is dramatically expanding its `black world' of covert operations," *Los Angeles Times* (Oct. 27, 2002)

242   NSC to be in charge: David Isenberg, "`P2OG' allows Pentagon to fight dirty," *Asia Times Online* (Nov. 5, 2002); www.atimes.com/atimes/Middle_East/DI05AK02.html.

243   An endless night of black ops: Chris Floyd, "Global Eye – Into the Dark," *The Moscow Times* (Nov. 1, 2002); www.themoscowtimes.com/stories/2002/11/01/120.html.

243   Spc. Peterson's arrest: Noelle Phillips, "Fort Stewart soldier jailed in Florida on $5 million bond," *Savannah Morning News* (May 16, 2002)

243   Emad Salem: Ralph Blumenthal, "Tapes Depict Proposal to Thwart Bomb Used in Trade Centere Blast," *The New York Times* (Oct. 28, 1993)

War as an Economic Boost

244   "clear and predictable danger": *Report from Iron Mountain on the Possibility and Desirability of Peace* (New York: The Dial Press, Inc., 1967), p. 4.

245   The basic social system: Ibid.

245   Principal organizing force and economic stabilizer: Ibid.

245   Disestablishment catastrophic: Ibid.

245   Not be allowed to disappear: Ibid.

245   Elimination of national sovereignty: Ibid.

245   Necessary social classes: Ibid.

246   Reintroduction of slavery: Ibid.

246   War substitutes: Ibid.

247   Threat will have to be invented: Ibid.

244   Report unsettling: Ibid.

248   Iron Mountain Study not fiction: Radio interview transcript of Col. Donn de Grand Pre, "Former Pentagon Official Says 'No-Win Wars' Part of Plan for One World Government," *Spotlight* (April 23, 2001)

249   Plunge protection team: Richard Wachman, "Federal reserve Ready to Prop Up Wall Street With Billions," *The Observer* (Sept. 17, 2001)

249   John McCain on war profiteering: Julian E. Barnes, "Cashing In on the Defense Buildup," *U.S. News & World Report* (May 13, 2002)

250   Rick Santorum: Ibid.

250   Prince Bernhard: Jim Marrs, *Rule by Secrecy* (New York: HarperCollins, Publishers, 2000)

250   Lockheed bribery scandals: Christopher H. Schmitt, "Wages of Sin: Why lawbreakers still win government contracts," *U.S. News & World Report* (May 13, 2002)

250   F-35 contract to Lockheed: Ibid.

251   Law breaking by contractors: Ibid.

251   Rep. Peter DeFazio: Ibid.

PART V – *Qui bono?* WHO BENEFITS?

The Mass Media

252   Hamilton Peterson learned things: Russ Kick, "Associated Press Story Change: The Flight 93 Tape," *The Memory Hole*; www.thememoryhole.org/911/ap-93tape.htm

252   Bernie Saunders: Michael Collins Piper, "Bilderberger 'Blacks' Out D.C. Media," *American Free Press* (July 22, 2002)

253   Like railroad and oil trusts of 1890s: William Greider, *One World, Ready or Not* (New York: Simon & Schuster, 1997)

254   Uncritical passing of officials opinions: Michael Parenti, *Inventing Reality: The Politics of the Mass Media* (New York: St. Martin"s Press, 1986)

254   Britt Hume: Ibid.

255   CFR media members: *CFR/Trilateral Influence on the Carter/Reagan/Bush/Clinton Administration*, non-copyrighted material from the Fund to Restore an Educated Electorate, Kerrville, TX; obtained from *The United States Government Manual 1991/92*, Office of the Federal Register - National Archives and Records Administration; Standard & Poor's *Register of Corporations, Directors and Executives*, 1991; *Annual Report 1991/92*, Council on Foreign Relations, New York City.

255   Reed Irvine and AIM: Michael Collins Piper, "'Watchdog' Won't Bite," *The Spotlight* (May 7, 1990)

258   Walter Cronkite, Daniel Schorr and Morley Safer: Bill Kirtz, "Disgust with the ranks," *Quill* (a publication of the Society of Professional Journalists) (May, 1998)

258   Top censored stories of 2001-2002: Project Censored Press Release, Sonoma State University (Aug. 28, 2002); www.projectcensored.org.

A Dismal Foreign Policy Record

258   Gore Vidal: Cooper, op. cit.

259   Foreign adventurisms listed: Editors, *the new Encyclopedia Britannica* (Chicago: Encyclopedia Britannica, Inc., 15th Edition, 1991)

262   We are hated because of our government: Robert Bowman, "The Security Charade," *The National Catholic Reporter* (Oct. 2, 1998)

Manufactured Enemies

262   Ho Chi Minh as agent: Lloyd Shearer, "When Ho Chi Minh was an Intelligence Agent for the U.S." *Parade* (March 18, 1973); *The New Encyclopedia Britannica*, Vol. 5.

263   Greatest myth of contemporary history: Griffin, op. cit.

263   Trotsky and Wall Street: William T. Still, *New World Order: The Ancient Plan of Secret Societies* (Lafayette, LA: Huntington House Publishers, 1990)

263   Jacob Schiff's $20 million: Gary Allen, *None Dare Call It Conspiracy* (Seal Beach, CA: Concord Press, 1971)

263   Elihu Root's $20 million: David Icke, *...and the truth shall set you free* (Cambridge, England: Bridge of Love Publications, 1995),

263   Rich back Bolshevik Revolution: Allen, op. cit.
264   Churchill on worldwide conspiracy: A. Ralph Epperson, *The New World Order* (Tucson, AZ: Publius Press, 1990), pp. 104-105.

The Hegelian Dialectic

266   The key to understanding world history: Texe Marrs, *Circle of Intrigue* (Austin, TX: Living Truth Publishers, 1995)

Who's Who of the Elite

267   Foreign policy partly to blame: Stacy Humes-Schulz, "US 'was partly to blame' for terror attacks", *Financial Times*, September 4, 2002.

269   Normal security bypassed: L. Fletcher Prouty, "An Introduction to the Assassination Business," *Gallery* (September, 1975)

270   Michael Rivero quote: Robert Sterling, "Dubya Dubya Three – Are Americans The Victims Of A Hoax?" *The Konformist* (Oct. 23, 2001)

The War on Freedom

Index

60 Minutes .... -37-, -202-, -256-

60 Minutes II .... -37-

911 .... -21-, -69-, -70-, -85-, -295-

Abbott Laboratories .... -193-

ABC .... -55-, -91-, -104-, -115-, -252-, -253-, -255-, -256-, -278-, -282-, -290-

ABC News . -55-, -104-, -278-, -282-, -290-

ABFFE .... -174-

Abrams, Elliot .... -59-

ACLU .... -152-, -159-, -163-, -172-, -174-, -181-, -188-, -286-

Adams Mark Hotel .... -163-

Advanced Scientific Computing
Research .... -149-

Afghanistan .... -5-, -7-, -26-, -40-, -41-, -43-, -55-, -61--63-, -78--82-, -84-, -85-, -87-, -88-, -91-, -93-, -98-, -108--110-, -112--116-, -120-, -126-, -130-, -137-, -173-, -176-, -178-, -191-, -240-, -261-, -262-, -267-, -269-, -277-, -279-, -280-, -283-

Afghanmagazine.com .... -87-

African-Americans .... -93-

Agreed Framework .... -88-

Agroterrorism .... -147-, -148-

AIG Insurance .... -51-

Air Force .... -4-, -10--12-, -63-,-64-, -70-, -71-,-110-, -124-, -169-,-232-, -250-

Air Force One .... -12-, -124-

Air France Flight 8969 .... -26-, -275-

Airborne Warning and
Control System (AWAC) .... -66-

Airbus Industrie .... -187-

Akin Gump Straus's Hauer & Feld .... -112-

Aktion Adlerflug .... -233-

Al-Omari, Abdulaziz .... -13-

Albuquerque Journal .... -15-, -273-

Alcoa .... -192-

Alex. Brown .... -50-, -51-

Alfa Bank .... -111-

Alfa Eko .... -111-, -112-

Alfa Group .... -111-

Algiers .... -26-

Allied .... -3-, -90-, -110-, -143-, -226-, -227-, -233-, -236-

Allison Engine Co. .... -64-

Allstate .... -192-

Al-Jazeera .... -37-, -87-, -252-

al-Qaeda .... -5-, -22-, -23-, -25--29-, -31-, -32-, -37-, -40--43-, -45-, -48-, -57-, -91-, -115-, -116-, -119-, -121-, -123-, -129-, -133-, -134-, -137-, -146-, -176-, -178-, -186-, -252-, -253-, -271-, -272-, -276-, -283-

Amalgamated Bank .... -223-

Amdocs, Ltd. .... -57-

American Airlines .... -9-, -49-, -121-

American Association for
Research in Baghdad .... -104-

American Civil Liberties Union
.... -151-, -159-, -172-, -179-, -189-

American Council for Capital Formation -217-

American Flag .... -158-

American Flight 11 .... -9-, -11-, -13-

American Flight 77 .... -9-, -10-

American Historical Association .... -196-

American Legion National
Convention .... -212-

American Library
Association .... -164-, -173-

American Muslim Council .... -94-

American Office of Strategic Services -263-

American POWs .... -100-, -157-

American Society of Civil
Engineers (ASCE) .... -21-

American Special Forces .... -115-

America's Unocal Corporation .... -78-

Ameritech .... -253-

AMR Corp. .... -49-

Amylin Pharmaceutical .... -192-

Anarchist Club .... -162-

Ancient Weapons .... -104-

Anderson, Harold .... -255-

Anderson, Jack .... -61-, -73-

Anderson, John B. .... -208-, -211-

Anderson, Maxwell .... -105-

Andrew W. Mellon Foundation .... -217-

Angola .... -204-, -260-, -261-

Animal and Plant Health Inspection Service-148-

Antiterrorism .... -22-, -34-, -100-,
-131-, -133-, -168-, -170-, -172--174-, -176-
, -267-, -285-

Anti-Communism .... -144-, -264-

Anti-Semites .... -95-

AOL Time Warner .... -192-, -193-, -253-

Aon Corp. .... -17-

Applied Digital Solutions .... -184-, -289-

Arab Mujahideen .... -114-

Arabic .... -14-, -23-,
-28-, -29-, -44-,-54-, -63-, -94-,-101-, -117-,
-118-,-127-, -280-

Arabic Safa Trust .... -94-

Arbusto Energy .... -122-, -123-

Archer Daniels Midland .... -193-

Arctic National Wildlife
Reserve National Park .... -93-

Armed Services Committee .... -47-

Armitage, Richard .... -59-, -156-, -157-

Armonk .... -119-

Arms Control and
Disarmament Agency .... -201-, -210-

Army .... -27-, -29-, -30-, -56-,
-61-, -67-, -72-, -77-, -78-, -82-, -97-, -109-,
-123-, -137-, -140-, -141-, -143-, -144-,
-154-, -163-, -201-, -202-, -226-, -238-,
-242-, -243-, -246-, -279-, -286-

Army Group South .... -77-

Army's Intelligence and
Security Command (INSCOM) .... -143-

Arnold, Kenneth .... -4-

Art Student Scandal .... -56-

ARVN .... -154-

Aryan .... -76-

ASCE .... -21-

ASG .... -27-

Ashcroft, John Attorney General -36-, -39-,
-47-, -62-, -85-, -123-, -153-, -156-, -160-,
-167-, -168-, -172-, -175--179-, -181-, -192-
, -197-

Asia Times .... -242-, -294-

Asian .... -1-, -27-,-78-, -79-, -81-,
-82-, -84-, -109-,-260-, -280-

Assassination Records Review
Board .... -241-

Associated Press .... -50-, -69-, -95-,
-105-, -187-, -188-,-253-, -255-, -256-,-273-
, -274-, -276-,-277-, -281--287-,-289-, -295-

Association of American Physicians
and Surgeons .... -135-

Association of Art Museum
Directors .... -105-

AT&T .... -192-,-253-

ATF .... -4-, -35-,-101-, -102-

Atta, Mohammed .... -103-, -104-, -132-

Atwan, Abdel-Barri .... -29-

Austin Chronicle .... -199-, -290-

AWAC .... -66-

Axis .... -3-, -88-, -144-, -235-, -237-

Axis of Evil .... -88-

Baker Hughes .... -98-

Baker, James .... -123-, -126-, -213-,
-227-, -228-, -258-

Baker, Paul .... -57-

Baker, Raymond .... -108-

Balance of Power .... -59-, -227-, -266-

Balfour, Arthur .... -60-

Bank of America . -121-, -183-, -193-, -284-

Bank of International Settlements .... -235-

Bankers Trust .... -51-

Banque de Paris et des Pays-Bas .... -235-

Barak .... -73-, -196-

Barksdale Air Force Base .... -11-

Basmyia .... -104-

Bay of Pigs .... -51-, -240--242-,
-259-, -271-

BBC News .... -13-, -57-, -79-,
-88-, -130-, -273-,-274-, -278-, -280--286-

BCCI .... -123-,
-124-, -126-, -284-

Bechtel .... -208-

Bedard, Paul .... -104-

Beghal, Djamel .... -43-

Benevolence International .... -168-

Bennington .... -162-

Berger, Samuel R. .... -37-

Berlet, Chip .... -55-

Bernard, Marcel .... -66-

Bezalel Academy .... -56-

Bible .... -72-, -280-

Bilderberg Hotel .... -221-

Bilderberger Conference .... -223-

Bill of Rights .... -173-, -175-, -224-, -270-

Bin Laden, Abdullah .... -128-

Bin Laden, Mohammed Awad .... -113-

Bin Laden, Osama ... -5-, -6-, -12-, -22--24-,
-26--29-, -31--33-, -35-, -38-, -40--43-, -48-
, -50-, -51-, -61-, -66-, -74-, -76-, -81--85-,
-87-, -91-, -100-, -102-, -103-, -112--119-,
-121-, -122-, -126-, -127-, -129-, -130-,
-133-, -137-, -173-, -243-, -247-, -252-,
-253-, -257-, -258-, -267-, -271-, -272-

Family .... -12-, -51-, -114-,
-121--123-, -126--128-, -272-

Bin Laden, Salem .. -121--123-, -126-, -128-

Binladen Aviation .... -122-

Binladen Brothers Construction .... -126-

Binladen Group .... -126-

Bizarre Coincidence .... -131-

Black Operation .... -241-

Black Tuesday .... -49-

Bloomberg Business News .... -49-

BNL .... -229-

Bodansky, Yossef .... -25-

Bodine, Barbara .... -32-

Boeing .... -9-, -63--
65-, -122-, -124-,-193-, -249-, -250-

Bollyn, Christopher .... -105-

Bolshevik Revolution .... -263-, -296-

Bolshevism .... -263-

Bolton, John .... -59-

Border Patrol .... -138-

Bowie Maryland Freeway Airport .... -66-

BP Amoco .... -193-

Bradley International Airport .... -139-

Branch Davidian .... -138-

Braun, Harry .... -80-
Breen, Kenneth .... -33-
Breitweiser, Kristin .... -13-
Bristol-Myer's Squibb .... -217-
British Airways .... -65-
British Intelligence .... -91-
British Royal Family .... -222-
Brooke Army Medical Center .... -123-
Brown, A.J. .... -161-
Brown, Harold .... -210-, -258-
Brown, Willie .... -46-, -47-
Brownstein, Hyatt & Faber .... -193-
Brzezinski, Zbigniew .... -80-, -82-, -83-,
-207-, -208-, -210-,-212-, -223-, -258-
Bucca, Ronald P. Fire Marshal ..... -18-,-20-
Buchanan, Lyn .... -72-, -74-
Buddhas of Bamiyan .... -105-
Bureau of Diplomatic Security .... -130-
Burke's Peerage .... -206-
Bush, George Herbert Walker .... -51-,
-94-, -100-, -110-,-122--124-, -126-,129-, -
170-, -197-,-206-, -234-
        Administration .... -80-, -204-,
        -229-,-230-
        President -74-, -87-, -97-, -112-,
        -124-, -125-, -163-, -206-, -211-
        -214-, -219-, -227-, -228-, -231-,
        -236-, -260--262-, -267-
Bush, George W.
        Administration .... -23-, -24-,
        -31-, -39-, -47-, -53-, -59-, -60-,
        -77-, -80-, -86-, -88-, -89-, -91-
        -95-, -97-, -99-, -100-, -116-,
        -120-, -123-, -127--129-, -131-,
        -141-, -142-, -156-, -163-, -166-
        , -173-, -175--177-, -187-, -190-
        -196-, -198--200-, -252-, -257-, -
        267-
        President . -5-, -6-, -9--13-, -24-,

        -39-, -48-, -53-, -54-, -59-, -60-,
        -62-, -65-, -69-, -74--77-, -79-
        -81-, -87--98-, -106-, -110--112-
        , -117-, -119--123-, -125--129-,
        -131--133-, -137-, -140-, -146-,
        -150-, -151-, -153--155-, -157-
        -159-, -161--165-, -170-, -174-,
        -178-, -183-, -184-, -190--200-,
        -202-, -203-, -205-, -206-, -220-,
        -226-, -230-, -234-, -236-, -242-,
        -249-, -252-, -257-, -258-, -268-,
        -269-
Bush, Jeb .... -93-
Bush, Prescott .... -234-, -268-
Bush-Nazi Connection .... -51-
Business Roundtable .... -217-, -254-
Cable Splicer .... -141-, -285-
Cable Splicer II .... -141-
Cabots .... -109-
Cacchioli, Louie .... -16-
Calabrese, Prudence .... -74-
CALEA .... -57-,-58-
Calgene, Inc. .... -193-
Cameron, Carl .... -56-
CapCities .... -254-
Capitol .... -10-, -47-, -92-, -164-, -165-
Capitol Hill .... -92-
Card, Andrew .... -77-, -192-
Carew, Tom .... -109-, -110-
Cargill .... -193-
Carlisle .... -154-
Carlyle Group -51-, -94-, -126-, -127-, -284-
Carnivore .... -30-, -31-, -275-
Carnivore .... -31-
Carter, Jimmy President .... -82-,
-83-, -156-, -206-, -208--212-, -214-, -258-
Casey, William .... -51-, -203-, -219-
Castle, Michael .... -77-
Caucasian Oil Fields .... -77-

Cayman Islands-25-, -108-, -124--126-, -274-

CBS-47-, -80-, -89-, -191-, -252--256-, -277-

CBS News .... -47-, -80-, -191-, -277-

CCC .... -230-

CCFR .... -90-

CDR .... -159-

Center for International Affairs .... -201-

Center For Public Integrity
97-, -111-, -178-,-282-, -288-

Center for Responsive Politics .... -8-,
-192-, -273-, -289-

Centers for Disease Control and
Prevention .... -135-

CentGas .... -78-,-79-, -280-

Central Asia .... -61-, -78-, -80-,-81-

Central Asia Institute .... -81-

Central Asian Gas Pipeline, Ltd
. (CentGas) .... -78-

Central Command
.... -87-, -127-, -186-

Central Europe .... -83-

Central Intelligence Agency .... -4-, -41-,
-52-, -276-

Central Powers .... -215-

Century Association .... -216-

Century Group .... -237-

CFR -59-, -60-, -77-, -78-, -83-, -119-, -204-
-207-, -210--223-, -227-, -237-, -238-, -244-
, -255-, -258-, -263-, -268-, -284-, -290-
-295-

Channel One .... -117-

Charles Cogan .... -108-

Charles Higham .... -235-

Charles R. Smith .... -57-

Charles Schwab .... -192-

Chase .... -121-, -183-,
-210-, -220-, -228-, -235-, -293-

Chemical and Biological National
Security .... -149-

Cheney, Dick Vice President ...... -12-, -24-,
-47-, -69-, -74-, -79-, -80-, -86-, -96--100-,
-111-, -112-, -131--133-, -142-, -163-, -190-
, -191-, -196-, -197-, -206-, -258-, -267-
-269-

Chester Ward .... -217-

Chevron .... -98-,-192-

Chevron Oil .... -98-

Chicago Board of Options Exchange .... -49-

Chicago Council on Foreign
Relations (CCFR) .... -90-

Chicago Exchange .... -49-

Chicago Postal Inspector's Office ...... -158-

Chicago Tribune .... -192-, -287-

Chief Judge Royce Lamberth .... -31-

Children's Internet Protection Act ...... -173-

Children's TV Workshop .... -255-

ChipMobile .... -185-

Christian Science Monitor .... -17-, -274-

Christians .... -184-

Christopher Bollyn .... -18-, -105-

CIA .... -1-,
-4-, -6-, -11-, -23--27-, -31-, -35-, -39--43-,
-45-, -47--49-, -51-, -52-, -55-, -57-, -61-, -
62-, -66-, -72-, -73-, -82-, -88-, -99--101-, -
108--111-, -114-, -117-, -122--124-, -127-, -
128-, -130-, -131-, -142-, -143-, -152-, -
153-, -155-, -156-, -165-, -166-, -173-, -
187-, -188-, -202--204-, -211-, -214-, -216-,
-218-, -219-, -222-, -223-, -226-, -227-, -
234-, -235-, -240--242-, -257--261-, -267-, -
269--272-, -276-, -277-, -283-, -284-, -291-,
-292-

Citibank .... -51-, -108-, -283-

Citigroup .... -51-,-192-

Citizen Corps .... -158-, -160-, -286-

Clark, Wesley .... -258-

Clarke, Richard .... -31-, -32-, -37-,-187-

Clean Water Act .... -98-

Clifford, Clark .... -51-
Clinton, Bill .... -34-
       Administration .. -34-, -36-, -37-,
       -40-, -58-, -80-,-86-, -100-, -102-,
       -153-, -184-, -187-,-220-, -231-,
       -253-,-257-, -268-
       President .... -35--37-, -42-, -80-,
       -84-, -91-, -99-J12-, -115-, -116-,
       -138-, -190-, -196-, -198-, -199-,
       -205-, -206-, -221-, -231-, -257-,
       -258-, -262-, -267-
Clinton, Hillary .... -34-, -221-
Clorox .... -193-
CNN .... -14-, -17-,
-27-, -106-, -252-, -255-, -256-, -258-, -273-
-275-, -281-, -282-, -286-, -290-
COG .... -198-
Cogan, Charles .... -108-
Cogitek Corp. .... -65-
COINTEL .... -144-
Cointelpro .... -153-
Cold War .... -3-, -73-, -83-,
-108-, -145-, -166-, -198-, -244-
Coldren, Lee .... -84-
Colin Powell .... -133-, -192-
Cologne .... -235-
Columbia University .... -207-, -210-
Commission of European Communities-208-
Commodity Credit
 Corporation (CCC) .... -230-
Common Market .... -223-, -292-
Communications Assistance for
Law Enforcement Act (CALEA) .... -57-
Communist Party .... -111-, -232-, -263-
Compromised .... -110-, -283-
Computer Fraud and Abuse Act .... -167-
Computer Security Division .... -149-
Comverse Infosys .... -57-

Congress 6,
 -5-, -21-, -24-,-27-, -31-, -33-,-47-, -52-, -
58-,-59-, -77-, -83-,-87-, -92-, -93-,-96-, -
97-, -133-,-136--138-, -142--146-, -150-, -
153-, -154-, -164--167-, -170-, -173-, -176-,
-178-, -182-, -185-, -190-, -195-, -197-, -
199-, -200-, -203-, -211-, -215-, -229-, -
252-, -253-, -257-, -274-
Constitution .... -5-, -77-, -89-,
-92-, -93-, -95-, -145-, -151-, -153-, -157-,
-165--168-, -173-, -181-, -195-, -199-,
-202-, -206-, -224-, -268-, -270-, -281-,
-288-
Continuity of Government .... -198-
Contras .... -97-, -260-
Controlled Demolition, Inc. .... -19-
Cordier, Ericca .... 6, -74-
Corley, Dr. W. Gene .... -20--22-
Coulson, Danny .... -102-
Council of Economic Advisers .... -211-
Council on Foreign Relations .... -4-,
-14-, -31-, -58--60-, -74-, -77-, -81-, -83-,
-87-, -90-, -119-, -146-, -194-, -201-, -204-
-207-, -210--212-, -214-, -215-, -218-, -220-
, -221-, -226-, -234-, -236-, -248-, -252-, -
254-, -256-, -258-, -291-, -293-, -295-
Counterpunch .... -39-, -276-, -286-
Craig Roberts .... -100-, -145-
Cramer, Glen .... -69-
Crescent Group Of Pakistan .... -79-
Critical Infrastructure
Assurance Office .... -149-
Crogan, Jim .... -103-, -104-
Crossley, Richard .... -49-
Cuba .... -97-, -137-,-176-, -240--242-,-259-
Cuban Missile Crisis .... -145-, -240-
Custom House .... -18-
Customs Service .... -18-, -137-, -148-
Czech Republic .... -220-

C-130 .... -71-, -250-

C-Span .... -92-

Danang .... -156-

DARE .... -93-, -161-, -220-, -292-, -296-

DARPA .... -64-, -143-

Dasquie, Guillaume .... -55-, -80-, -84-

David Isenberg .... -242-

Davidians .... -138-

Davis, Jayna .... -102-

Davis, John W. .... -216-

DCS-1000 .... -30-

De Grand Pre, Donn .... -67-, -248-

DEA .... -4-, -55-, -56-,
-58-, -110-, -124-, -161-, -171-, -278-,
-283-

Dean, Lisa .... -58-

Declaration of Independence .... -136-

Defense Advanced Projects
Agency (DARPA) .... -64-

Defense Intelligence Agency ....
.... -4-, -72-, -73-,
-110-

Defense Policy Board .... -59-, -60-

Defense Science Board (DSB) .... -242-

Delmart "Mike" Vreeland .... -44-

Delray Beach .... -56-

Delta Oil Company Limited of Saudi Arabia
.... -78-

Delta Petroleum .... -193-

Democrat .... -47-, -72-, -91--
93-, -108-, -146-,-165-, -193-, -199-,-220-, -
251-, -268-,-281-, -292-

Democratic Party .... -62-, -91-, -93-,
-95-, -156-, -211-

Department of Commerce .... -149-

Department of Defense .... -4-, -47-, -58-,
-105-, -124-, -138-, -149-, -241-, -279-

Department of Energy's
National Laboratories .... -149-

Department of Government .... -201-

Department of Health and
Human Services .... -135-, -147-

Department of Motor Vehicles .... -182-

Department of State .... -148-, -201-

Department of Transportation .... -182-

Desert Storm .... -125-, -226-, -231-

Deutch, John .... -51-, -99-, -219-, -258-

Deutsche Bank .... -50-, -51-, -233-, -277-

Deutsche Bank Alex. Brown ....
.... -50-

DIA .... -4-, -73-

Dial Press .... -244-, -245-, -294-

Diamandis, Alex .... -53-

Dick Eastman .... -61-

Die Zeit .... -57-,
-278-

Digital Angel .... -189-

Dillion Fund .... -217-

Dintilhac, Jean-Pierre .... -39-

Disarmament Agency .... -201-, -210-

Disney .... -11-,
-253-

DNA .... -167-, -179-,
-190-

DOD .... -44-

Doherty, David .... -51-

Dole Food .... -193-

Domestic Emergency Support Teams
of the Department of Justice .... -147-

Domestic Security Enhancement
Act of 2003 .... -179-, -288-

Dominican Republic .... -7-, -259-

Don Eslinger .... -189-

Donn de Grand Pre .... -67-, -248-

Douglas Valentine .... -155-

Douri, Riyadh Al- .... -104-

Dr. Joseph Hieronim Retinger, ... -221-

Dr. W. Gene Corley .... -20-, -21-

Dresser-Rand .... -99-

Driver's License Modernization
Act of 2002 .... -182-, -183-

Drug Abuse Resistance Education (DARE) -161-

Drug Enforcement Agency .. -4-, -55-, -108-

DSB .... -242-

dTective .... -188-,-289-

Dulles International Airport .... -9-, -131-

Dulles, Allen .... -219-, -222-, -234-,
-235-, -259-

Dulles, John Foster .... -216-, -222-, -234-,
-235-, -259-

Durenberger, David .... -40-

Durham Tech .... -161-

Dutch Shell Oil .... -222-, -244-

Eastern European .... -73-

Eastman Kodak .... -192-

Eastman, Dick .... -61-

Echelon .... -12-,
-39-, -40-, -53-, -186-, -187-, -276-, -278-, -
289-

Economist .... -208-, -209-, -228-

Ecstasy .... -55-, -108-

Edinburgh Air Force Base .... -63-

Edward S. Herman .... -203-

Edward Spannaus .... -163-

Edwards Air Force Base .... -63-

EFF .... -165-, -287-

Effective Death Penalty Act of 1996 .. -100-

Egyptian .... -25-, -28-, -118-, -127-,
-243-, -250-, -275-

Eiffel Tower .... -26-

Eisenhower, General Dwight D. .. -3-, -222-

El Pais .... -90-

El Paso Times .... -183-, -288-

Elaine Scarry .... -71-

Electronic Frontier Foundation (EFF) . -165-

Electronic Privacy Information
Center .... -30-, -167-

Electronic Warfare .... -71-

Electro-Magnetic Pulsing [EMP] .... -67-

Elgin Air Force Base .... -11-

Elgindy, Amr Ibrahim .... -33-

Eli Lilly .... -192-

Ellen Schrecker, ... -163-

Elliott, Tom .... -17-

Ellner, Oded .... -54-

Elmendorf AFB .... -145-

Emergency Czar .... -151-

Enabling Act .... -232-

Encase .... -188-,-289-

Enchanted Valley .... -122-

Energy Task Force
-93-, -99-, -197-, -285-

Enron .... -93-, -98-, -99-, -125-,
-133-, -268-, -271-

Enterprise Rent-A-Car .... -192-

Environmental Protection Agency -98-, -211-

EO .... -145-

Eric Hufschmid .... -20-

European Union .... -39-, -223-

Evian .... -224-

eWorldtrack .... -189-

Executive Branch .... -4-, -172-, -178-,
-179-, -195-, -198-, -266-, -289-

Executive Order .... -150-, -151-,
-196-, -198-, -249-

Export-Import Bank of the United States -18-

Extremist .... -22-, -101-

Exxon .... -208-

FAA .... -9-, -10-, -12-, -32-, -46-, -111-

FACA .... -152-

Fairness & Accuracy In
Reporting (FAIR) .... -252-

Faisal, Saud Al- Prince ... -13-, -113-, -120-,
-121-

FBI .... -1-, -3-, -4-,
-11--15-, -20-,-23-, -27-, -30--42-, -44-, -46-

-304-

-48-,-51--53-, -55-,-57-, -58-, -61-,-63-, -69-
-71-,-80-, -95-, -101--104-, -111-, -121-,-
127-, -128-, -130-,-134-, -144-, -147-,-149-,
-152-, -153-,-159-, -165--167-,-169-, -171-
-175-,-182-, -188-, -214-,-229-, -238-, -243-,
-244-, -257-, -267-,-269-, -274--278-,-284-,
-289-

FBIHQ .... -33-,-38-

FCI .... -55-

Federal Advisory Act (FACA) .... -152-

Federal Bureau of Investigation .... -4-

Federal Communications
 Commission .... -192-, -195-, -257-

Federal Computer Incident
Response Center .... -149-

Federal Election Commission .... -8-

Federal Emergency Management
 Agency -4-, -20-, -131-, -135-, -151-, -209-

Federal Network .... -192-

Federal Register Web .... -145-

Federal Research Division .... -41-

Federal Reserve .... -124-, -211-,
-219-, -237-, -248-, -255-, -256-, -295-

Federal Reserve System .... -219-, -255-

Federal Trade Commissions .... -195-

Federation of American Scientists
 .... -198-, -242-

Feith, Doug .... -59-

FEMA .... -4-, -11-,
-18-, -20-, -21-,-72-, -131-, -135-,-140-, -
144-, -145-,-147-, -150-, -151-,-159-, -285-,
-290-

Fifth Columnists .... -115-

Financial Services Authority ....
 .... -49-

Financial Times .... -90-, -109-, -119-,
-225-, -282--284-,-296-

Fire Engineering .... -20-, -21-, -274-

First Amendment .... -33-, -96-, -153-,
-164-, -167-, -168-,-170-, -171-

FISA .... -38-, -166-,-287-

FISC .... -166-, -167-, -179-, -287-

Fisher-Rosemount .... -98-

Fisk, Robert .... -106-

Fleischer, Ari .... -23-, -116-, -195-, -252-

Flowserve .... -98-

Fluent .... -188-, -289-

Flying Tigers .... -237-

Focus ..... -42-, -59-, -81-, -88-, -134-, -141-

FOIA .... -152-

Forbeses .... -109-

Ford Foundation .... -208-, -217-

Ford Motor Co. .... -192-, -193-, -234-

Foreign Affairs ..... -31-, -204-, -207-, -218-,
-219-, -290-

Foreign Counterintelligence
Investigation (FCI) .... -55-

Foreign Intelligence Surveillance
Court (FISC) .... -166-, -179-

Foreign Policy .... -2-, -60-, -82-, -83-, -90-,
-200-, -201-, -204-, -208-, -210-, -212-,
-220-, -227-, -257--259-, -261-, -262-,
-272-, -291-, -295-, -296-

Fort Belvoir .... -143-

Fort Benning .... -146-

Fort Bragg .... -127-, -284-

Fort Hood .... -138-

Fort Meade .... -39-

Fort Stewart .... -243-, -294-

Fort Worth Federal Correctional
 Institution .... -170-

Foundation for Relief and
Development .... -168-

Founding Fathers .... -171-, -178-, -195-

Fox 5 News .... -17-

Fox News .... -51-, -56--58-, -90-, -275-

Fox, Mike .... -80-

Frank Serpico .... -136-

Frankfurter Allgemeine Zeitung .. -40-, -53-

Fred Hubbell .... -139-

Freedom of Information Act .... -30-, -152-, -153-, -172-

Freemason .... -265-

French Revolution .... -264-

G. Edward Griffin .... -263-

Galati, Rocco .... -45-

Garden Plot .... -141-, -285-

Garrison, Jim .... -101-

GE .... -253-, -254-

Gene Matthews .... -135-

General Accounting Office .... -99-, -130-

General Dwight D. Eisenhower .... -222-

General Dynamics .... -192-

General Hameed Gul .... -61-

General Vo Nguyen Giap .... -263-

Geneva Conventions .... -155-

Georg Wilhelm Friedrich Hegel. .... -265-

George Washington University
.... -155-, -176-, -196-

Georgetown University Law School ... -178-

Gerald Ford .... -213-

German Marshall Fund ... -90-, -208-, -217-

German Parliament .... -232-

German Sixth Army .... -77-

Gestapo .... -159-, -234-, -235-, -239-,-294-

Get Chipped .... -184-, -185-

Ghamdi, Saeed Al- .... -13-

Gibson, McGuire .... -104-, -105-

Gilead Sciences .... -192-

Gilgamesh .... -104-

Glass, Randy .... -35-

Global Hawk ...... -63--65-, -67-, -68-, -71-, -272-, -279-

Global Options LLC .... -46-

Global Positioning System (GPS) .... -189-

Global Relief Foundation .... -168-, -287-

GMF .... -90-

Golden Triangle .... -108-, -157-

Goldman Sachs .... -204-, -205-, -249-

GOP .... -92-, -126-, -228-, -282-

Gordon, Steven .... -55-

GPS .... -189-, -190-, -289-

Graham, Bob .... -24-

Grants Pass Daily Courier .... -163-

Green Berets .... -127-

Greenburg, Hank .... -51-

Greyhound .... -193-

Grillflame .... -72-

Ground Zero .... -11-

Guantanamo Bay Naval Base ....
.... -137-, -176-

Guardian .... -83--85-, -96-, -128-,-276-, -277-, -281-,-282-, -284-

Guinness .... -191-

Guinness World Records 2000 .... -191-

Gul, Hameed .... -61-, -62-

Gulf International Bank .... -230-

Gulf of Tonkin .... -60-, -77-

Gulf of Tonkin Resolution .... -77-

Gulf War .... -2-, -32-, -78-, -80-, -96--98-, -100-, -101-, -104-, -119-, -126-, -226-, -229-, -230-, -232-, -246-, -261-, -280-, -292-

Gulf War Syndrome .... -232-

Gulfstream Aerospace .... -192-

Gunderson, Ted L. .... -40-

Hadith .... -120-

Haig, Alexander .... -14-, -203-, -213-, -258-

Haji .... -113-

Halliburton ... -79-, -96--100-, -111-, -112-, -191-, -282-

Hamas .... -52-, -94-, -101-, -129-, -186-

Hamilton, Bill .... -52-

Hanging Gardens of Babylon .... -106-

Hanjour, Hani .... -66-

Hanssen, Robert .... -38-, -51-

Harken Bahrain Energy Company ...... -125-

Harken Energy .... -98-, -123-, -125-, -126-, -129-, -191-

Harper's Magazine .... -201-

Harry Braun .... -80-

Harvard .... -71-, -154-, -201-, -209-,-247-, -248-

Harvard College .... -201-

Harvard Defense Studies Program ..... -201-

Harvard International Seminar .... -201-

Hazmi, Nawaf Al- .... -121-, -169-

HCA .... -193-

Hegelian Dialectic .... -2-, -264-, -265-,-296-

Hegelian System .... -265-

Heinrich Himmler .... -233-

Henry Kissinger .... -202-

Henry Stimson .... -219-

Herndon .... -128-

Heroin   -61-,-108-, -109-, -112-,-157-, -283-

Hersh, Seymour .... -60-

Herzliya .... -50-

Hezbollah .... -94-

HHS .... -147-

Higginsons .... -109-

High-Powered Microwave (HPM) .... -69-

Hill, Eleanor .... -23-, -24-

Hillary Clinton .... -34-, -221-

Hilton Hotel .... -40-

Hogan's Heroes .... -139-

Holland American Trading Company . -234-

Holocaust .... -236-

Holy Land .... -168-

Homeland Security .... -1-, -35-, -60-, -131-, -134--137-, -145--155-, -158--160-, -163-, -183-, -185-, -186-, -199-, -233-, -268-, -285-, -286-

Hoover Institution .... -217-

Hoover, Edgar .... -3-, -238-

Hopsicker, Daniel .... -110-, -111-

Hotel Maison Rouge .... -233-

House Government Reform Committee .... -196-

House Judiciary Committee .... -178-, -229-

House of Representatives .... -164-, -212-

Houston Gulf Airport .... -122-

Houston Post .... -124-, -125-

Howe, Carol .... -102-

HPM .... -69-

Hufschmid, Eric .... -20-

Hussein, Dr. Abdel El M. .... -117-

Hussein, Saddam .... -31-, -59-, -78-, -86-, -88-, -90-,-91-, -96-, -97-,-100-, -102-, -104-, -106-, -114-, -126-, -187-, -226--231-, -247-, -264-, -267-, -268-, -271-, -272-

Hydrogen Political Action Committee .... -80-, -280-

I.G. Farben .... -222-, -233-, -235-

IAEA .... -89-, -90-, -281-

IASPS .... -59-, -279-

ID Card .... -182-, -183-, -185-, -288-

Illegal Immigration Reform .... -184-

Illuminati .... -262-, -264-, -265-, -271-

ILWU .... -157-

Imle, John F. Jr. .... -78-

Immigration Reform Caucus .... -146-

Immigration Responsibility Act .... -184-

inalshibh, Ramzi .... -57-

Independent ...... -24-, -26-, -66-, -81-, -92-, -117-, -120-, -165-, -253-, -254-, -274-, -279-

Independent Digital .... -26-

Inderfurth, Karl "Rick" .... -84-, -85-

Indian News Agency .... -82-

Indochinese Communist Party .... -263-

Indonesia Petroleum Ltd. Of Japan .... -78-

Ingersoll-Dresser Pump .... -99-
INS .... -32-, -58-,
-138-, -148-, -152-
INSCOM .... -73-, -143-
Insight Magazine .... -56-, -58-, -165-,
-170-, -287-
Inspector General's Office .... -130-
Institute for Advanced
Strategic and Political
Studies (IASPS) .... -59-
Institute of International
  Affairs .... -215-, -222-, -223-
Institute of Macroeconomic Researches -28-
Intelligence and Security
Command (INSCOM) .... -73-, -143-
Intelligence Committees .... -23-, -133-
Intelligence Online .... -55-
Internal Revenue Service .... -4-
International Institute of Islamic Thought 28-
International Longshore
and Warehouse Union (ILWU) .... -157-
International Monetary Fund .... -209-
International Paper .... -192-
International Relations Committee .... -92-
International Society for
Individual Liberty .... -174-, -287-
Internet .... -6-, -12-, -14-, -39-, -40-,
-43-, -45-, -52--54-, -61-, -66-, -68-, -69-,
 -71-, -84-, -87-, -116-, -134-, -144-, -145-,
 -163-, -164-, -167-, -172--174-, -179-,
 -181-, -185-, -187--189-, -197-, -201-,
-249-, -253-, -270-, -277-
Internet Service Providers .... -167-, -172-
Intimidation in the First Degree .... -163-
Investment Bankers .... -235-
Investment Dealers Association
of Canada .... -50-
Iraq .... -1-, -5-, -28-,
-59-, -80-, -85-,-86-, -88--92-,-96--101-, -

104--106-, -117-, -119-,-143-, -157-, -158-,
-191-, -195-, -225-,-227-, -228-, -230-,
-231-, -236-, -246-,-267-, -281--283-,-292-,
-293-
Iraqi .... -7-, -56-, -78-, -86-,
-88-, -89-, -91-, -92-, -100--102-, -104-,
-105-, -125-, -126-, -157-, -226--228-,
-230-, -231-, -261-, -282-
Iron Curtain .... -73-
IRS ..... -4-, -171-, -188-, -189-, -196-, -198-
Isaiah .... -73-
Isikoff, Michael .... -53-
Islam .... -25-, -114-, -117-, -120-, -285-
Islamic .... -25-, -26-, -34-, -62-, -79-,
-80-, -82-, -101-, -113-, -115-, -118-,
-127-129-, -276-
Islamic Fundamentalists .... -62-
Islamic Jihad .... -25-, -101-, -127-
Isle of Man .... -129-
ISP .... -167-
Israel .... -29-, -30-, -53--63-, -67-,
-78-, -88-, -95-, -117-, -120-, -227-, -278-,
-279-
Israel Corp. .... -54-
Israeli Foreign Ministry .... -55-
Israeli Parliament .... -59-
Italian Parliament .... -39-
ITOCHU Oil Exploration Co. Ltd. .... -79-
ITT .... -234-, -293-
Ivanov, Igor .... -82-
Izvestia .... -45-,-216-
J. Anthony Lucas .... -216-, -217-
J. Edgar Hoover .... -153-, -217-
Jabin .... -73-
Jackson, C.D. .... -222-
Jackson, Jesse .... -106-
Jacksonville .... -243-
James Bamford .... -241-
James Pavitt .... -43-

James, Charles Sr. .... -194-
James, Chuck .... -194-
James, Kay Coles .... -194-
James, Valerie .... -32-
Jane's Aerospace .... -63-, -279-
Jansen, Brad .... -58-
Jeddah .... -113-, -114-, -130-
Jefferson, Thomas .... -5-
Jekyll Island .... -219-, -221-, -280-
Jerusalem Post .... -54-, -278-
Jewish World Review .... -58-, -278-
Jews for the Preservation of
  Firearms Ownership (JPFO) .... -233-
JFK Assassination -20-, -112-, -201-, -214-,
  -256-, -269-
Job Corps .... -247-
Joe Vialls .... -67-
John Ashcroft .... -85-, -175-
John Birch Society .... -212-
John F. Kennedy Special
Warfare Center and School .... -127-
John J. McCloy .... -220-
Johns Hopkins University .... -81-
Johnson, Larry .... -127-, -174-
Johnson, Lyndon President . -77-, -78-, -97-,
  -187-, -259-, -269-
Johnson, W. Thomas .... -255-
Joint Chiefs of Staff -70-, -127-, -201-,-241-
Joint Strike Fighter .... -250-
JP Morgan Chase .... -121-, -183-
JPFO .... -233-, -293-
Judah .... -73-
Judicial Watch .... -99-, -100-, -127-,
  -197-, -199-, -282-,-284-
Justice Department .... -13-, -18-, -23-, -25-,
  -36-, -58-, -129-, -137-, -159-, -167-, -168-,
  -175-, -176-, -178-, -179-, -195-, -229-,
  -288-
Justice Department's Office of

Public Affairs .... -178-
Karzai, Hamid .... -79-
Katz, David .... -26-
Katzman, Kenneth .... -22-
Kazakhstan .... -82-
KBR .... -97-, -98-
Keating, Frank .... -74-, -101-
Kellogg .... -97-, -111-, -192-, -282-
Kellogg Brown & Root .... -97-, -111-, -282-
Kennedy, John F. President ..... -94-, -101-,
-127-, -145-, -224-, -240-, -241-, -244-,
-247-, -268--270-
Kennedy, Robert .... -101-
Kennedy-Kassenbaum Health
Care Reform Acts .... -184-
Kent State University .... -261-
Kerik, Bernard .... -14-
Kernel of Evil .... -119-
Key, Charles .... -100-, -101-
KGB .... -111-, -186-
Khalilzad, Zalmay .... -59-, -79-, -80-
Khost .... -115-
Kick, Russ .... -46-, -190-
Kimmel, Rear Admiral Husband .... -77-
King .... -101-
King Abdul-Aziz University .... -113-
King Ahaz .... -73-
King Hezakiah .... -73-
King Nebuchadnezzar .... -106-
King Saud IV .... -113-
King Uzziah .... -73-
King, Martin Luther .... -261-
King, Rachel .... -159-
Kissinger Associates .... -200-, -204-, -228-,
  -229-, -292-
Kissinger, Henry ..... -14-, -31-, -200--205-,
  -211-, -218-, -224-, -228-, -229-, -248-,
  -257-, -258-, -260-, -268-
Knights of Malta .... -203-

Knights Templar .... -223-
Knokke .... -207-, -290-
Koran .... -14-, -72-, -120-
Korean Airlines 007 .... -212-
Koryagina, Dr. Tatyana .... -28-
Kosovo .... -5-, -7-, -33-, -261-
Kraft .... -193-, -255-
Kreindler, Jim .... -100-
Krongard, A.B. "Buzzy" .... -51-
Kuhn, Loeb & Company .... -263-
Kurzberg, Paul .... -54-
Kurzberg, Sivan .... -54-
Kuwait, -7-, -114-, -119-, -125-, -126-, -226-
-228-, -230-, -231-
Kuwait Investment Office .... -230-
L3 Com .... -64-
LA Weekly .... -103-, -281-, -282-
Labor Department .... -194-
Lahood, Ray .... -24-
Lamberth, Royce Chief Judge .... -31-
Lamont-Doherty Earth Observatory ...... -19-
Langley Air Force Base .... -10-
LAPD .... -45-,-277-
LaRouche, Lyndon H. .... -58--60-, -175-
Le Figaro .... -42-, -277-
Le Monde .... -56-, -57-, -278-
League of Nations .... -60-, -215-
Lear Corp. .... -193-
Lenin .... -266-
Lerner-Lam, Arthur .... -19-
Levin, Carl .... -108-
Liaotung Peninsula .... -239-
Liberation Army .... -27-, -29-, -61-
Lieberman, Joseph .... -24-, -133-, -153-
Life Magazine .... -222-
Lilly Endowment .... -208-
Links Club .... -216-
Livingston, Neil .... -46-
Lockerbie .... -169-

Lockheed Martin . -192-, -193-, -250-, -251-
Loizeaux, Mark .... -19-
Lone Star .... -122-
Lord, Day and Lord .... -205-
Los Angeles International Airport .... -139-
Los Angeles Times ... -23-, -25-, -45-, -192-,
-199-, -241-, -274-, -276-, -288-, -294-
Lowells .... -109-
Lucent Technologies .... -192-
Ludwig Von Mises Institute .... -183-
Lufthansa .... -64-
Luftwaffe .... -232-, -236-
M.A. Bank .... -283-
Macover, Micha .... -53-
Mafia .... -203-,-284-
Magic Lantern .... -188-
Magley, Robb .... -69-
Magna Carta .... -167-
Mahon, Dennis .... -102-
Main Bank .... -123-, -124-, -284-
Majestic Hotel .... -215-
MAK .... -113-
Maktab al-Khidimat (MAK) .... -113-
Manila Times .... -27-, -275-
Manning, Bayless .... -208-
Manning, Bill .... -20-, -21-
Manning, Paul .... -235-
Manufacturers Hanover Trust .... -244-
Maresca, John J. .... -79-, -219-
Mariel Boatlift of 1980 .... -144-
Marijuana .... -107-, -184-
Marine Corps School .... -204-
Mark of the Beast .... -184-
Marmari, Omer .... -54-
Martyrdom Battalion .... -41-
Marxist .... -215-, -260-
Masonic Lodge .... -203-
Matriculas .... -183-, -288-
MBC .... -29-, -275-

-310-

McCain, John .... -24-, -249-, -250-

McCarthy, Joseph .... -3-

McGuire Gibson .... -105-

MCI .... -253-

McKnight Foundation .... -217-

McRae, Ron .... -73-

McVeigh, Timothy .... -101--104-, -131-

Meese, Ed .... -52-, -110-

Mena .... -110-

Merck .... -192-,
-193-

Meridian Plaza .... -20-

Merrill Lynch .... -49-, -50-, -249-

Metropolitan Medical
Response System .... -147-

Mexican Consul .... -183-

Mexican War of 184 .... -259-

Mexico's Foreign Ministry .... -183-

Michigan .... -44-, -91-, -108-, -193-

Microsoft .... -188-, -192-

Microsoft Corp. .... -188-

Middle East .... -13-, -29-, -52-, -58-,
-68-, -77-, -81-, -86-, -91-, -102-, -120-,
-122-, -133-, -142-, -169-, -225-, -248-

Midhar, Khalid AH 3-, -24-, -41-, -67-, -121-

Midwest University .... -244-

Milanytch, Ross .... -16-

Miley, John .... -109-

Military Intelligence Reserve .... -201-

Miller, Doreen .... -173-, -175-, -176-

Miller, Wally .... -70-

Ministry of Defense .... -231-

Mission Impossible .... -68-

Model State Emergency
Health Powers Act .... -135-, -285-

Modern American Knights .... -203-

Mohammed, Khalid Shaikh .... -41-, -42-

Monotheism .... -76-

Monsanto .... -192-, -193-

Moore, Michael .... -27-

Morgan Stanley Dean Witter & Co ...... -50-

Moscow, Alvin .... -31-, -218-

Mossad .... -57-,
-61--63-, -74-,-75-, -267-, -279-

Motorola .... -192-

Mount Holyoke College .... -143-

Mount Rainier .... -4-

Mount Rushmore .... -11-

Moussaoui, Zacarias
-18-, -36--38-, -103-, -104-

Moyers, Bill .... -6-, -198-, -255-

MSNBC .... -25-, -273-, -274-

Mubarak, Hosni Egyptian President 28-, -29-

Mueller .... -38-

Mujahideen .... -26-, -40-, -82-, -108--110-,
-113-, -114-, -126-

Murad, Abdul Hakin .... -26-

Murrah Federal Building .... -27-, -36-,
-100-, -101-, -133-, -138-

Muslim .... -9-, -25-, -26-, -33-,
-79-, -83-, -94-, -101-, -113-, -116-, -117-,
-119-, -120-, -127--129-, -168-, -266-,
-275-, -287-

Muttawakil, Wakil Ahmed .... -26-

Muwafaq Foundation .... -121-

Myers, Richard .... -70-, -82-, -83-

NAFTA .... -251-, -257-

Naik, Niaz .... -82-, -84-, -85-

NASA .... -69-

Nasdaq .... -249-

National Archives .... -241-, -295-

National Commerce Bank
.. -121-, -123-, -124-

National Commission on
Marijuana and Drug Abuse .... -107-

National Communications
System of the Department of Defense -149-

National Counterintelligence

Center (NCIC) .... -56-
National Disaster Medical System ...... -147-
National Domestic Preparedness
Office .... -147-
National Emergencies Act .... -5-
National Emergency . -5-, -145-, -148-,-157-
National Flight Emergency
Response System (NFERS) .... -65-
National Football League .... -247-
National Guard -100-, -114-, -122-, -124-, -140-
National ID System .... -182-, -184-, -288-
National Infrastructure Protection Center149-
National Infrastructure Simulation
and Analysis Center .... -149-
National Institute of Standards
and Technology .... -22-, -149-
National Intelligence Council (NIC) ..... -41-
National Oceanic and
Atmospheric Administration .... -194-
National Public Radio .... -47-
National Reconnaissance Office-, -72-, -131-
National Security .... -1-, -4-, -12-, -23-,
-31-, -32-, -34-, -36-, -37-, -39-, -48-, -56-,
-58--60-, -67-, -71-, -72-, -76-, -79-, -80-,
-82-, -87-, -88-, -115-, -128-, -136-, -137-,
-143-, -148--150-, -152-, -172-, -175-,
-181-, -186-, -192-, -196--198-, -200--202-,
-204-, -209-, -210-, -241-, -242-, -251-, -
252-, -260-, -266-, -269-, -287-
National Security Act .... -4-, -36-, -136-,
-198-, -266-
National Security Agency ..... -4-, -23-, -39-,
-72-, -186-, -241-
National Security Archive .... -196-
National Security Archives ...... -197-, -202-
National Security Council .... -4-, -59-, -79-,
-80-, -150-, -201-,-209-, -242-, -260-
National Security
Council (NSC) .... -4-, -150-, -242-

National Security Division .. -32-, -34-, -56-
National Strategy to Secure Cyberspace-187-
National Union for the Total
Independence of Angola .... -261-
NATO .... -68-, -86-, -222-
Navy .... -44-, -45-, -88-, -97-,
-98-, -176-, -217-, -237-, -239-, -261-
Nazi Party .... -233-
Nazi Schutzstaffel (SS) .... -222-
Nazis .... -129-, -215-, -232-,
-233-, -235-, -236-, -268-, -271-, -293-
NBC's Meet the Press .... -69-
NCIC .... -56-
NEADS .... -9-
Nelson, Dr. Brendan .... -64-
Nestle .... -193-
Net .... -81-, -140-, -184-, -187-,
-273-, -275-, -277-, -280-, -283-, -285-,
-288-, -289-
Neue Presse .... -29-
Nevada Supreme Court .... -186-
New Delhi .... -78-
New Hitler .... -78-, -230-
New Mexico Institute of Mining
and Technology .... -15-
New World Order .... -145-, -205-, -227-,
-267-, -292-, -296-
New York Daily News .... -10-, -286-
New York Fire Department .... -20-
New York Police Department .... -20-
New York Stock Exchange .... -51-, -249-
New York Times .... -14-, -15-, -18-, -28-,
-29-, -32-, -42-, -54-, -65-, -73-, -80-, -97-,
-106-, -120-, -126-, -142-, -177-, -191-,
-199-, -200-, -216-, -226-, -243-, -254-,
-255-, -258-, -275-, -276-, -279-, -282-,
-284-, -285-, -289-, -291-, -293-, -294-
New York University .... -172-

New Yorker .... -12-, -31-, -32-, -60-, -273-, -275-

Newark Airport .... -9-

Newburyport .... -109-

Newsday .... -110-, -287-

NewsInsight.net .... -81-

NewsMax.com .... -57-, -274-, -275-, -278-, -281-

Newsweek Magazine .... -47-

NFERS .... -65-,-67-, -279-

NIC .... -41-, -276-

Nichols, Terry .... -27-, -102-, -103-

Nidal, Abu .... -62-

Nigerian Mobile Police .... -98-

Night Stalkers .... -140-

Nixon, Richard President .... -97-, -107-, -119-, -144-, -151-, -187-, -197-, -201--203-, -220-, -224-, -258-, -261-, -268-

NL Industries .... -193-

No Child Left Behind Act .... -162-

Nobel Peace Prize .... -201-

Nobel, Alfred .... -76-

Nobel, Ludwig .... -76-

NORAD .... -9-, -11-, -72-, -270-

Normandy .... -233-

North, Oliver Lieutenant Colonel-150-, -151-

Northeast Air Defense Sector (NEADS) -9-

Northern Alliance .... -61-, -82-

Northwest Airlines .... -193-

NRO .... -4-, -131-, -132-, -267-, -285-

NSC .... -4-, -150-, -151-, -242-, -294-

Nuclear Hideout .... -244-

Nuclear Weapon .... -89-

Nuclear Weapons and Foreign Policy .... -201-, -204-

Nuremberg War Crimes Trials .... -236-

NYC .... -10-, -17-, -46-, -72-

Nynex .... -253-

NYPD .... -10-, -182-, -288-

Oasis .... -188-, -289-

October Surprise .... -132-, -230-

Odigo .... -53-, -278-

Office for Domestic Preparedness ...... -147-

Office of Emergency Preparedness ..... -147-

Office of Information Awareness (OIA) .... -143-

Office of Intelligence .... -35-

Office of Management and Budget .... -192-, -194-

Office of Naval Intelligence .... -44-

Office of Personnel Management .... -194-

Office of Strategic Information -142-, -286-

Office of Strategic Services (OSS) ..... -222-

OIA .... -143-

Oil & Gas Journal .... -97-

Oklahoma City .... -27-, -34-, -36-, -100--104-, -131-, -138-, -282-

Oklahoma City Fire Department .... -101-

Olberg, Ralph .... -40-

Old Dominion University .... -136-

Omar, Mullah .... -82-, -84-

Omari, Abdulaziz Al- .... -13-

Oosterbeek .... -221-

OPEC .... -86-, -227-

Operation Desert Storm .... -226-

Operation Eagle Flight .... -233-, -293-

Operation Mongoose .... -240-

Operation Northwoods .... -240--242-

Operation Rescue .... -179-, -180-

Operation TIPS .... -158--160-, -286-

Operations Research Office ..... -201-, -248-

Opium .... -61-, -108-, -109-, -283-

Opium Wars .... -109-

Organization of American Historians . -196-

Organization of Petroleum
Exporting Countries (OPEC) .... -86-
Oriental Institute of the University
of Chicago .... -104-
Oriental Mysticism .... -72-
Orlando Sentinel .... -94-, -281-
Orwellian .... -52-, -134-
Osman, Tim .... -40-
OSS .... -222-
Otis Air National Guard Base .... -10-
Oval Office .... -137-, -196-, -213-, -283-
O'Hare Airport .... -178-
O'Neill, John16-, -31-, -32-, -37-, -80-, -102-
O'Neill, Paul .... -129-, -192-, -194-
O'Toole, Pam .... -109-
P2 .... -203-
P2OG .... -242-
Pacific Equity Investigations .... -33-
Pacific Fleet .... -237-, -238-
Pacific Maritime Association (PMA) . -157-
Pacific Ocean .... -64-
Palestine Liberation Organization .... -260-
Palmer, Orio J. Battalion Chief .... -18-
Pan Am Flight 103 .... -169-
Panama Canal .... -239-
Parade Magazine .... -12-, -47-
Paris Peace Conference .... -215-
Parliament .... -39-, -59-, -60-,
-111-, -203-, -232-,-236-
Patriot Act .... -1-, -163--168-,
-170--174-, -178-,-179-, -181-, -185-,-195-,
-287-, -288-
Pavitt, James .... -43-
Pax Americana .... -86-, -267-
PBS .... -70-, -113-, -114-, -116-, -118-
PBS's Frontline .... -112-
PCA .... -138-, -139-
Peabody Energy .... -194-
Peace Corps. .... -193-

Pearl Harbor .... -2-, -76-, -77-,
-87-, -136-, -237--239-, -269-, -293-
Pentagon .... -5-, -9-, -10-, -12-,
-26-, -41-, -44-, -47-, -49-, -54-, -62-, -66-,
-69-, -82-, -85-, -87-, -94-, -97-, -98-,
-100-, -104-, -105-, -112-, -117-, -118-,
-127-, -132-, -141--143-, -227-, -231-,
-240-, -242-, -248-, -269-, -277--279-,
-283-, -286-, -294-, -295-
People Finder .... -53-
People's Almanac #3 .... -210-, -290-
People's Liberation Army .... -27-, -61-
Perelman, Marc .... -55-
Perkins, Handasyd .... -109-
Perle, Richard .... -59-, -60-, -267-
Perry, Philip .... -194-
Perry, Steve .... -39-
Persian Gulf .... -27-, -78-, -80-,
-125-, -126-, -226-,-230-, -232-, -246-,-261-
Persian Gulf War .... -78-, -80-, -126-,
-226-, -230-, -246-,-261-
Peshawar .... -113-
Petroleum Finance Company .... -98-
Pew Charitable Trusts .... -217-
Pharmacia .... -192-, -193-
Philip Morris .... -193-
Phoenix Program .... -155-, -156-, -242-
Pinyun Lu-shun .... -239-
Pipes, Daniel .... -58-
Plum Island Disease Facility .... -148-
PMA .... -157-
PNAC .... -86-
Pocantico Hilla .... -204-
Pol Pot .... -204-
Political Research Associates .... -55-
Pollard, Jonathan .... -57-
Polo, Marco .... -76-
Popovic, Alex .... -50-
Popular Mechanics .... -186-, -289-

-314-

Port Arthur .... -239-
Posse Comitatus Act (PCA) .... -138-
Post .... -23-, -32-, -43-, -54-, -58-,
-63-, -66-, -73-, -80-, -81-, -87-, -113-,
-124-, -125-, -128-, -158-, -173-, -194-,
-195-, -198-, -199-, -210-, -214-, -215-,
-246-, -254-, -255-, -273-, -276-,
-278--280-, -285--289-, -291-
Postal Service .... -137-, -158-, -159-,-286-
Powell, Colin .... -47-, -82-, -90-,
-91-, -133-, -139-,-156-, -191-, -192-,-194-,
-195-, -258-
Pravda .... -28-,-216-
Predator .... -40-,-276-
Presbyterian Church .... -220-
President Franklin Delano Roosevelt .. -237-
Presidential Decision Directive (PDD) -140-
Presidential Medal of Freedom .... -97-
Presidential Order .... -209-
Presidential Powers and War Powers Act140-
Presidential Records Act .... -196-, -197-
Presidential Review Memorandum ..... -209-
President's Commission on
Organized Crime .... -111-
Princeton University .... -51-
Proactive, Preemptive
Operations Group (P2OG) .... -242-
Problems Solutions Innovations .... -74-
Prohibition .... -107-
Project Bojinka .... -26-
Project Censored .... -256-, -257-, -295-
Project for the New American
Century (PNAC) .... -86-
PROMIS .... -40-, -48-, -51-, -52-, -275-
Propaganda Masonica Due .... -203-
Psychic Spies .... -73-
Psychological Strategy Board .... -201-
Public Citizen .... -196-, -197-
Public Health Emergency

Preparedness .... -147-
Public Policy Center .... -217-
Pushtan .... -43-
QTC Medical .... -192-
Qualcomm Inc. .... -192-
Radio Kabul .... -87-
Radlauer, Don .... -52-
Raghead Collaborator .... -163-
Rainbow Bookstore Cooperative .... -174-
Rand Corporation .... -94-, -201-, -244-
RAO Gazprom .... -79-
Ratigan, Dylan .... -49-
Raytheon Systems .... -64-
Razim, Mohammad Alim .... -79-
RCMP .... -44-
RCMP [Royal Canadian Mounted Police]44-
Red Brigade .... -203-
Red Sea .... -60-, -113-
Reichsleiter .... -235-
Remote Viewers .... -1-, -72--74-, -280-
Remote Viewing .... -72--75-
Reno, Janet .... -47-, -136-, -137-
Report From Iron
Mountain .... -244-, -245-, -247-, -294-
Reporter's Committee for
Freedom of the Press .... -197-
Republic of El Salvador .... -260-
Republican .... -7-, -24-, -40-,
-72-, -92-, -94-, -102-, -119-, -127--129-,
-141-, -146-, -162-, -194--196-, -198-,
-199-, -212-, -213-, -220-, -271-, -291-
Reuters News Service .... -29-
RFIM .... -247-
Rhodes, Cecil .... -60-, -265-
Rice, Condoleezza .... -80-, -87-, -192-,
-194-, -252-, -258-
Riconosciuto, Michael .... -40-
Riyadh .... -104-,-114-, -284-
Roberts, Craig .... -100-, -101-, -145-

Rockefeller Brothers Fund
.... -201-, -208-, -290-
Rockefeller, David .... -31-, -50-, -204-,
-207-, -208-, -210--212-, -214-, -219-,-220-,
-223-, -228-
Rockefeller, John D. -76-, -201-, -204-,-217-
Rockefeller, Nelson .... -204-, -222-, -248-
Rodman, Peter .... -59-
Rodriguez, Paul .... -56-, -58-
Romero, Van .... -15-
Rome-Berlin Axis .... -235-
Rommel, Erwin Field Marshal .... -77-
Roosevelt, Franklin Delano President ....
-76-, -77-, -87-, -195-, -237--240-
Roswell .... -4-, -94-, -281-
Rothschild, 2nd Lord Lionel Walter ..... -60-
Rothschild, Baron Edmond de ... -60-, -223-
Rotterdam Bank .... -234-
Round Table Group .... -60-, -219-
Rowley, Coleen M. .... -38-, -39-
Royal Australian Air Force .... -64-
Royal Institute of
International Affairs ...... -215-, -222-, -223-
Royer, Jeffrey A. .... -33-
RPG .... -116-
RQ-4A Global Hawk UAV .... -63-
Rubenstein, Howard J. .... -54-
Rubin Foundation .... -205-
Ruby Ridge .... -101-, -136-, -169-
Rule By Secrecy .... 4, -4-, -51-, -106-,
-279-, -290-, -295-
Rumaila .... -226-
Rumsfeld, Donald Defense Secretary .. -12-,
-40-, -47-, -59-,-86-, -87-, -89-,-119-, -142-,
-143-,-146-, -191-, -192-,-242-, -267-
Ruppert, Michael .... -45-, -49--52-,-127-
Ruppert, Michael C. ..... -45-, -49--52-,-127-
Russell and Company .... -109-
Russian Empire .... -44-

Russian Intelligence Service .... -45-
Russian Ministry of
Economic Development .... -28-
Russian Revolution .... -263-
Russian Studies Department .... -207-
Russia's Lower House of Parliament .. -111-
Russo-Afghan War .... -83-, -112-
Russo-Japanese War .... -240-
SAAR Foundation .... -128-
Safa Trust .... -94-, -128-, -129-
Saleh, Ali Abdullah .... -32-
San Antonio International Airport ...... -122-
San Francisco Chronicle .... -50-, -277-
Sarandon, Susan .... -106-
Saudi Arabian Airlines .... -13-
Saudi Embassy .... -120-, -121-
SAVAK Secret Police .... -259-
Sayed, Abdelkader Mahmoud Es .... -25-
Sayreville School District .... -163-
Sayyaf, Abu .... -27-
Scarry, Elaine .... -71-
Schafer, Raymond P. .... -107-
Schippers, David .... -36-, -52-
Schlumberger .... -98-, -99-
School of the Americas .... -146-
Seal, Barry .... -110-, -111-
Sears .... -26-, -192-
Sears Tower .... -26-
Seattle Space Needle .... -11-
SEC .... -50-, -125-,
-126-, -277-, -278-,-282-
Secret Government .... -72-, -150-,
-166-, -175-, -198-
Secret Service .... -12-, -29-, -44-,
-62-, -150-, -152-, -161-, -163-, -170-,
-287-
Secret Team .... -198-
Secretary of Defense . -40-, -47-, -59-, -64-,
-86-, -89-, -97-, -126-, -142-, -157-, -213-,

Securities Industry Association .... -51-

Seismic Evidence .... -69-, -274-

Selective Service System .... -246-

Seminole County .... -189-

Senate Foreign Relations Committee -66-, -228-

Senate Iran-Contra Committee .... -150-

Senate Judiciary Committee .... -175-, -288-

Sesame Street .... -255-

Shadow Government .... -5-, -150-, -151-, -198-, -199-, -209-,-289-, -290-

Shanksville .... -10-

Shaw, Bruce .... -101-

Shehhi, Marwan-Al- .... -66-, -103-

Shehri, Waleed Al- .... -13-

Shelby, Richard .... -24-

Shelton, Ike .... -47-

Shibh, Ramzi Ben Al- .... -37-, -132-

Shmuel, Yaron .... -54-

Short, Walter Major General .... -77-

Siemens .... -189-,-289-

Sierra Magazine .... -194-, -289-

Silesian-American Corporation .... -234-

Silk Road .... -78-

Silverstein, Larry A. .... -50-

Simons, Tom .... -84-, -85-

Singh, Jaswant .... -82-

Sisera .... -73-

Sissonville High School .... -162-

Sixth Army .... -77-, -141-

Skull and Bones .... -109-, -205-, -206-, -234-, -244-

Slatkin, Nora .... -51-

Smith, Charles R. .... -57-

Smith, Gerald .... -210-

Smith, Patti .... -106-

Smith, Walter Bedell ..... -222-, -223-, -259-

Smith, William French .... -150-

Snitch Culture .... -160-, -161-

Sobel, David .... -30-, -31-

Socialists .... -262-, -264-

Society of Licenced Aeronautical Engineers .... -64-

Soft Money .... -62-

Solarz, Stephen .... -59-

Solntsevo Crime Family .... -112-

Sonic Boom .... -69-

Sorbi's Flying Club .... -67-

Southern Poverty Law Center .... -161-

Soviet Empire .... -83-, -280-

Soviet Union .... -78-

Spanish-American War .... -7-, -259-

Special Studies Project .... -201-

Special Study Group .... -244-

Special Weapons and Tactics .... -141-

Sperry, Pau .... -34-

Spotlight .... -221-, -229-, -276-, -292-, -293-, -295-

Springfield .... -170-

SRI .... -73-

SS .... -222-, -233-, -234-

St. Louis's Gateway Arch .... -11-

Standard & Poor's .... -254-, -255-, -295-

Standard Oil .... -76-, -216-, -235-, -244-

Stanford Research Institute (SRI) .... -73-

Stargate .... -72-

Starr Foundation .... -217-

Starr, S. Fredrick .... -81-

State Department -22-, -31-, -41-, -52-, -59-, -80-, -84-, -85-, -100-, -105-, -120-, -127-, -130-, -204-, -219-, -228-, -293-

State of Emergency .... -5-, -273-

Statue of Liberty .... -158-, -183-

Stewart, Jim .... -47-

Stewart, Payne .... -11-

Stoffer, Irit .... -55-

Stoltz, Dick .... -35-

Strassmier, Andreas .... -102-

Strategic National Stockpile of HHS .. -147-

Sturgises .... -109-

Subcommittee on Constitutional
Rights .... -140-, -144-

Subcommittee on Narcotics
and Drug Interdiction .... -111-

Sullivan, Martin E. .... -106-

Sullivan, William ....⁻ -212-

Sunday Times .... -109-

Suter, Dominick .... -55-

SWAT .... -141-

Sweeney, Madeline Amy .... -15-

Syntek Technologies .... -143-

Taft-Hartley Act .... -157-

Tagesspiegel .... -64-

Talbot, Strobe .... -14-, -205-, -258-

Taliban .... -26-, -35-, -61-, -79--85-,
-87-, -105-, -109-, -114-, -115-, -120-,
-137-, -176-, -178-, -267-, -274-, -276-,
-280-, -281-, -283-

TCI .... -253-

Technologists .... -64-, -229-

Tempest .... -186-, -187-, -289-

Terrorism Information and
Prevention System .... -158-

Terrorist Task Force .... -102-

Terrorists .... -7-, -9-, -12-, -14-, -23--25-,
-27-, -28-, -30--36-, -38-, -40-, -41-, -49-,
-50-, -56-, -57-, -62-, -70-, -71-, -79-, -88-,
-103-, -108-, -119--121-, -123-, -129-, -132-
-134-, -137-, -143-, -148-, -150-, -156-,
-160-, -164-, -166--168-, -174-, -185-, -187-
, -232-, -242-, -243-, -262-, -273-, -275-, -
279-

Texaco .... -217-,-250-

Texas Air National Guard .... -122-

Texas City Sun .... -163-

Texas Commerce Bank .... -123-

Texas Commerce Bank Tower .... -123-

Texas Instruments .... -208-

Texas Rangers .... -125-

Texas Research & Information Bureau . -74-

The Electronic Privacy Information
Center .... -30-

The Guardian .... -83--85-, -128-,
-276-, -277-, -281-,-282-, -284-

The Houston Chronicle .... -122-, -162-

The Inquiry .... -122-, -215-, -291-

The Law To Remove The
Distress of the People and State .... -165-

The National Commerce B
ank in Saudi Arabia .... -121-

The National Neighborhood
Watch Institute .... -160-

The Net .... -184-, -187-

The Spirit of Justice .... -176-

The State of Israel .... -54-, -60-

The Wall Street Journal . -49-, -126-, -212-,
-224-, -255-

Thessalonica .... -73-

Third Reich .... -165-, -272-, -293-

Thomson-CSF .... -187-

Three Mile Island .... -44-, -45-, -209-

Tiananmen Square .... -261-

Time Magazin d 5-, -123-, -124-, -205-, -235-

Time Warner .... -192-, -193-, -253-

Time, Inc. .... -208-

TIPS .... -15-, -41-, -158--161-, -286-

Titanic .... -81-

TMBR/Sharp Drilling .... -193-

Tokyo .... -7-, -208-

Tom Brown, Inc. .... -193-

Toronto Star .... -45-, -277-

Trading With the Enemy Act .... -234-

Transamerica Corp. .... -192-

Transamerica Tower .... -26-

TransDimensional Systems .... -74-

Transportation Security Administration -148-

Treaty of Versailles .... -215-

Trialogue .... -208-, -290-

Tribeca Grill .... -35-

Tribune Company .... -192-

Trilateral Commission83-, -194-, -204--212-, -214-, -220-, -221-, -223-, -225-, -236-, -255-, -256-, -290-

Trilateralist .... -206-, -209-, -227-,-244-

Trireme Partners .... -60-

Truman, Harry S. President .... -4-, -157-

Truth .... -6-, -38-, -75-, -77-, -83-,-119-, -134-, -142-,-180-, -191-, -216-,-247-, -252-, -256-,-262-, -269-, -278-,-296-

Tucker, James P. .... -77-, -223-, -225-

TWA 800 .... -249-

Tyumen Oil Co. .... -111-

U.S. Air Force .... -64-

U.S. Alien Property Custodian .... -234-

U.S. Army .... -67-, -72-, -141-, -143-, -201-, -238-, -286-

U.S. Army Counter-Intelligence Corps -201-

U.S. Army's School of Advanced Military Studies .... -63-

U.S. Coast Guard .... -148-

U.S. Department of Justice Nazi War Crimes .... -234-

U.S. Destroyer Cole .... -32-

U.S. Embassies .... -41-, -80-

U.S. Embassy .... -6-, -29-, -43-

U.S. Export-Import Bank .... -111-

U.S. Government -4-, -12-, -22-, -25-, -32-, -44-, -56-, -58-, -59-, -87-, -112-, -115-, -117-, -126-, -132-, -137-, -147-, -157-, -162-, -183-, -187-, -201-, -211-, -217--219-, -229-, -231-, -247-, -250-, -257-, -260--262-, -285-, -288-

U.S. Gun Control Act .... -233-

U.S. Justice Department .... -13-, -18-

U.S. Navy .... -44-, -45-, -217-,-261-

U.S. News & World Report -78-, -87-, -97-, -104-, -137-, -210-,-211-, -231-, -251-,-255-, -261-, -274-,-276-, -281--285-,-293-, -295-

U.S. Securities and Exchange Commission .... -50-

U.S. Senate .... -154-, -175-, -215-

U.S. Sixth Fleet .... -77-

U.S. Treasury -49-, -52-, -209-,-249-, -277-

UAL Corp. .... -49-

UAV .... -63-, -65-

UBC .... -234-

Ummat .... -117-, -283-

UN .... -68-, -82-, -88--92-, -96-, -98-, -106-, -157-, -161-, -164-, -224-, -231-, -232-, -246-, -268-, -281-, -287-

Union Pacific .... -193-

United Airlines ... -9-, -13-, -49-, -74-, -193-

United Catholic Church .... -262-

United Command Plan .... -145-

United Flight 175 .... -9--11-

United Flight 93 .... -9-, -10-, -13-

United Fruit .... -259-

United Nations ... -3-, -11-, -14-, -26-, -90-, -92-, -211-, -227-, -231-, -259-, -268-

United Nations Special Commission (UNSCOM) .... -231-

United States Arms Control .... -201-

United States Army Special Operations Command .... -140-

United Way .... -193-

University Club .... -216-

University of Chicago .... -80-, -104-

University of Jerusalem .... -56-

University of Maryland School of Law .... -51-

University of Pennsylvania .... -203-

University of San Francisco .... -95-

University of Southern California .... -169-

University of Texas at Austin .... -162-
University of Texas Health
Science Center .... -169
Unocal .... -78-,-79-
UNSCOM .... -231-
UPI .... -61-, -281-
Urban Moving Systems .... -55-
USA Patriot Act .. -163-, -165--167-, -173-,
-174-, -181-, -185-, -195-, -287-, -288-
USAR .... -145-
USNORTHCOM .... -145-, -146-
Utah .... -135-
Uzbekistan .... -81-, -82-, -97-
Vankin, Johnathan .... -78-, -203-, -227-
Vatican Bank .... -203-
Veliz, Teresa .... -16-
Verfassungsschutz .... -62-
VeriChip .... -185-, -289-
VeriChip Centers .... -185-
VeriTracks .... -189-
Vermont Vanguard .... -156-
Veronis, Suhler & Associates .... -254-
Versailles Peace Conference .... -262-
Veterans of Foreign Wars (VFW) ...... -212-
VFW .... -212-
Viacom .... -253-
Vialls, Joe .... -64-, -67-
Vienna .... -90-
Vieques Island .... -179-
Vietcong .... -154-
Vietnam Veterans Memorial .... -106-
Vietnam War .... -77-, -78-, -106-,
-109-, -155-, -187-,-203-, -219-, -261-,-262-
Vietnamese Communist Party .... -263-
Village Voice .... -190-, -289-
Vinson & Elkins .... -192-
Von Buelow, Andreas .... -62--64-
Vornado Realty Trust .... -50-
Vreeland, Delmart "Mike" .... -44-, -45-

Waco .... -101-,
-136-, -138-, -169-
Wahabbi .... -120-
Wahabbis .... -120-, -284-
Wall Street .... -49-, -51-, -52-, -77-,
-81-, -126-, -212-, -220-, -224-, -249-, -255-
, -263-, -277-, -291-, -295-, -296-
Wall Street Journal -49-, -126-, -212-, -224-,
-255-, -291-
Walt Disney Co. .... -253-
Walt Disney World .... -11-
WAMY .... -128-
War Between The States -136-, -138-, -181-
War Department .... -7-
War On Drugs .... -6-, -7-, -35-, -39-,
-107-, -108-, -138-, -146-
War on Poverty .... -7-
War on Terrorism3-, -6-, -7-, -24-, -35-, -43-,
-79-, -93-, -97-, -127-, -131-, -133--135-,
137-, -141-, -146-, -160-, -177-, -178-, -
188-, -190-, -250-, -267-, -271-, -285-
Warren Commission-51-, -201-, -220-, -235-
Washington Post .... -23-, -43-, -54-,
-66-, -73-, -80-,-81-, -87-, -128-,-194-, -
199-, -210-,-214-, -254-, -255-,-273-, -276-,
-278--280-, -285-, -287-,-289-, -291-
Washington Times .... -28-, -63-, -255-,
-279-, -281-, -286-,-289-
Washington's Metropolitan Club .... -216-
Weapons of Mass Destruction
.... -25-, -27-, -88-,
-90-, -138-, -149-,-231-, -242-, -293-
Weapons Systems Evaluation
Group of the Joint Chiefs of Staff .... -201-
Weehawken .... -55-
Weekly .... -77-, -103-, -156-, -278-,
-280--282-, -291-
Welfare Reform Act .... -184-
Wells Fargo .... -183-, -208-

Welna, David .... -47-

Werthebach, Ekehardt .... -62-

West Virginia .... -89-, -146-, -162-, -281-

Western Front .... -215-

Westfield America, Inc. .... -50-

Westfields Marriott .... -225-

Whalen, John .... -78-, -203-, -227-

Wharton School .... -203-

Whistleblower Protection Act (WPA) . -152-

White House .... -6-, -9-, -10-, -12-,
-23-, -26-, -31-, -37-, -41-, -59-, -66-, -72-,
-77-, -89-, -92-, -93-, -100-, -106-, -116-,
-123-, -129-, -132-, -153-, -192-, -194-,
-196-, -197-, -199-, -200-, -210-, -214-,
-225-, -239-, -240-, -252-, -253-, -260-,
-273-, -276-, -280-, -289-, -291-, -294-

White House Cultural Property
Advisory Committee .... -106-

White House Weekly .... -77-

Whitewater .... -170-

Wilderness Society .... -217-

Wildes, Michael .... -41-

Williams, Anthony A. .... -186-

Williams, Kenneth J. .... -33-

Wingate, Lynn .... -33-

Wiretapping .... -39-, -57-, -58-,-179-

WMD .... -149-

Wolfowitz, Paul .... -59-, -70-, -80-,
-86-, -87-, -267-

Worden, Carl .... -177-

Worden, Robert L. .... -41-

Working Group on Financial Markets -248-

World Assembly of
Muslim Youth (WAMY) .... -128-

World Trade Center   -5-, -6-, -9-, -10-, -14-,
-15-, -17-, -20-, -21-, -26-, -27-, -29--35-,
-37-, -46-, -50-, -54-, -61-, -82-, -85-, -100
, -102-, -130-, -132-, -232-, -237-, -243-, -
279-

World Trade Organization .... -27-, -257-

World War I . -7-, -60-, -136-, -215-, -262-,
-263-, -266-

World War II .... -3-, -7-, -31-, -77-, -78-,
-81-, -106-, -113-, -115-, -137-, -139-,
-144-, -145-, -195-, -217-, -221-, -235-,
-236-, -246-, -250-, -258-, -259-

World War III .... -46-

WorldCom .... -125-, -268-

WorldNetDaily .... -102-, -126-, -273-,
-276-, -282-, -284-

Worms Bank .... -235-

WPA .... -152-

Wright, Bill .... -70-

Wright, Lawrence .... -31-, -32-

Wright, Robert G. Jr. .... -33-, -34-, -36-

WTC .... -10--21-,
-26-, -27-, -44-,-46-, -49-, -50-,-53-, -54-, -
61-,-69-, -74-, -75-,-85-, -112-, -119-,-127-,
-168-, -240-,-243-, -269-, -274-,-276-, -278-
, -279-

Wurmser, David .... -59-

Xerox .... -217-

Xinhau .... -89-

Y2K .... -34-

Yale -109-, -205-, -206-, -209-, -234-, -248-

Yale School of Management .... -205-

Yamani, Ahmad Zaki Al- .... -80-

YellowTimes .... -173-, -288-

Yildash, Tahir .... -26-

York Foundation .... -129-

York International Trust .... -129-

Yousef, Ramzi . -26-, -27-, -30-, -31-, -102-

Zim American Israeli Shipping Co. ...... -54-

Zoroaster .... -76-

Zoubeida, Abou .... -43-

Zubaydah, Abu .... -41-

[China's] People's Liberation Army ..... -61-

Be sure and visit JimMarrs.com for updates and other information.